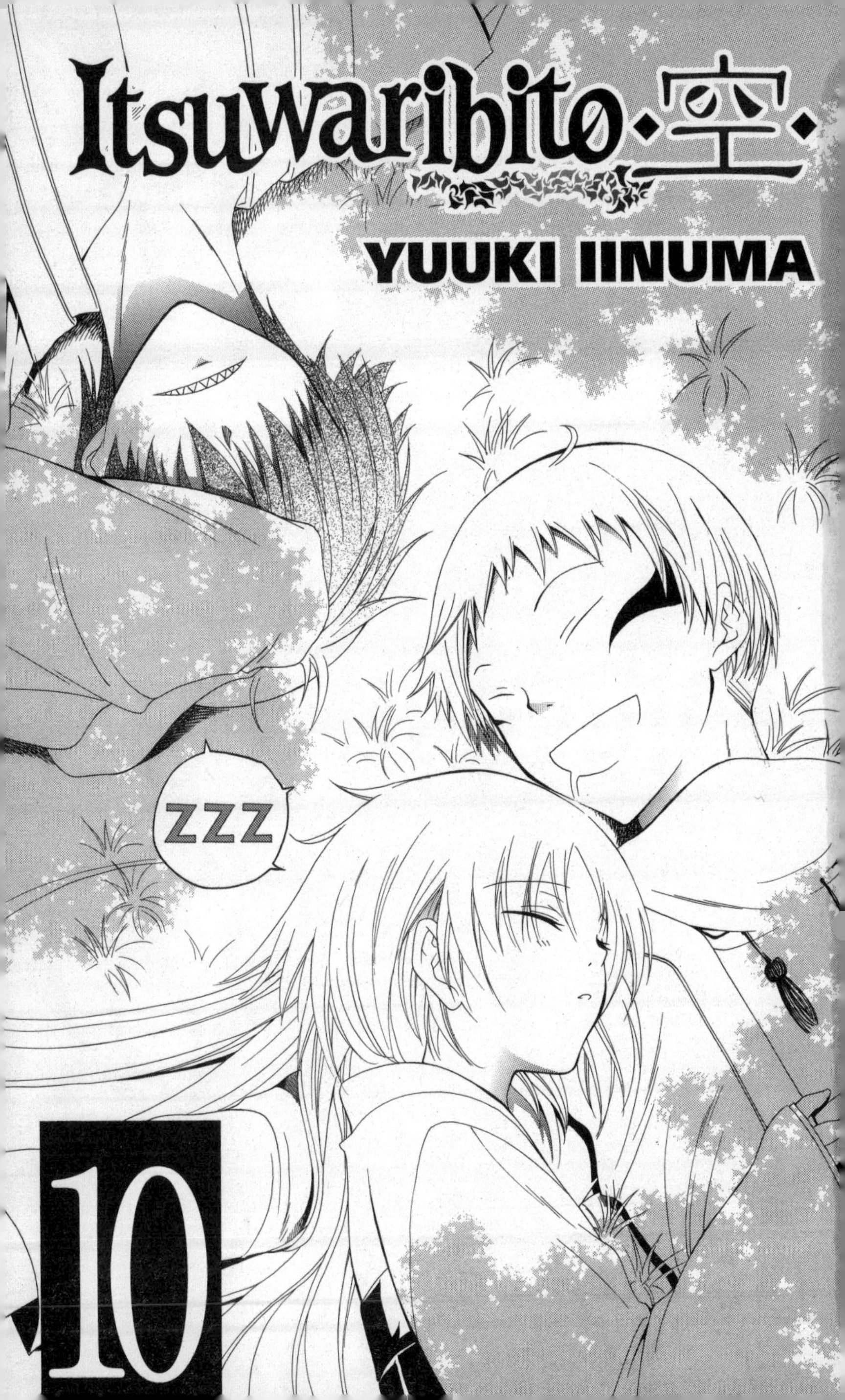
Itsuwaribito ·空·
YUUKI IINUMA
ZZZ
10

Contents

Chapter 88 Onihime

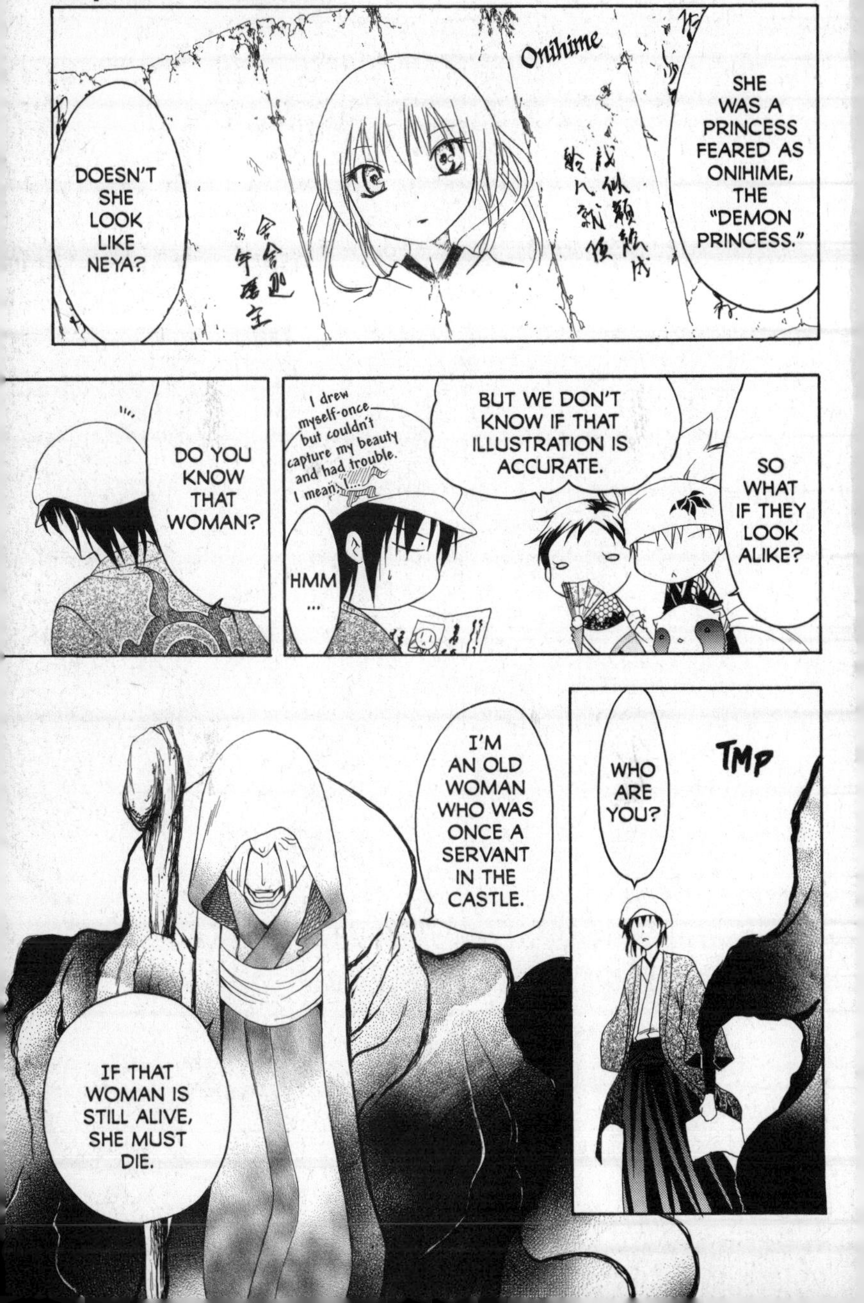
Onihime
SHE WAS A PRINCESS FEARED AS ONIHIME, THE "DEMON PRINCESS."
DOESN'T SHE LOOK LIKE NEYA?
SO WHAT IF THEY LOOK ALIKE?
BUT WE DON'T KNOW IF THAT ILLUSTRATION IS ACCURATE.
I drew myself-once but couldn't capture my beauty and had trouble. I mean, I...
HMM ...
DO YOU KNOW THAT WOMAN?
TMP
WHO ARE YOU?
I'M AN OLD WOMAN WHO WAS ONCE A SERVANT IN THE CASTLE.
IF THAT WOMAN IS STILL ALIVE, SHE MUST DIE.

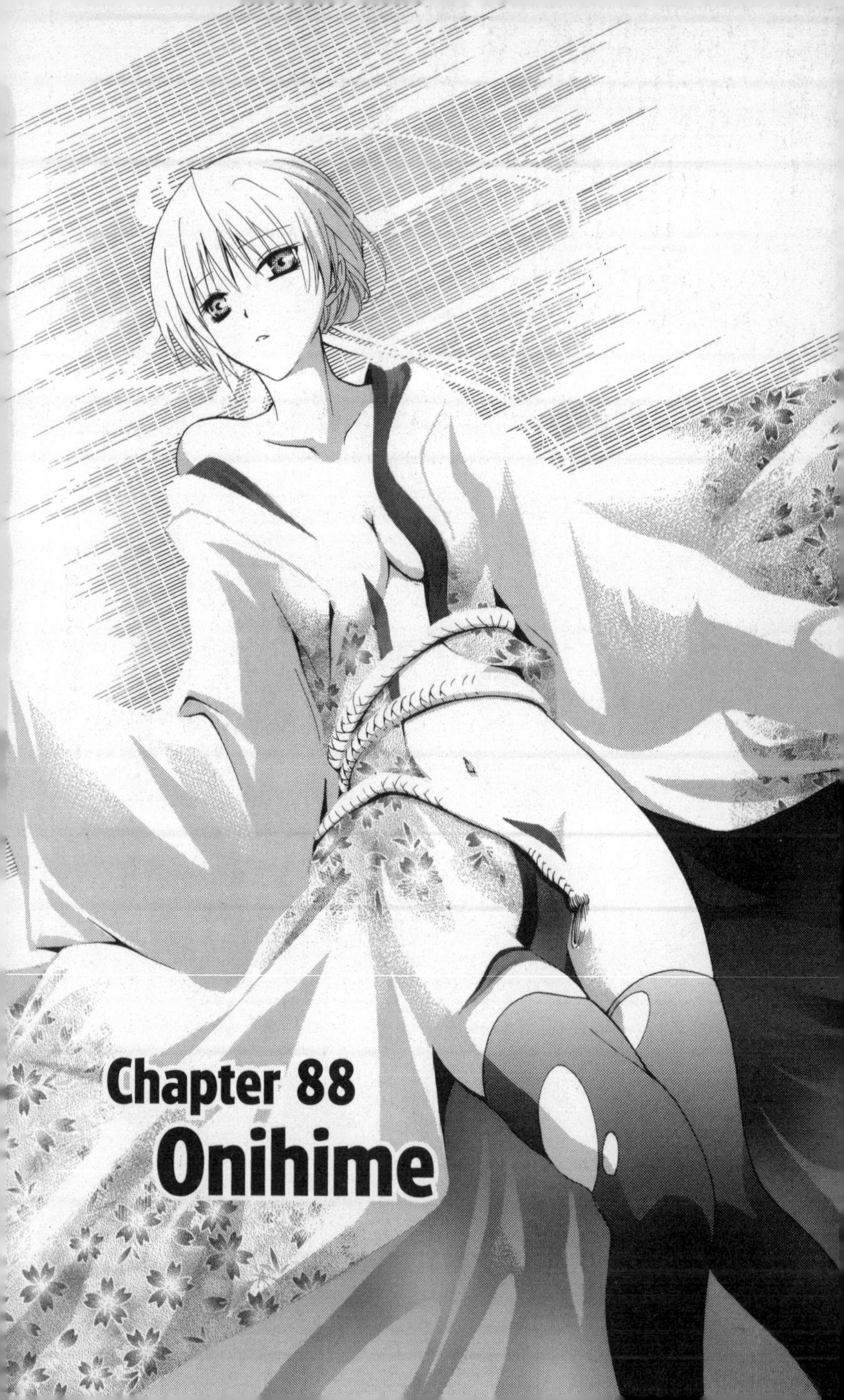
Chapter 88
Onihime

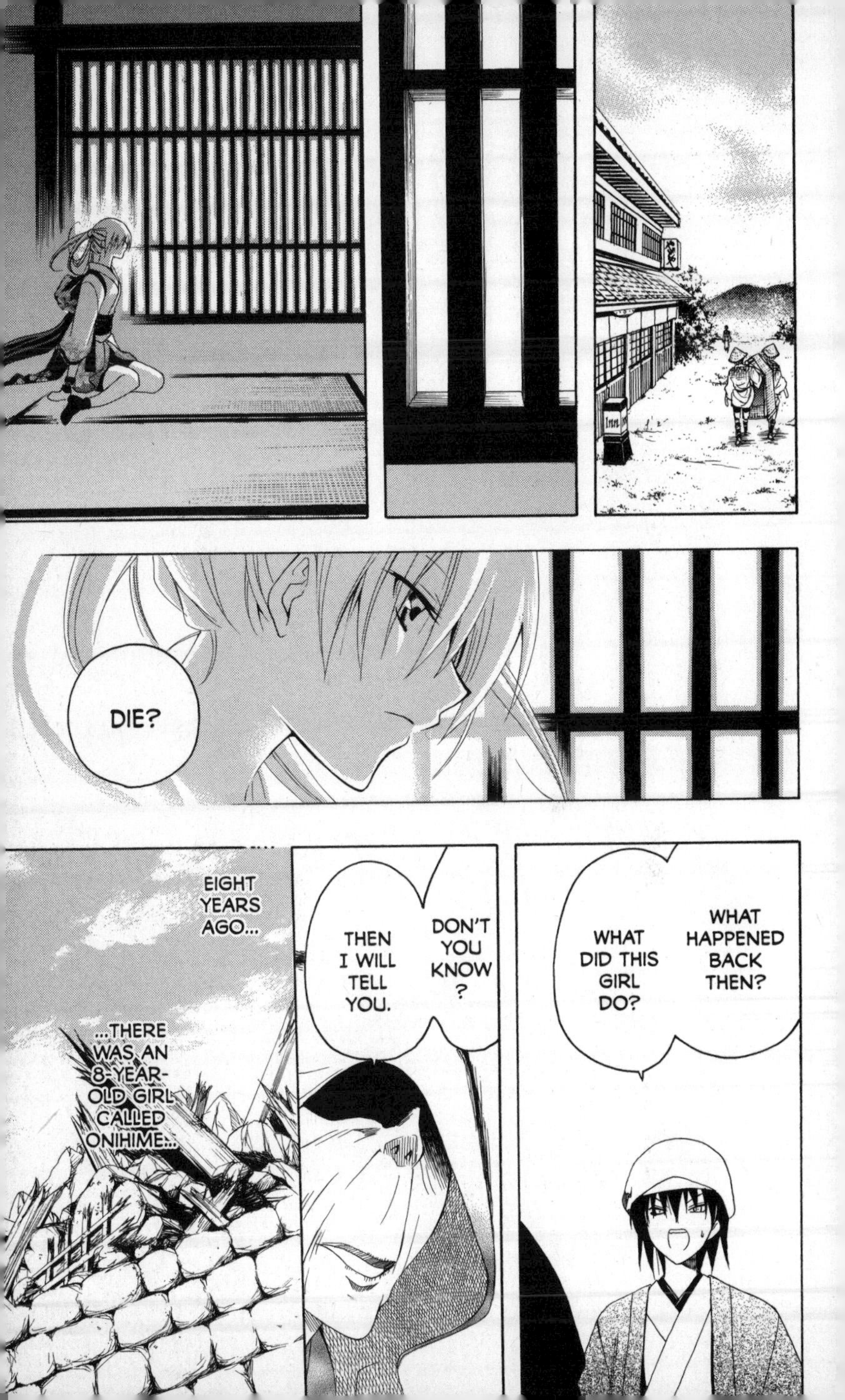

Inn
DIE?
WHAT HAPPENED BACK THEN?
WHAT DID THIS GIRL DO?
DON'T YOU KNOW?
THEN I WILL TELL YOU.
EIGHT YEARS AGO...
...THERE WAS AN 8-YEAR-OLD GIRL CALLED ONIHIME...

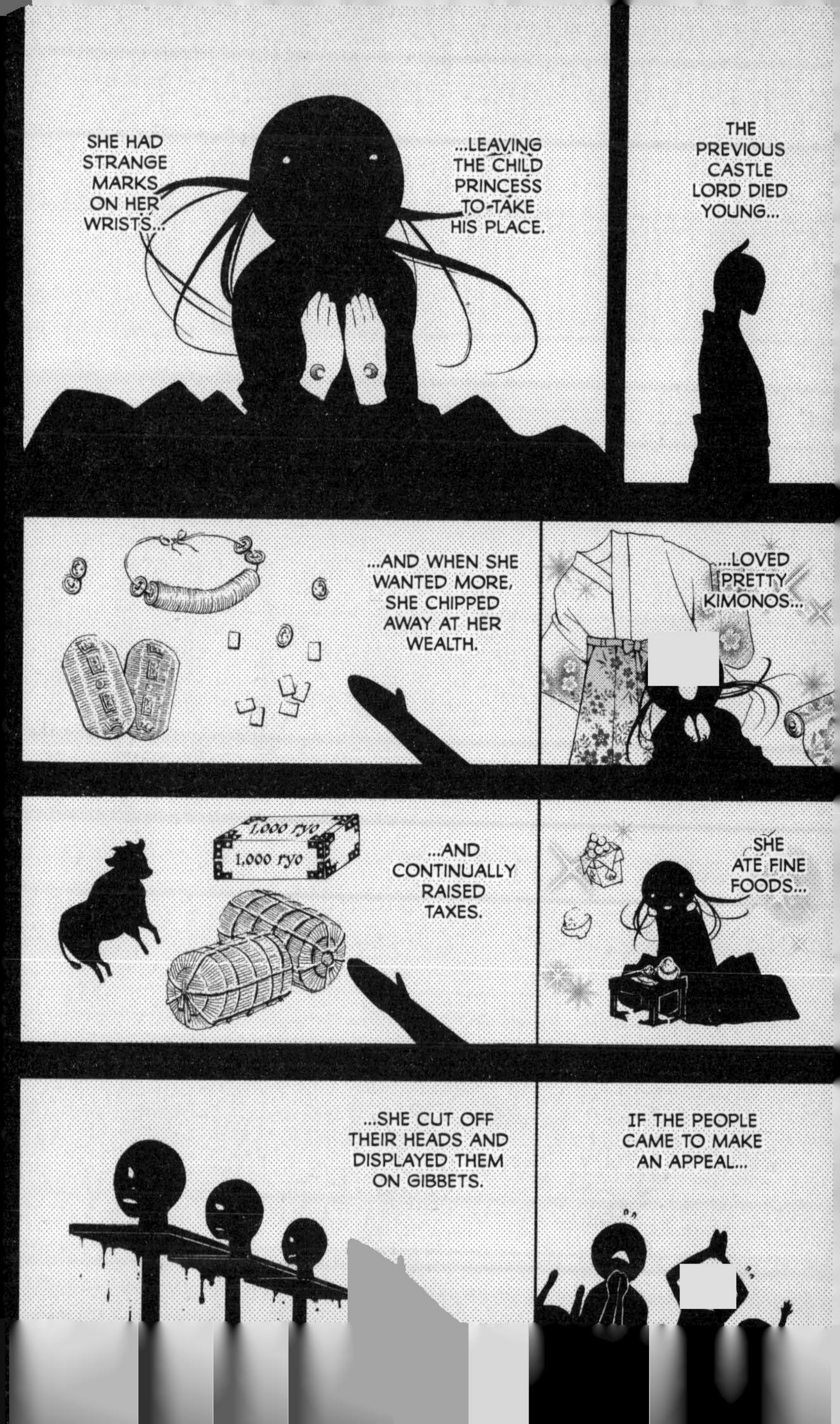
THE PREVIOUS CASTLE LORD DIED YOUNG...
...LEAVING THE CHILD PRINCESS TO TAKE HIS PLACE.
SHE HAD STRANGE MARKS ON HER WRISTS...
...LOVED PRETTY KIMONOS...
...AND WHEN SHE WANTED MORE, SHE CHIPPED AWAY AT HER WEALTH.
SHE ATE FINE FOODS...
1,000 ryo
1,000 ryo
...AND CONTINUALLY RAISED TAXES.
IF THE PEOPLE CAME TO MAKE AN APPEAL...
...SHE CUT OFF THEIR HEADS AND DISPLAYED THEM ON GIBBETS.

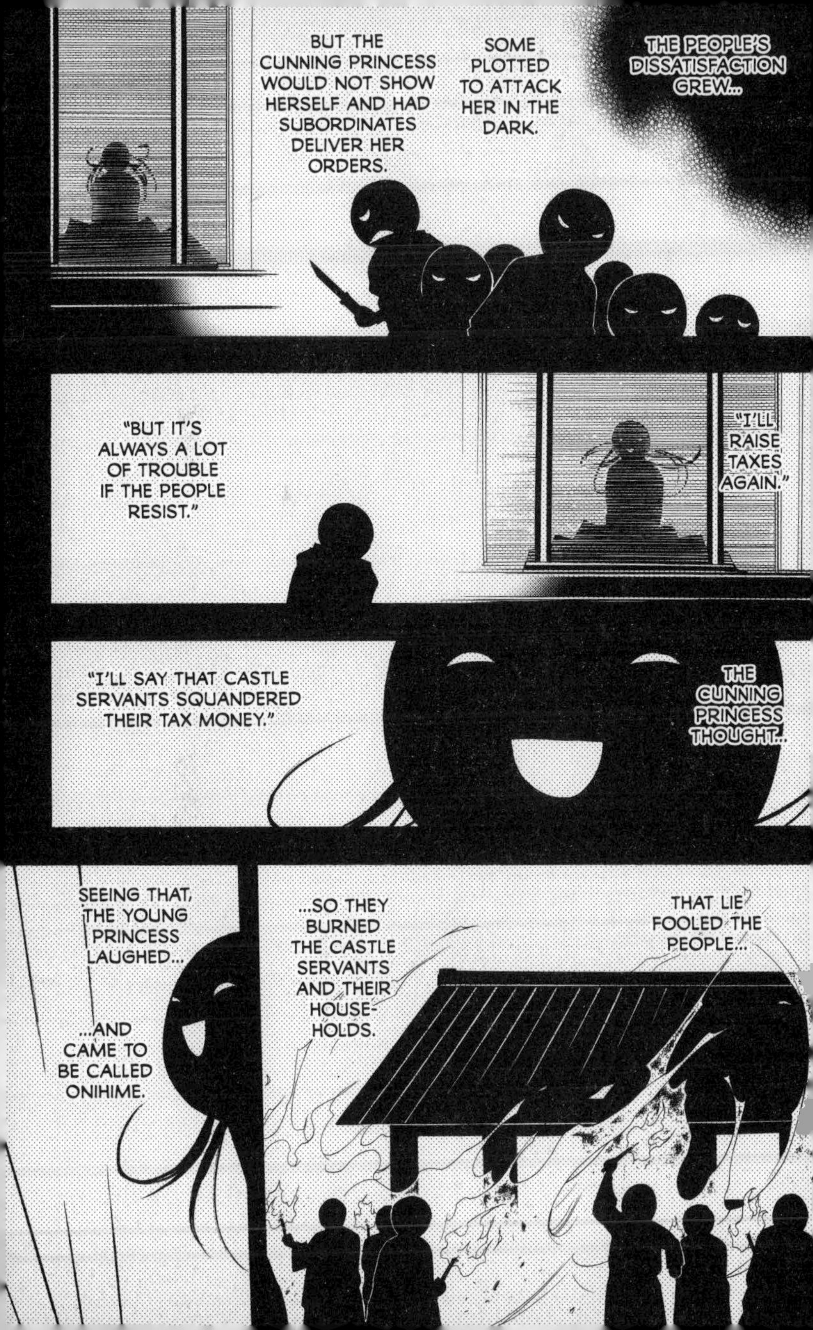
THE PEOPLE'S DISSATISFACTION GREW...
SOME PLOTTED TO ATTACK HER IN THE DARK.
BUT THE CUNNING PRINCESS WOULD NOT SHOW HERSELF AND HAD SUBORDINATES DELIVER HER ORDERS.
"I'LL RAISE TAXES AGAIN."
"BUT IT'S ALWAYS A LOT OF TROUBLE IF THE PEOPLE RESIST."
THE CUNNING PRINCESS THOUGHT...
"I'LL SAY THAT CASTLE SERVANTS SQUANDERED THEIR TAX MONEY."
THAT LIE FOOLED THE PEOPLE...
...SO THEY BURNED THE CASTLE SERVANTS AND THEIR HOUSE-HOLDS.
SEEING THAT, THE YOUNG PRINCESS LAUGHED...
...AND CAME TO BE CALLED ONIHIME.

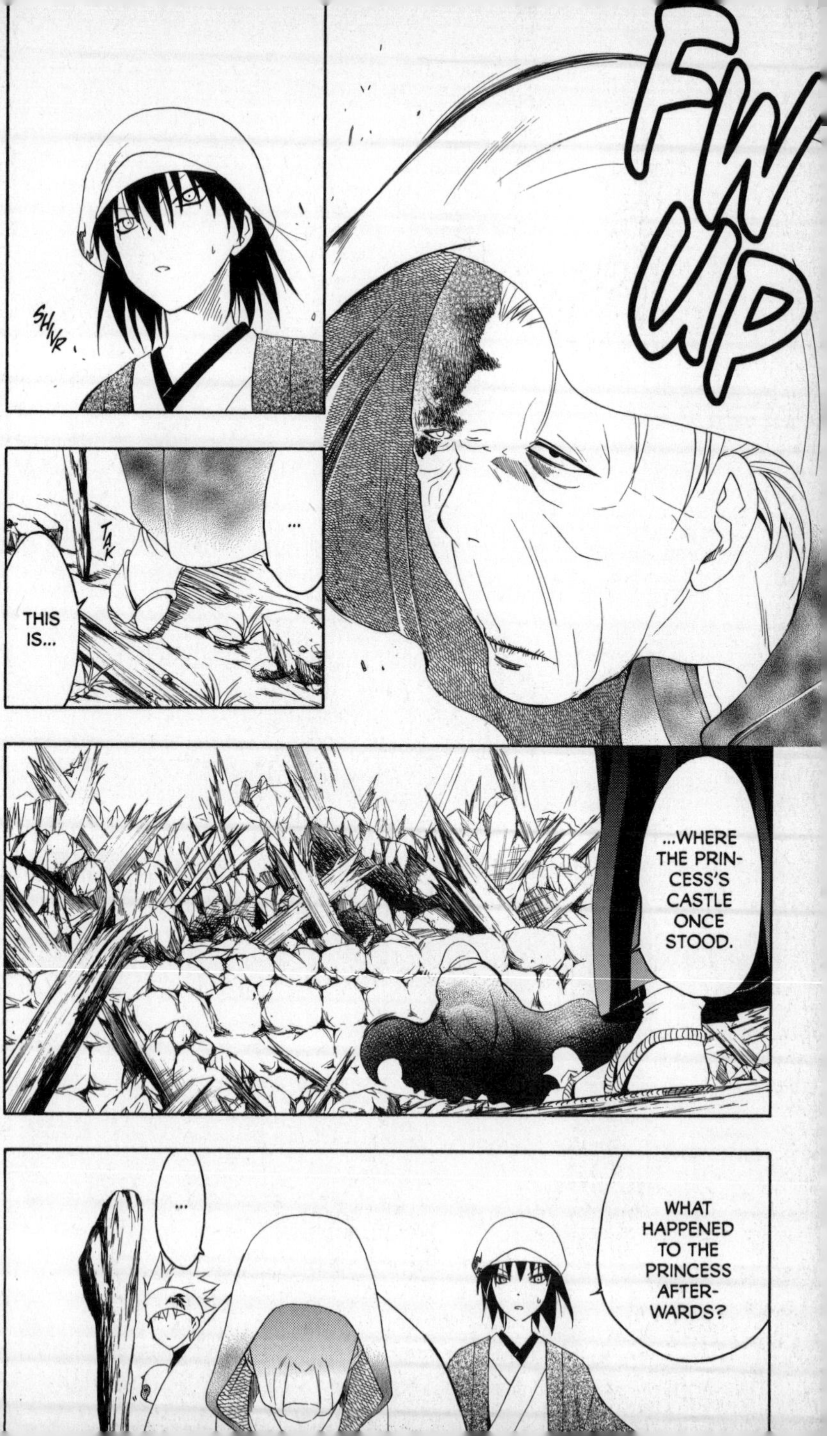
FWUP
SHWR
...
TAK
THIS IS...
...WHERE THE PRIN-CESS'S CASTLE ONCE STOOD.
WHAT HAPPENED TO THE PRINCESS AFTER-WARDS?
...

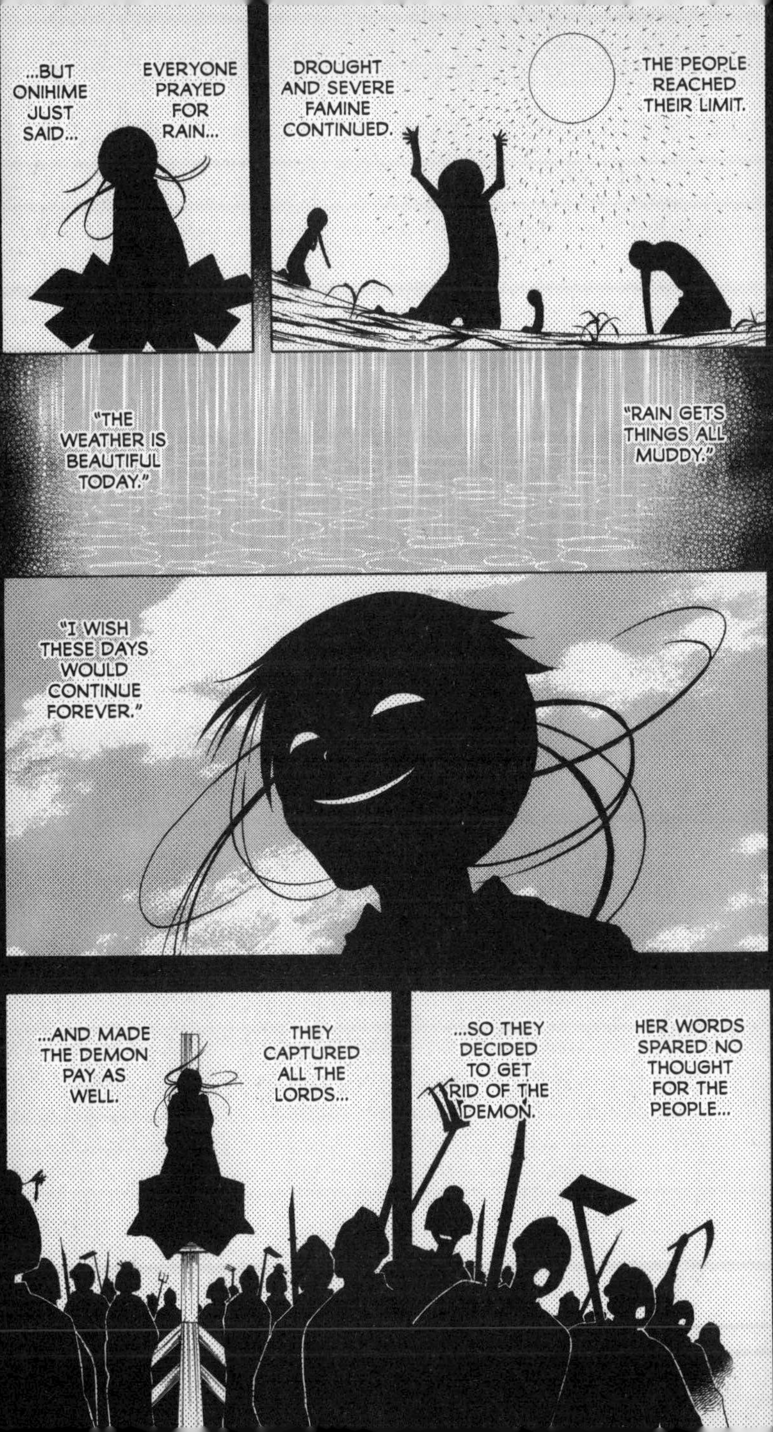
THE PEOPLE REACHED THEIR LIMIT.
DROUGHT AND SEVERE FAMINE CONTINUED.
EVERYONE PRAYED FOR RAIN...
...BUT ONIHIME JUST SAID...
"RAIN GETS THINGS ALL MUDDY."
"THE WEATHER IS BEAUTIFUL TODAY."
"I WISH THESE DAYS WOULD CONTINUE FOREVER."
HER WORDS SPARED NO THOUGHT FOR THE PEOPLE...
...SO THEY DECIDED TO GET RID OF THE DEMON.
THEY CAPTURED ALL THE LORDS...
...AND MADE THE DEMON PAY AS WELL.

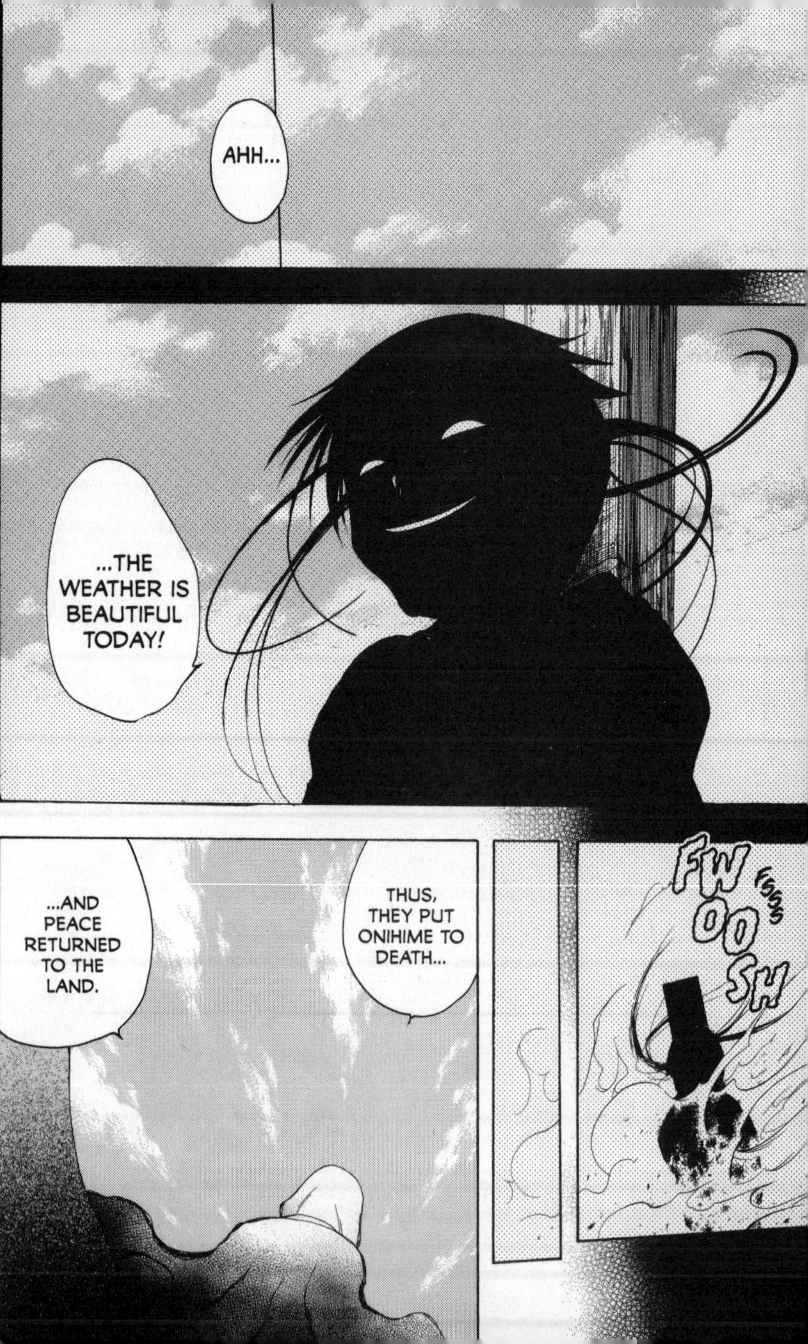
AHH...
...THE WEATHER IS BEAUTIFUL TODAY!
FWOOSH
FSSSS
THUS, THEY PUT ONIHIME TO DEATH...
...AND PEACE RETURNED TO THE LAND.

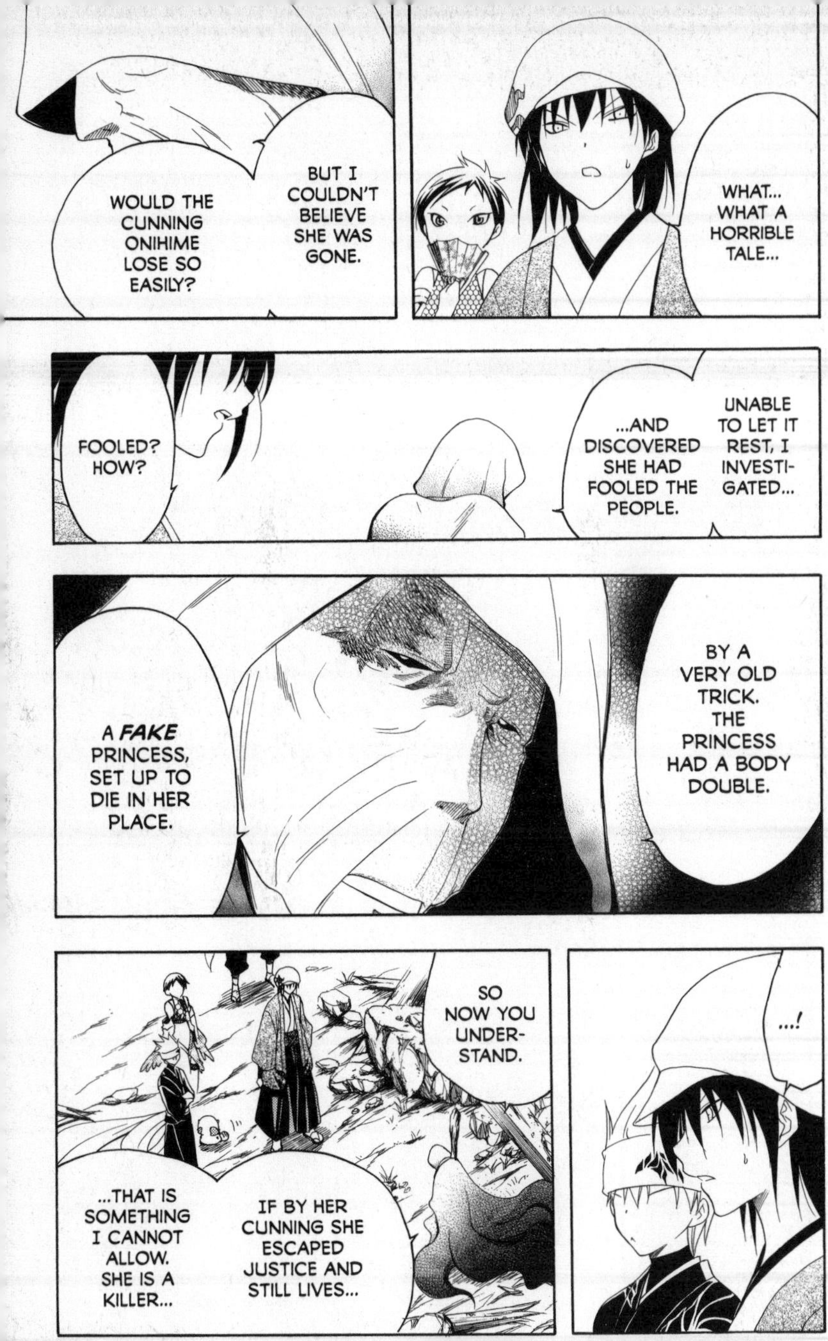
WHAT... WHAT A HORRIBLE TALE...
BUT I COULDN'T BELIEVE SHE WAS GONE.
WOULD THE CUNNING ONIHIME LOSE SO EASILY?
UNABLE TO LET IT REST, I INVESTIGATED...
...AND DISCOVERED SHE HAD FOOLED THE PEOPLE.
FOOLED? HOW?
BY A VERY OLD TRICK. THE PRINCESS HAD A BODY DOUBLE.
A *FAKE* PRINCESS, SET UP TO DIE IN HER PLACE.
...!
SO NOW YOU UNDERSTAND.
IF BY HER CUNNING SHE ESCAPED JUSTICE AND STILL LIVES...
...THAT IS SOMETHING I CANNOT ALLOW. SHE IS A KILLER...

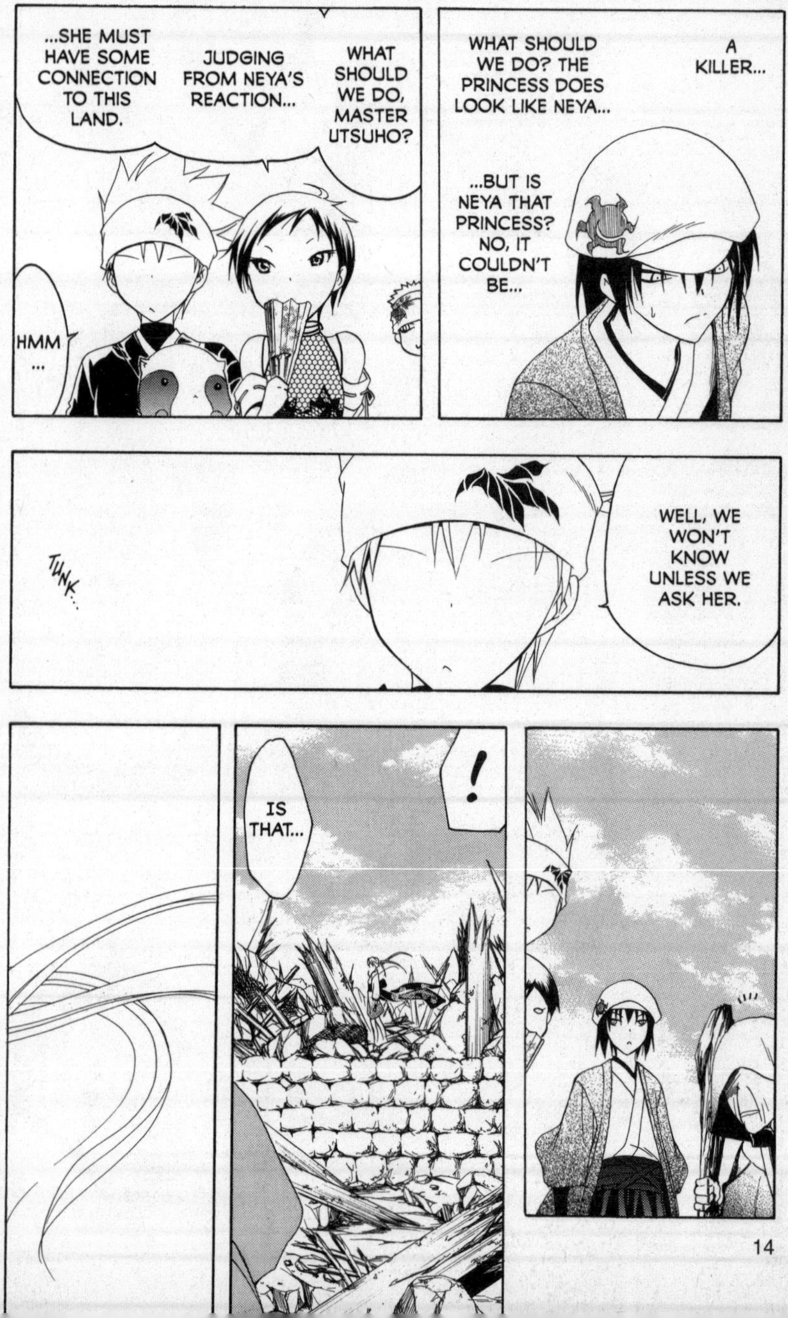
A KILLER...
WHAT SHOULD WE DO? THE PRINCESS DOES LOOK LIKE NEYA...
...BUT IS NEYA THAT PRINCESS? NO, IT COULDN'T BE...
WHAT SHOULD WE DO, MASTER UTSUHO?
JUDGING FROM NEYA'S REACTION...
...SHE MUST HAVE SOME CONNECTION TO THIS LAND.
HMM...
WELL, WE WON'T KNOW UNLESS WE ASK HER.
TUNK...
!
IS THAT...

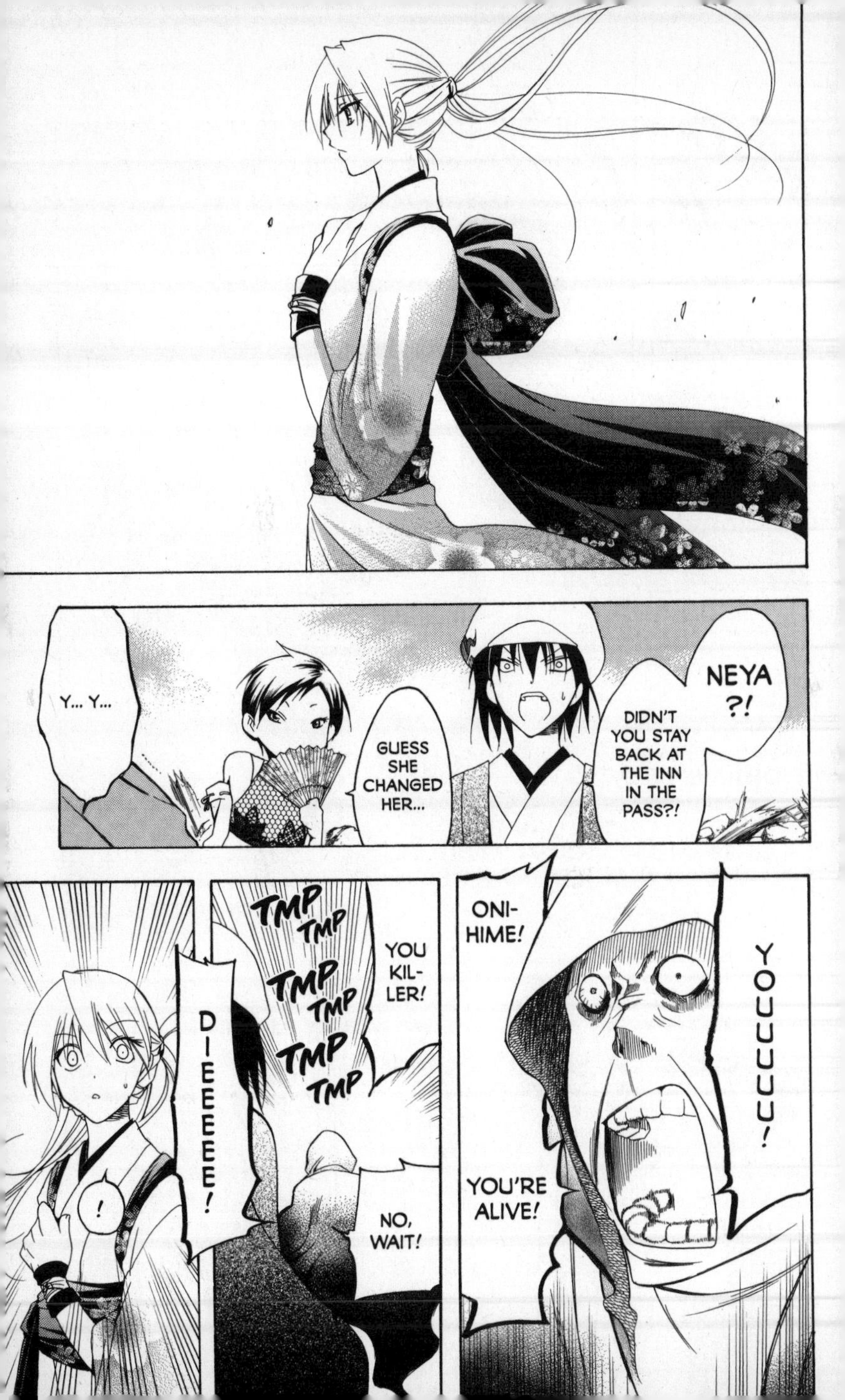
NEYA ?!
DIDN'T YOU STAY BACK AT THE INN IN THE PASS?!
GUESS SHE CHANGED HER...
Y... Y...
YOUUUUU!
ONI-HIME!
YOU'RE ALIVE!
YOU KIL-LER!
TMP TMP TMP TMP TMP TMP
NO, WAIT!
DIEEEEEE!
!

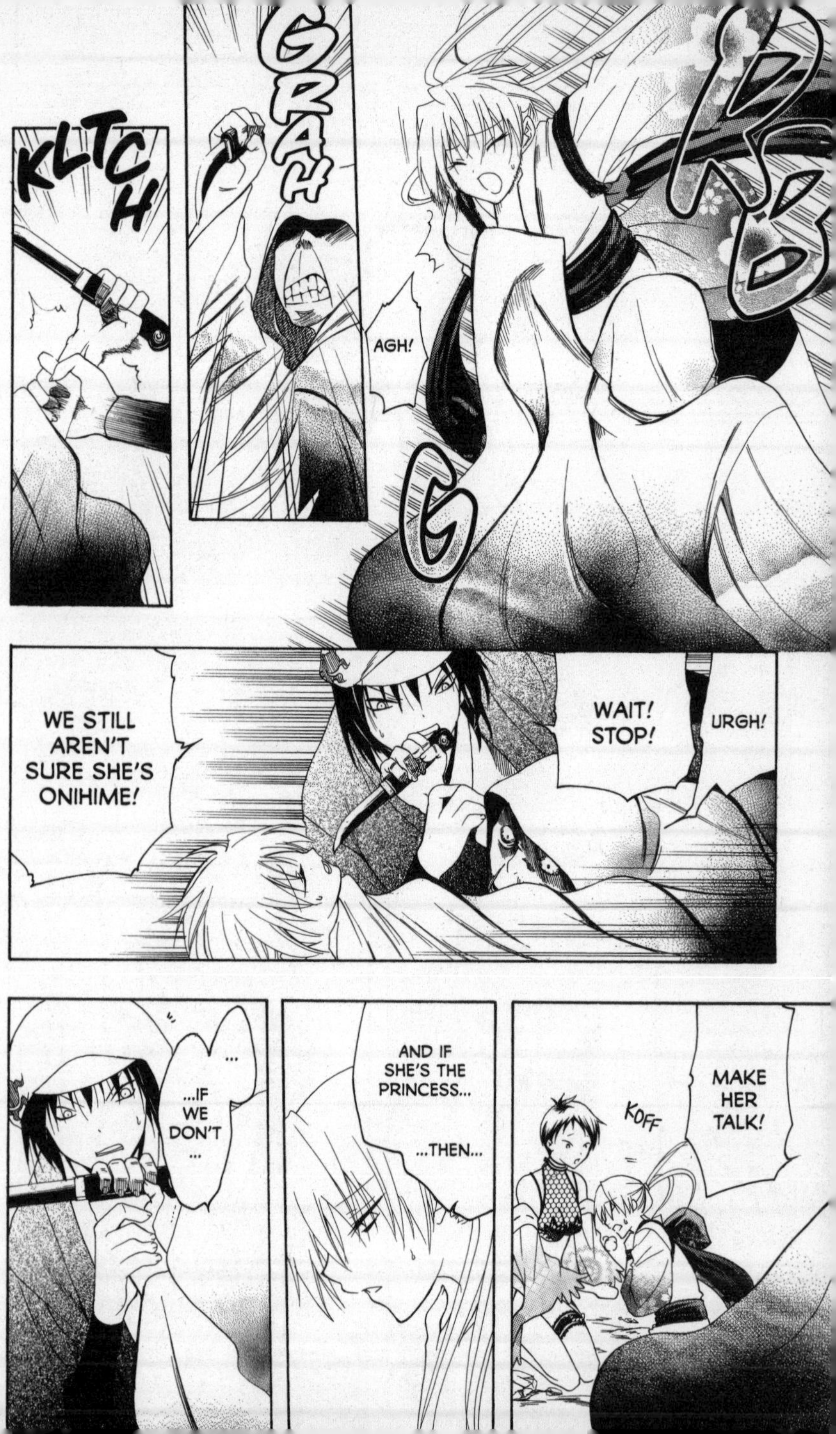
AGH!
GRAH
KLTCH
WAIT! STOP!
URGH!
WE STILL AREN'T SURE SHE'S ONIHIME!
MAKE HER TALK!
KOFF
AND IF SHE'S THE PRINCESS...
...THEN...
...
...IF WE DON'T ...

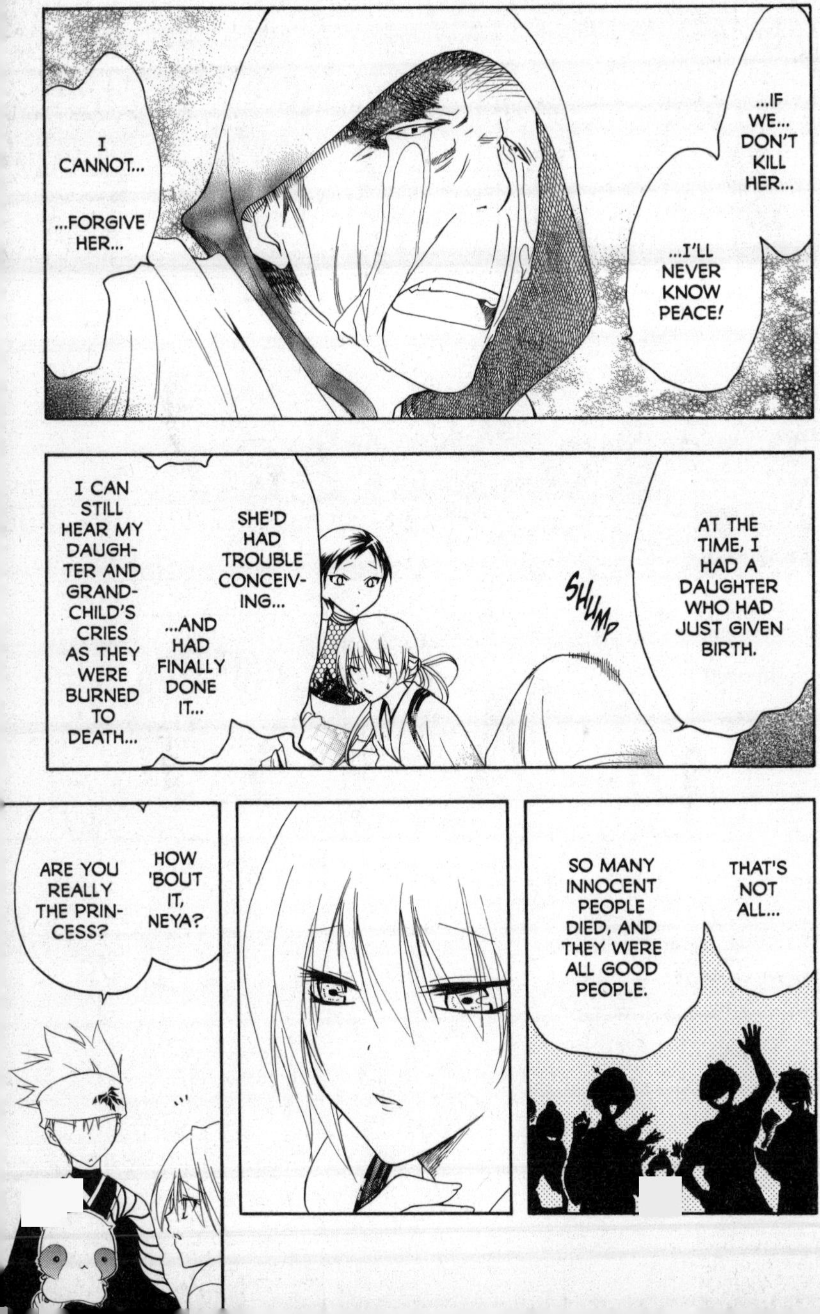
...IF WE... DON'T KILL HER...
...I'LL NEVER KNOW PEACE!
I CANNOT...
...FORGIVE HER...
AT THE TIME, I HAD A DAUGHTER WHO HAD JUST GIVEN BIRTH.
SHUMP
SHE'D HAD TROUBLE CONCEIV-ING...
...AND HAD FINALLY DONE IT...
I CAN STILL HEAR MY DAUGH-TER AND GRAND-CHILD'S CRIES AS THEY WERE BURNED TO DEATH...
THAT'S NOT ALL...
SO MANY INNOCENT PEOPLE DIED, AND THEY WERE ALL GOOD PEOPLE.
HOW 'BOUT IT, NEYA?
ARE YOU REALLY THE PRIN-CESS?
...

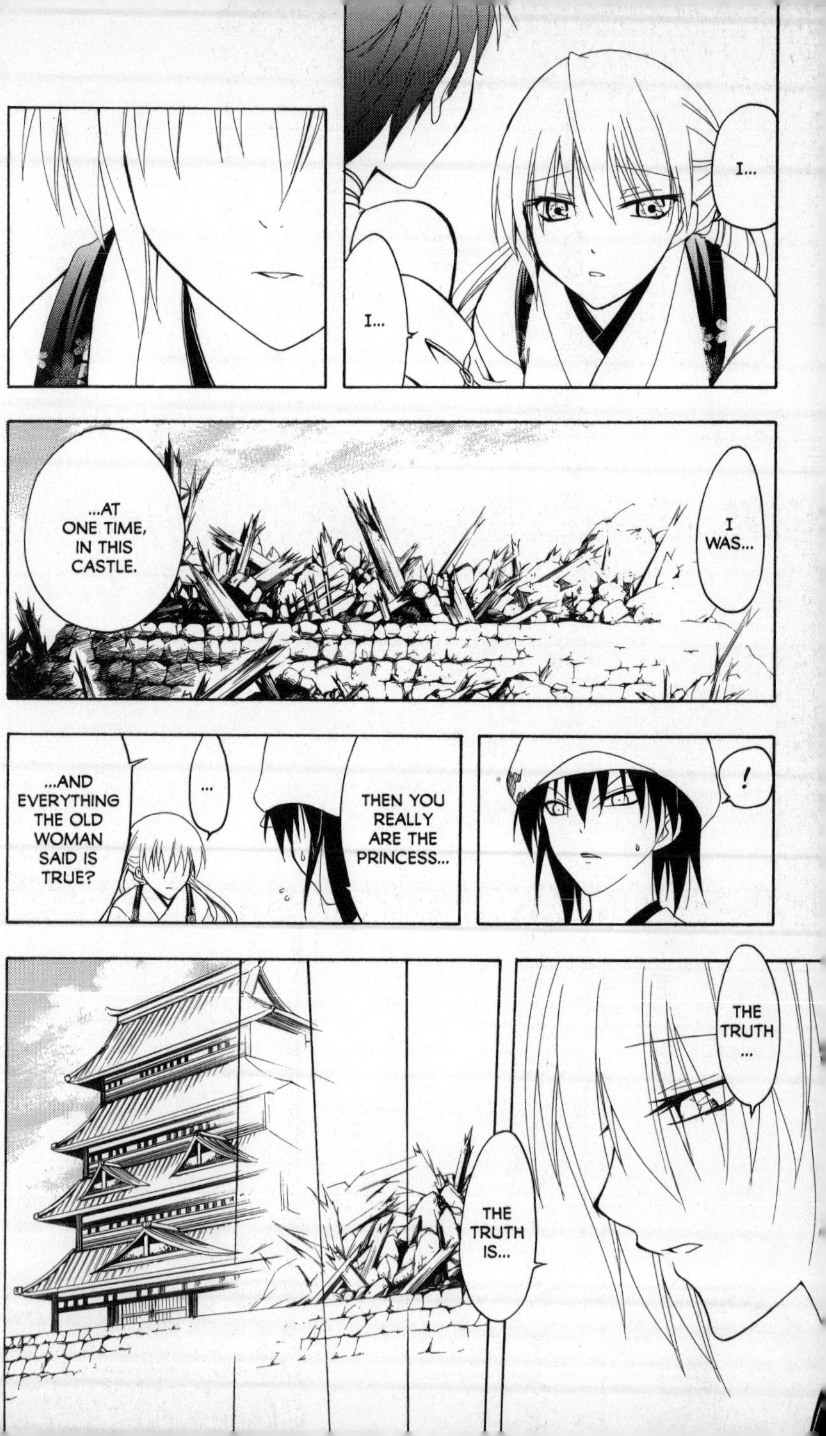
I...
I...
I WAS...
...AT ONE TIME, IN THIS CASTLE.
!
THEN YOU REALLY ARE THE PRINCESS...
...
...AND EVERYTHING THE OLD WOMAN SAID IS TRUE?
THE TRUTH ...
THE TRUTH IS...

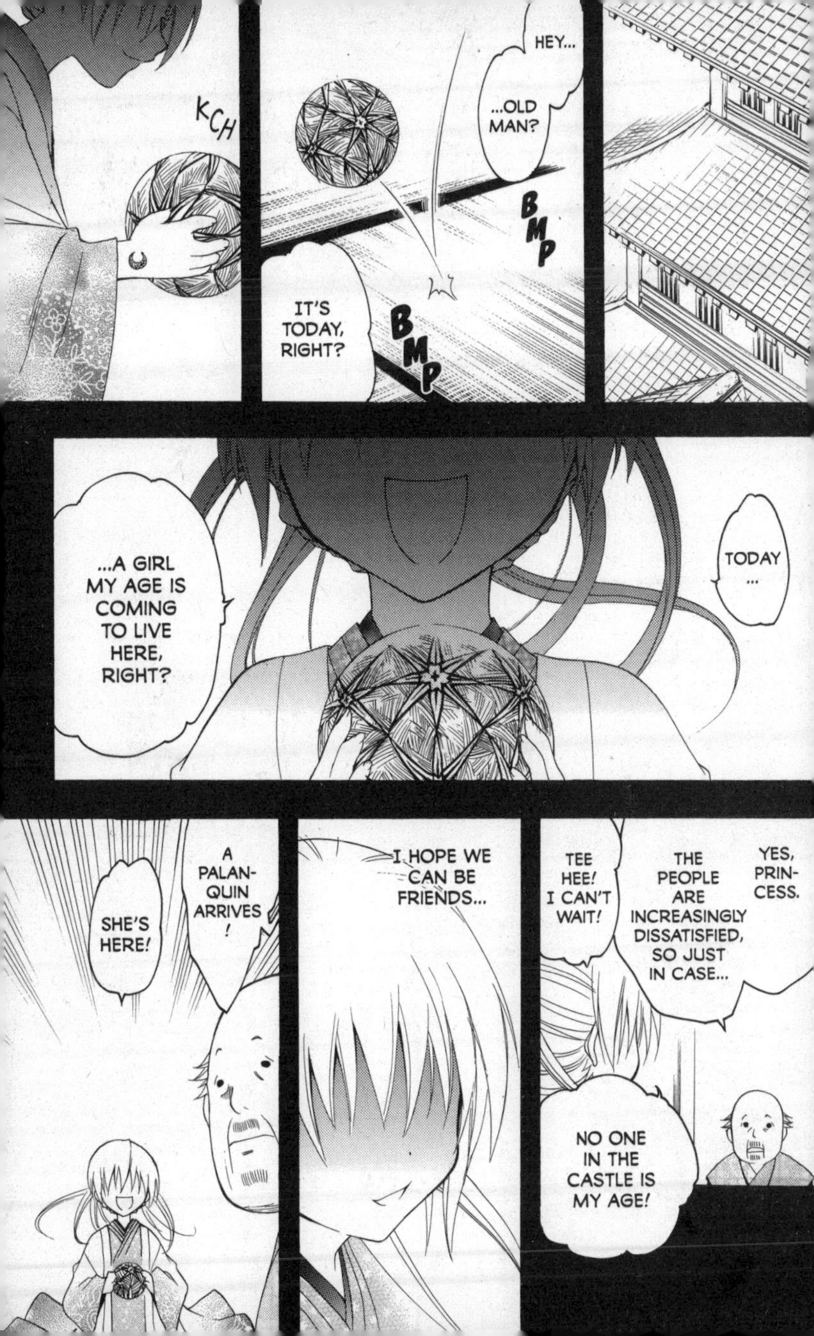
HEY...
...OLD MAN?
BMP
IT'S TODAY, RIGHT?
BMP
KCH
TODAY ...
...A GIRL MY AGE IS COMING TO LIVE HERE, RIGHT?
YES, PRINCESS.
THE PEOPLE ARE INCREASINGLY DISSATISFIED, SO JUST IN CASE...
TEE HEE! I CAN'T WAIT!
NO ONE IN THE CASTLE IS MY AGE!
I HOPE WE CAN BE FRIENDS...
A PALANQUIN ARRIVES!
SHE'S HERE!

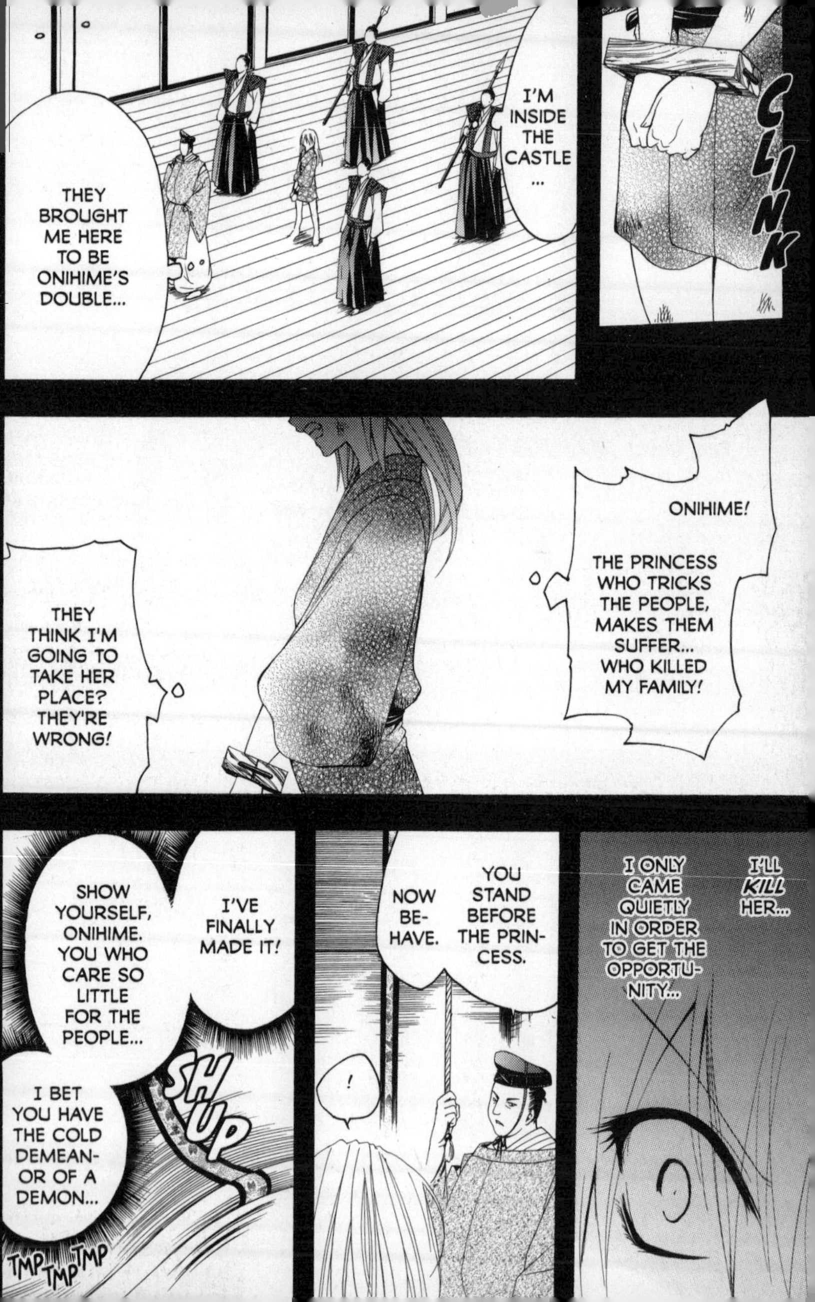
CLINK
I'M INSIDE THE CASTLE...
THEY BROUGHT ME HERE TO BE ONIHIME'S DOUBLE...
ONIHIME!
THE PRINCESS WHO TRICKS THE PEOPLE, MAKES THEM SUFFER... WHO KILLED MY FAMILY!
THEY THINK I'M GOING TO TAKE HER PLACE? THEY'RE WRONG!
I'LL KILL HER...
I ONLY CAME QUIETLY IN ORDER TO GET THE OPPORTU-NITY...
YOU STAND BEFORE THE PRIN-CESS.
NOW BE-HAVE.
!
I'VE FINALLY MADE IT!
SHOW YOURSELF, ONIHIME. YOU WHO CARE SO LITTLE FOR THE PEOPLE...
SHUP
I BET YOU HAVE THE COLD DEMEAN-OR OF A DEMON...
TMP TMP TMP

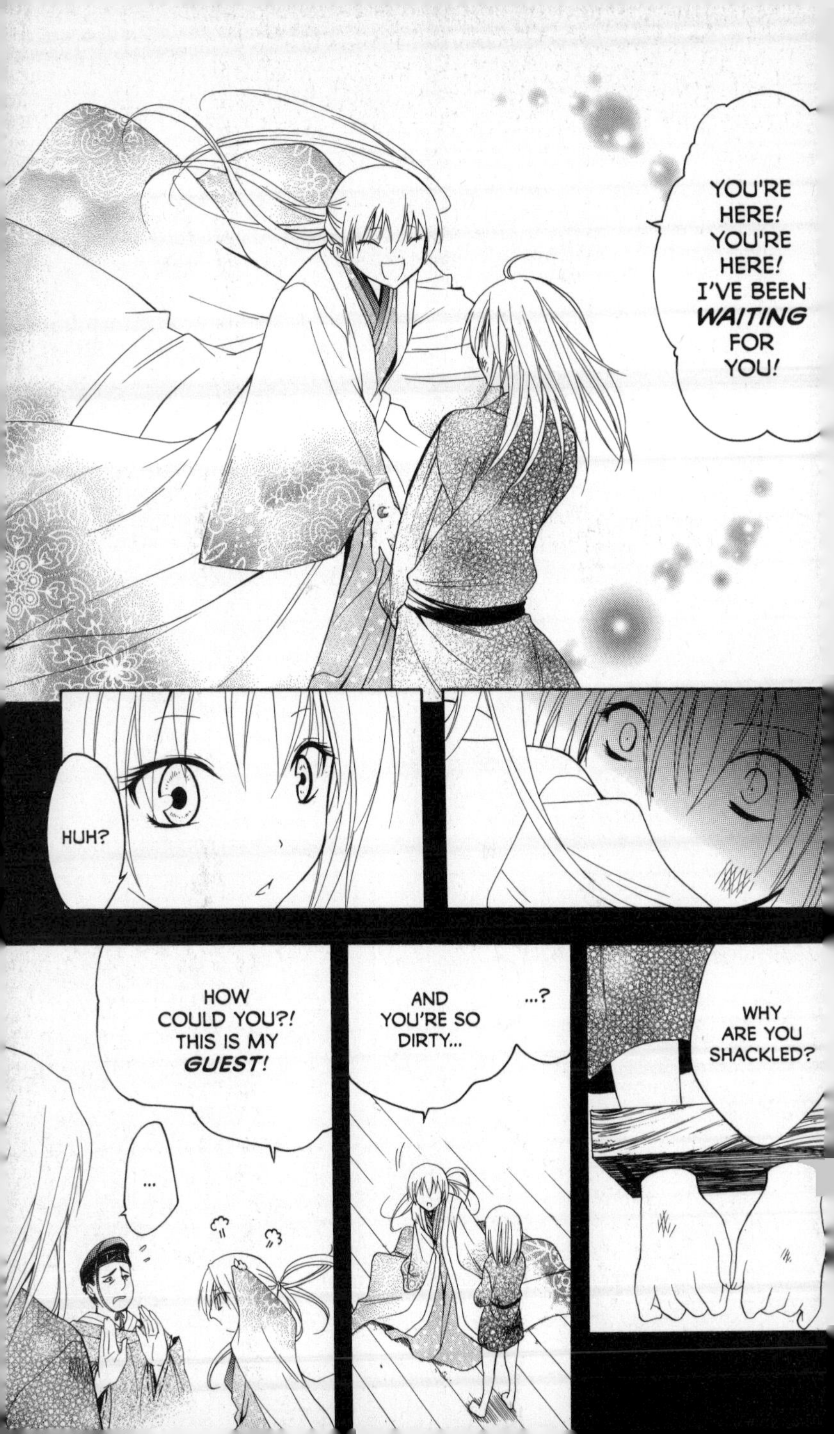
YOU'RE HERE! YOU'RE HERE! I'VE BEEN *WAITING* FOR YOU!
HUH?
WHY ARE YOU SHACKLED?
...?
AND YOU'RE SO DIRTY...
HOW COULD YOU?! THIS IS MY *GUEST*!
...

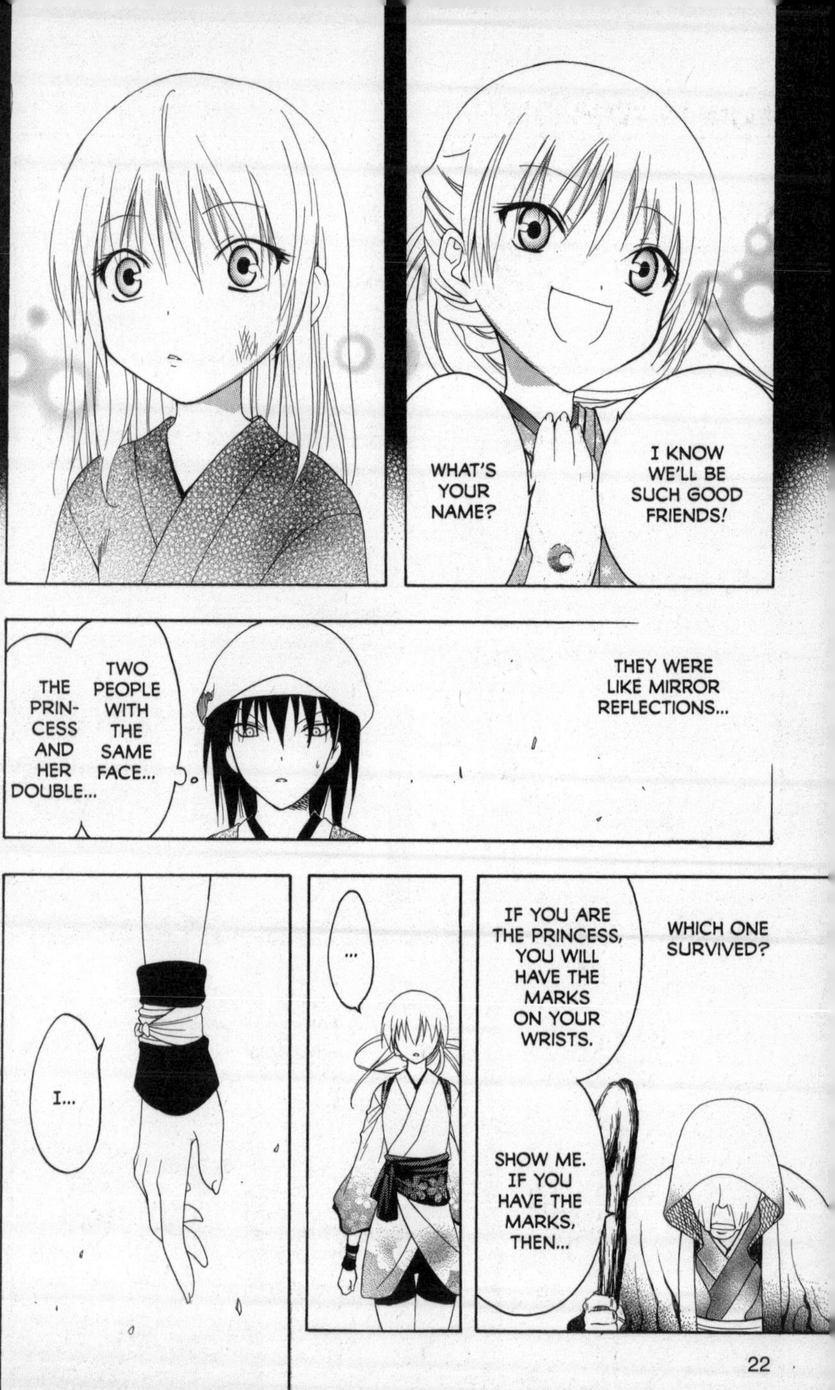
I KNOW WE'LL BE SUCH GOOD FRIENDS!
WHAT'S YOUR NAME?
THEY WERE LIKE MIRROR REFLECTIONS...
TWO PEOPLE WITH THE SAME FACE...
THE PRINCESS AND HER DOUBLE...
WHICH ONE SURVIVED?
IF YOU ARE THE PRINCESS, YOU WILL HAVE THE MARKS ON YOUR WRISTS.
SHOW ME. IF YOU HAVE THE MARKS, THEN...
...
I...

Chapter 89 Weather

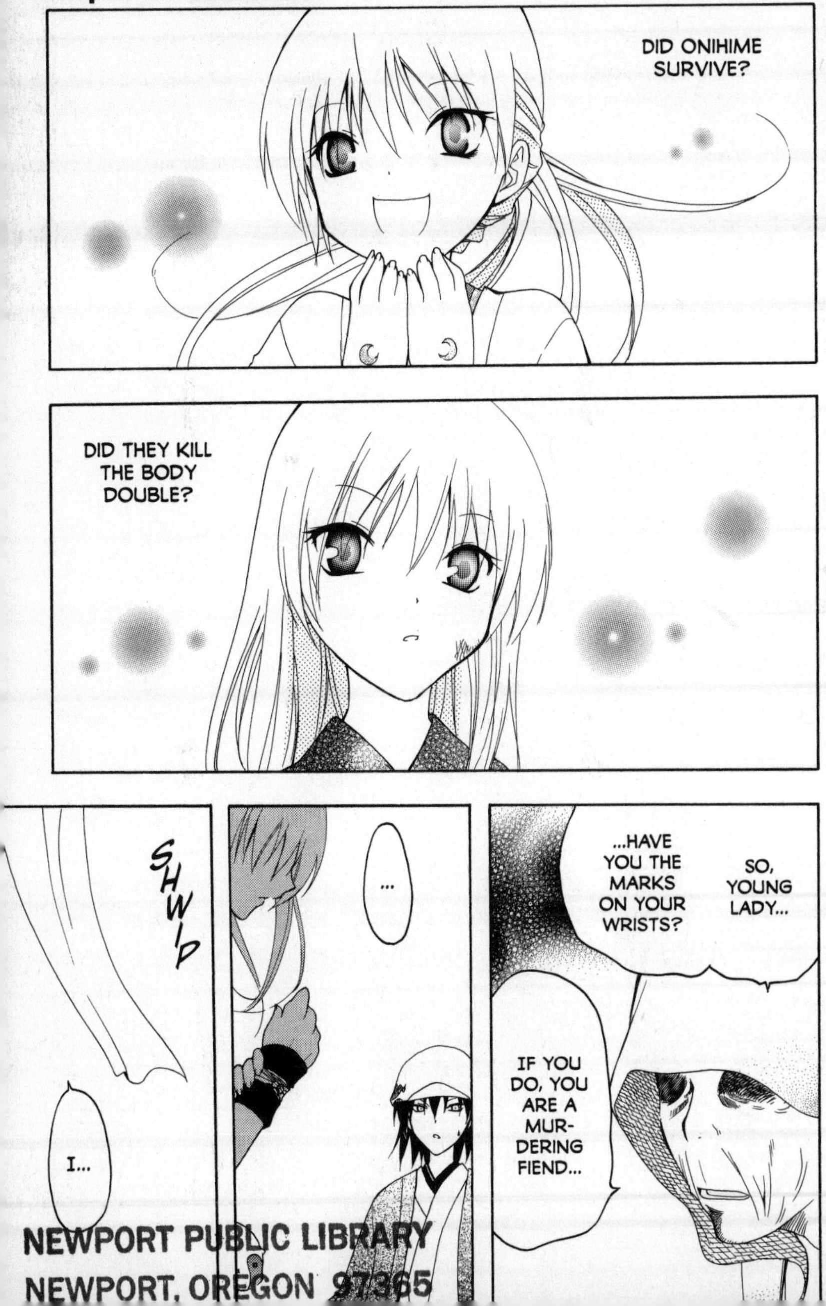

DID ONIHIME SURVIVE?
DID THEY KILL THE BODY DOUBLE?
SO, YOUNG LADY...
...HAVE YOU THE MARKS ON YOUR WRISTS?
IF YOU DO, YOU ARE A MUR-DERING FIEND...
...
SHWIP
I...

Chapter 89
Weather

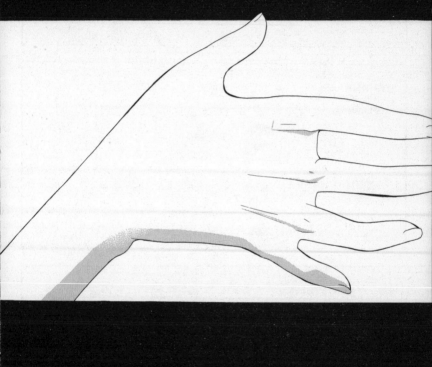

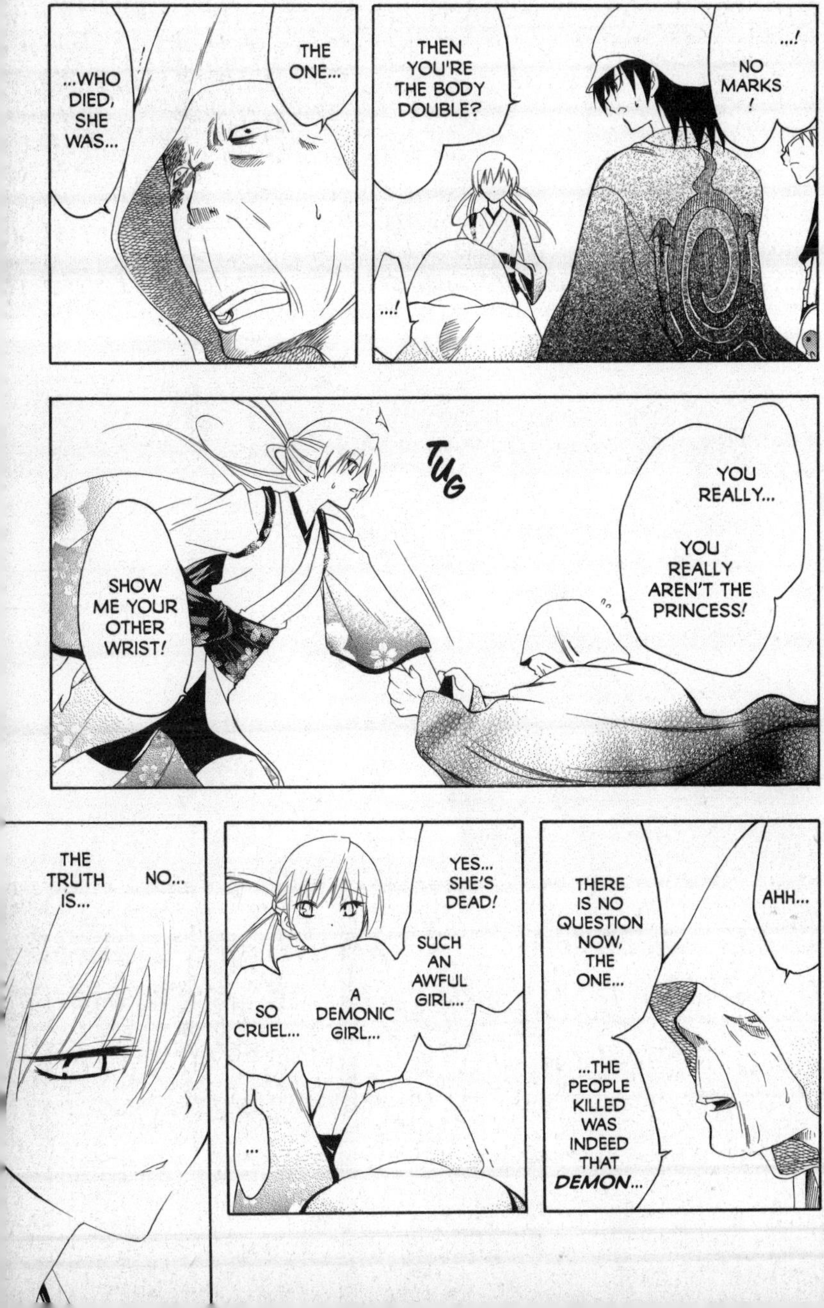
...!
NO MARKS!
THEN YOU'RE THE BODY DOUBLE?
...!
THE ONE...
...WHO DIED, SHE WAS...
TUG
YOU REALLY...
YOU REALLY AREN'T THE PRINCESS!
SHOW ME YOUR OTHER WRIST!
AHH...
THERE IS NO QUESTION NOW, THE ONE...
...THE PEOPLE KILLED WAS INDEED THAT *DEMON*...
YES... SHE'S DEAD!
SUCH AN AWFUL GIRL...
A DEMONIC GIRL...
SO CRUEL...
...
NO...
THE TRUTH IS...

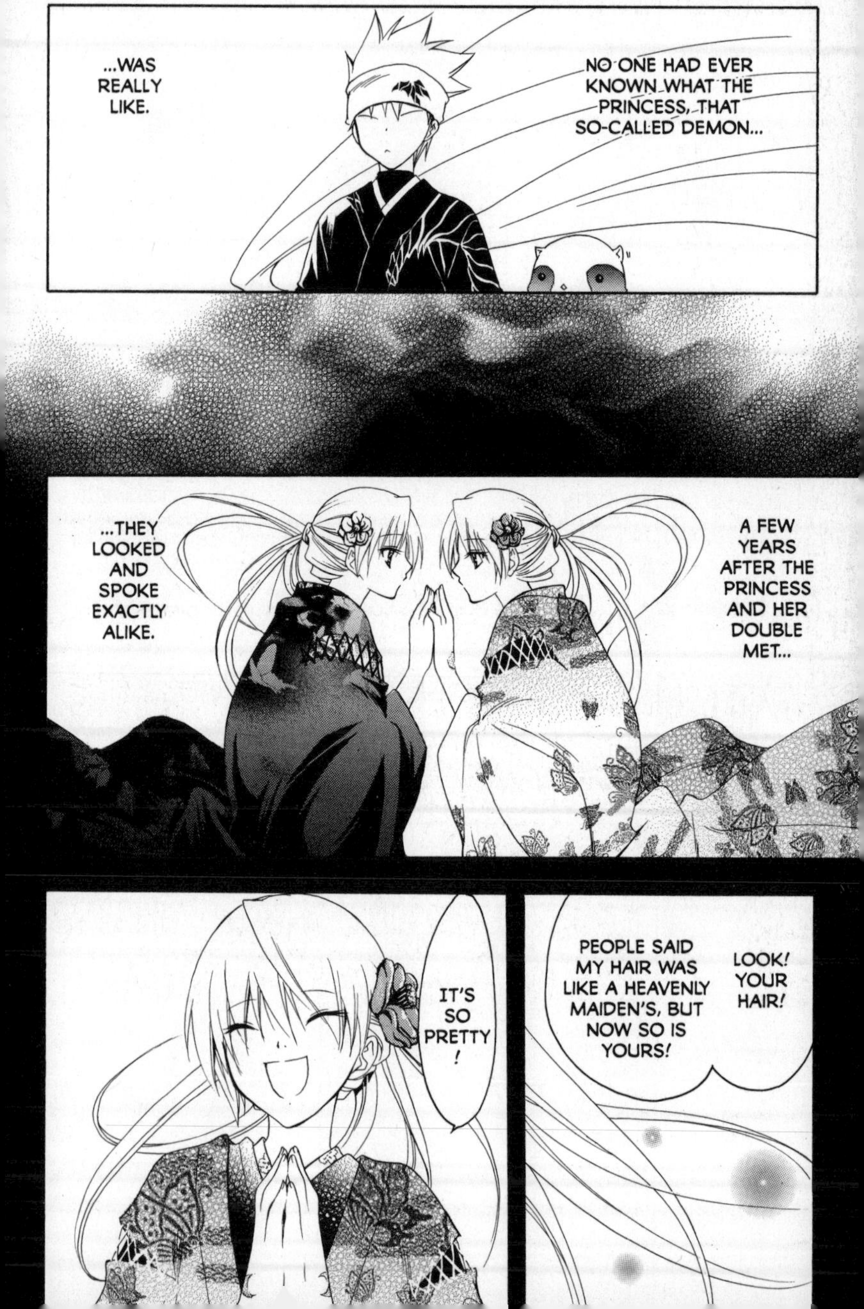
NO ONE HAD EVER KNOWN WHAT THE PRINCESS, THAT SO-CALLED DEMON...
...WAS REALLY LIKE.
A FEW YEARS AFTER THE PRINCESS AND HER DOUBLE MET...
...THEY LOOKED AND SPOKE EXACTLY ALIKE.
LOOK! YOUR HAIR!
PEOPLE SAID MY HAIR WAS LIKE A HEAVENLY MAIDEN'S, BUT NOW SO IS YOURS!
IT'S SO PRETTY!

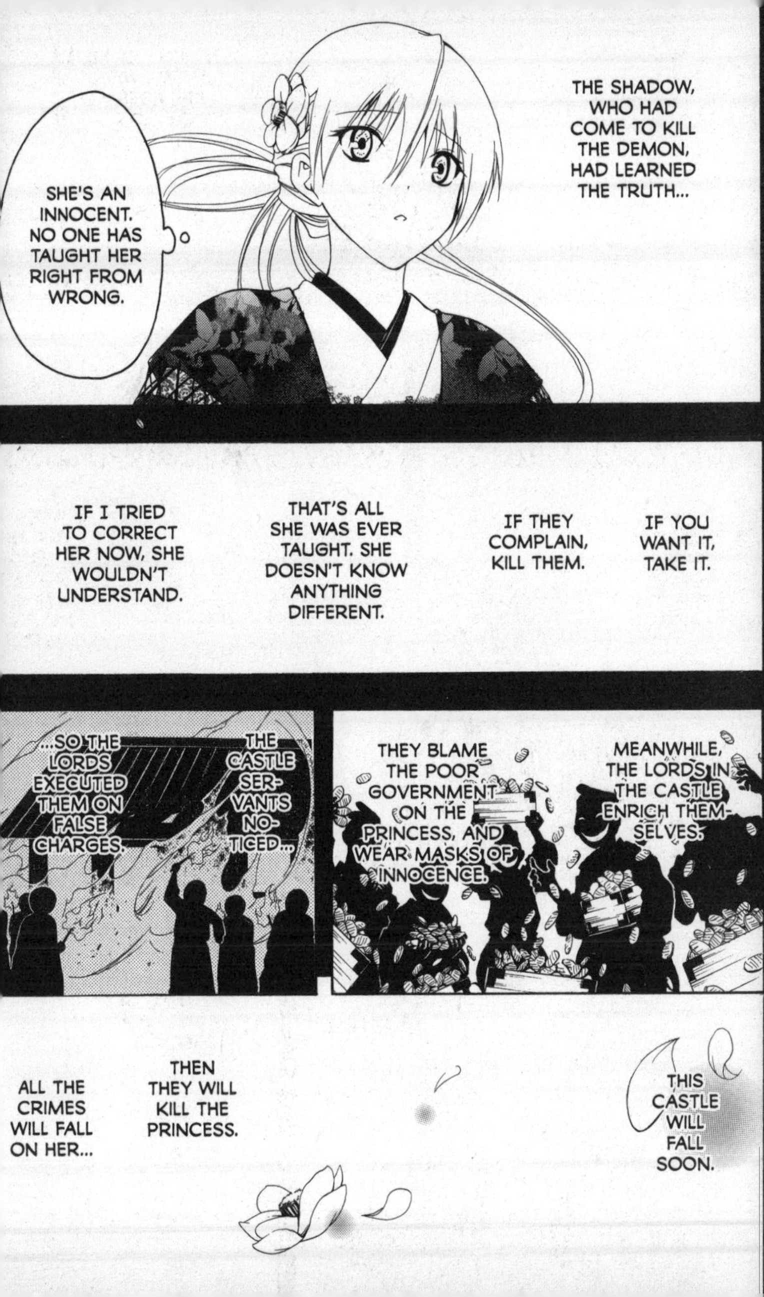
THE SHADOW, WHO HAD COME TO KILL THE DEMON, HAD LEARNED THE TRUTH...
SHE'S AN INNOCENT. NO ONE HAS TAUGHT HER RIGHT FROM WRONG.
IF YOU WANT IT, TAKE IT.
IF THEY COMPLAIN, KILL THEM.
THAT'S ALL SHE WAS EVER TAUGHT. SHE DOESN'T KNOW ANYTHING DIFFERENT.
IF I TRIED TO CORRECT HER NOW, SHE WOULDN'T UNDERSTAND.
MEANWHILE, THE LORDS IN THE CASTLE ENRICH THEMSELVES.
THEY BLAME THE POOR GOVERNMENT ON THE PRINCESS, AND WEAR MASKS OF INNOCENCE.
THE CASTLE SERVANTS NOTICED...
...SO THE LORDS EXECUTED THEM ON FALSE CHARGES.
THIS CASTLE WILL FALL SOON.
THEN THEY WILL KILL THE PRINCESS.
ALL THE CRIMES WILL FALL ON HER...

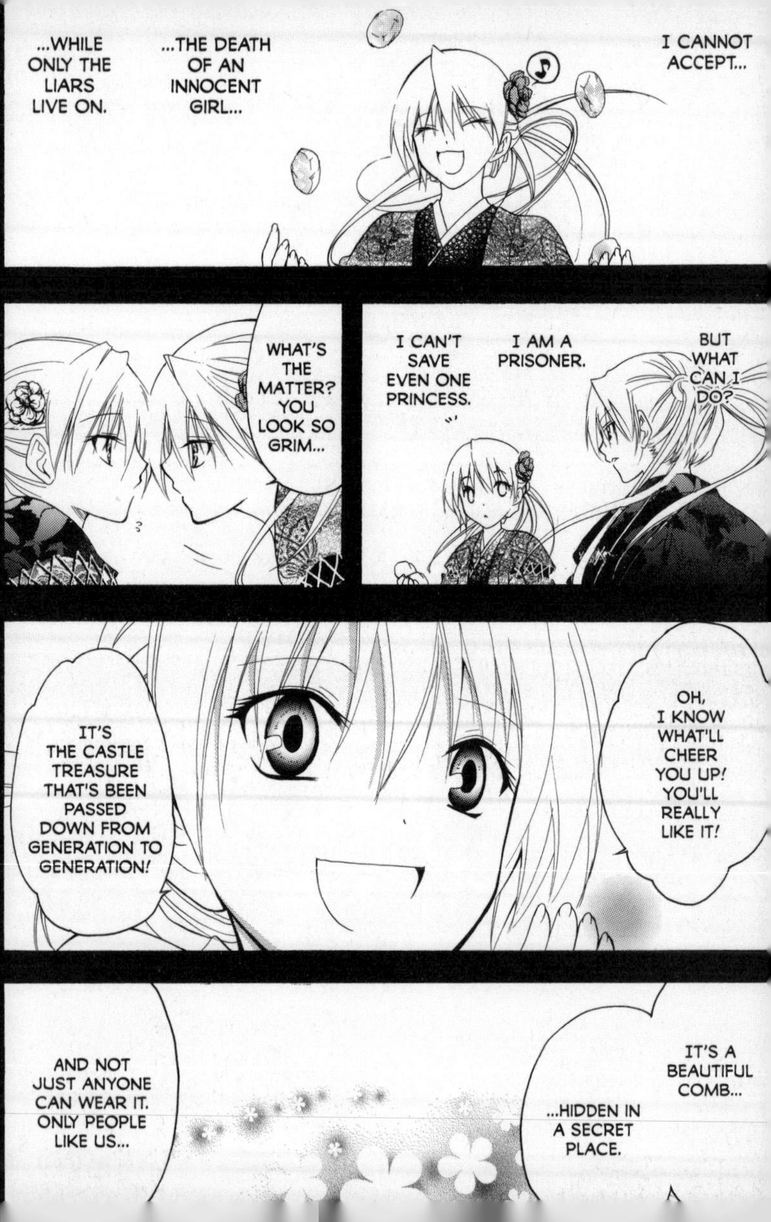
I CANNOT ACCEPT...
...THE DEATH OF AN INNOCENT GIRL...
...WHILE ONLY THE LIARS LIVE ON.
BUT WHAT CAN I DO?
I AM A PRISONER.
I CAN'T SAVE EVEN ONE PRINCESS.
WHAT'S THE MATTER? YOU LOOK SO GRIM...
OH, I KNOW WHAT'LL CHEER YOU UP! YOU'LL REALLY LIKE IT!
IT'S THE CASTLE TREASURE THAT'S BEEN PASSED DOWN FROM GENERATION TO GENERATION!
IT'S A BEAUTIFUL COMB...
...HIDDEN IN A SECRET PLACE.
AND NOT JUST ANYONE CAN WEAR IT. ONLY PEOPLE LIKE US...

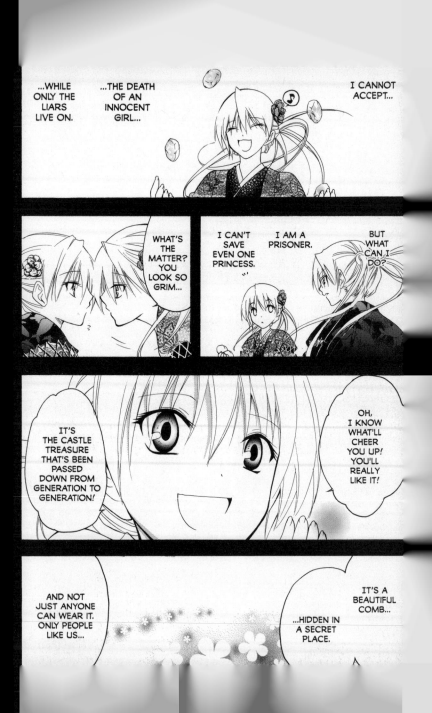

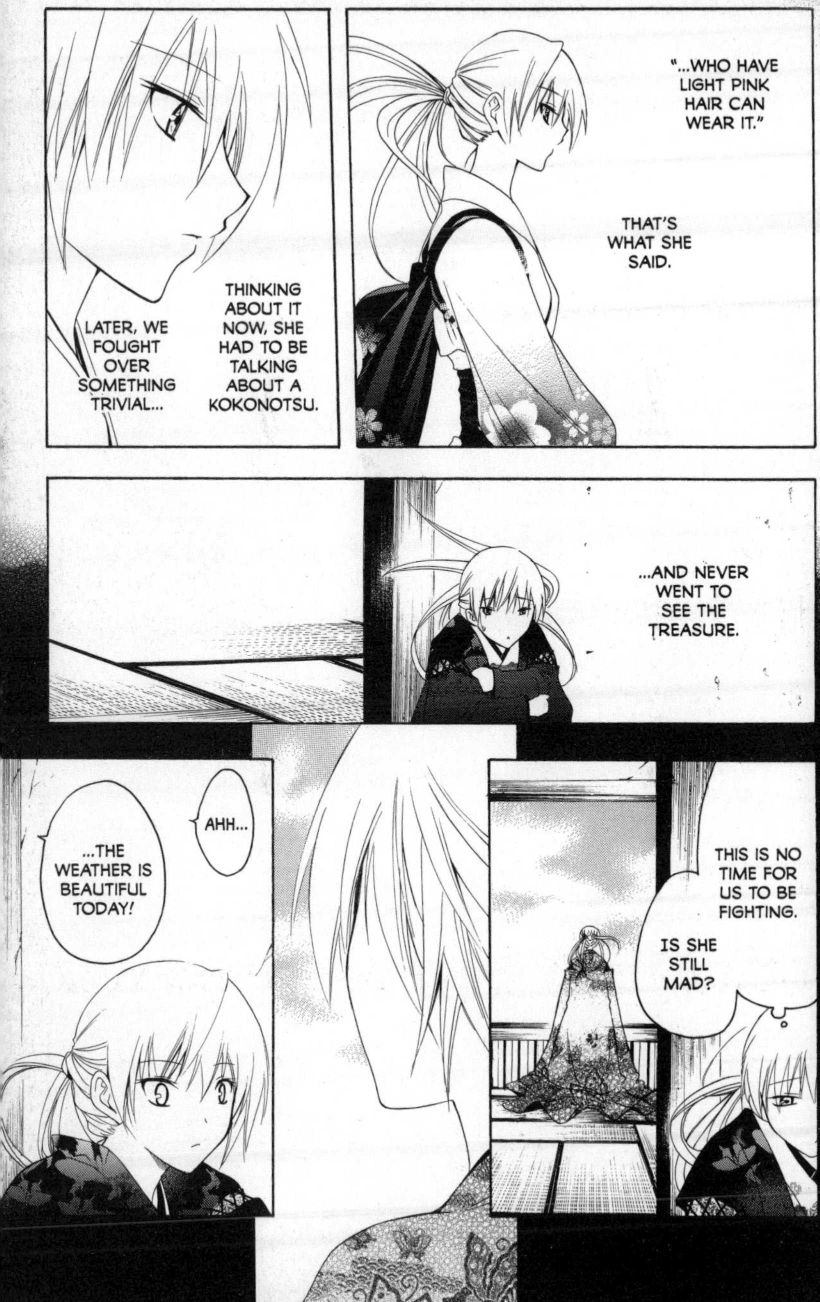
"...WHO HAVE LIGHT PINK HAIR CAN WEAR IT."
THAT'S WHAT SHE SAID.
THINKING ABOUT IT NOW, SHE HAD TO BE TALKING ABOUT A KOKONOTSU.
LATER, WE FOUGHT OVER SOMETHING TRIVIAL...
...AND NEVER WENT TO SEE THE TREASURE.
THIS IS NO TIME FOR US TO BE FIGHTING.
IS SHE STILL MAD?
AHH...
...THE WEATHER IS BEAUTIFUL TODAY!

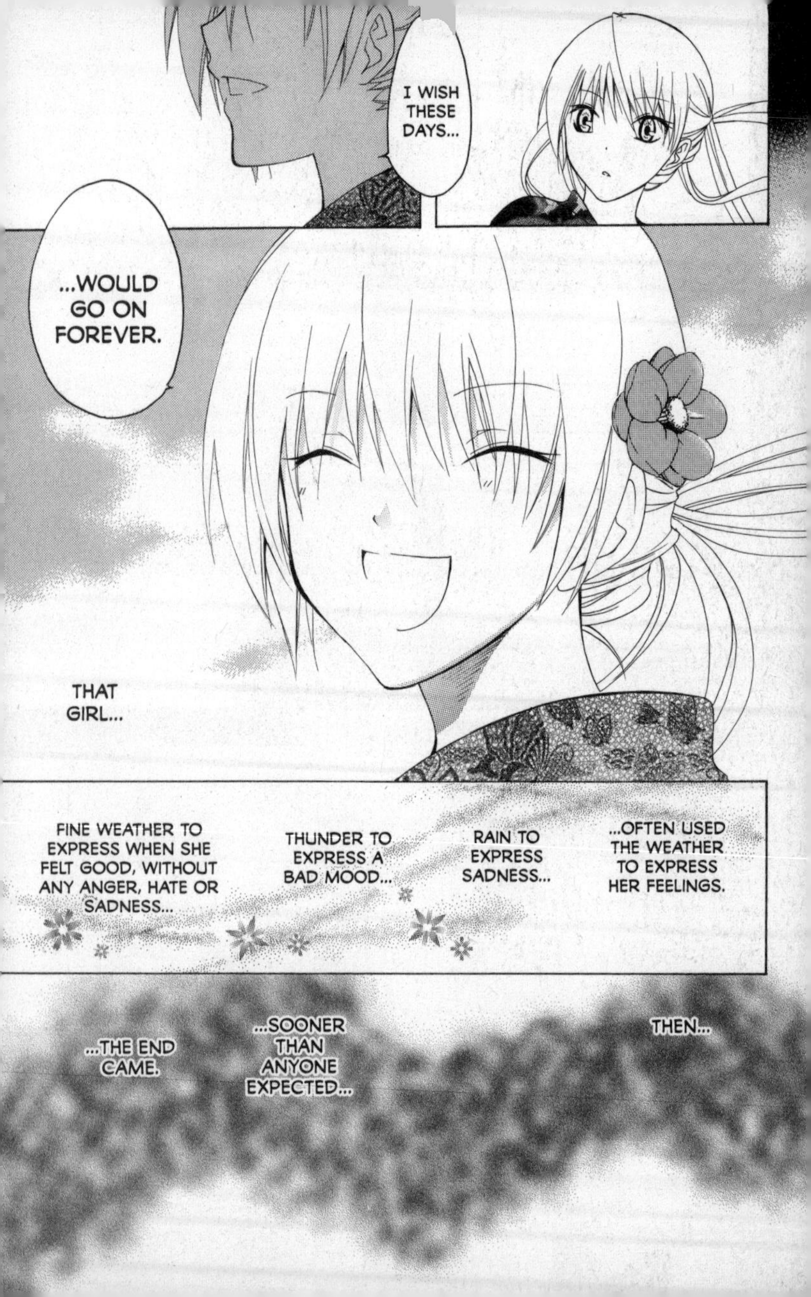
I WISH THESE DAYS...
...WOULD GO ON FOREVER.
THAT GIRL...
...OFTEN USED THE WEATHER TO EXPRESS HER FEELINGS.
RAIN TO EXPRESS SADNESS...
THUNDER TO EXPRESS A BAD MOOD...
FINE WEATHER TO EXPRESS WHEN SHE FELT GOOD, WITHOUT ANY ANGER, HATE OR SADNESS...
THEN...
...SOONER THAN ANYONE EXPECTED...
...THE END CAME.

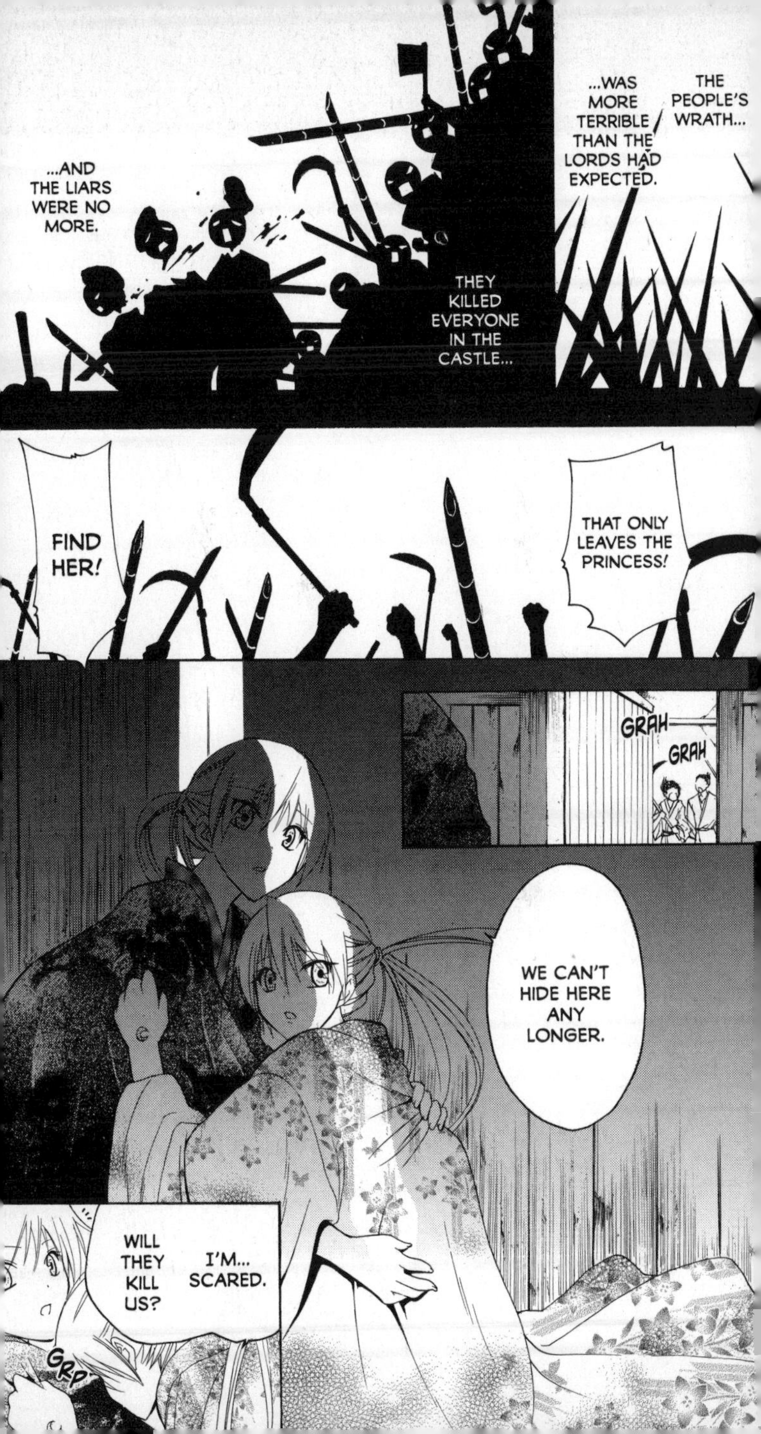
THE PEOPLE'S WRATH...
...WAS MORE TERRIBLE THAN THE LORDS HAD EXPECTED.
THEY KILLED EVERYONE IN THE CASTLE...
...AND THE LIARS WERE NO MORE.
THAT ONLY LEAVES THE PRINCESS!
FIND HER!
GRAH
GRAH
WE CAN'T HIDE HERE ANY LONGER.
I'M... SCARED.
WILL THEY KILL US?
GRP

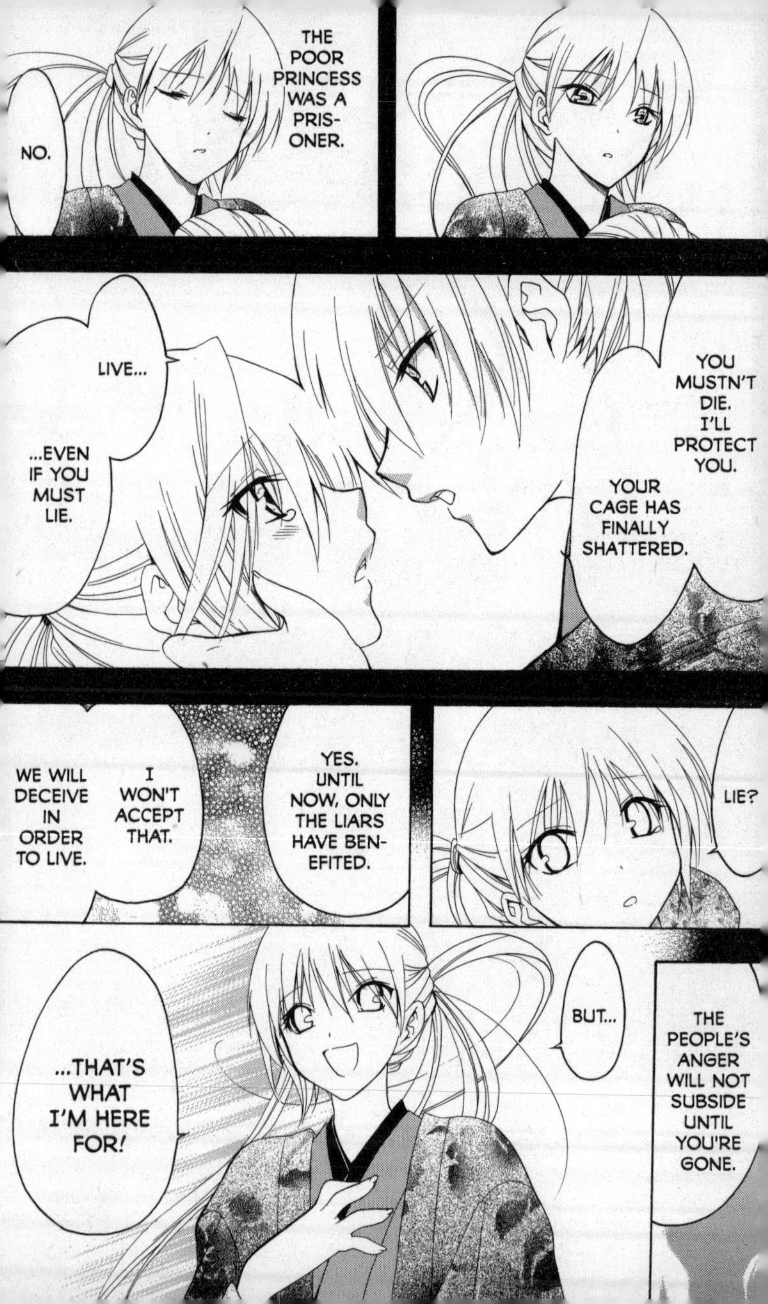
THE POOR PRINCESS WAS A PRISONER.
NO.
YOU MUSTN'T DIE. I'LL PROTECT YOU.
YOUR CAGE HAS FINALLY SHATTERED.
LIVE...
...EVEN IF YOU MUST LIE.
LIE?
YES. UNTIL NOW, ONLY THE LIARS HAVE BENEFITED.
I WON'T ACCEPT THAT.
WE WILL DECEIVE IN ORDER TO LIVE.
THE PEOPLE'S ANGER WILL NOT SUBSIDE UNTIL YOU'RE GONE.
BUT...
...THAT'S WHAT I'M HERE FOR!

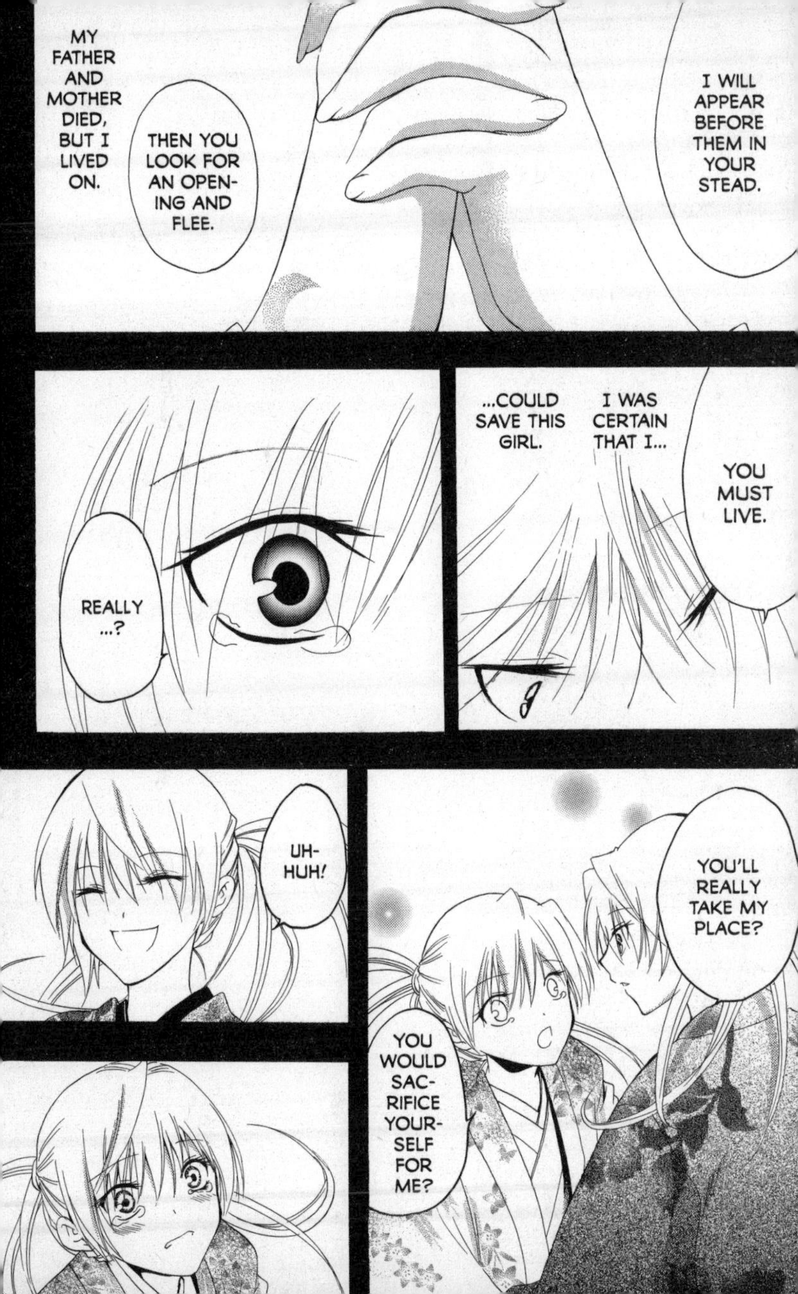
I WILL APPEAR BEFORE THEM IN YOUR STEAD.
THEN YOU LOOK FOR AN OPENING AND FLEE.
MY FATHER AND MOTHER DIED, BUT I LIVED ON.
YOU MUST LIVE.
I WAS CERTAIN THAT I...
...COULD SAVE THIS GIRL.
REALLY ...?
YOU'LL REALLY TAKE MY PLACE?
YOU WOULD SACRIFICE YOURSELF FOR ME?
UH-HUH!

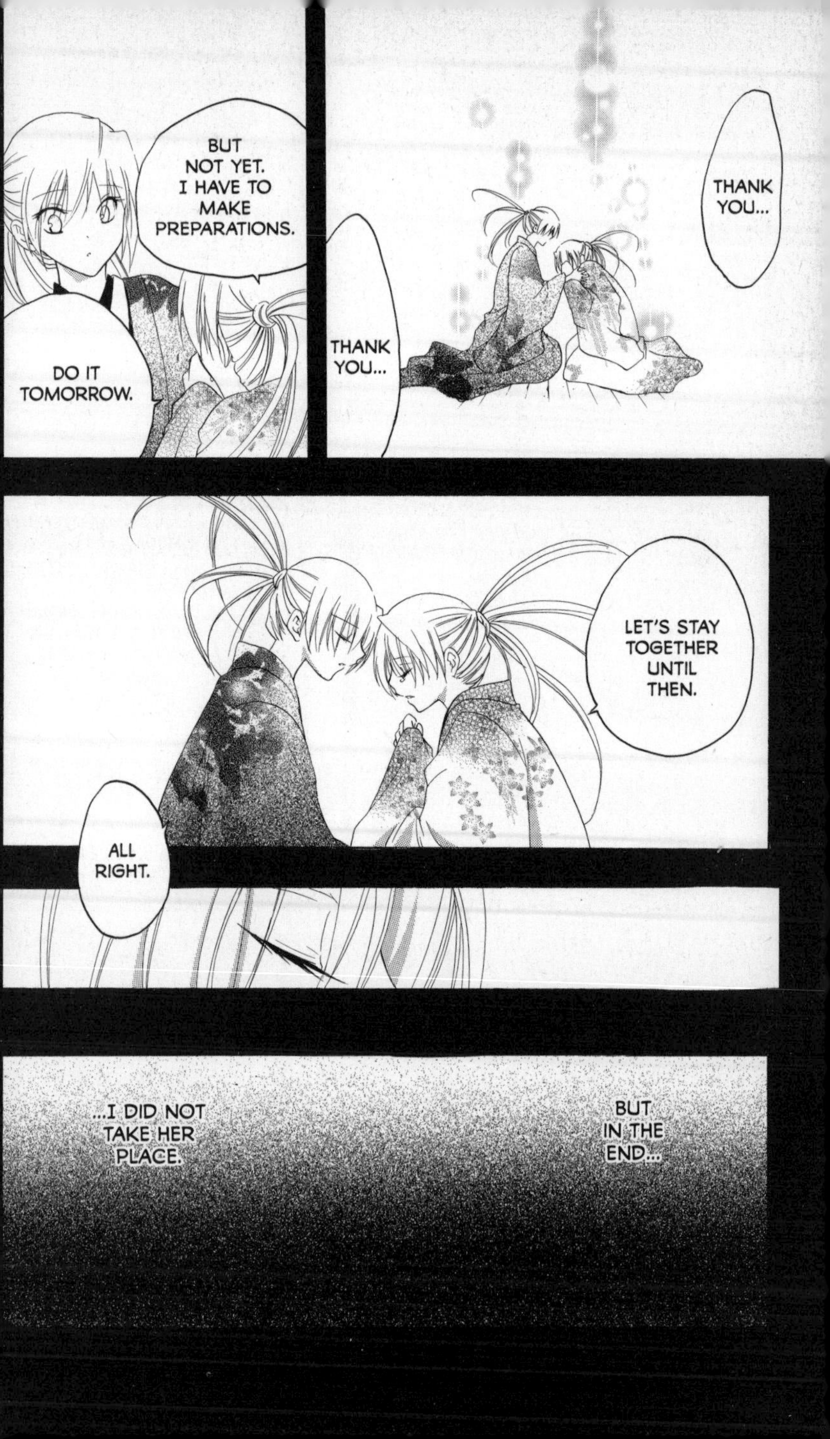
THANK YOU...
THANK YOU...
BUT NOT YET. I HAVE TO MAKE PREPARATIONS.
DO IT TOMORROW.
LET'S STAY TOGETHER UNTIL THEN.
ALL RIGHT.
BUT IN THE END...
...I DID NOT TAKE HER PLACE.

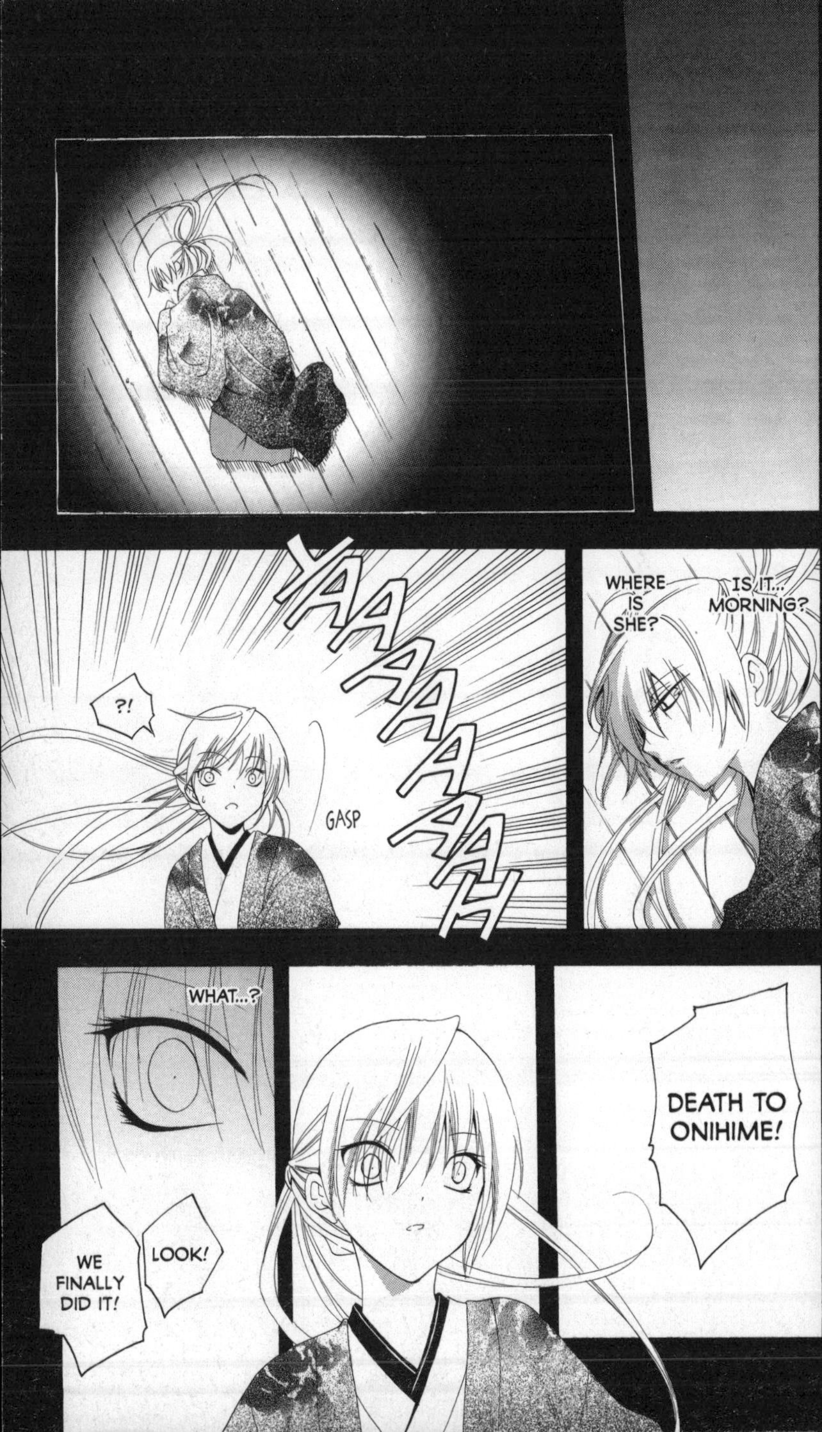
IS IT... MORNING?
WHERE IS SHE?
YAAAAAAAH
?!
GASP
DEATH TO ONIHIME!
WHAT...?
LOOK!
WE FINALLY DID IT!

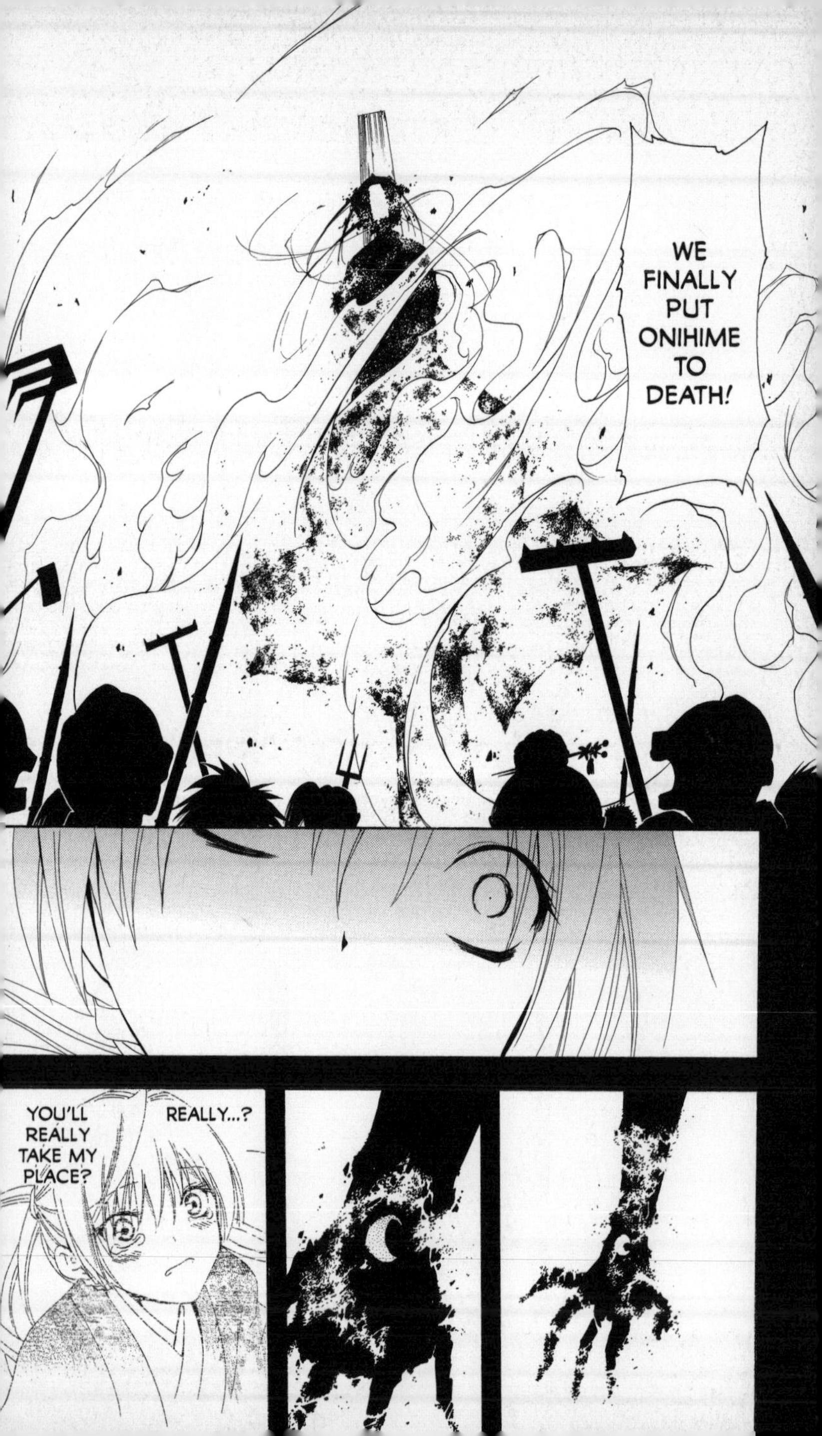
WE FINALLY PUT ONIHIME TO DEATH!
REALLY...?
YOU'LL REALLY TAKE MY PLACE?

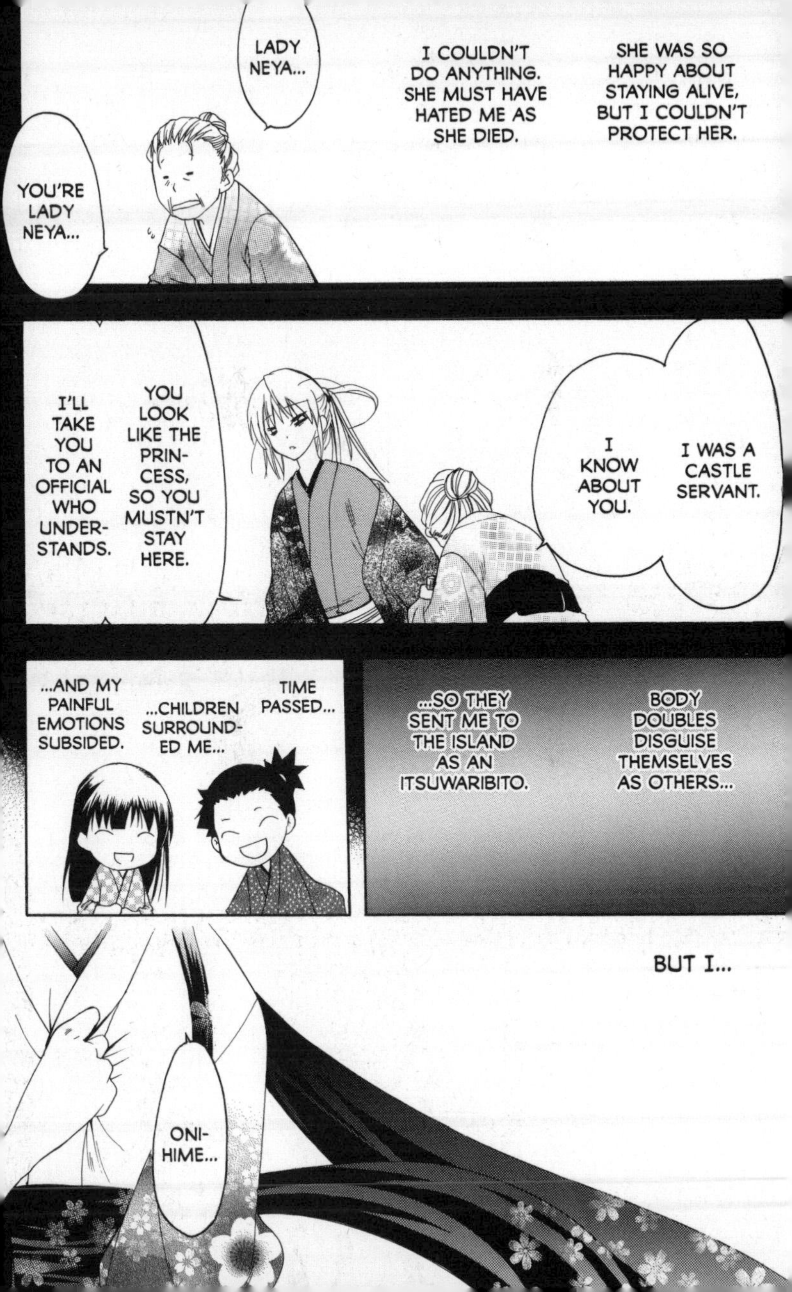
SHE WAS SO HAPPY ABOUT STAYING ALIVE, BUT I COULDN'T PROTECT HER.
I COULDN'T DO ANYTHING. SHE MUST HAVE HATED ME AS SHE DIED.
LADY NEYA...
YOU'RE LADY NEYA...
I WAS A CASTLE SERVANT.
I KNOW ABOUT YOU.
YOU LOOK LIKE THE PRIN-CESS, SO YOU MUSTN'T STAY HERE.
I'LL TAKE YOU TO AN OFFICIAL WHO UNDER-STANDS.
BODY DOUBLES DISGUISE THEMSELVES AS OTHERS...
...SO THEY SENT ME TO THE ISLAND AS AN ITSUWARIBITO.
TIME PASSED...
...CHILDREN SURROUND-ED ME...
...AND MY PAINFUL EMOTIONS SUBSIDED.
BUT I...
ONI-HIME...

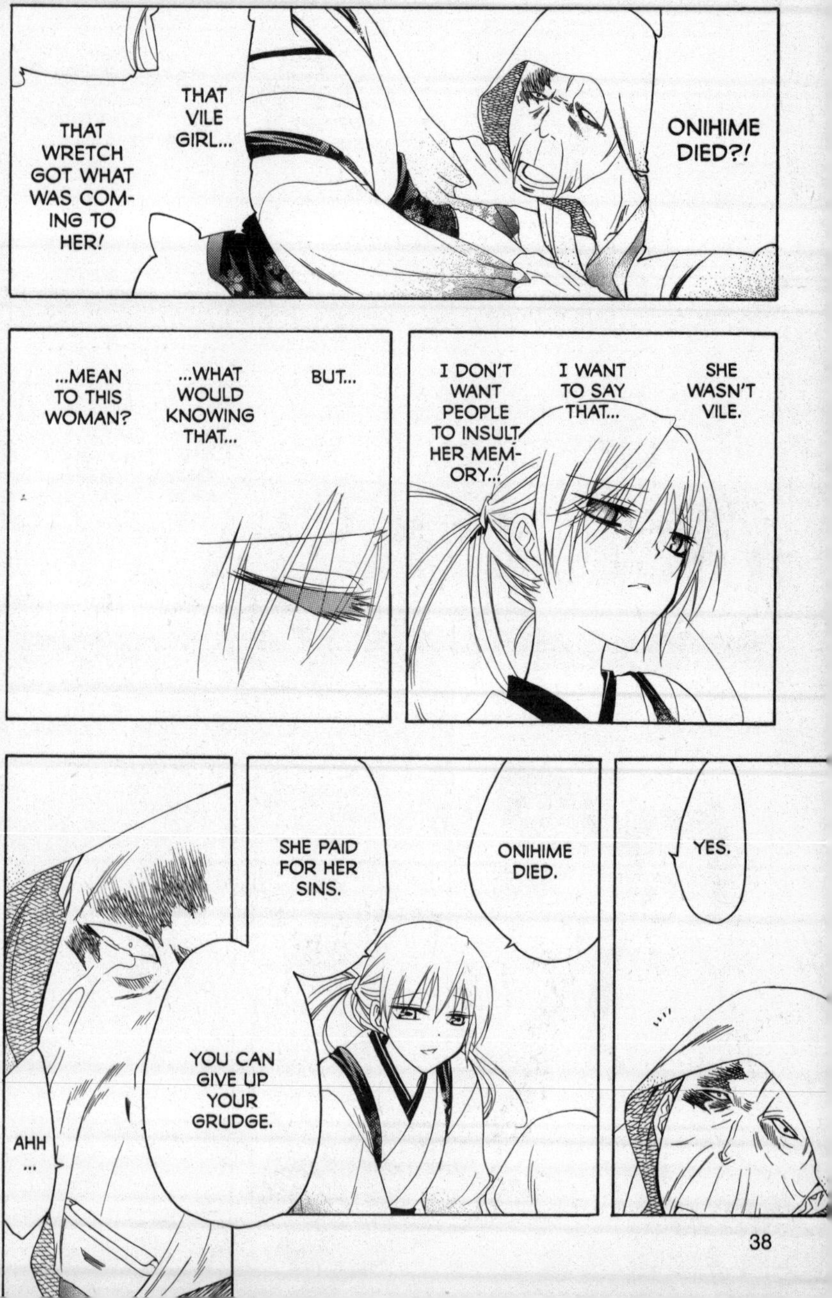
ONIHIME DIED?!
THAT VILE GIRL...
THAT WRETCH GOT WHAT WAS COMING TO HER!
SHE WASN'T VILE.
I WANT TO SAY THAT...
I DON'T WANT PEOPLE TO INSULT HER MEMORY...
BUT...
...WHAT WOULD KNOWING THAT...
...MEAN TO THIS WOMAN?
YES.
ONIHIME DIED.
SHE PAID FOR HER SINS.
YOU CAN GIVE UP YOUR GRUDGE.
AHH...

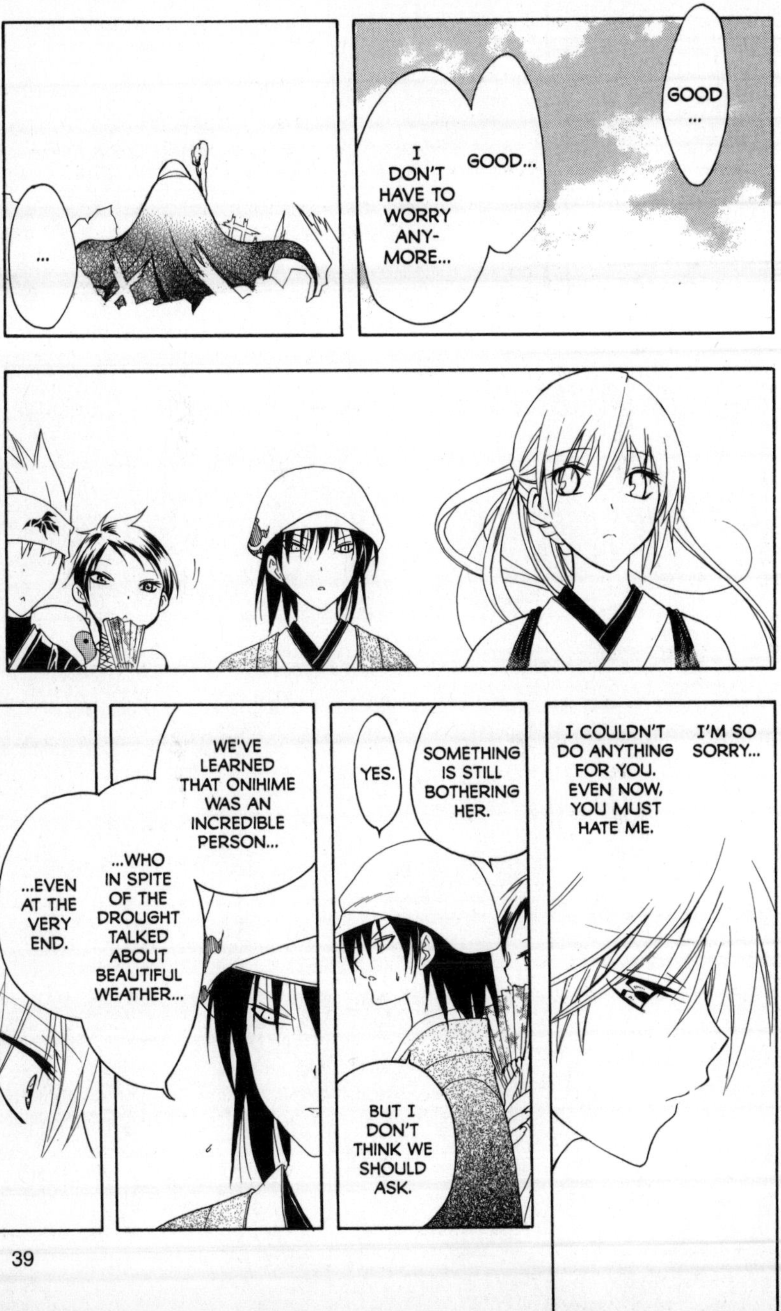
GOOD ...
GOOD...
I DON'T HAVE TO WORRY ANY-MORE...
...
I'M SO SORRY...
I COULDN'T DO ANYTHING FOR YOU. EVEN NOW, YOU MUST HATE ME.
SOMETHING IS STILL BOTHERING HER.
YES.
BUT I DON'T THINK WE SHOULD ASK.
WE'VE LEARNED THAT ONIHIME WAS AN INCREDIBLE PERSON...
...WHO IN SPITE OF THE DROUGHT TALKED ABOUT BEAUTIFUL WEATHER...
...EVEN AT THE VERY END.

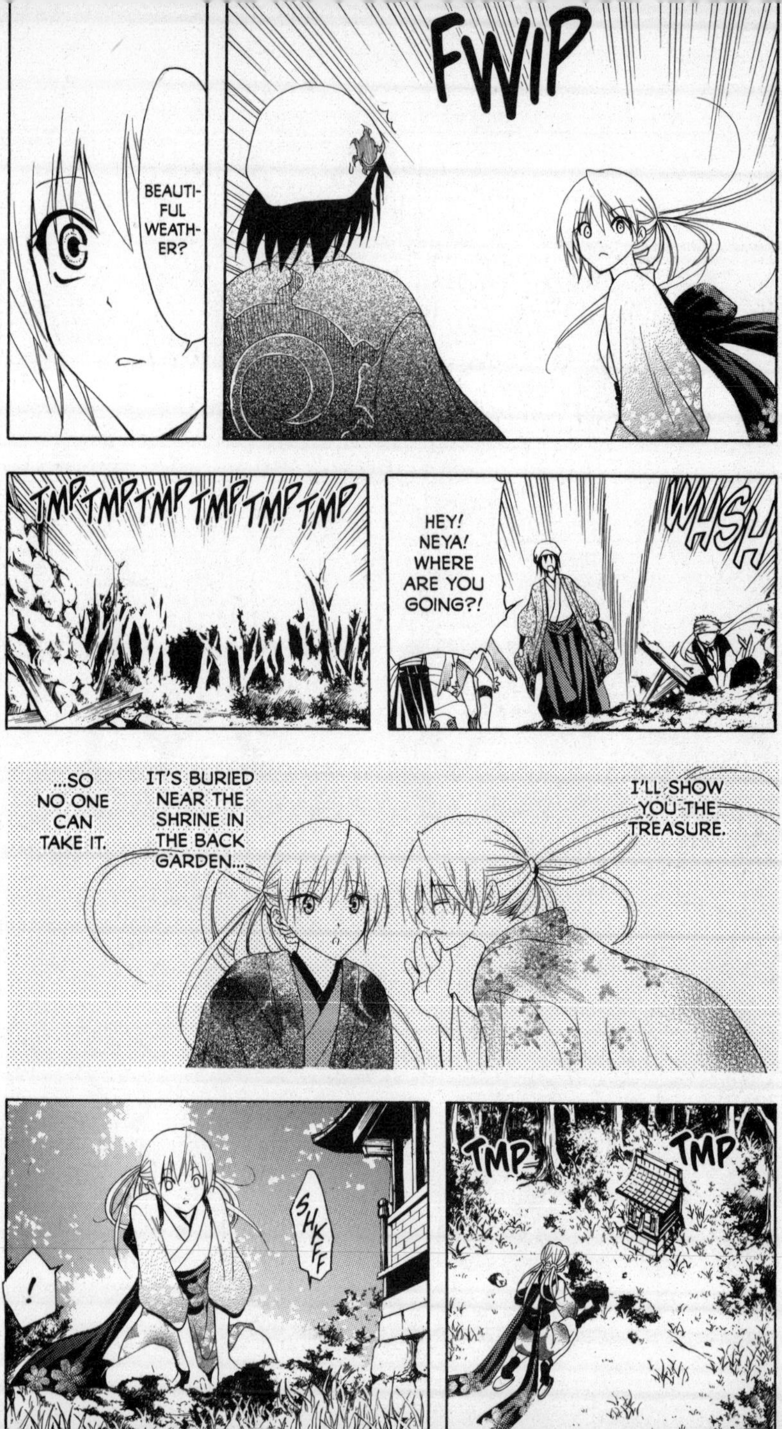
FWIP
BEAUTIFUL WEATHER?
WHSH
HEY! NEYA! WHERE ARE YOU GOING?!
TMP TMP TMP TMP TMP TMP
I'LL SHOW YOU THE TREASURE.
IT'S BURIED NEAR THE SHRINE IN THE BACK GARDEN...
...SO NO ONE CAN TAKE IT.
TMP
TMP
SHKFF
!

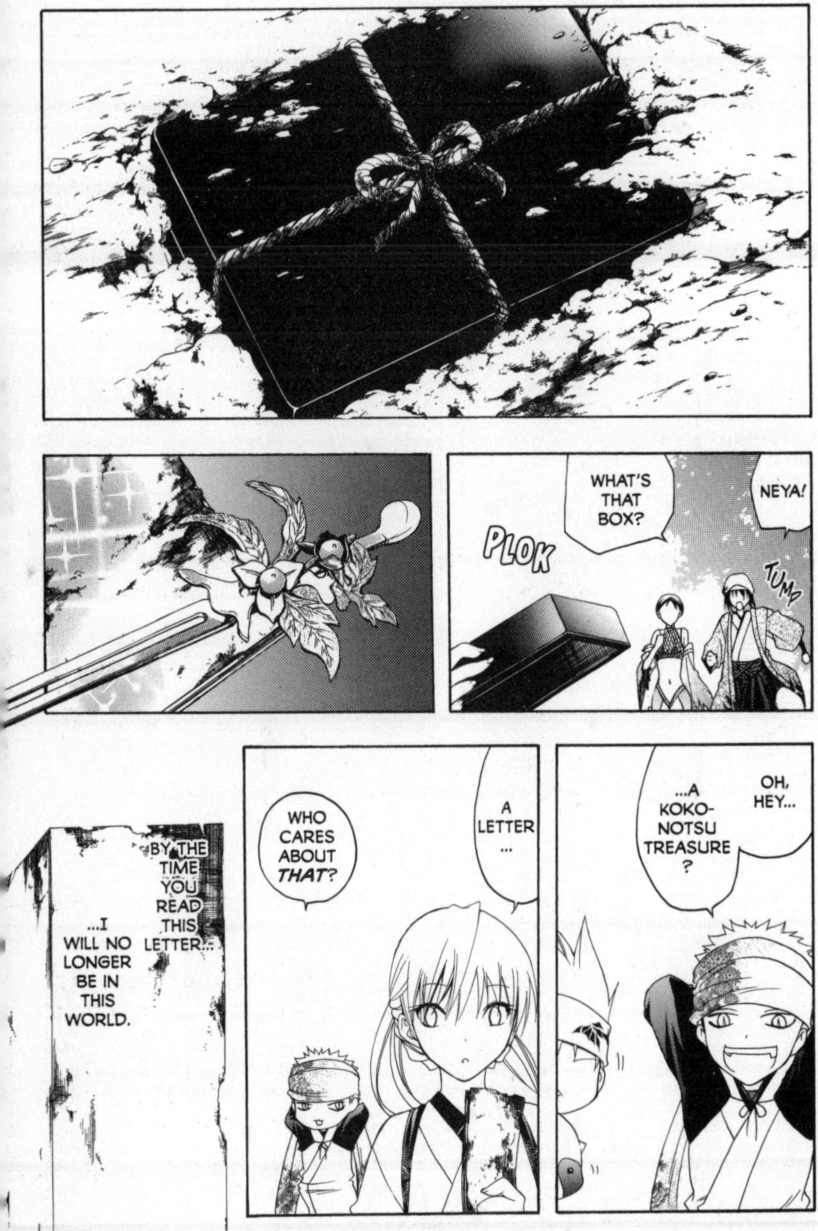
NEYA!
WHAT'S THAT BOX?
TUMP
PLOK
OH, HEY...
...A KOKO-NOTSU TREASURE?
A LETTER...
WHO CARES ABOUT *THAT*?
BY THE TIME YOU READ THIS LETTER...
...I WILL NO LONGER BE IN THIS WORLD.

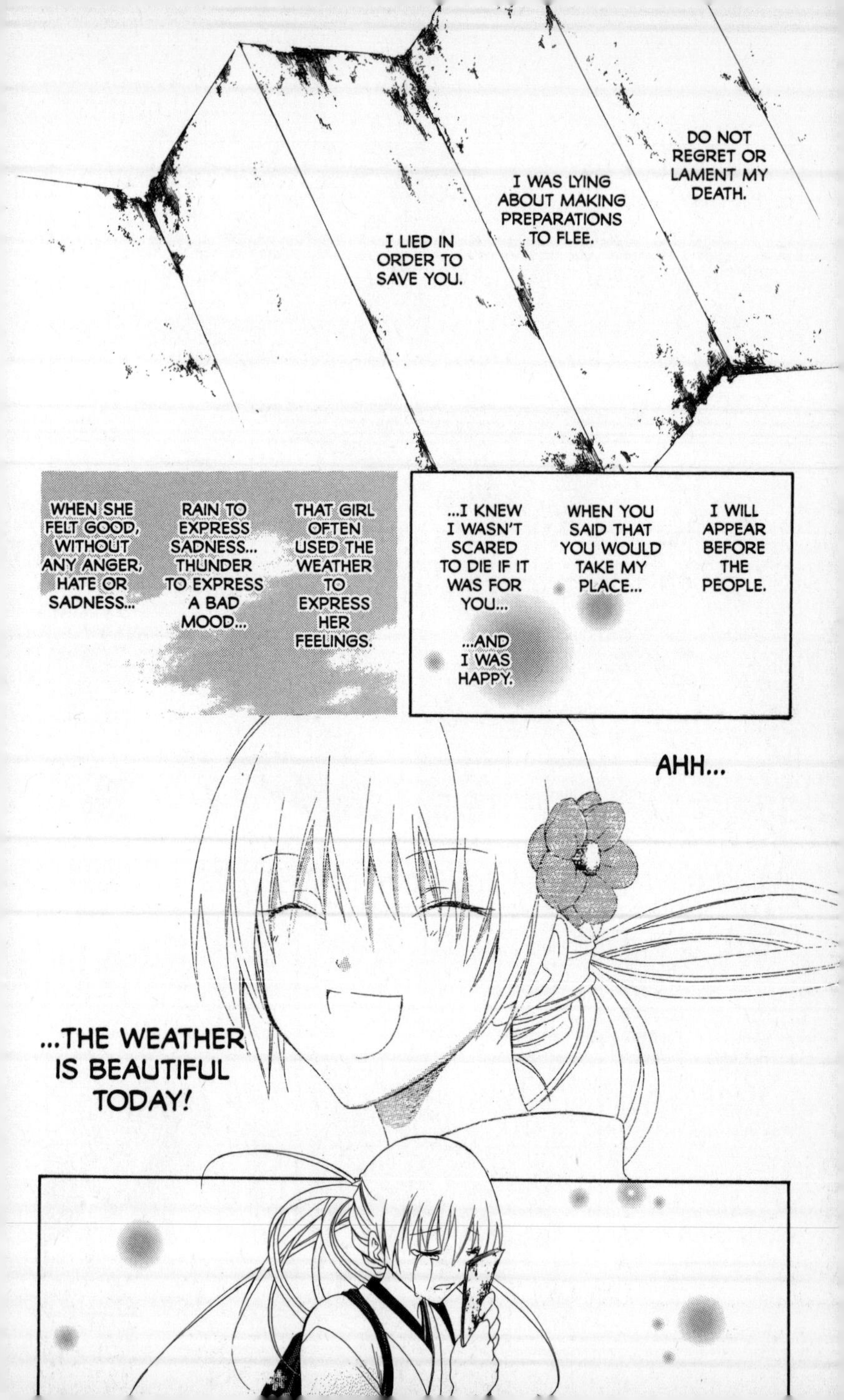
DO NOT REGRET OR LAMENT MY DEATH.
I WAS LYING ABOUT MAKING PREPARATIONS TO FLEE.
I LIED IN ORDER TO SAVE YOU.
I WILL APPEAR BEFORE THE PEOPLE.
WHEN YOU SAID THAT YOU WOULD TAKE MY PLACE...
...I KNEW I WASN'T SCARED TO DIE IF IT WAS FOR YOU...
...AND I WAS HAPPY.
THAT GIRL OFTEN USED THE WEATHER TO EXPRESS HER FEELINGS.
RAIN TO EXPRESS SADNESS... THUNDER TO EXPRESS A BAD MOOD...
WHEN SHE FELT GOOD, WITHOUT ANY ANGER, HATE OR SADNESS...
AHH...
...THE WEATHER IS BEAUTIFUL TODAY!

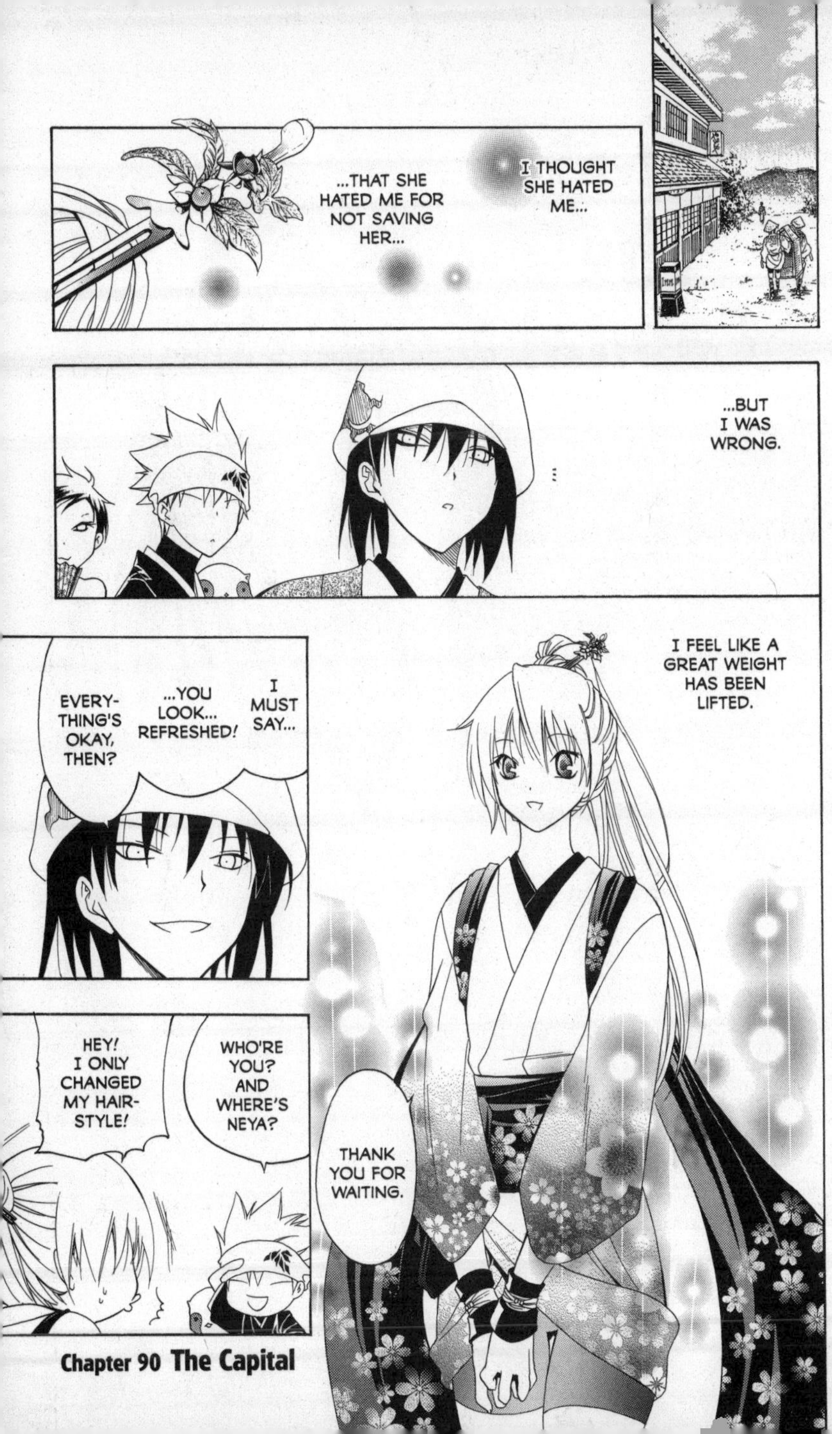
I THOUGHT SHE HATED ME...
...THAT SHE HATED ME FOR NOT SAVING HER...
...BUT I WAS WRONG.
...
I FEEL LIKE A GREAT WEIGHT HAS BEEN LIFTED.
THANK YOU FOR WAITING.
I MUST SAY...
...YOU LOOK... REFRESHED!
EVERY-THING'S OKAY, THEN?
WHO'RE YOU? AND WHERE'S NEYA?
HEY! I ONLY CHANGED MY HAIR-STYLE!

Chapter 90 The Capital

Chapter 90
The Capital

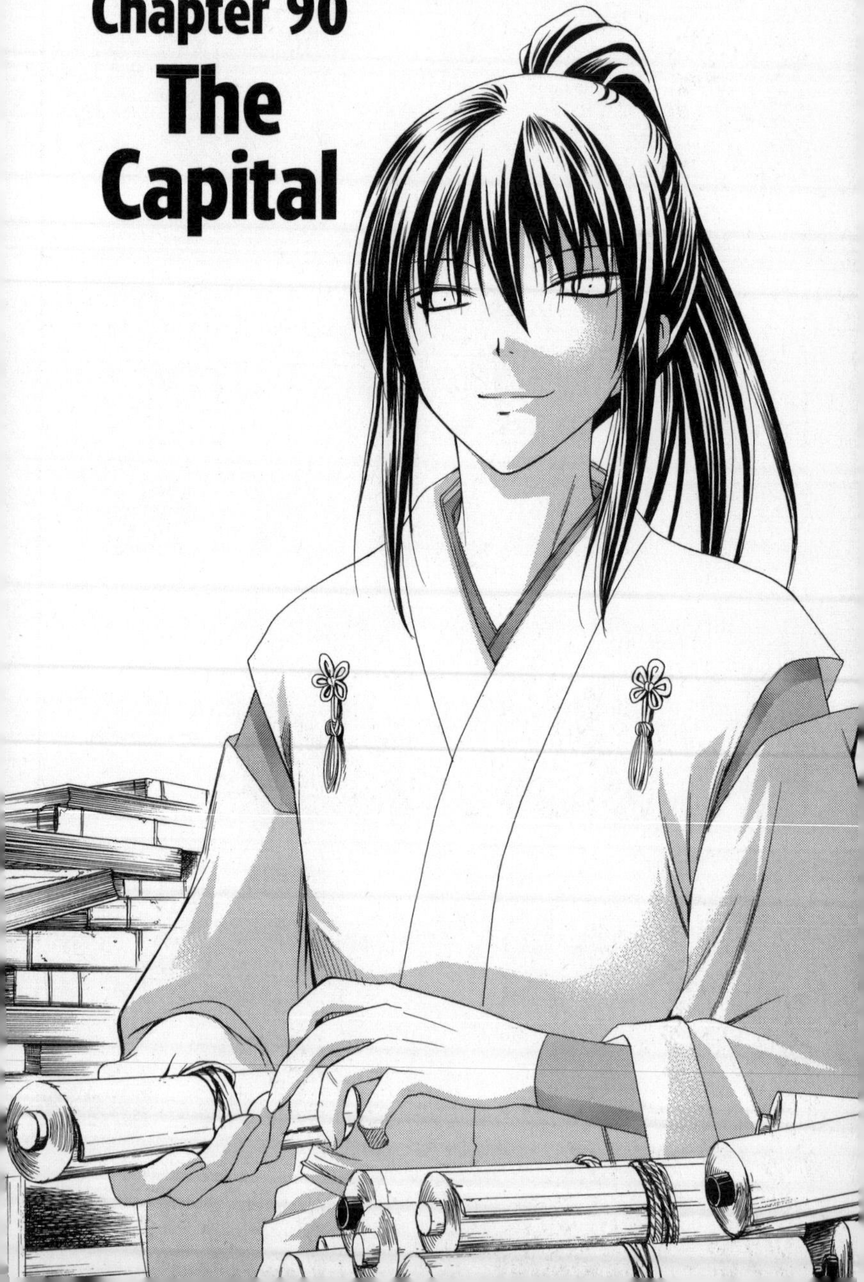

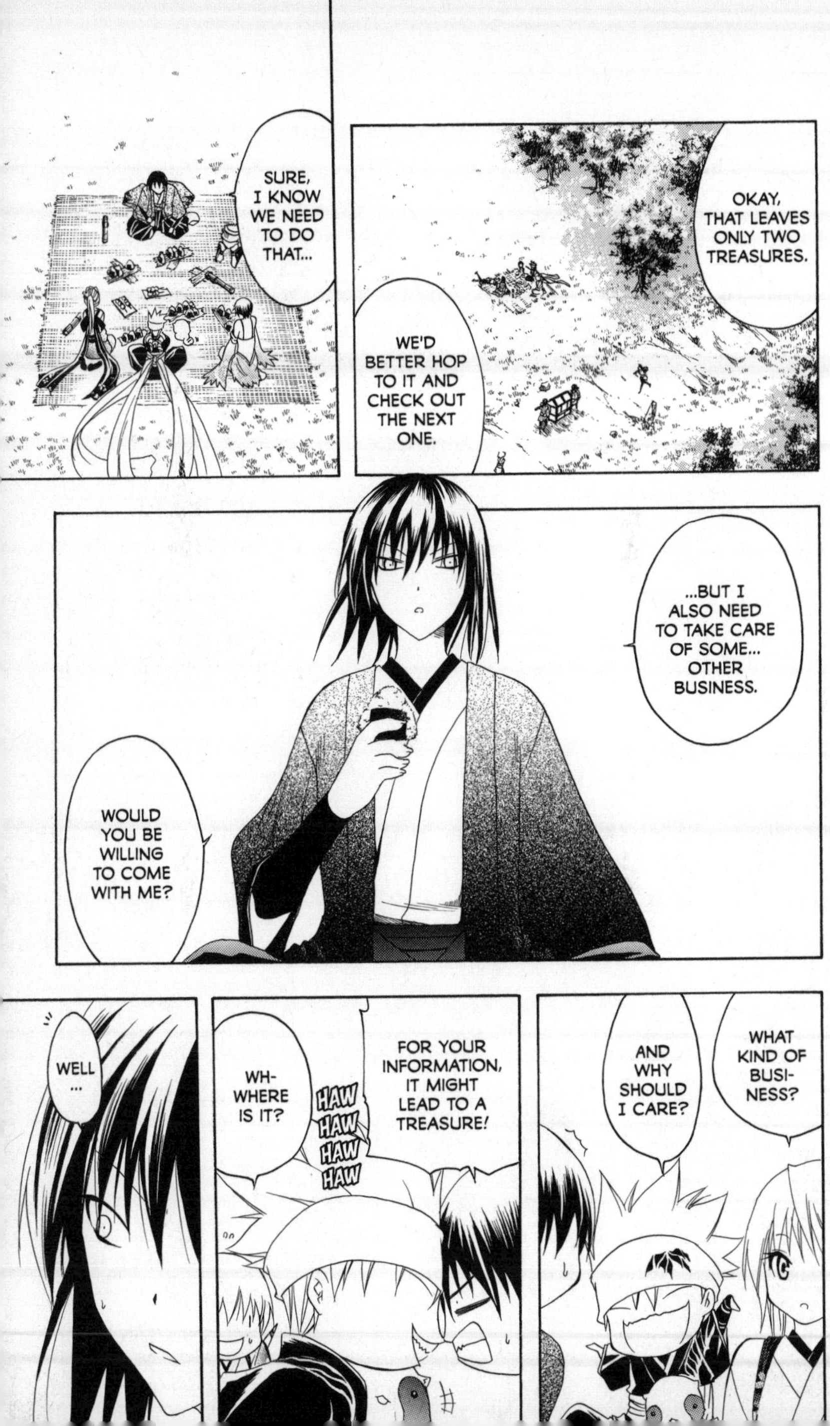
OKAY, THAT LEAVES ONLY TWO TREASURES.
WE'D BETTER HOP TO IT AND CHECK OUT THE NEXT ONE.
SURE, I KNOW WE NEED TO DO THAT...
...BUT I ALSO NEED TO TAKE CARE OF SOME... OTHER BUSINESS.
WOULD YOU BE WILLING TO COME WITH ME?
WHAT KIND OF BUSI-NESS?
AND WHY SHOULD I CARE?
FOR YOUR INFORMATION, IT MIGHT LEAD TO A TREASURE!
HAW HAW HAW HAW
WH-WHERE IS IT?
WELL ...

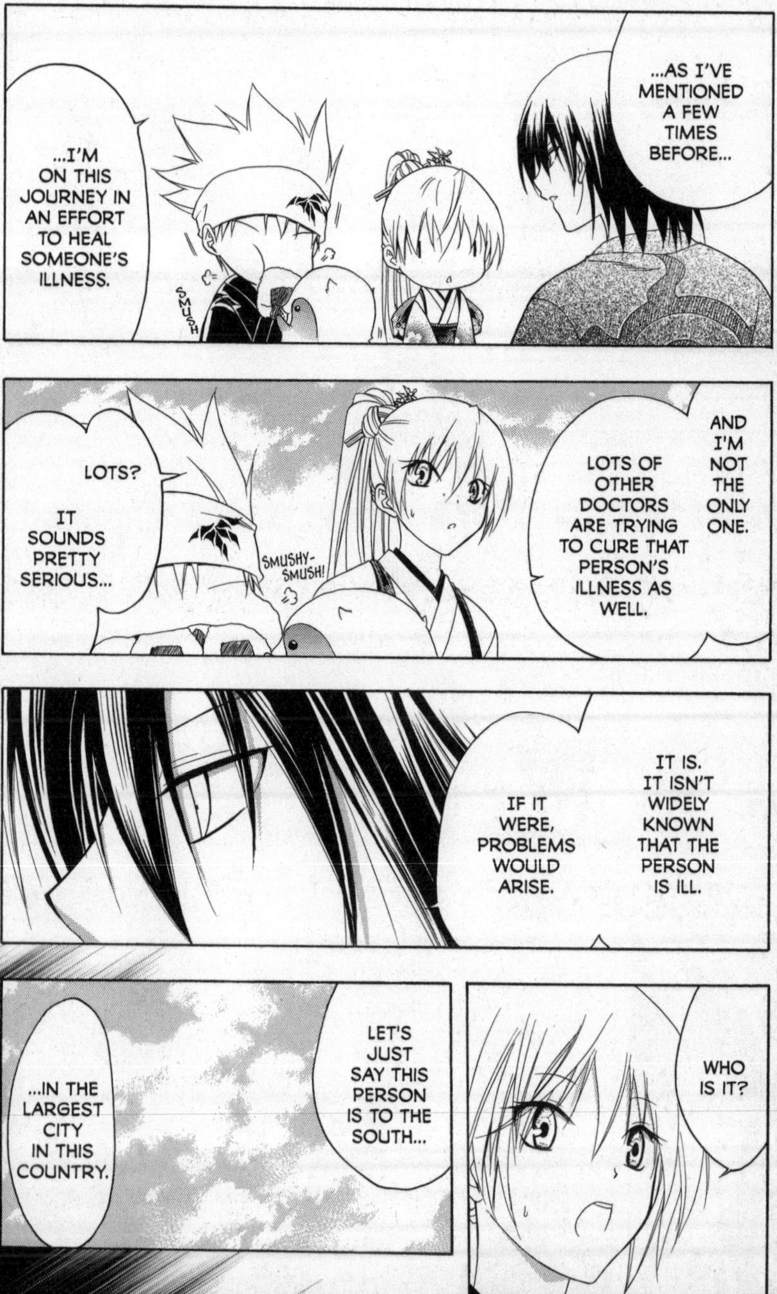
...AS I'VE MENTIONED A FEW TIMES BEFORE...
...I'M ON THIS JOURNEY IN AN EFFORT TO HEAL SOMEONE'S ILLNESS.
SMUSH
AND I'M NOT THE ONLY ONE.
LOTS OF OTHER DOCTORS ARE TRYING TO CURE THAT PERSON'S ILLNESS AS WELL.
SMUSHY-SMUSH!
LOTS?
IT SOUNDS PRETTY SERIOUS...
IT IS. IT ISN'T WIDELY KNOWN THAT THE PERSON IS ILL.
IF IT WERE, PROBLEMS WOULD ARISE.
WHO IS IT?
LET'S JUST SAY THIS PERSON IS TO THE SOUTH...
...IN THE LARGEST CITY IN THIS COUNTRY.

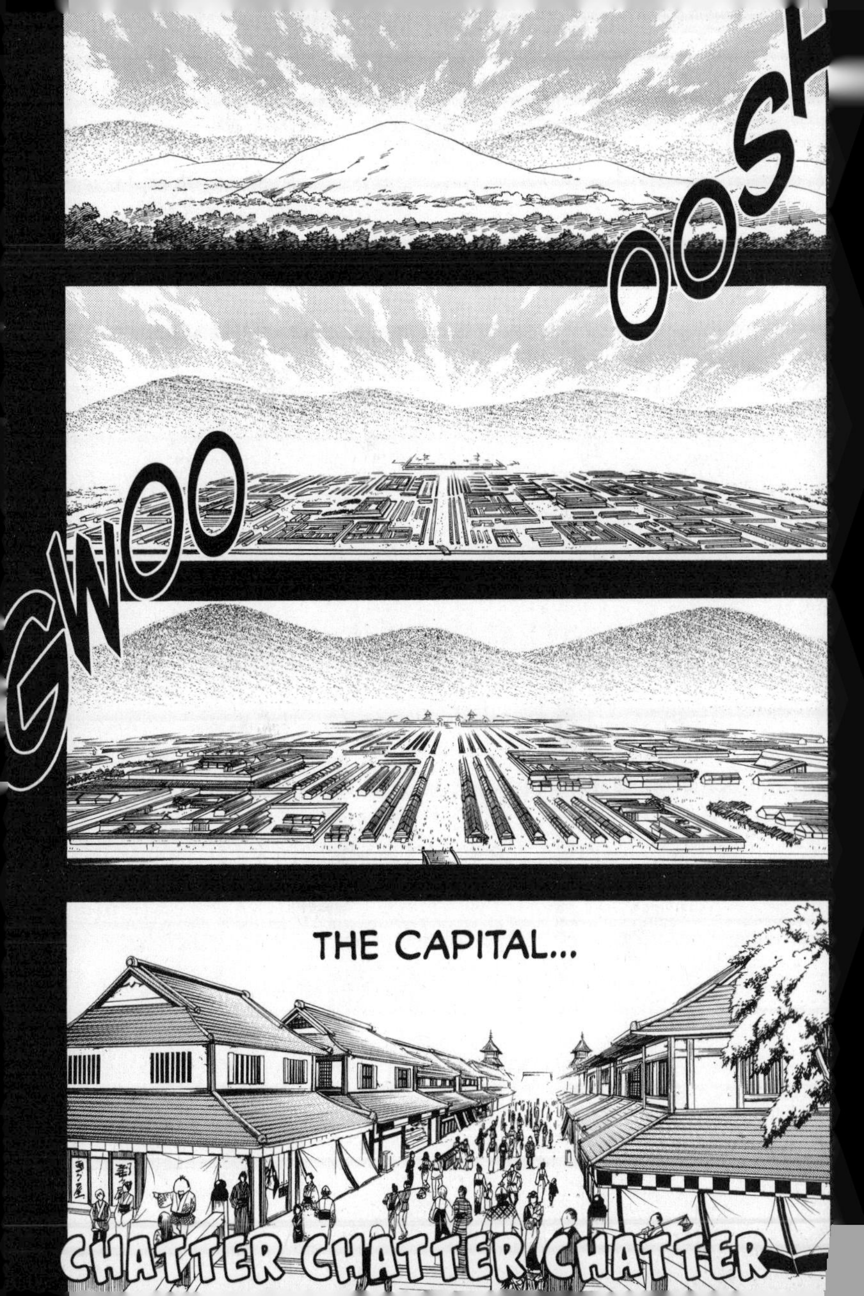
GWOO
OOSH
THE CAPITAL...
CHATTER CHATTER CHATTER

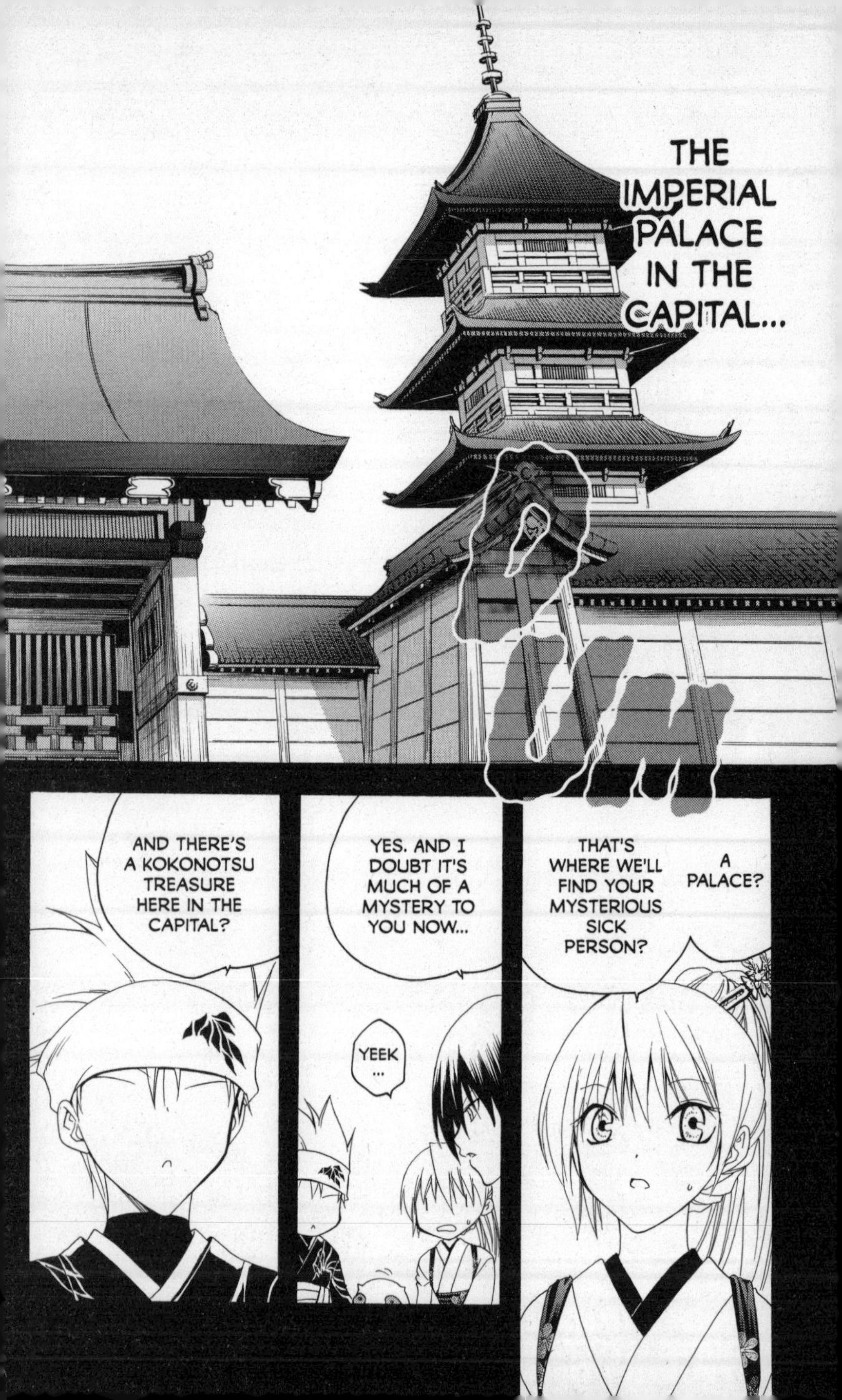
THE IMPERIAL PALACE IN THE CAPITAL...
A PALACE?
THAT'S WHERE WE'LL FIND YOUR MYSTERIOUS SICK PERSON?
YES. AND I DOUBT IT'S MUCH OF A MYSTERY TO YOU NOW...
YEEK ...
AND THERE'S A KOKONOTSU TREASURE HERE IN THE CAPITAL?

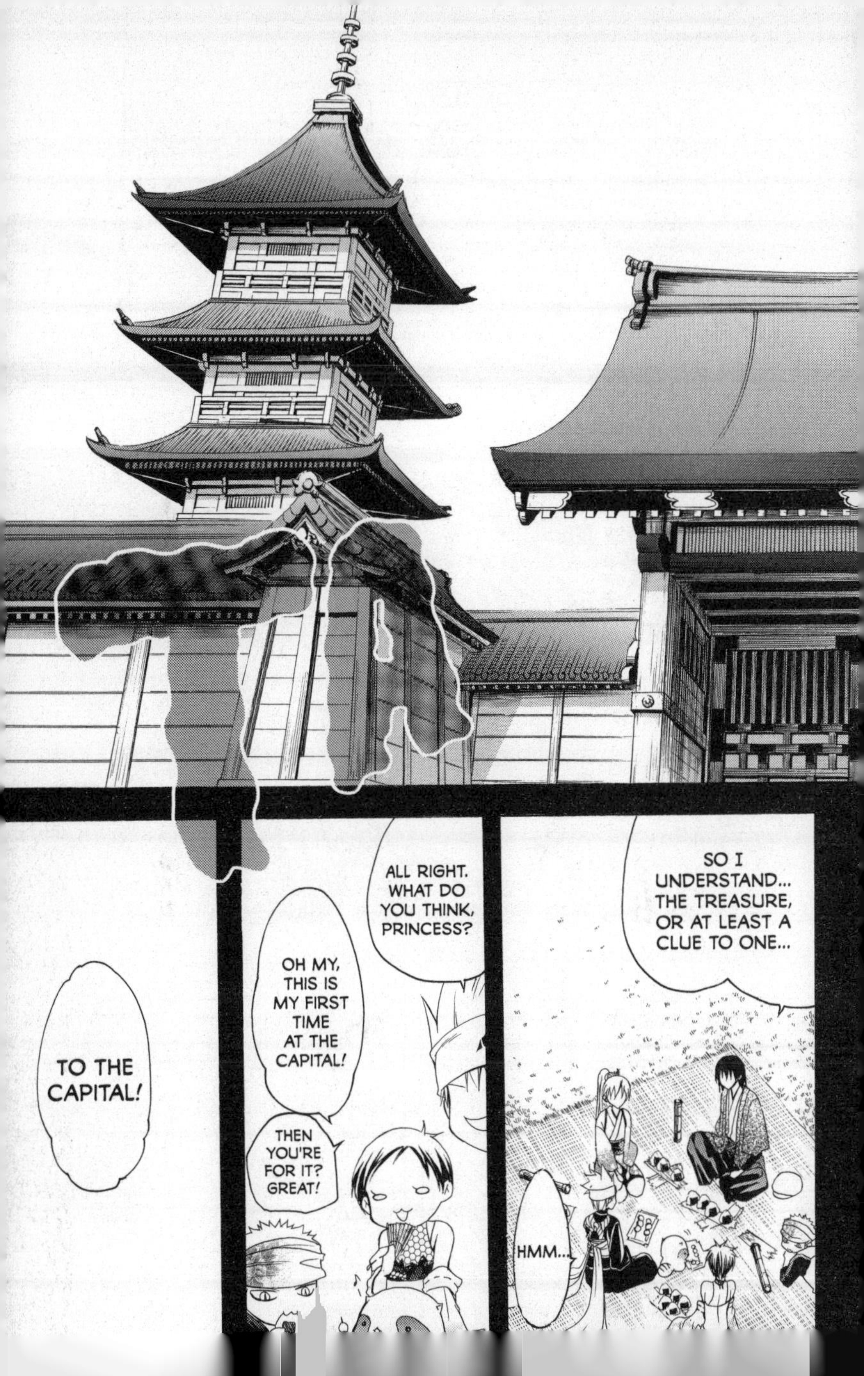
SO I UNDERSTAND... THE TREASURE, OR AT LEAST A CLUE TO ONE...
HMM...
ALL RIGHT. WHAT DO YOU THINK, PRINCESS?
OH MY, THIS IS MY FIRST TIME AT THE CAPITAL!
THEN YOU'RE FOR IT? GREAT!
TO THE CAPITAL!

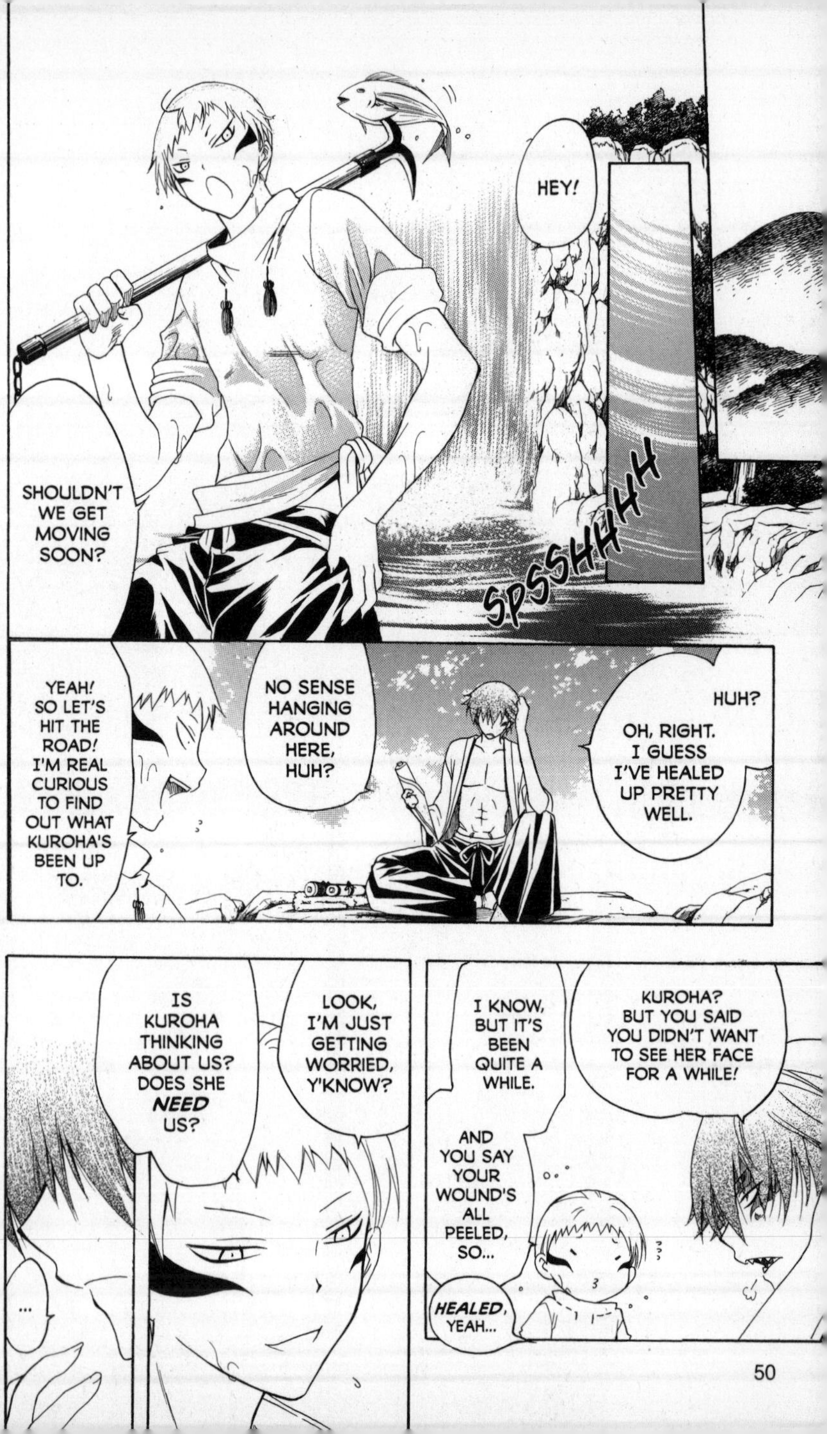
HEY!
SPSSHHHH
SHOULDN'T WE GET MOVING SOON?
HUH?
OH, RIGHT. I GUESS I'VE HEALED UP PRETTY WELL.
NO SENSE HANGING AROUND HERE, HUH?
YEAH! SO LET'S HIT THE ROAD! I'M REAL CURIOUS TO FIND OUT WHAT KUROHA'S BEEN UP TO.
KUROHA? BUT YOU SAID YOU DIDN'T WANT TO SEE HER FACE FOR A WHILE!
I KNOW, BUT IT'S BEEN QUITE A WHILE.
AND YOU SAY YOUR WOUND'S ALL PEELED, SO...
HEALED, YEAH...
LOOK, I'M JUST GETTING WORRIED, Y'KNOW?
IS KUROHA THINKING ABOUT US? DOES SHE ***NEED*** US?
...

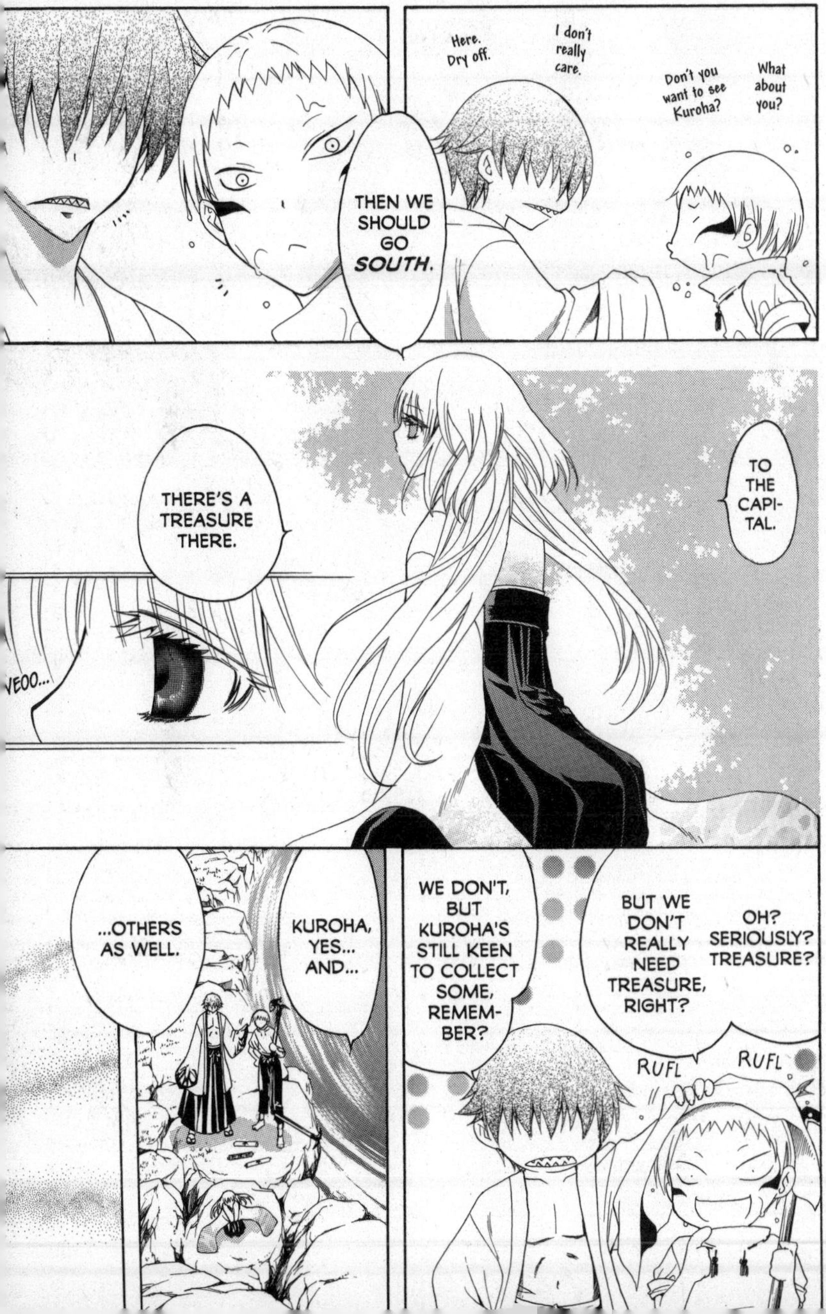
What about you?
Don't you want to see Kuroha?
I don't really care.
Here. Dry off.
THEN WE SHOULD GO *SOUTH*.
TO THE CAPITAL.
THERE'S A TREASURE THERE.
VEOO...
OH? SERIOUSLY? TREASURE?
BUT WE DON'T REALLY NEED TREASURE, RIGHT?
WE DON'T, BUT KUROHA'S STILL KEEN TO COLLECT SOME, REMEMBER?
RUFL
RUFL
KUROHA, YES... AND...
...OTHERS AS WELL.

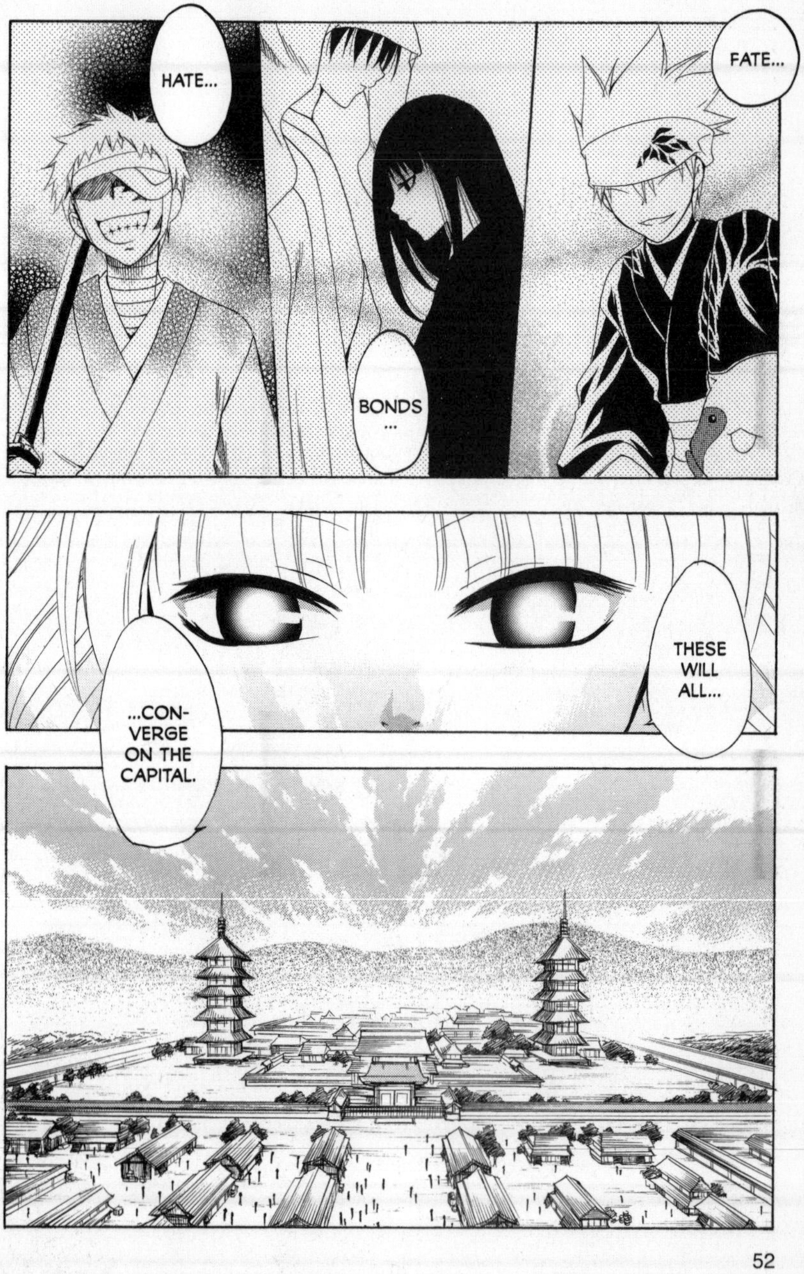
FATE...
BONDS ...
HATE...
THESE WILL ALL...
...CON-VERGE ON THE CAPITAL.

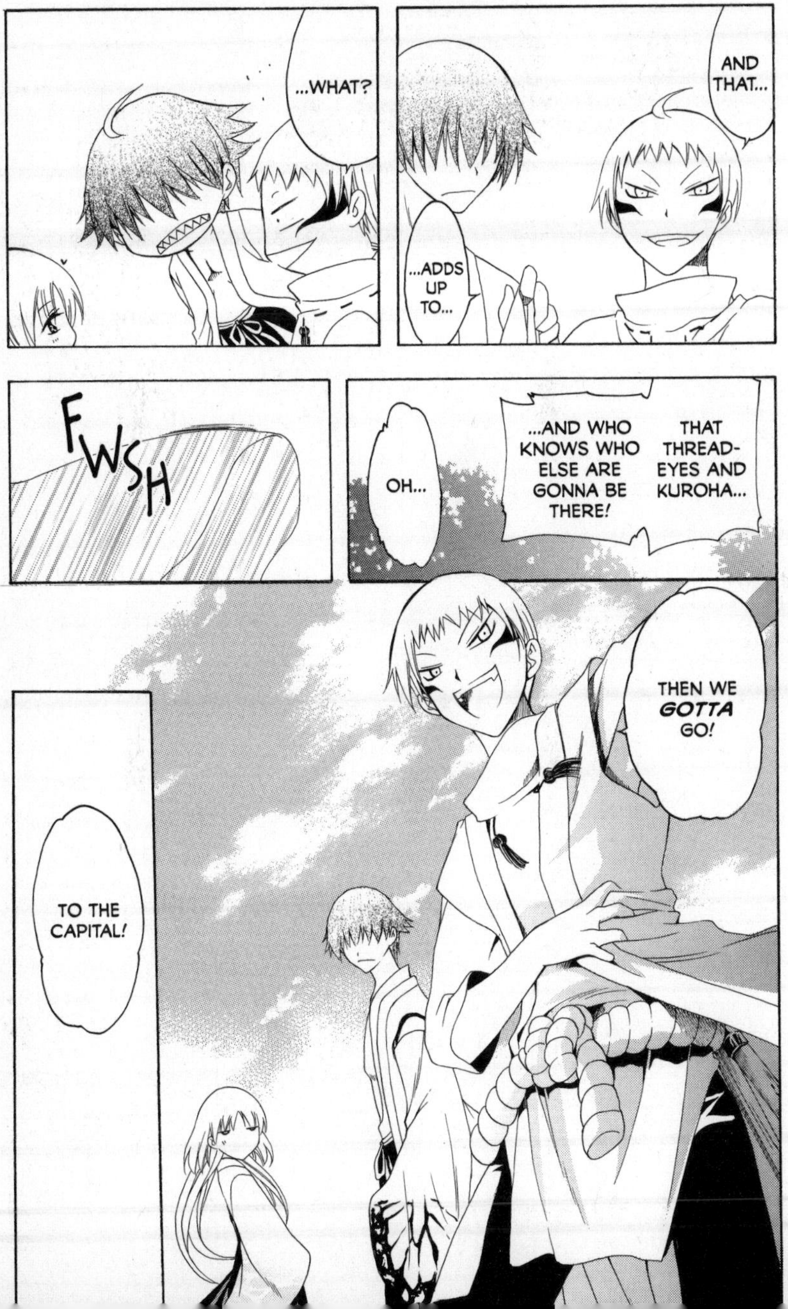
AND THAT...
...ADDS UP TO...
...WHAT?
THAT THREAD-EYES AND KUROHA...
...AND WHO KNOWS WHO ELSE ARE GONNA BE THERE!
OH...
FWSH
THEN WE *GOTTA* GO!
TO THE CAPITAL!

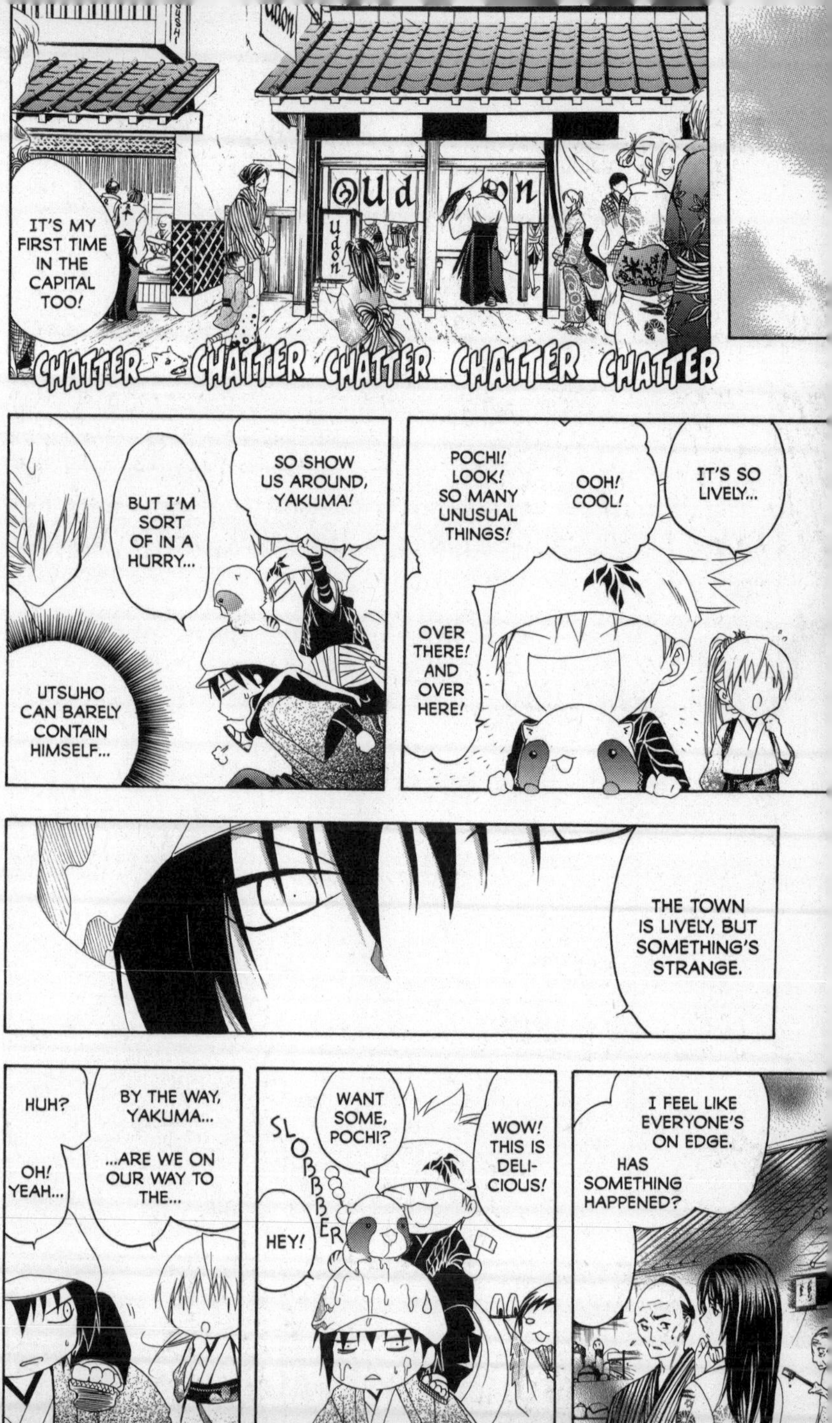
udon
IT'S MY FIRST TIME IN THE CAPITAL TOO!
CHATTER CHATTER CHATTER CHATTER CHATTER
IT'S SO LIVELY...
OOH! COOL!
POCHI! LOOK! SO MANY UNUSUAL THINGS!
OVER THERE! AND OVER HERE!
SO SHOW US AROUND, YAKUMA!
BUT I'M SORT OF IN A HURRY...
UTSUHO CAN BARELY CONTAIN HIMSELF...
THE TOWN IS LIVELY, BUT SOMETHING'S STRANGE.
I FEEL LIKE EVERYONE'S ON EDGE.
HAS SOMETHING HAPPENED?
WOW! THIS IS DELICIOUS!
WANT SOME, POCHI?
SLOBBBER
HEY!
BY THE WAY, YAKUMA...
...ARE WE ON OUR WAY TO THE...
HUH?
OH! YEAH...

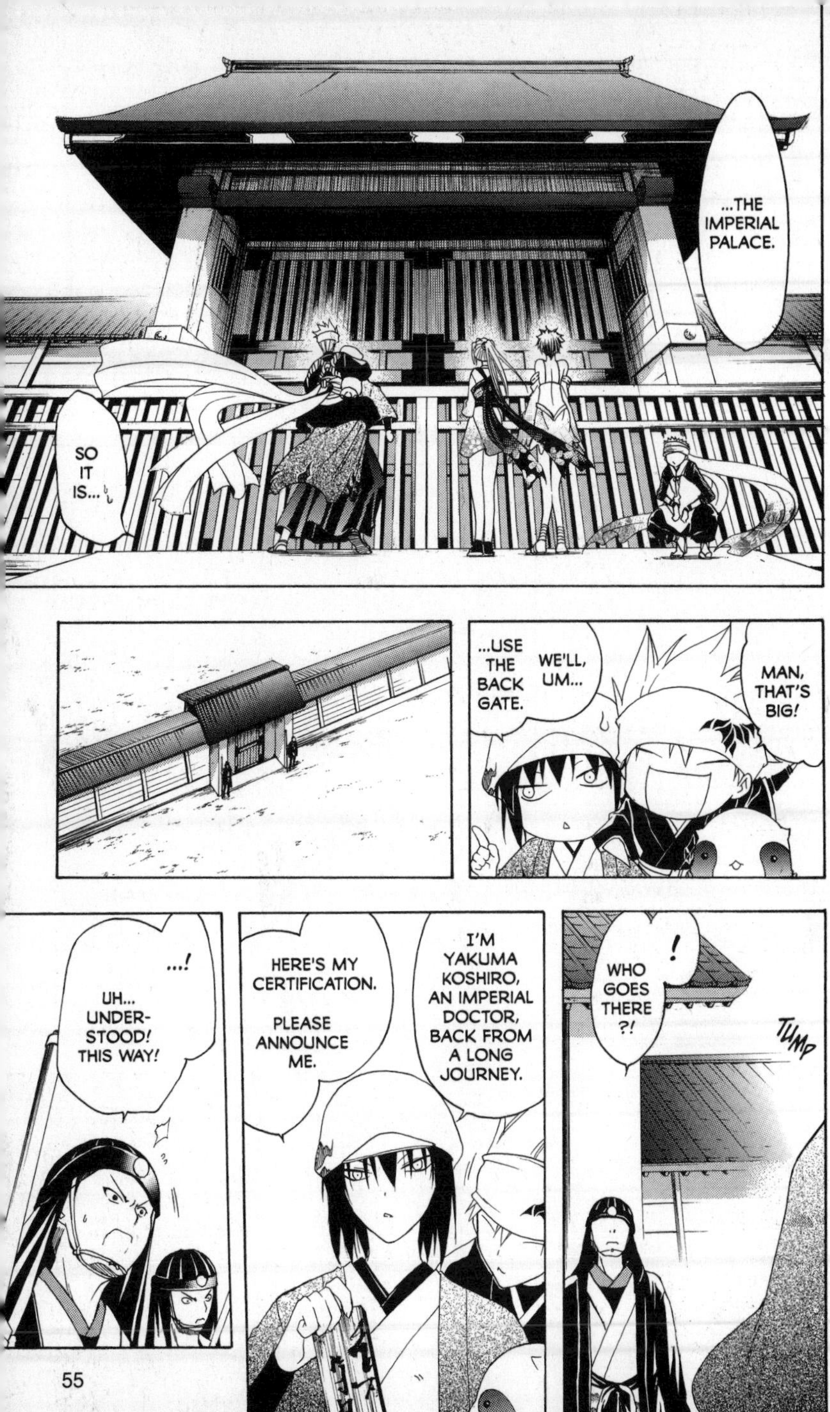
...THE IMPERIAL PALACE.
SO IT IS...
MAN, THAT'S BIG!
WE'LL, UM...
...USE THE BACK GATE.
!
WHO GOES THERE ?!
TUMP
I'M YAKUMA KOSHIRO, AN IMPERIAL DOCTOR, BACK FROM A LONG JOURNEY.
HERE'S MY CERTIFICATION.
PLEASE ANNOUNCE ME.
...!
UH... UNDERSTOOD! THIS WAY!

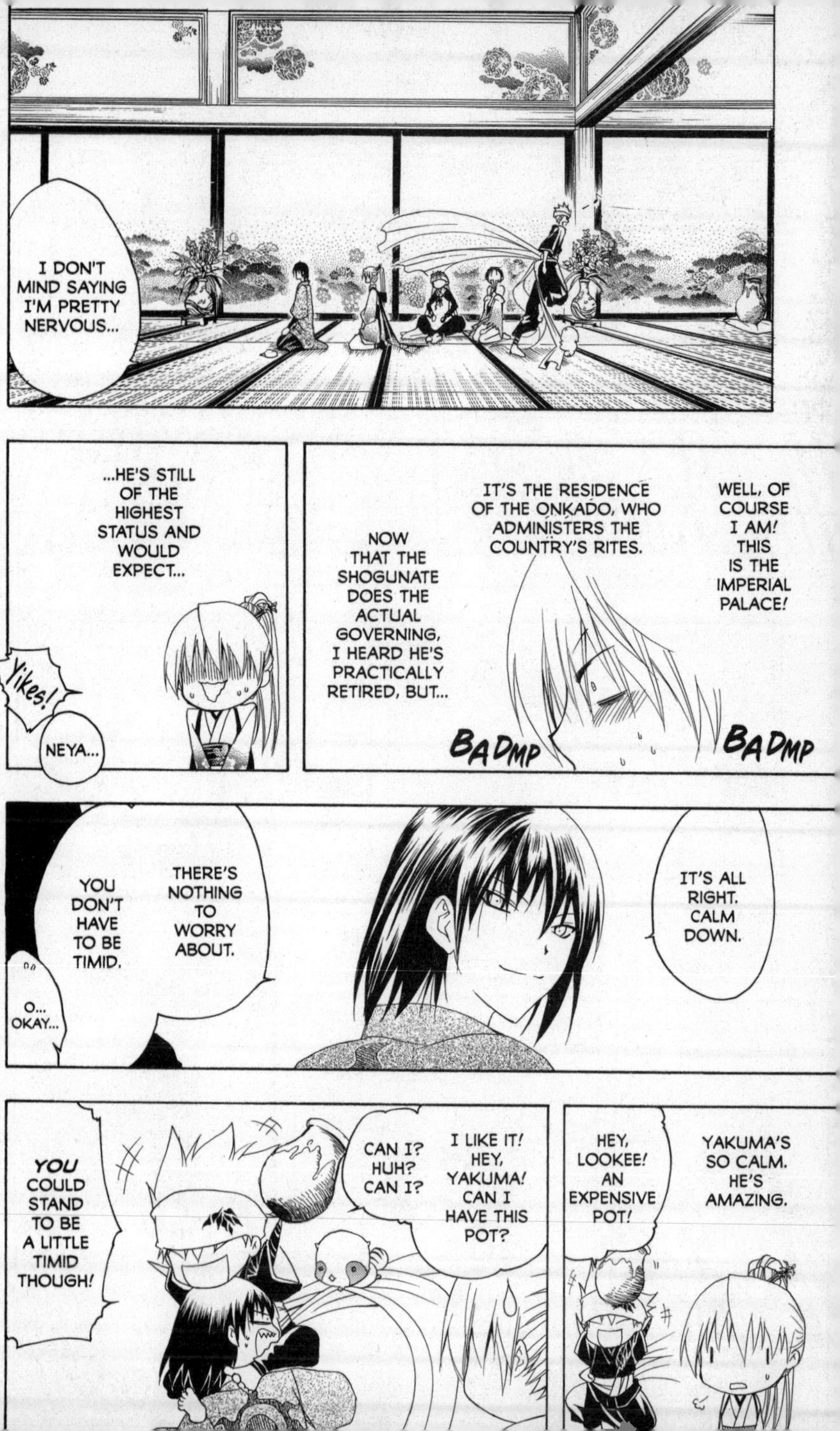
I DON'T MIND SAYING I'M PRETTY NERVOUS...
WELL, OF COURSE I AM! THIS IS THE IMPERIAL PALACE!
IT'S THE RESIDENCE OF THE ONKADO, WHO ADMINISTERS THE COUNTRY'S RITES.
NOW THAT THE SHOGUNATE DOES THE ACTUAL GOVERNING, I HEARD HE'S PRACTICALLY RETIRED, BUT...
BADMP
BADMP
...HE'S STILL OF THE HIGHEST STATUS AND WOULD EXPECT...
Yikes!
NEYA...
IT'S ALL RIGHT. CALM DOWN.
THERE'S NOTHING TO WORRY ABOUT.
YOU DON'T HAVE TO BE TIMID.
O... OKAY...
YAKUMA'S SO CALM. HE'S AMAZING.
HEY, LOOKEE! AN EXPENSIVE POT!
I LIKE IT! HEY, YAKUMA! CAN I HAVE THIS POT?
CAN I? HUH? CAN I?
YOU COULD STAND TO BE A LITTLE TIMID THOUGH!

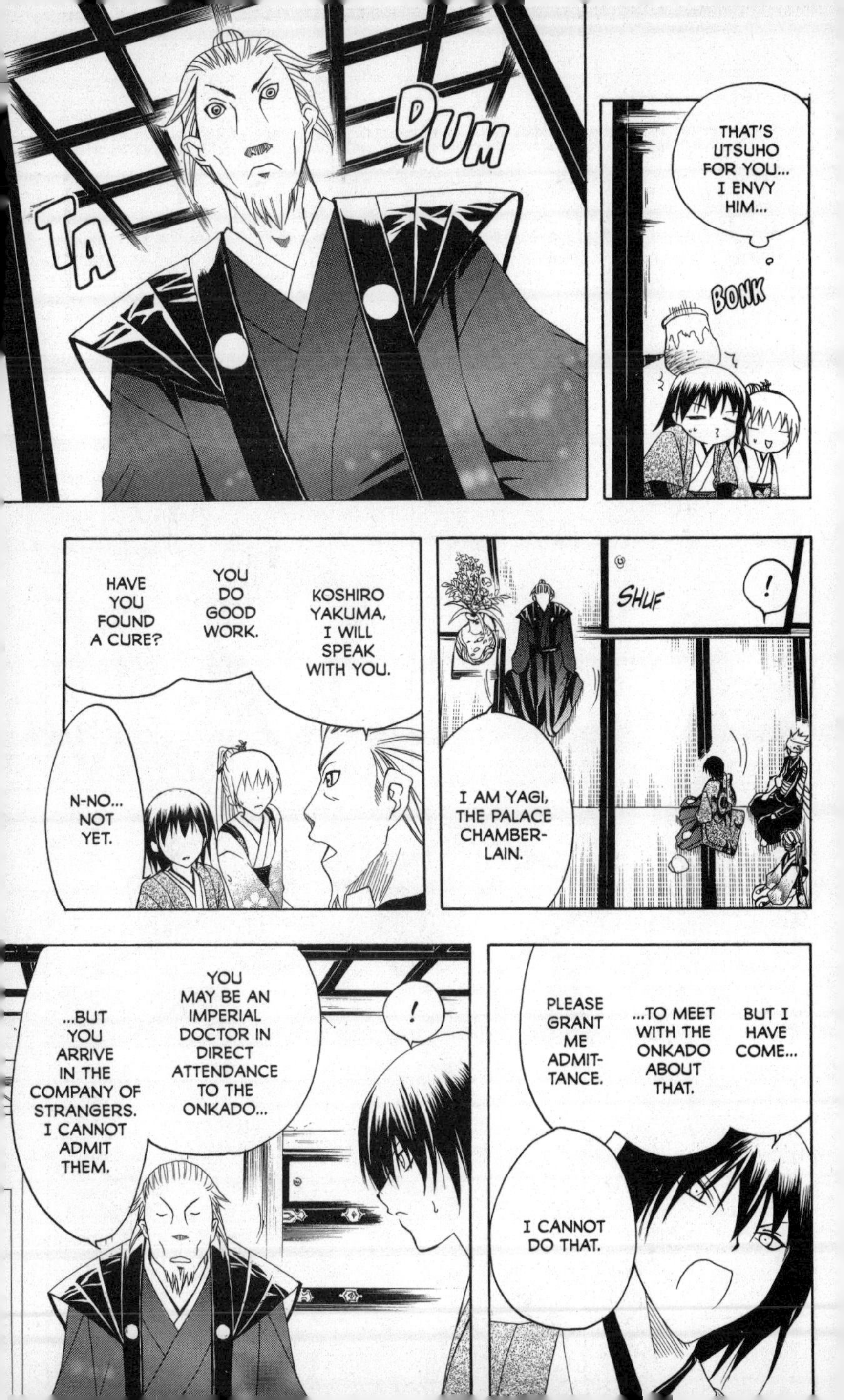
THAT'S UTSUHO FOR YOU... I ENVY HIM...
BONK
DUM
TA
!
SHUF
I AM YAGI, THE PALACE CHAMBERLAIN.
KOSHIRO YAKUMA, I WILL SPEAK WITH YOU.
YOU DO GOOD WORK.
HAVE YOU FOUND A CURE?
N-NO... NOT YET.
BUT I HAVE COME...
...TO MEET WITH THE ONKADO ABOUT THAT.
PLEASE GRANT ME ADMITTANCE.
I CANNOT DO THAT.
!
YOU MAY BE AN IMPERIAL DOCTOR IN DIRECT ATTENDANCE TO THE ONKADO...
...BUT YOU ARRIVE IN THE COMPANY OF STRANGERS. I CANNOT ADMIT THEM.

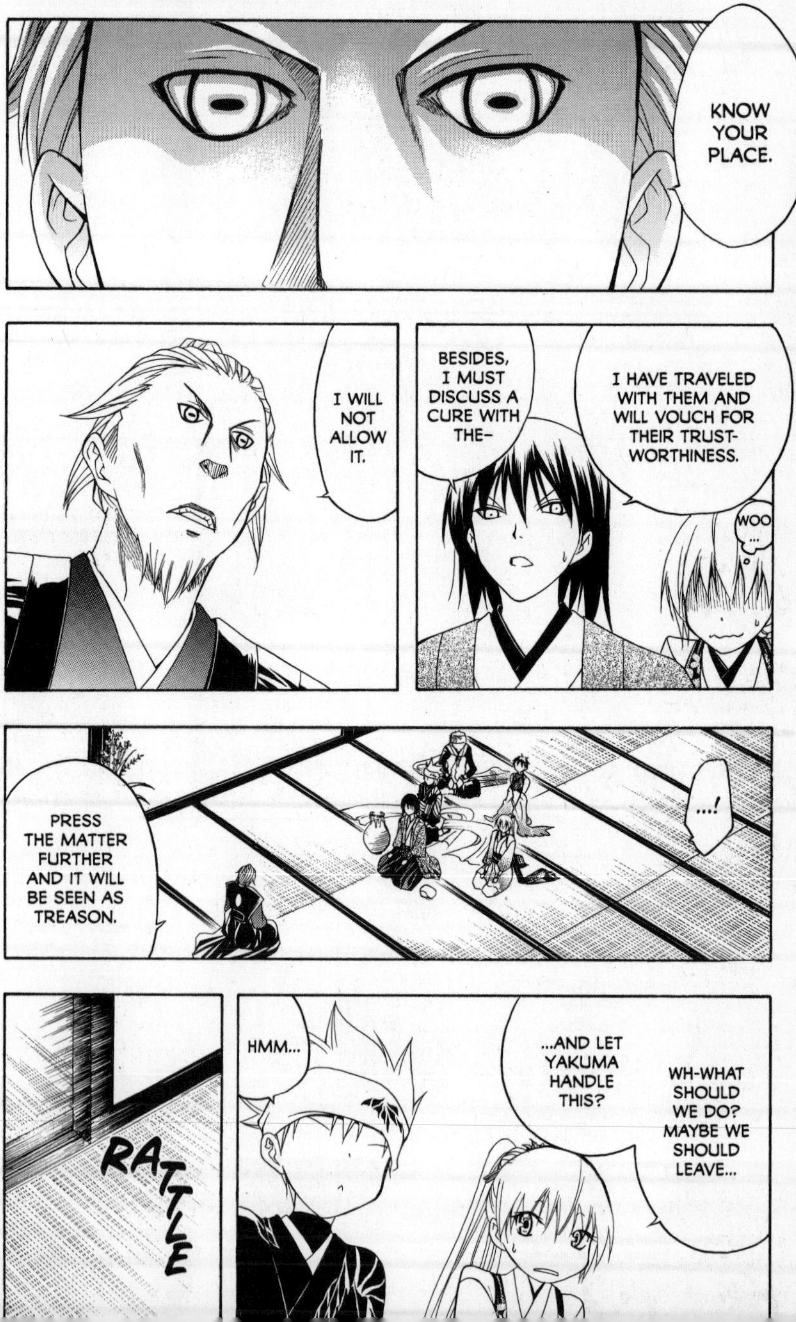
KNOW YOUR PLACE.
I HAVE TRAVELED WITH THEM AND WILL VOUCH FOR THEIR TRUST-WORTHINESS.
BESIDES, I MUST DISCUSS A CURE WITH THE–
WOO...
I WILL NOT ALLOW IT.
...!
PRESS THE MATTER FURTHER AND IT WILL BE SEEN AS TREASON.
WH-WHAT SHOULD WE DO? MAYBE WE SHOULD LEAVE...
...AND LET YAKUMA HANDLE THIS?
HMM...
RATTLE

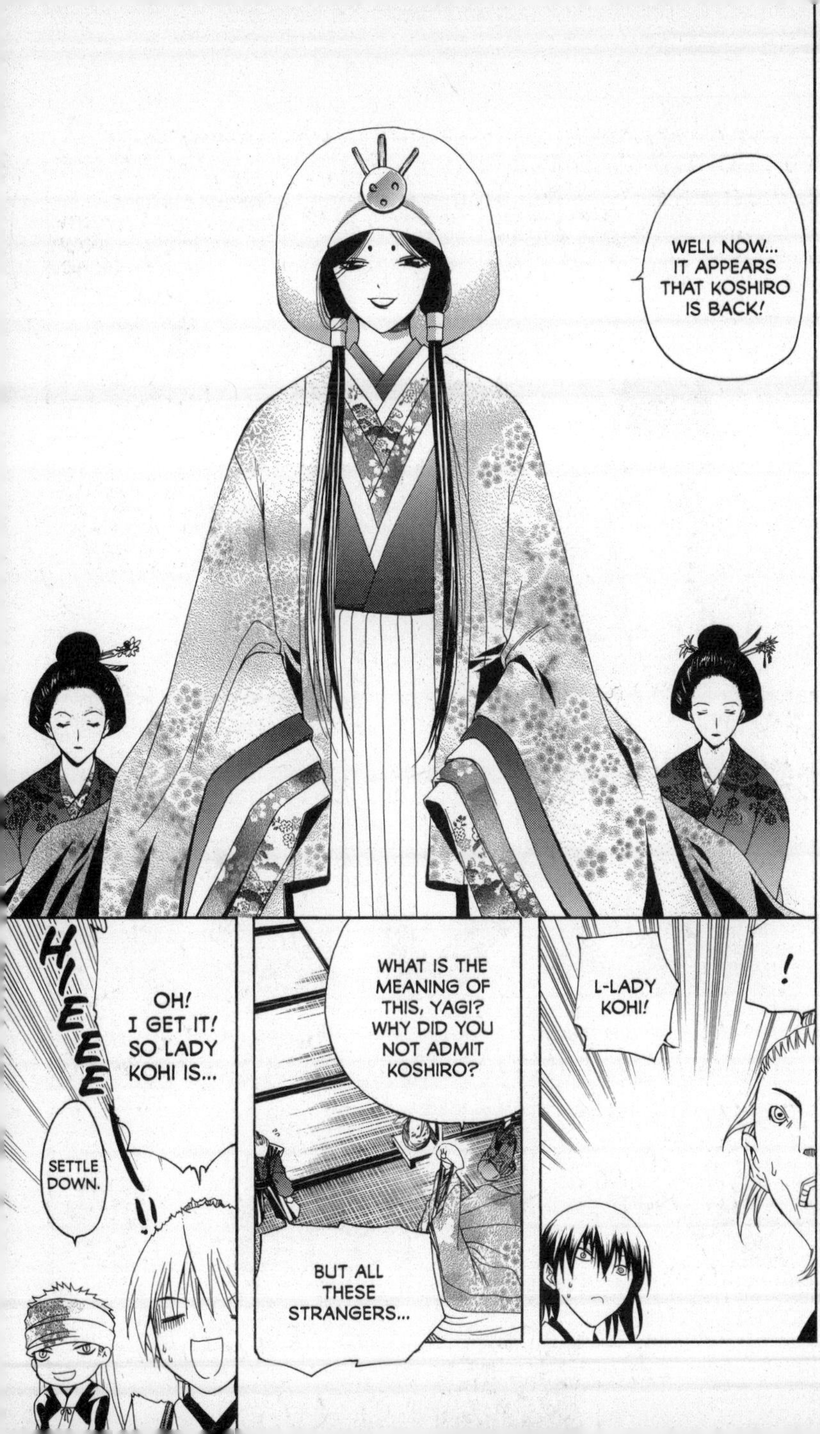
WELL NOW... IT APPEARS THAT KOSHIRO IS BACK!
!
L-LADY KOHI!
WHAT IS THE MEANING OF THIS, YAGI? WHY DID YOU NOT ADMIT KOSHIRO?
BUT ALL THESE STRANGERS...
OH! I GET IT! SO LADY KOHI IS...
HIEEE
SETTLE DOWN.
!!

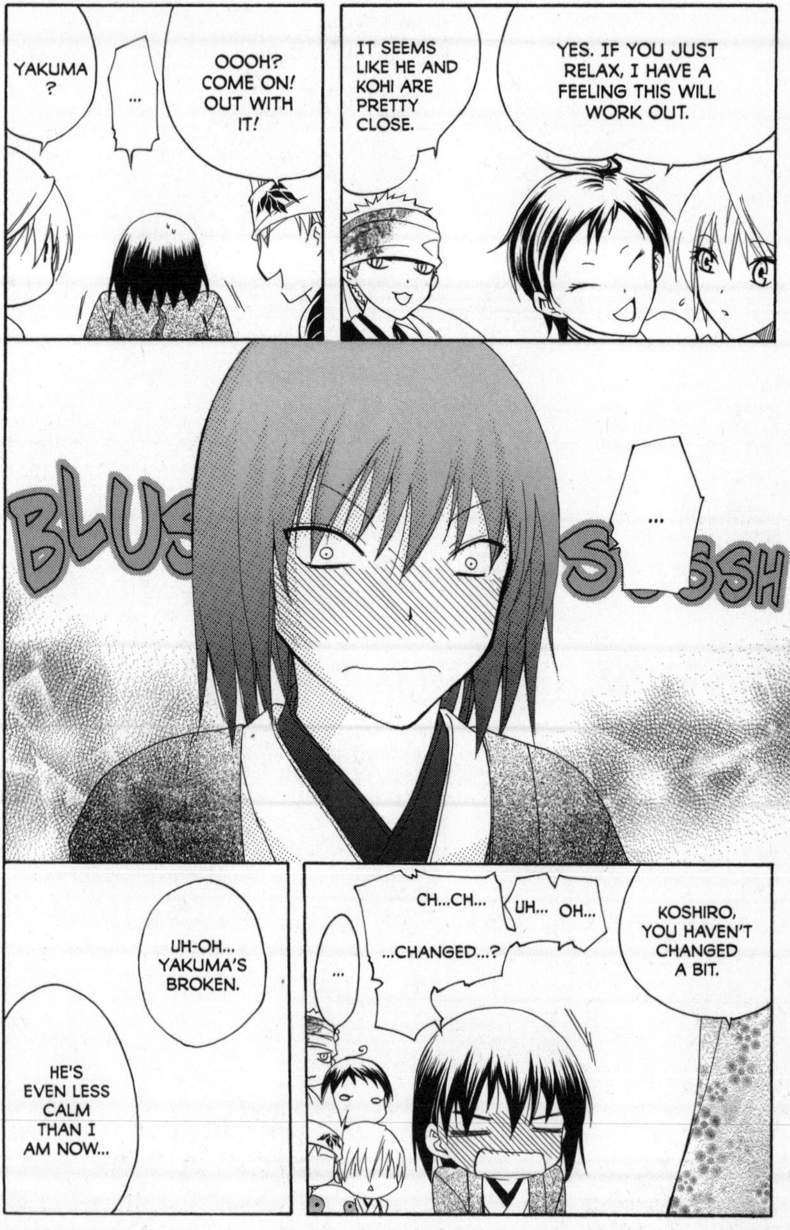
YES. IF YOU JUST RELAX, I HAVE A FEELING THIS WILL WORK OUT.
IT SEEMS LIKE HE AND KOHI ARE PRETTY CLOSE.
OOOH? COME ON! OUT WITH IT!
...
YAKUMA?
...
BLUS
SSSH
KOSHIRO, YOU HAVEN'T CHANGED A BIT.
UH... OH...
CH...CH...
...CHANGED...?
...
UH-OH... YAKUMA'S BROKEN.
HE'S EVEN LESS CALM THAN I AM NOW...

Chapter 91 Onkado

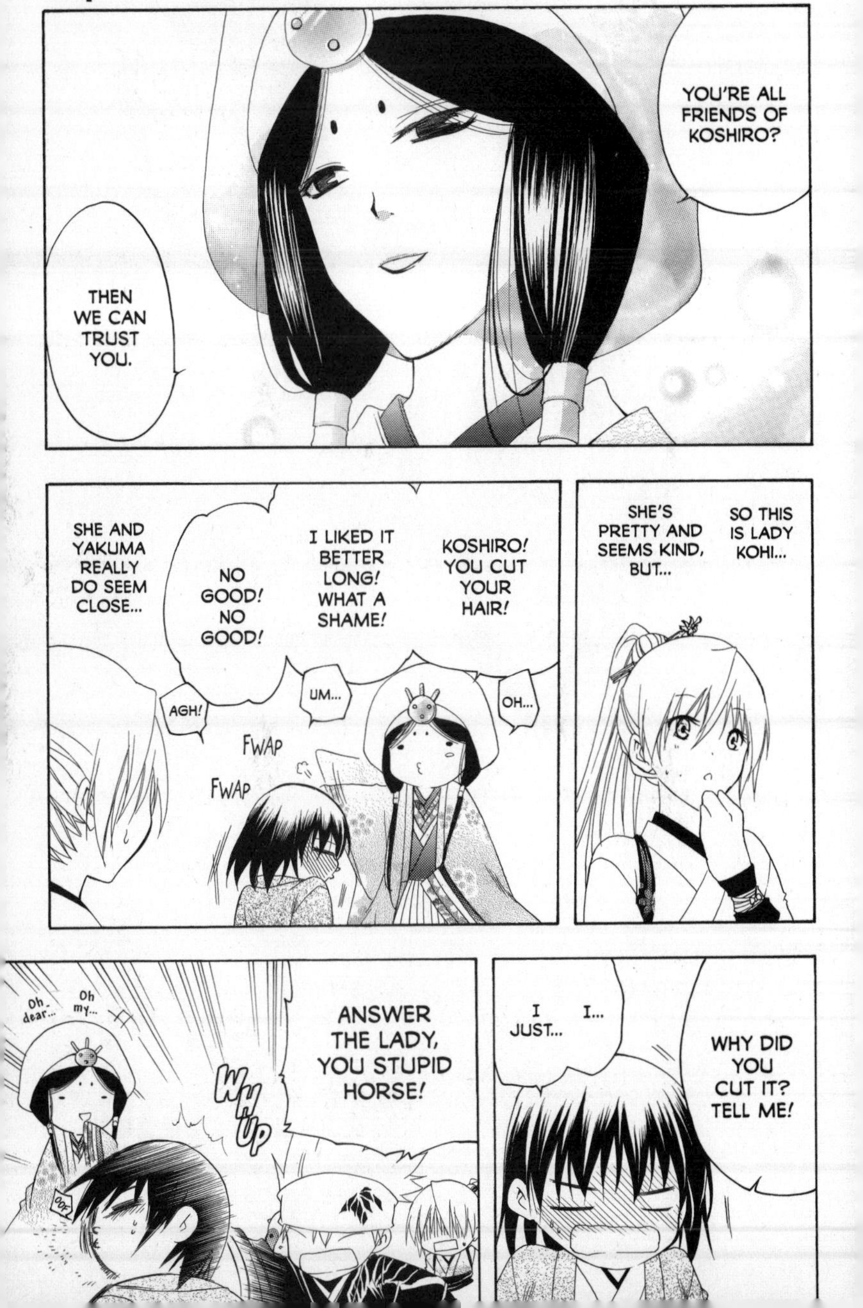

YOU'RE ALL FRIENDS OF KOSHIRO?
THEN WE CAN TRUST YOU.
SO THIS IS LADY KOHI...
SHE'S PRETTY AND SEEMS KIND, BUT...
KOSHIRO! YOU CUT YOUR HAIR!
I LIKED IT BETTER LONG! WHAT A SHAME!
NO GOOD! NO GOOD!
SHE AND YAKUMA REALLY DO SEEM CLOSE...
OH...
UM...
AGH!
FWAP
FWAP
WHY DID YOU CUT IT? TELL ME!
I...
I JUST...
ANSWER THE LADY, YOU STUPID HORSE!
WHUP
Oh my...
Oh dear...
OOF

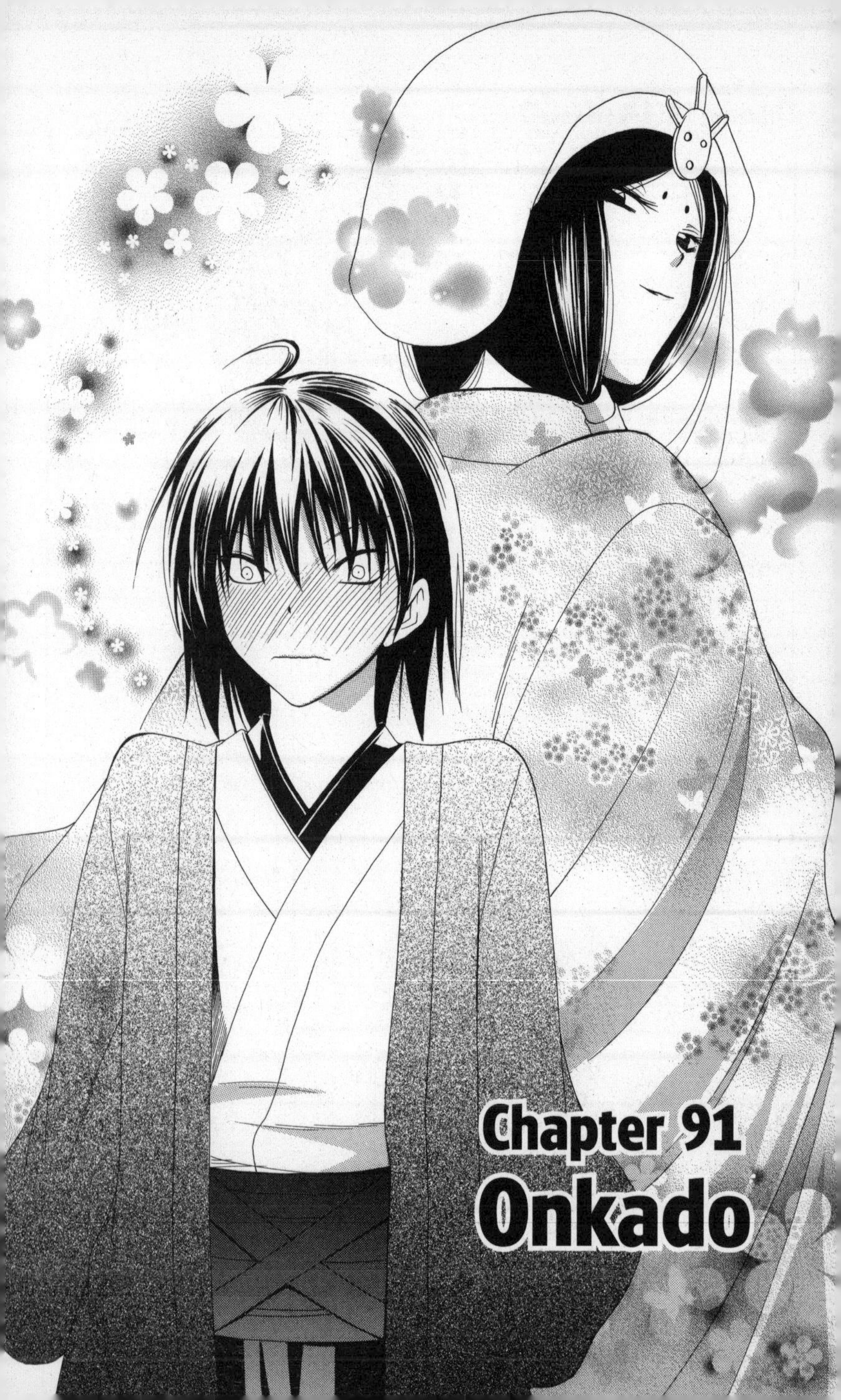
Chapter 91
Onkado

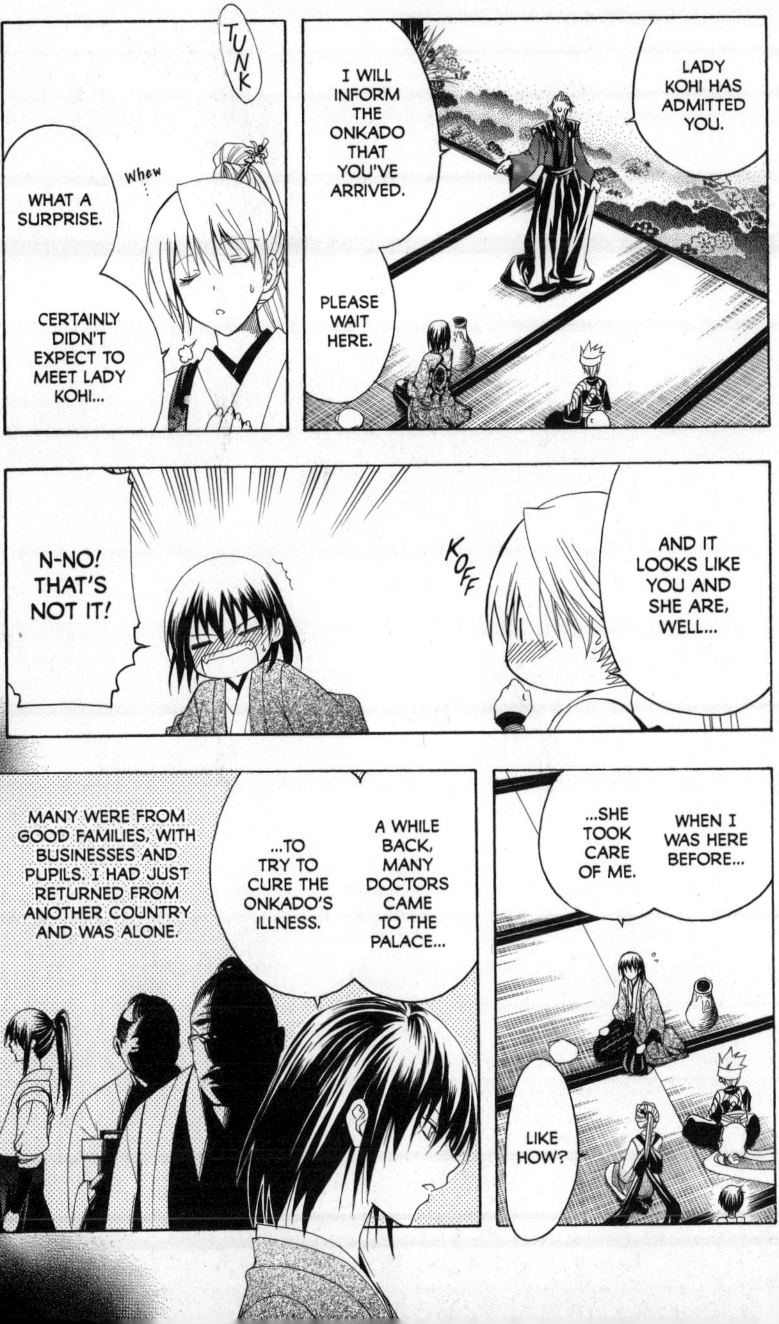
LADY KOHI HAS ADMITTED YOU.
I WILL INFORM THE ONKADO THAT YOU'VE ARRIVED.
PLEASE WAIT HERE.
TUNK
WHAT A SURPRISE.
Whew...
CERTAINLY DIDN'T EXPECT TO MEET LADY KOHI...
AND IT LOOKS LIKE YOU AND SHE ARE, WELL...
KOFF
N-NO! THAT'S NOT IT!
WHEN I WAS HERE BEFORE...
...SHE TOOK CARE OF ME.
LIKE HOW?
A WHILE BACK, MANY DOCTORS CAME TO THE PALACE...
...TO TRY TO CURE THE ONKADO'S ILLNESS.
MANY WERE FROM GOOD FAMILIES, WITH BUSINESSES AND PUPILS. I HAD JUST RETURNED FROM ANOTHER COUNTRY AND WAS ALONE.

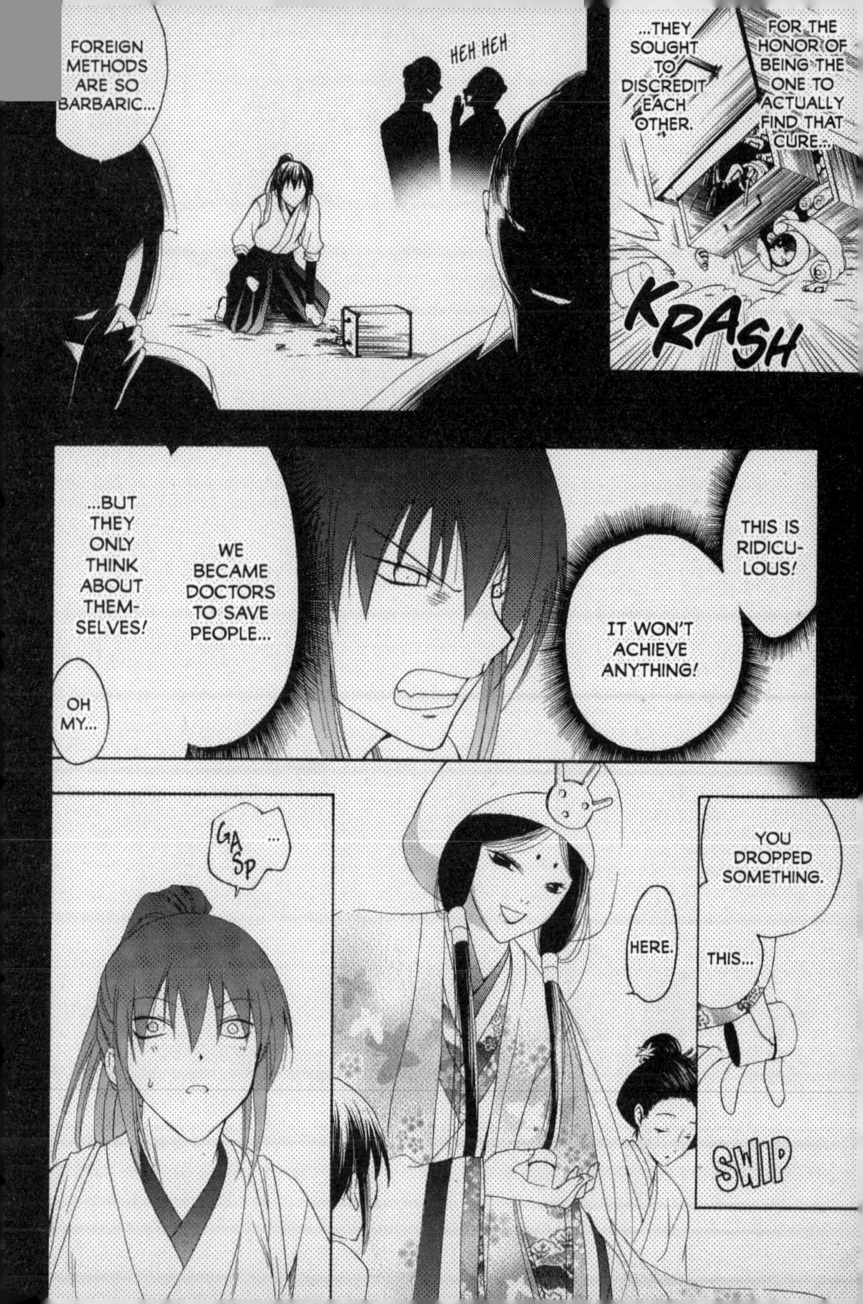
FOR THE HONOR OF BEING THE ONE TO ACTUALLY FIND THAT CURE...
...THEY SOUGHT TO DISCREDIT EACH OTHER.
KRASH
HEH HEH
FOREIGN METHODS ARE SO BARBARIC...
THIS IS RIDICU-LOUS!
IT WON'T ACHIEVE ANYTHING!
WE BECAME DOCTORS TO SAVE PEOPLE...
...BUT THEY ONLY THINK ABOUT THEM-SELVES!
OH MY...
YOU DROPPED SOMETHING.
THIS...
SWIP
HERE.
GASP...

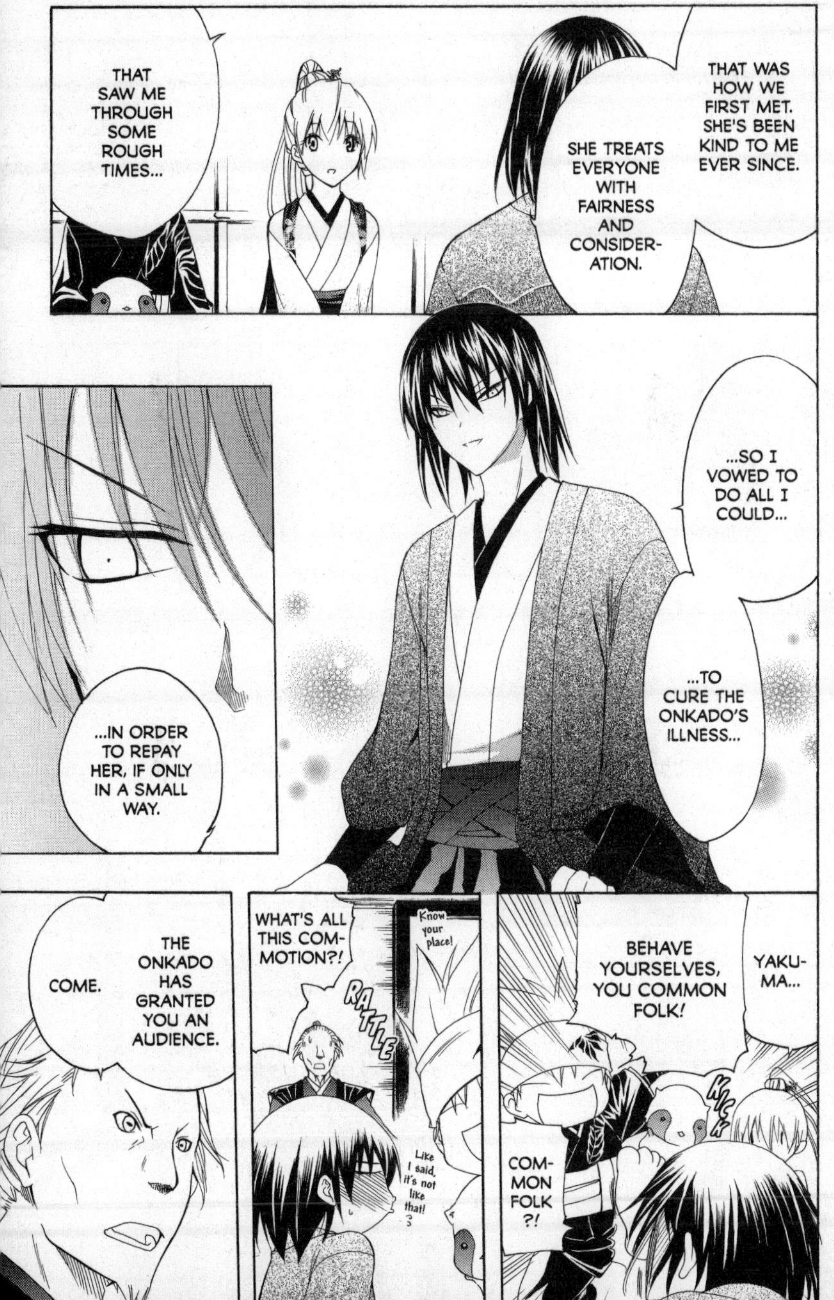
THAT WAS HOW WE FIRST MET. SHE'S BEEN KIND TO ME EVER SINCE.
SHE TREATS EVERYONE WITH FAIRNESS AND CONSIDER-ATION.
THAT SAW ME THROUGH SOME ROUGH TIMES...
...SO I VOWED TO DO ALL I COULD...
...TO CURE THE ONKADO'S ILLNESS...
...IN ORDER TO REPAY HER, IF ONLY IN A SMALL WAY.
YAKU-MA...
BEHAVE YOURSELVES, YOU COMMON FOLK!
KICK
COM-MON FOLK ?!
Know your place!
WHAT'S ALL THIS COM-MOTION?!
RATTLE
Like I said, it's not like that!
THE ONKADO HAS GRANTED YOU AN AUDIENCE.
COME.

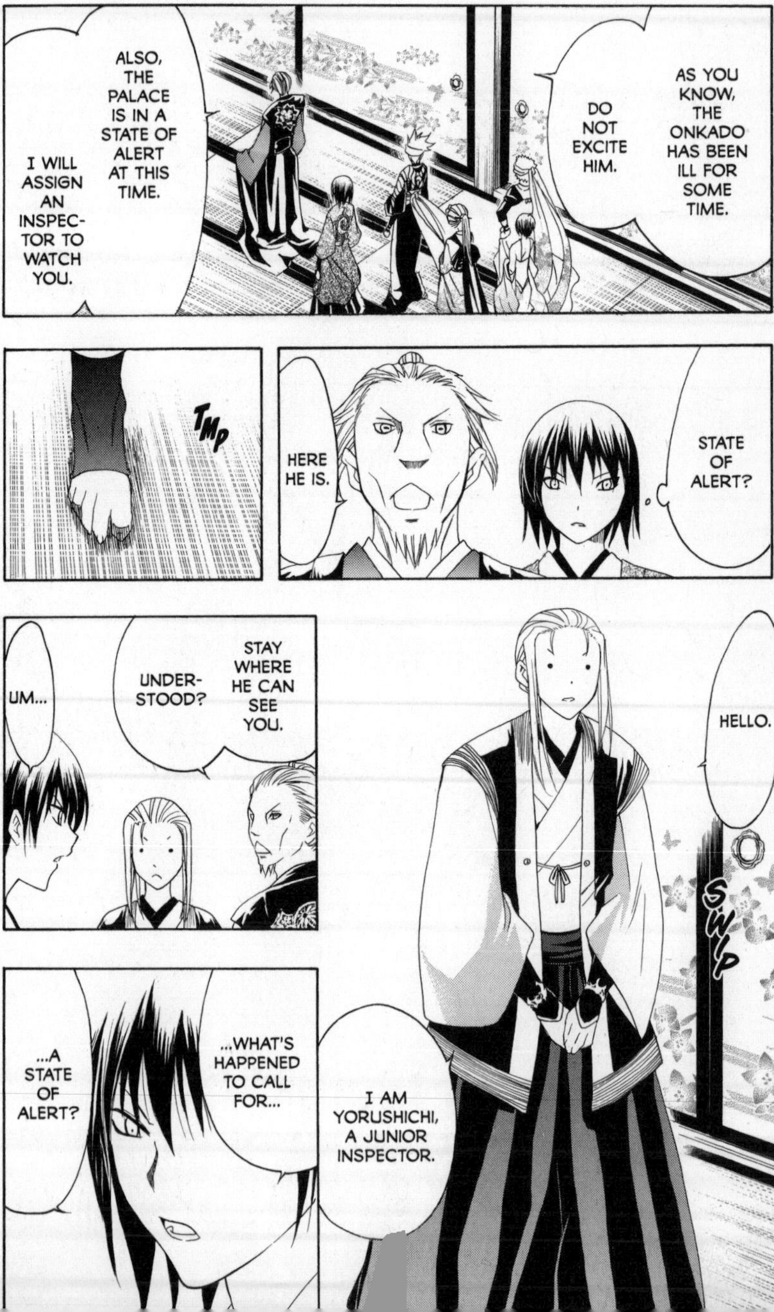
AS YOU KNOW, THE ONKADO HAS BEEN ILL FOR SOME TIME.
DO NOT EXCITE HIM.
ALSO, THE PALACE IS IN A STATE OF ALERT AT THIS TIME.
I WILL ASSIGN AN INSPEC-TOR TO WATCH YOU.
STATE OF ALERT?
HERE HE IS.
TMP
HELLO.
SWIP
I AM YORUSHICHI, A JUNIOR INSPECTOR.
STAY WHERE HE CAN SEE YOU.
UNDER-STOOD?
UM...
...WHAT'S HAPPENED TO CALL FOR...
...A STATE OF ALERT?

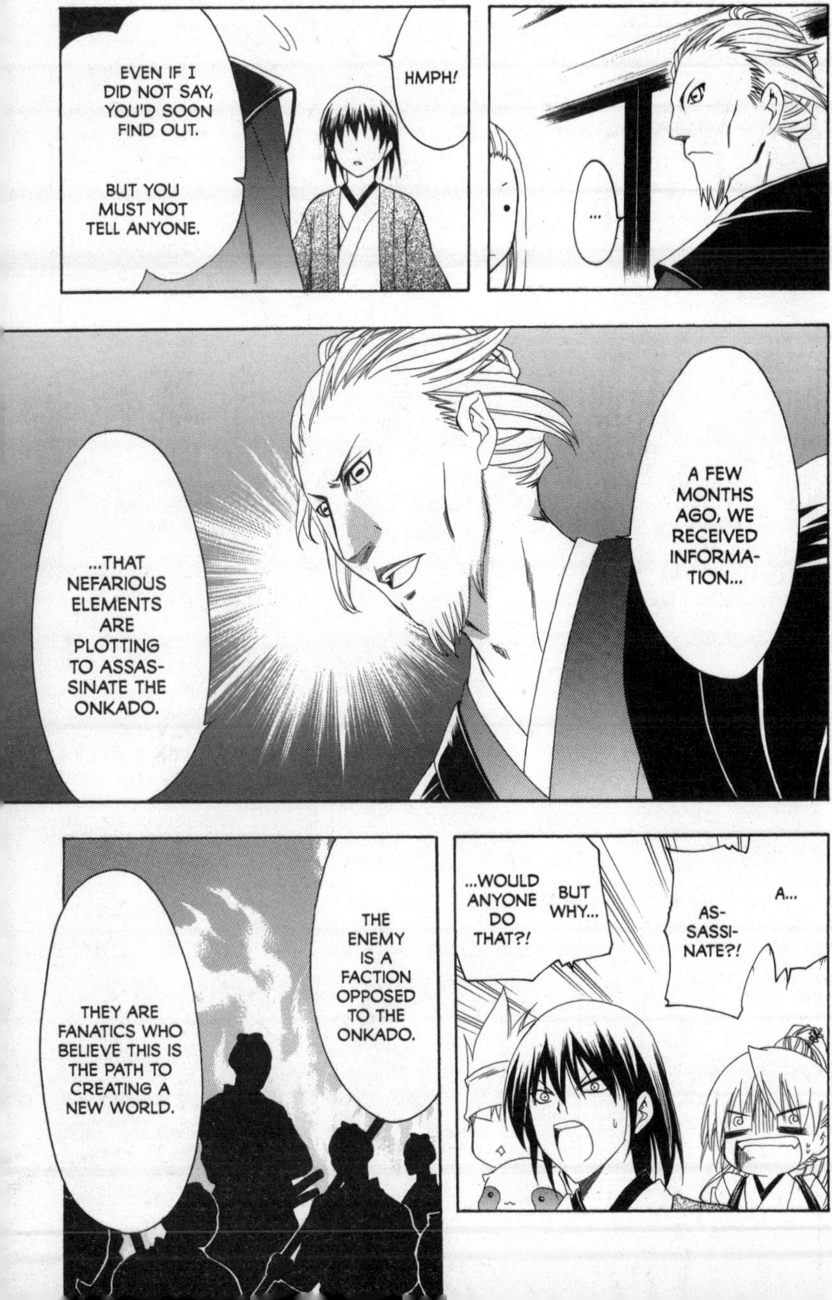
...
HMPH!
EVEN IF I DID NOT SAY, YOU'D SOON FIND OUT.
BUT YOU MUST NOT TELL ANYONE.
A FEW MONTHS AGO, WE RECEIVED INFORMATION...
...THAT NEFARIOUS ELEMENTS ARE PLOTTING TO ASSASSINATE THE ONKADO.
A...
ASSASSINATE?!
BUT WHY...
...WOULD ANYONE DO THAT?!
THE ENEMY IS A FACTION OPPOSED TO THE ONKADO.
THEY ARE FANATICS WHO BELIEVE THIS IS THE PATH TO CREATING A NEW WORLD.

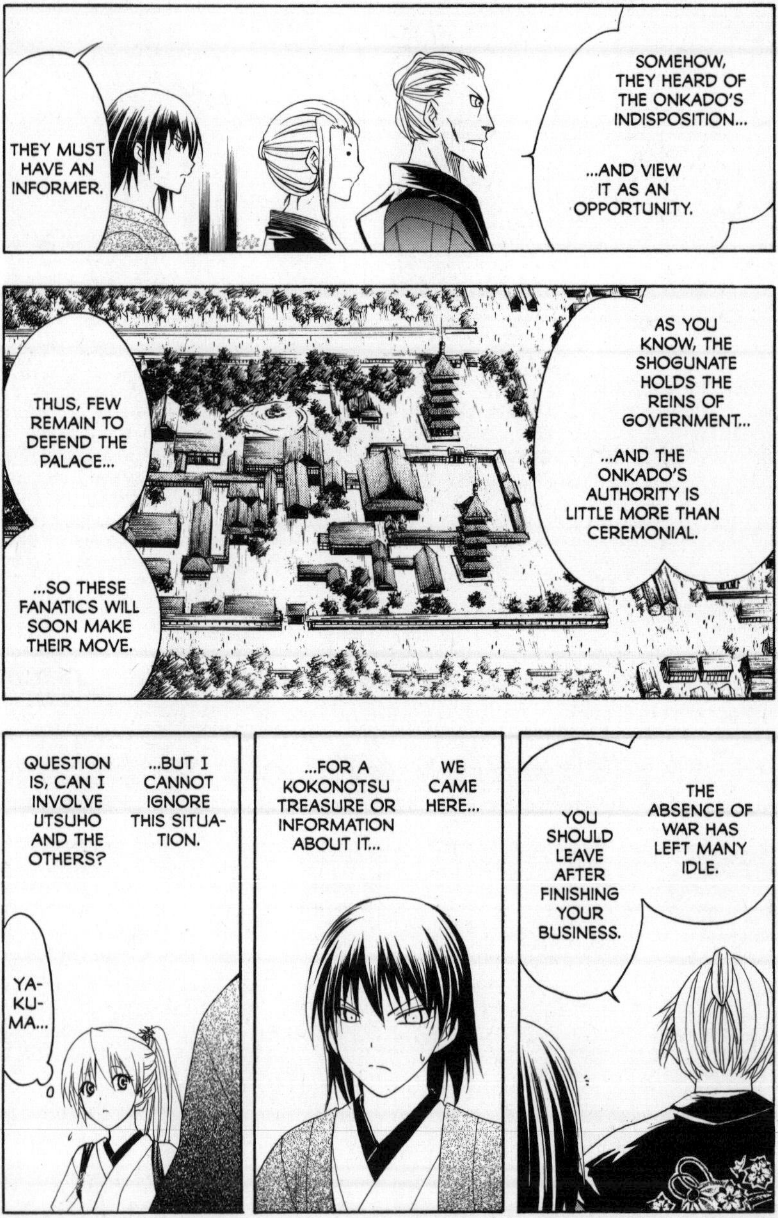
SOMEHOW, THEY HEARD OF THE ONKADO'S INDISPOSITION...
...AND VIEW IT AS AN OPPORTUNITY.
THEY MUST HAVE AN INFORMER.
AS YOU KNOW, THE SHOGUNATE HOLDS THE REINS OF GOVERNMENT...
...AND THE ONKADO'S AUTHORITY IS LITTLE MORE THAN CEREMONIAL.
THUS, FEW REMAIN TO DEFEND THE PALACE...
...SO THESE FANATICS WILL SOON MAKE THEIR MOVE.
THE ABSENCE OF WAR HAS LEFT MANY IDLE.
YOU SHOULD LEAVE AFTER FINISHING YOUR BUSINESS.
WE CAME HERE...
...FOR A KOKONOTSU TREASURE OR INFORMATION ABOUT IT...
...BUT I CANNOT IGNORE THIS SITUATION.
QUESTION IS, CAN I INVOLVE UTSUHO AND THE OTHERS?
YA-KU-MA...

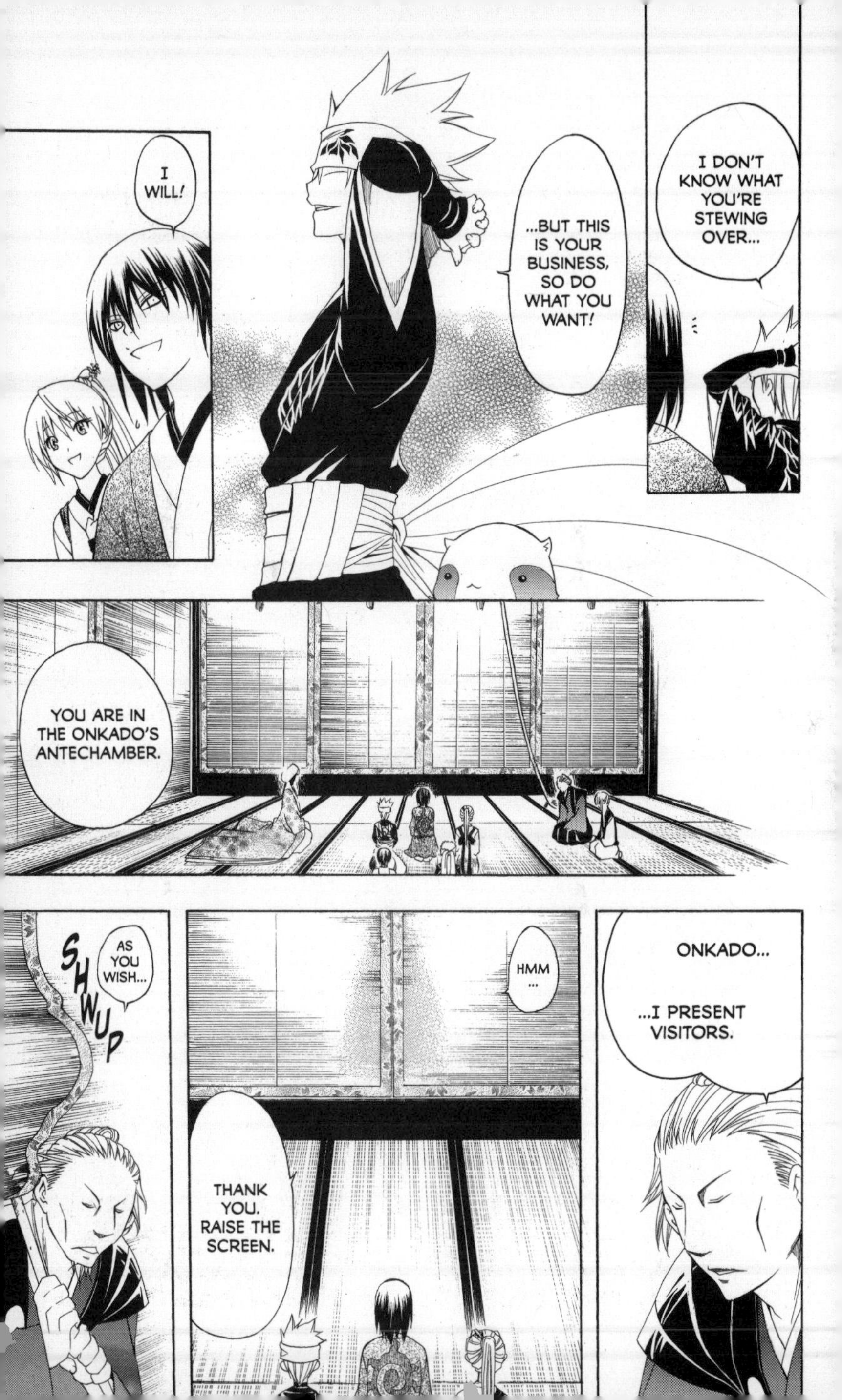
I DON'T KNOW WHAT YOU'RE STEWING OVER...
...BUT THIS IS YOUR BUSINESS, SO DO WHAT YOU WANT!
I WILL!
YOU ARE IN THE ONKADO'S ANTECHAMBER.
ONKADO...
...I PRESENT VISITORS.
HMM...
THANK YOU. RAISE THE SCREEN.
AS YOU WISH...
SHWUP

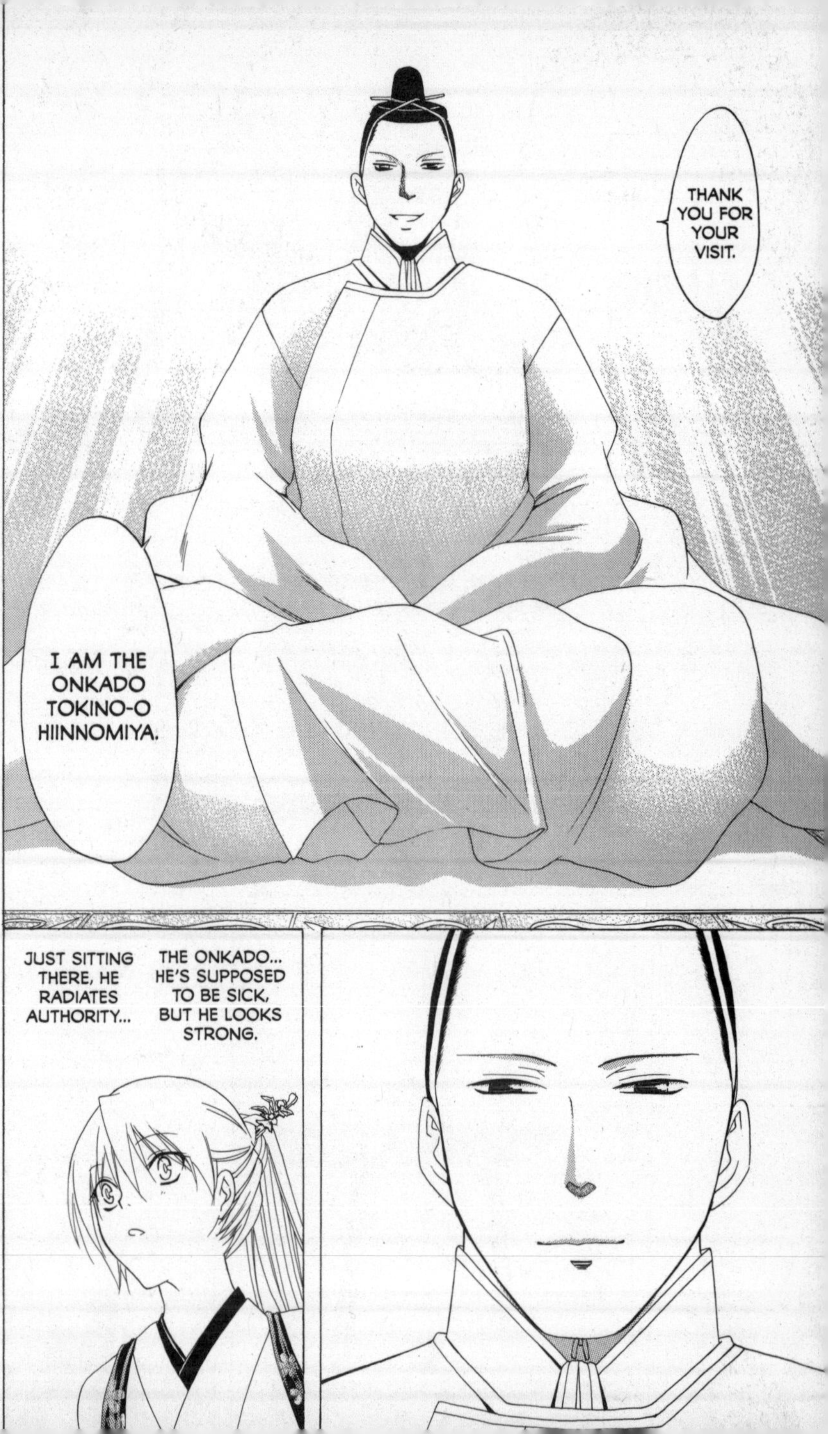
THANK YOU FOR YOUR VISIT.
I AM THE ONKADO TOKINO-O HIINNOMIYA.
THE ONKADO... HE'S SUPPOSED TO BE SICK, BUT HE LOOKS STRONG.
JUST SITTING THERE, HE RADIATES AUTHORITY...

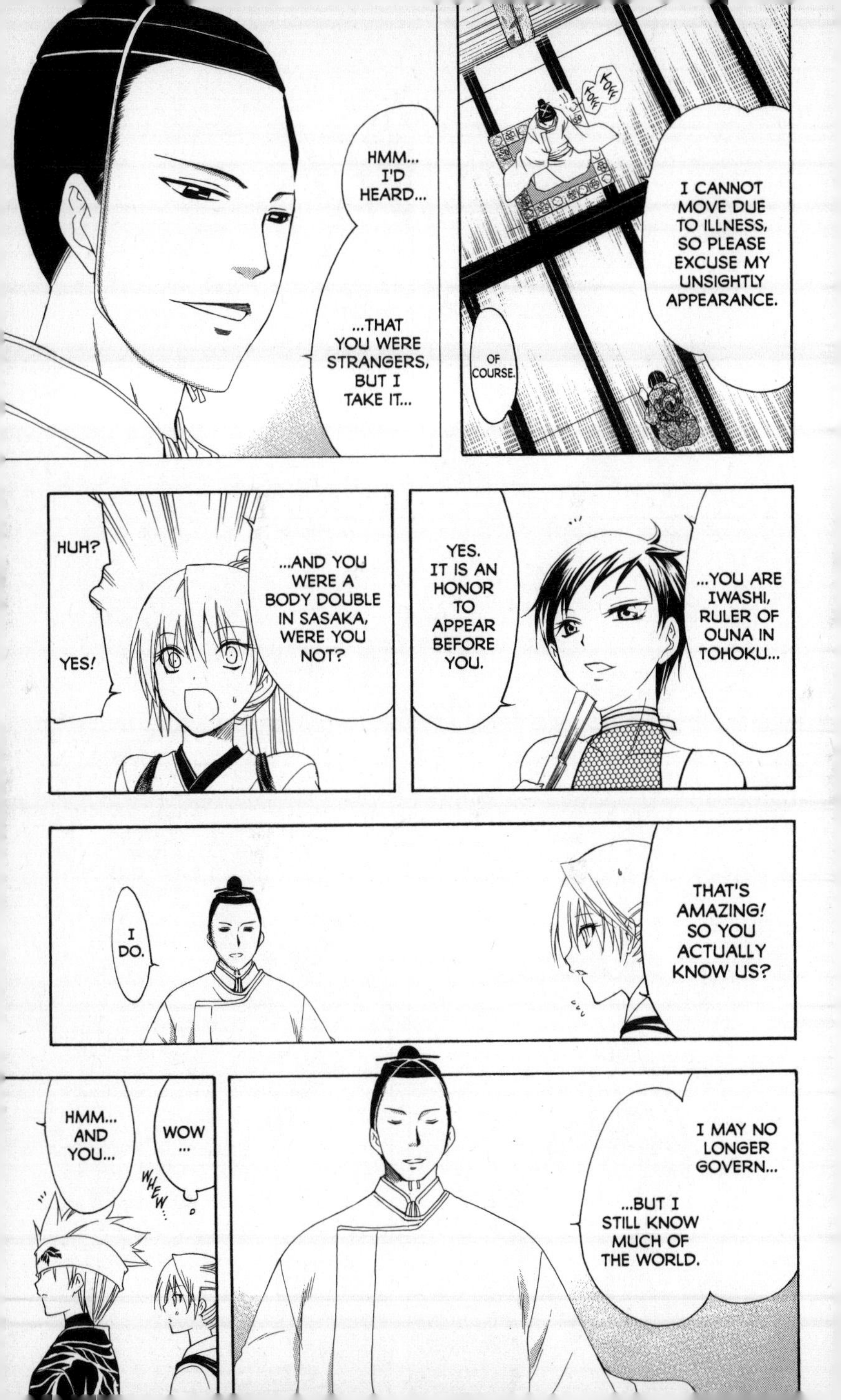
TOK TOK
I CANNOT MOVE DUE TO ILLNESS, SO PLEASE EXCUSE MY UNSIGHTLY APPEARANCE.
OF COURSE.
HMM... I'D HEARD...
...THAT YOU WERE STRANGERS, BUT I TAKE IT...
...YOU ARE IWASHI, RULER OF OUNA IN TOHOKU...
YES. IT IS AN HONOR TO APPEAR BEFORE YOU.
...AND YOU WERE A BODY DOUBLE IN SASAKA, WERE YOU NOT?
HUH?
YES!
THAT'S AMAZING! SO YOU ACTUALLY KNOW US?
I DO.
I MAY NO LONGER GOVERN...
...BUT I STILL KNOW MUCH OF THE WORLD.
WOW...
WHEW...
HMM... AND YOU...

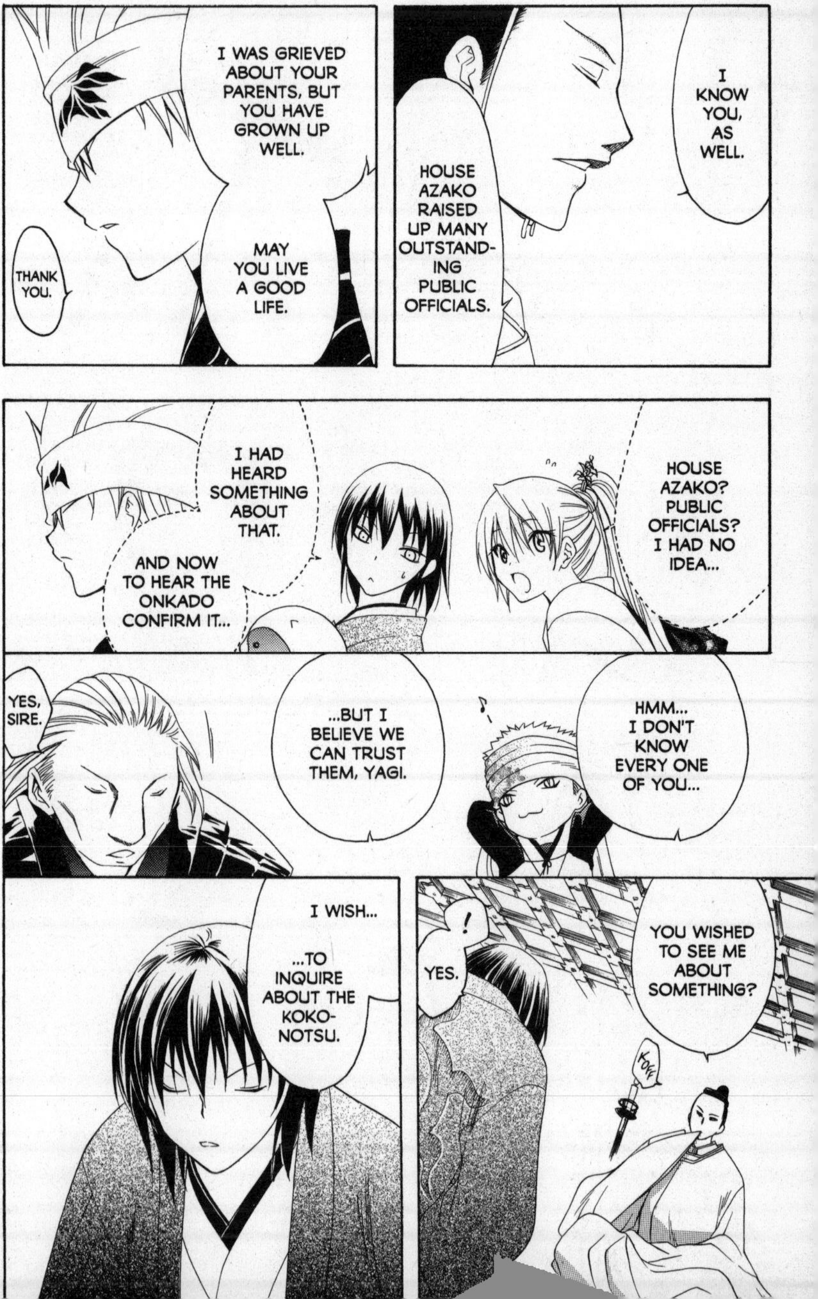
I KNOW YOU, AS WELL.
HOUSE AZAKO RAISED UP MANY OUTSTANDING PUBLIC OFFICIALS.
I WAS GRIEVED ABOUT YOUR PARENTS, BUT YOU HAVE GROWN UP WELL.
MAY YOU LIVE A GOOD LIFE.
THANK YOU.
HOUSE AZAKO? PUBLIC OFFICIALS? I HAD NO IDEA...
I HAD HEARD SOMETHING ABOUT THAT.
AND NOW TO HEAR THE ONKADO CONFIRM IT...
HMM... I DON'T KNOW EVERY ONE OF YOU...
...BUT I BELIEVE WE CAN TRUST THEM, YAGI.
YES, SIRE.
YOU WISHED TO SEE ME ABOUT SOMETHING?
!
YES.
I WISH...
...TO INQUIRE ABOUT THE KOKONOTSU.

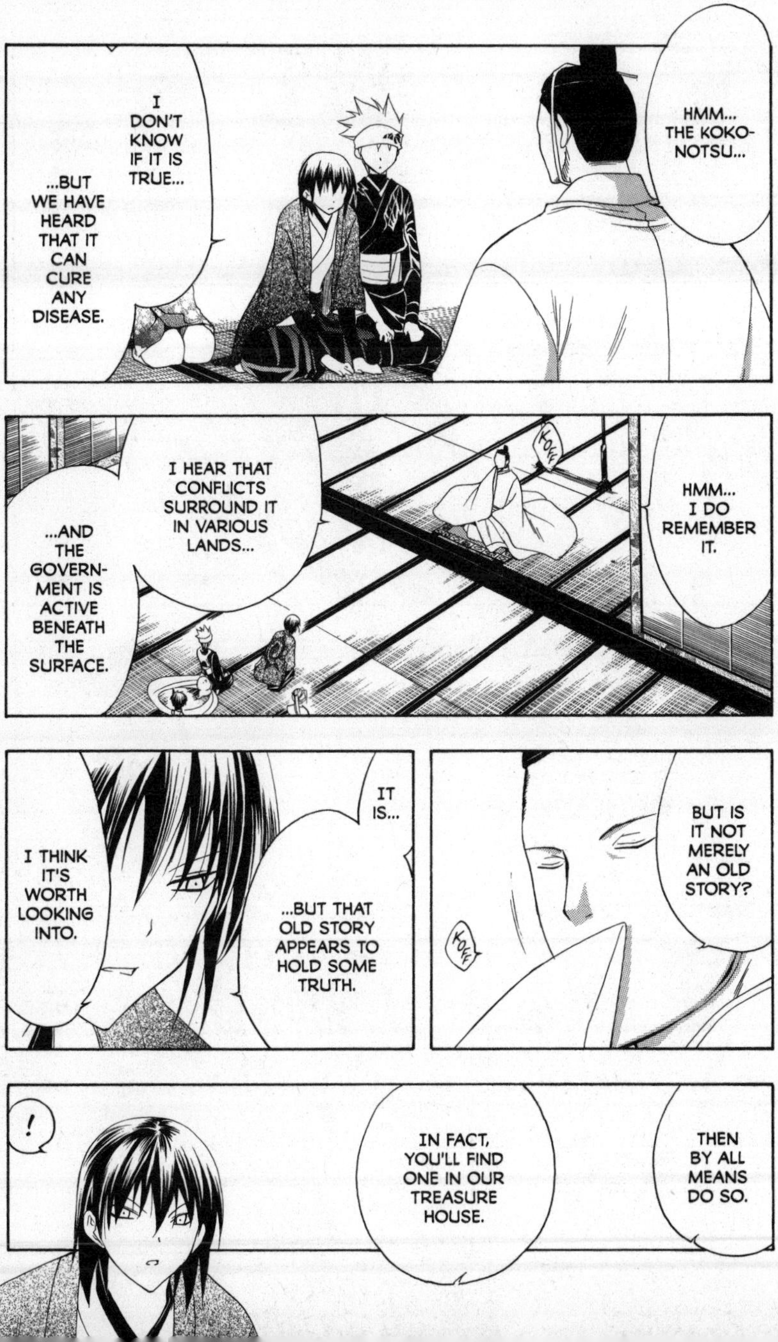
HMM... THE KOKO-NOTSU...
I DON'T KNOW IF IT IS TRUE...
...BUT WE HAVE HEARD THAT IT CAN CURE ANY DISEASE.
HMM... I DO REMEMBER IT.
KOFF
I HEAR THAT CONFLICTS SURROUND IT IN VARIOUS LANDS...
...AND THE GOVERNMENT IS ACTIVE BENEATH THE SURFACE.
BUT IS IT NOT MERELY AN OLD STORY?
KOFF
IT IS...
...BUT THAT OLD STORY APPEARS TO HOLD SOME TRUTH.
I THINK IT'S WORTH LOOKING INTO.
THEN BY ALL MEANS DO SO.
IN FACT, YOU'LL FIND ONE IN OUR TREASURE HOUSE.
!

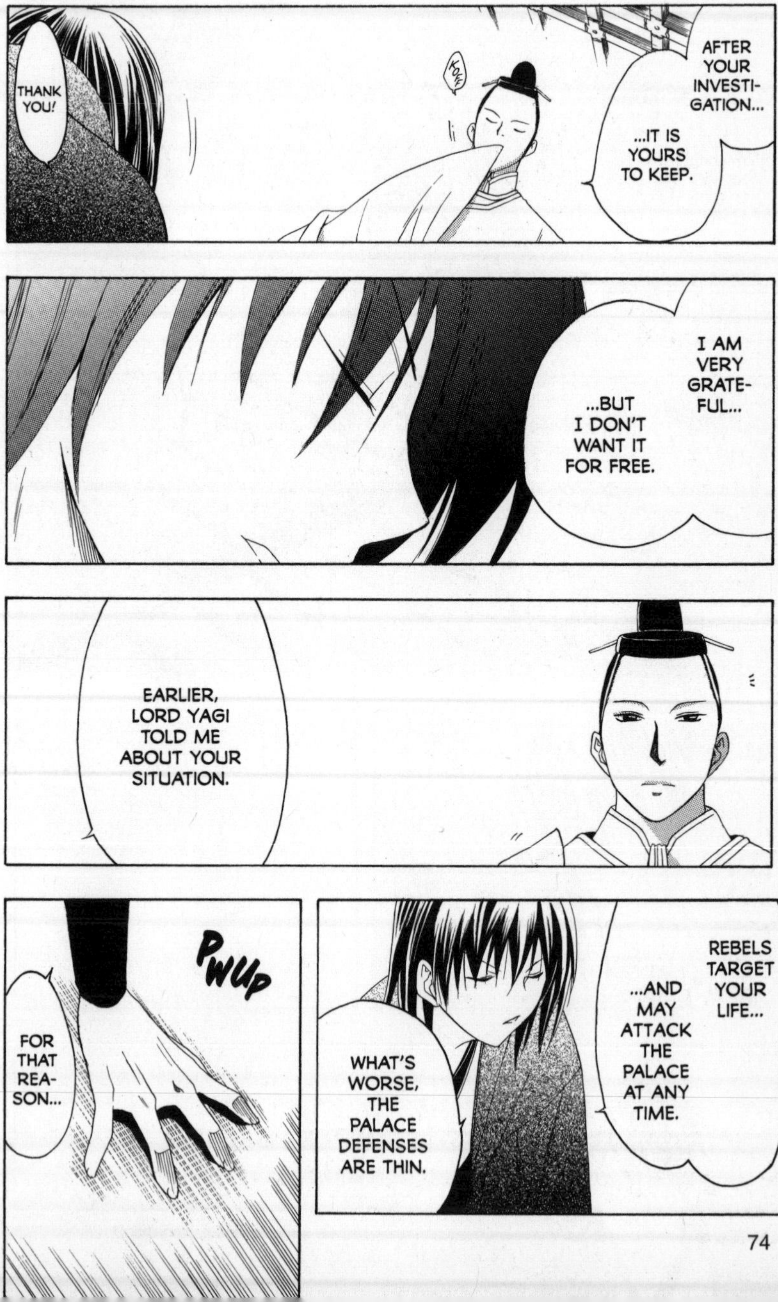
AFTER YOUR INVESTIGATION...
...IT IS YOURS TO KEEP.
KOFF
THANK YOU!
I AM VERY GRATEFUL...
...BUT I DON'T WANT IT FOR FREE.
EARLIER, LORD YAGI TOLD ME ABOUT YOUR SITUATION.
REBELS TARGET YOUR LIFE...
...AND MAY ATTACK THE PALACE AT ANY TIME.
WHAT'S WORSE, THE PALACE DEFENSES ARE THIN.
PWUP
FOR THAT REASON...

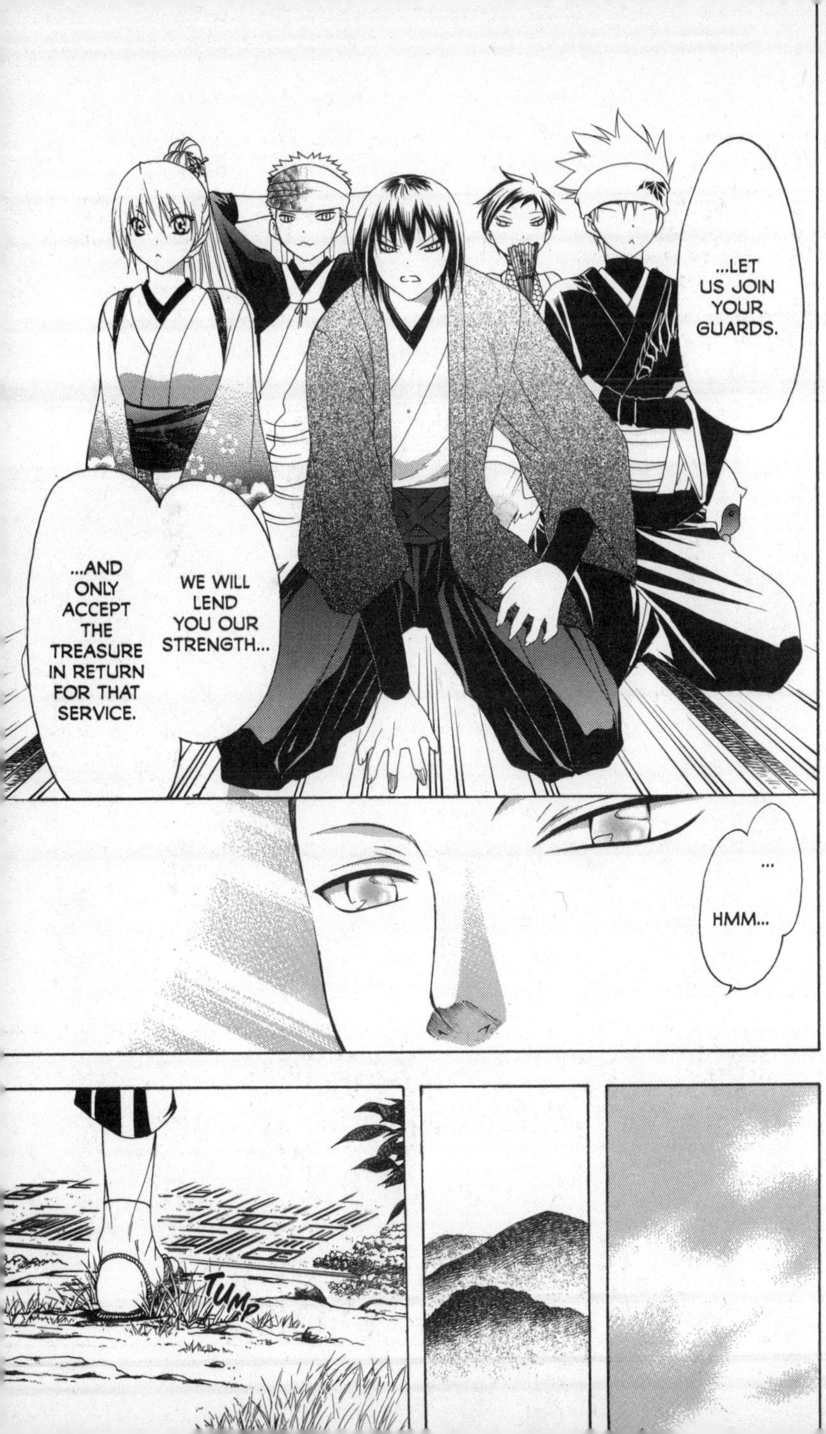
...LET US JOIN YOUR GUARDS.
WE WILL LEND YOU OUR STRENGTH...
...AND ONLY ACCEPT THE TREASURE IN RETURN FOR THAT SERVICE.
... HMM...
TUMP

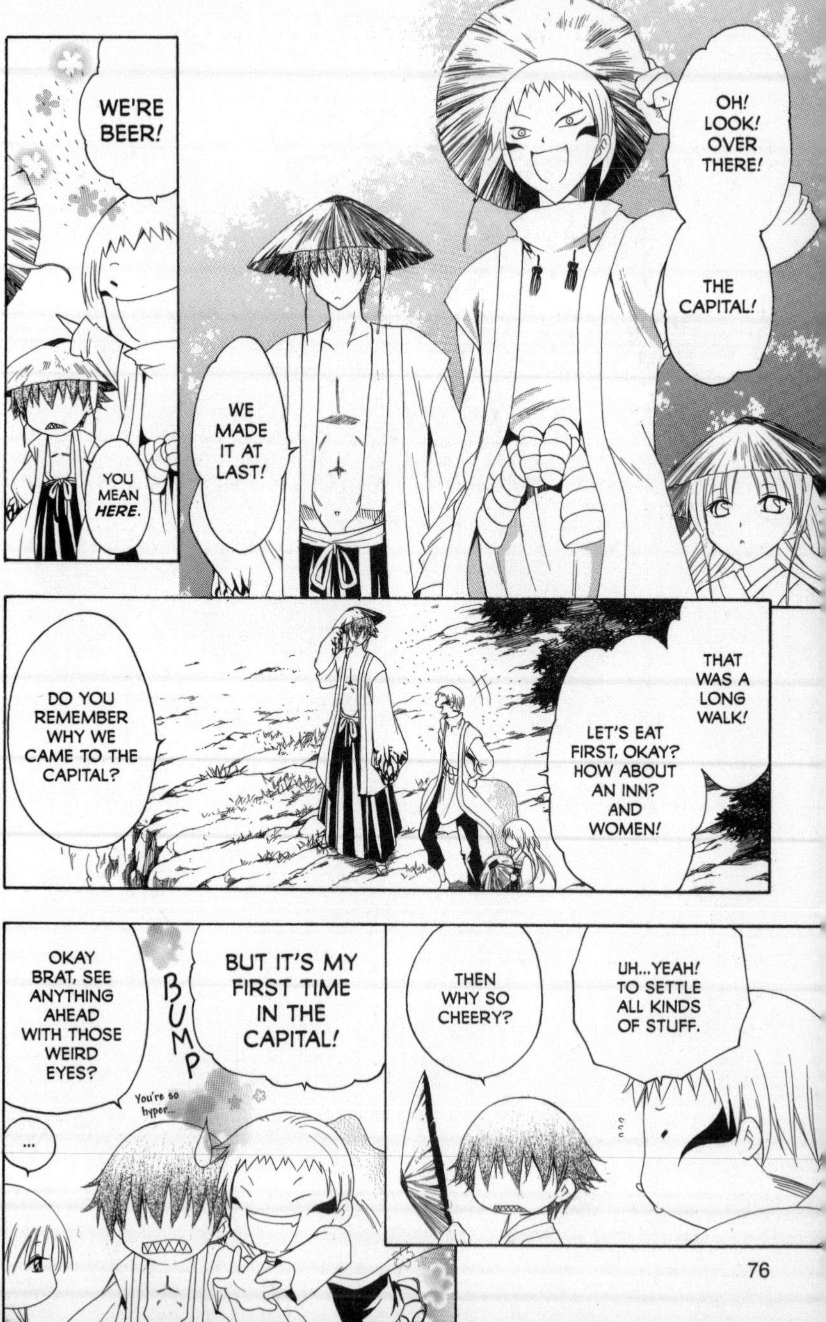
OH! LOOK! OVER THERE!
THE CAPITAL!
WE MADE IT AT LAST!
WE'RE BEER!
YOU MEAN *HERE*.
THAT WAS A LONG WALK!
LET'S EAT FIRST, OKAY? HOW ABOUT AN INN? AND WOMEN!
DO YOU REMEMBER WHY WE CAME TO THE CAPITAL?
UH...YEAH! TO SETTLE ALL KINDS OF STUFF.
THEN WHY SO CHEERY?
BUT IT'S MY FIRST TIME IN THE CAPITAL!
BUMP
OKAY BRAT, SEE ANYTHING AHEAD WITH THOSE WEIRD EYES?
You're so hyper...
...

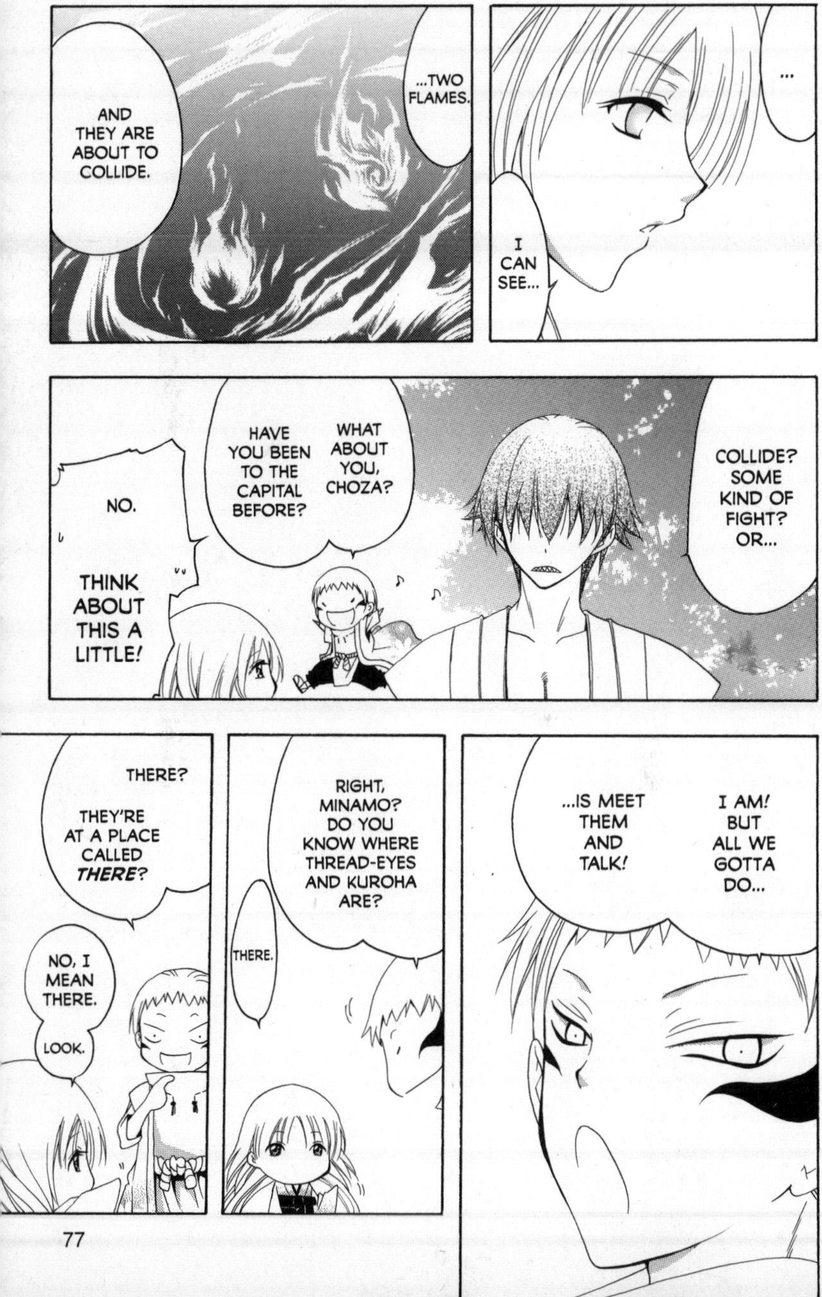
...
I CAN SEE...
...TWO FLAMES.
AND THEY ARE ABOUT TO COLLIDE.
COLLIDE? SOME KIND OF FIGHT? OR...
WHAT ABOUT YOU, CHOZA?
HAVE YOU BEEN TO THE CAPITAL BEFORE?
NO.
THINK ABOUT THIS A LITTLE!
I AM! BUT ALL WE GOTTA DO...
...IS MEET THEM AND TALK!
RIGHT, MINAMO? DO YOU KNOW WHERE THREAD-EYES AND KUROHA ARE?
THERE.
THERE?
THEY'RE AT A PLACE CALLED *THERE*?
NO, I MEAN THERE.
LOOK.

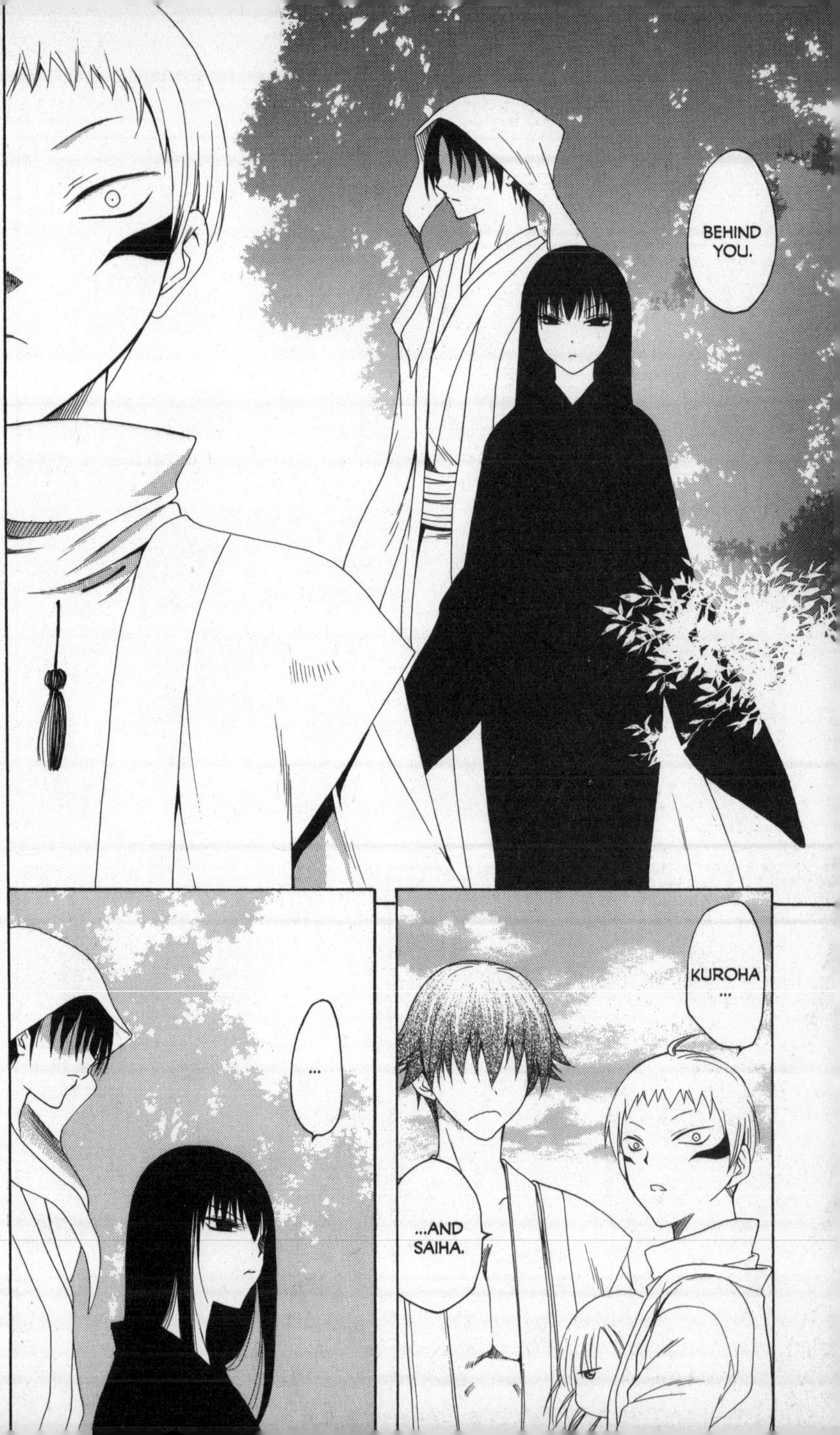
BEHIND YOU.
KUROHA ...
...AND SAIHA.
...

Chapter 92 Comrades

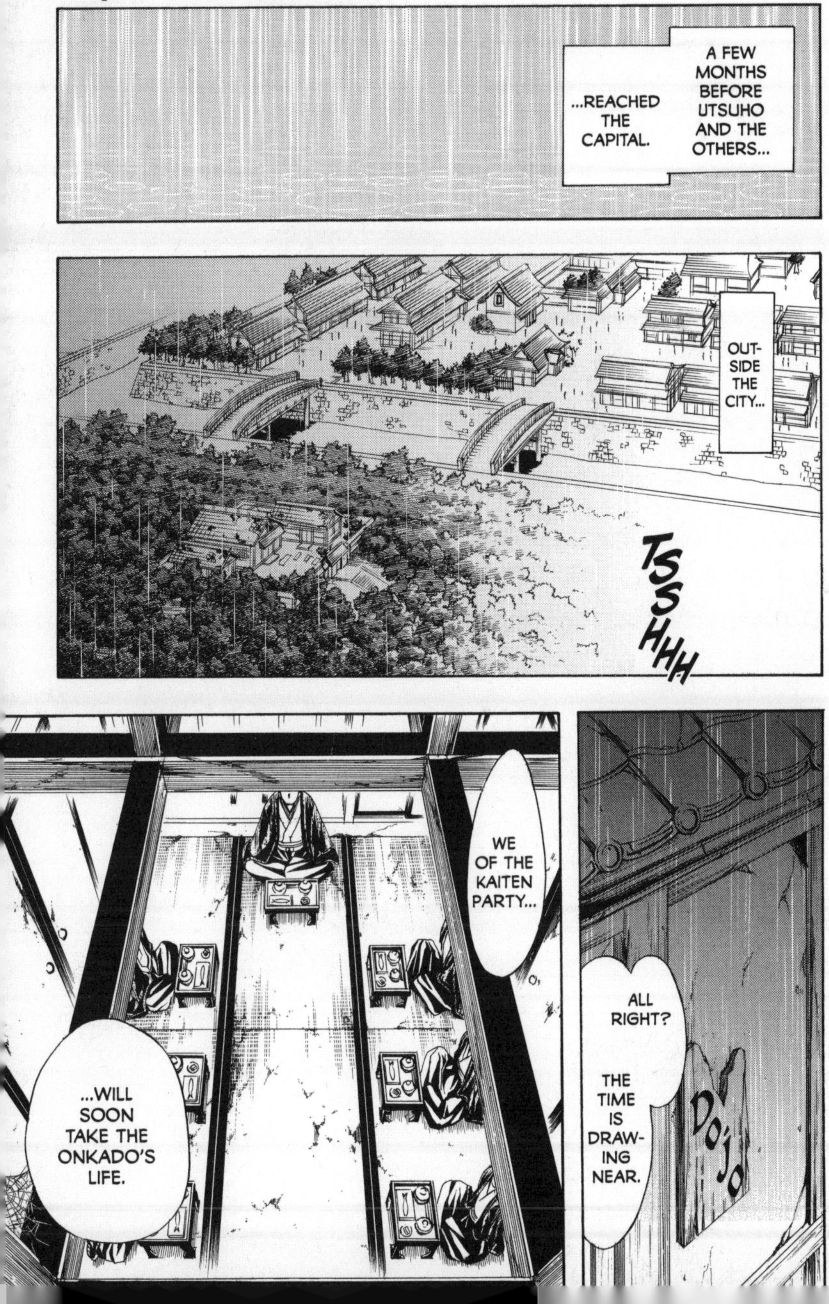
A FEW MONTHS BEFORE UTSUHO AND THE OTHERS...
...REACHED THE CAPITAL.
OUT-SIDE THE CITY...
TSSHHH
ALL RIGHT?
THE TIME IS DRAW-ING NEAR.
Dojo
WE OF THE KAITEN PARTY...
...WILL SOON TAKE THE ONKADO'S LIFE.

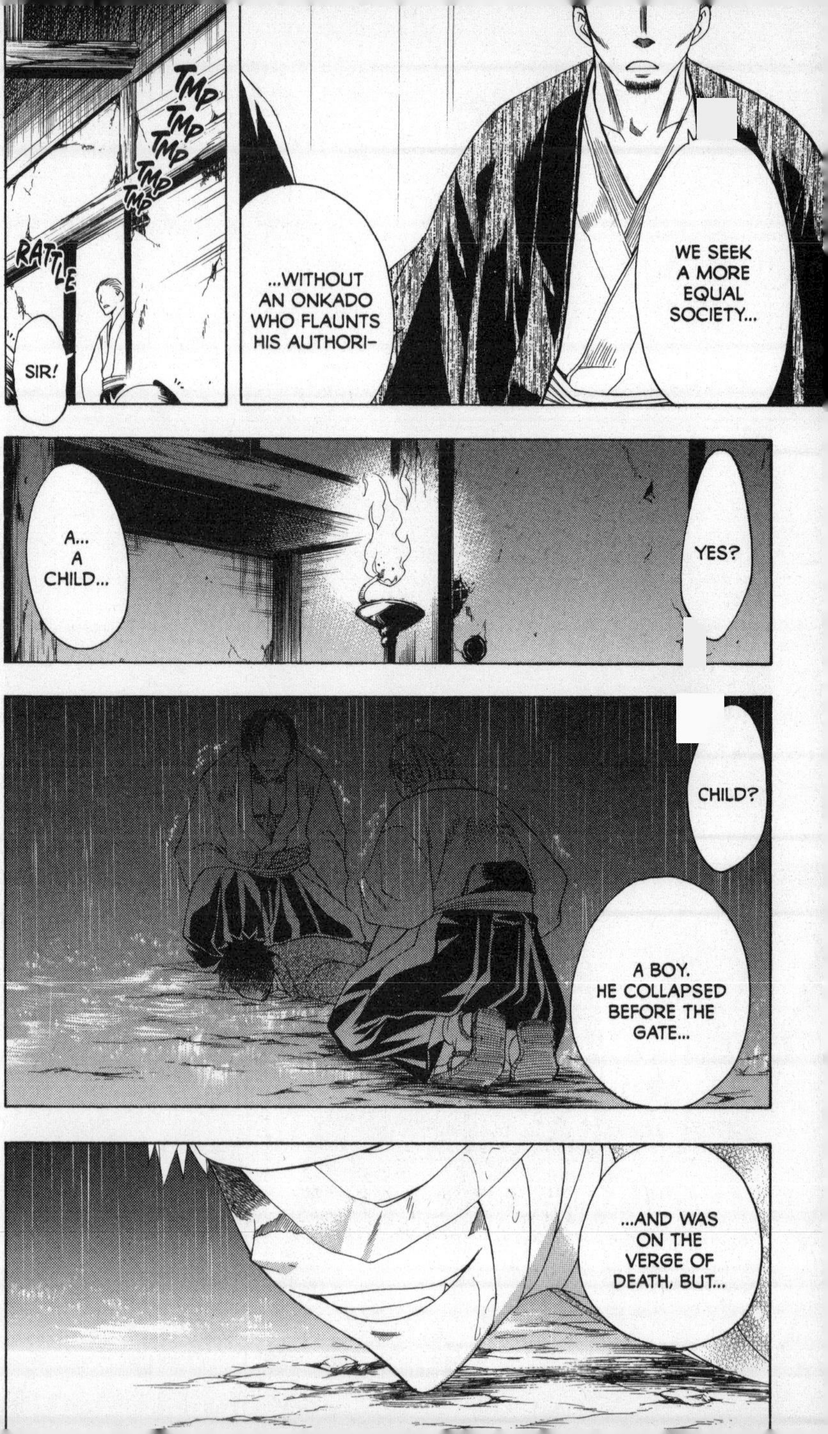
WE SEEK A MORE EQUAL SOCIETY...
...WITHOUT AN ONKADO WHO FLAUNTS HIS AUTHORI-
TMP TMP TMP TMP TMP
RATTLE
SIR!
YES?
A... A CHILD...
CHILD?
A BOY. HE COLLAPSED BEFORE THE GATE...
...AND WAS ON THE VERGE OF DEATH, BUT...

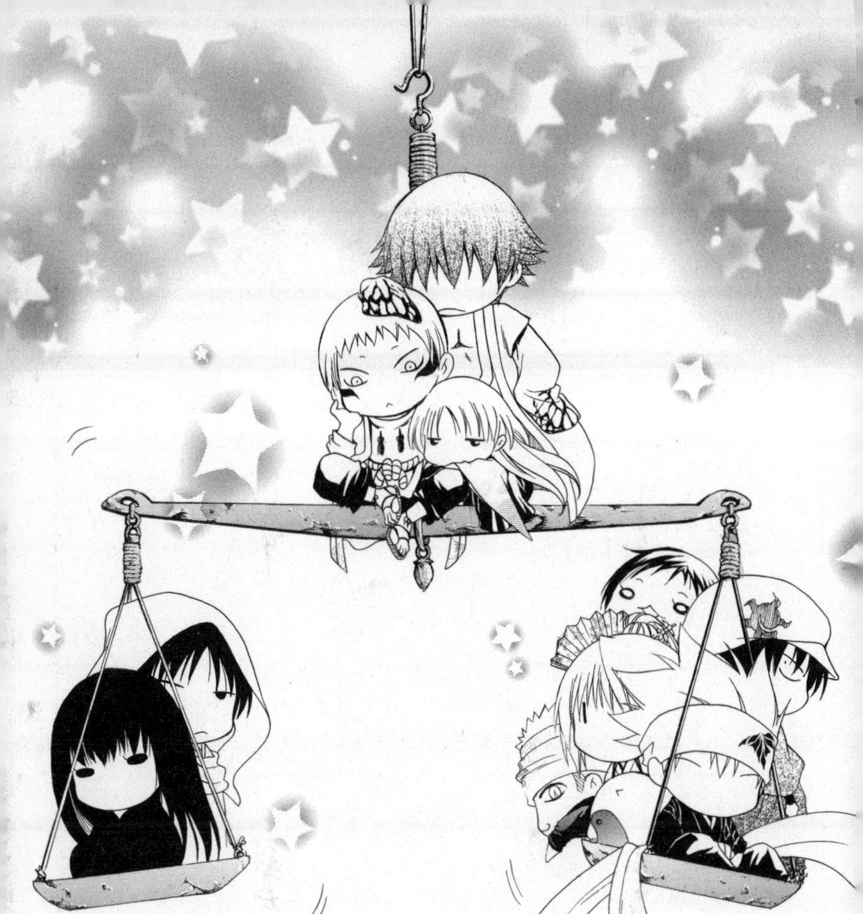

Chapter 92
Comrades

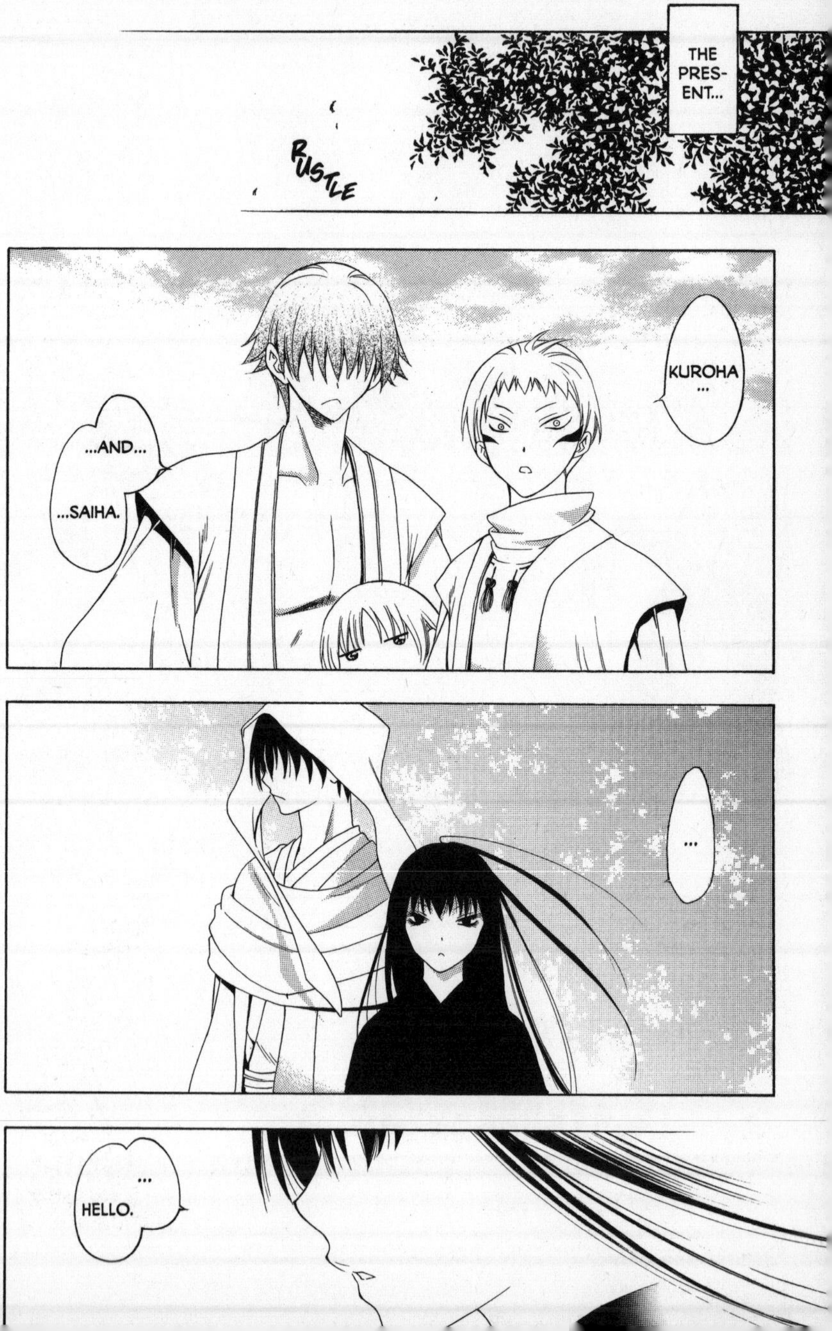
THE PRESENT...
RUSTLE
KUROHA ...
...AND...
...SAIHA.
...
... HELLO.

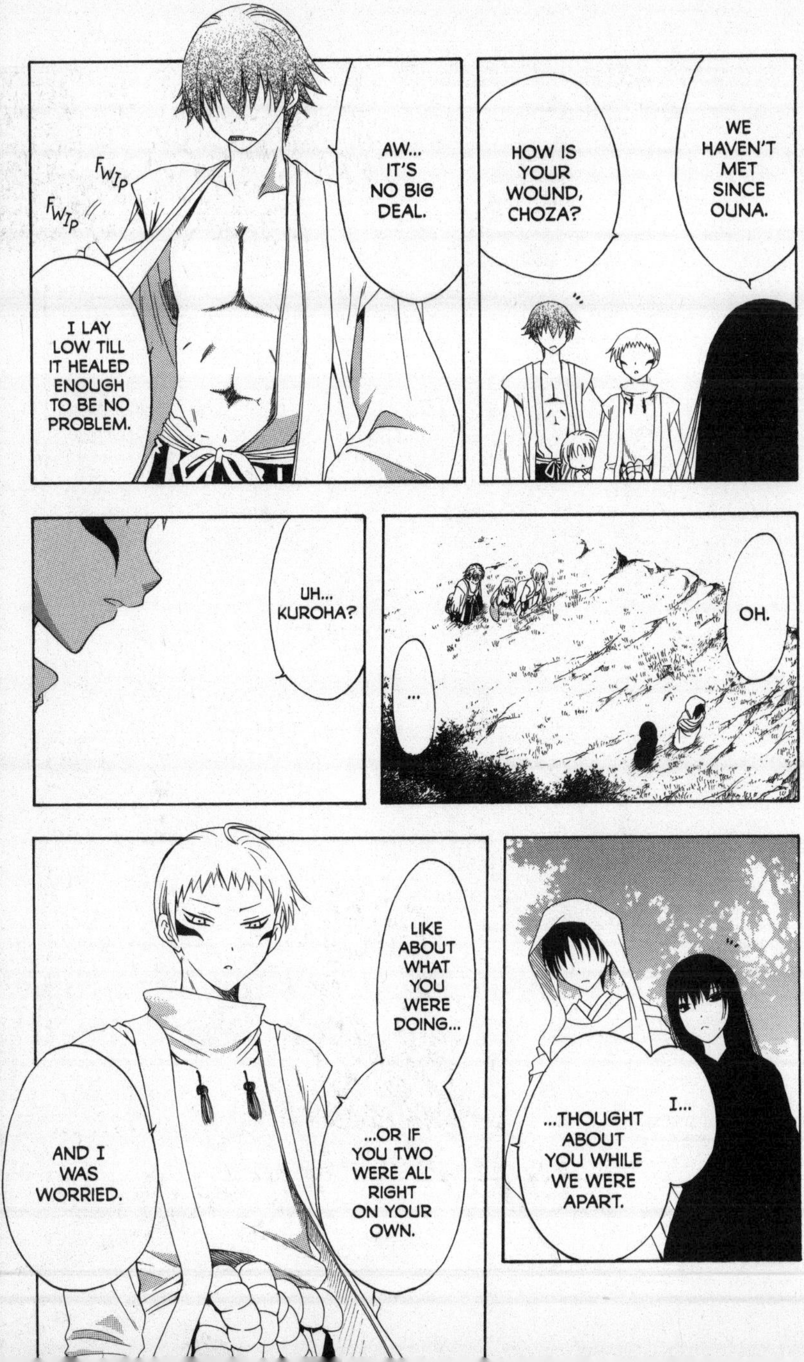
WE HAVEN'T MET SINCE OUNA.
HOW IS YOUR WOUND, CHOZA?
AW... IT'S NO BIG DEAL.
FWIP
FWIP
I LAY LOW TILL IT HEALED ENOUGH TO BE NO PROBLEM.
OH.
...
UH... KUROHA?
I...
...THOUGHT ABOUT YOU WHILE WE WERE APART.
LIKE ABOUT WHAT YOU WERE DOING...
...OR IF YOU TWO WERE ALL RIGHT ON YOUR OWN.
AND I WAS WORRIED.

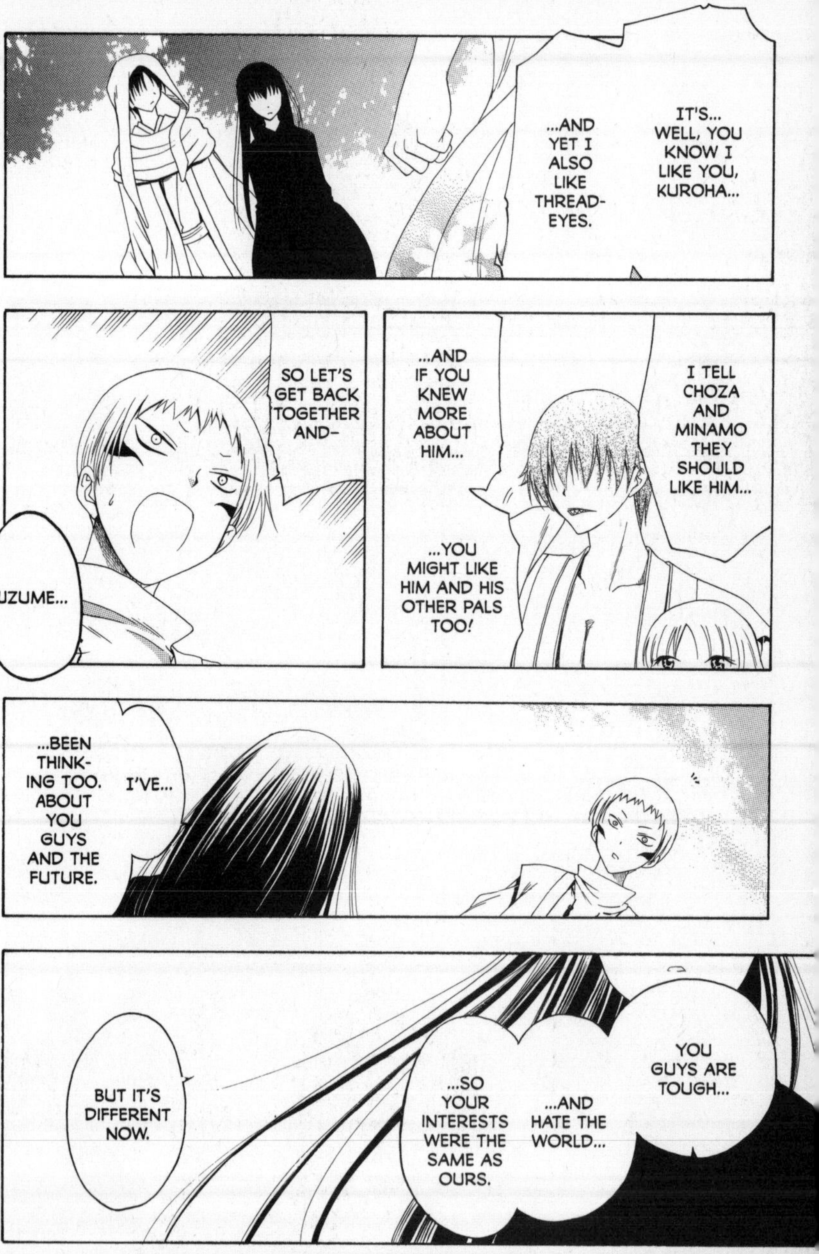
IT'S... WELL, YOU KNOW I LIKE YOU, KUROHA...
...AND YET I ALSO LIKE THREAD-EYES.
I TELL CHOZA AND MINAMO THEY SHOULD LIKE HIM...
...AND IF YOU KNEW MORE ABOUT HIM...
...YOU MIGHT LIKE HIM AND HIS OTHER PALS TOO!
SO LET'S GET BACK TOGETHER AND–
UZUME...
I'VE...
...BEEN THINKING TOO. ABOUT YOU GUYS AND THE FUTURE.
YOU GUYS ARE TOUGH...
...AND HATE THE WORLD...
...SO YOUR INTERESTS WERE THE SAME AS OURS.
BUT IT'S DIFFERENT NOW.

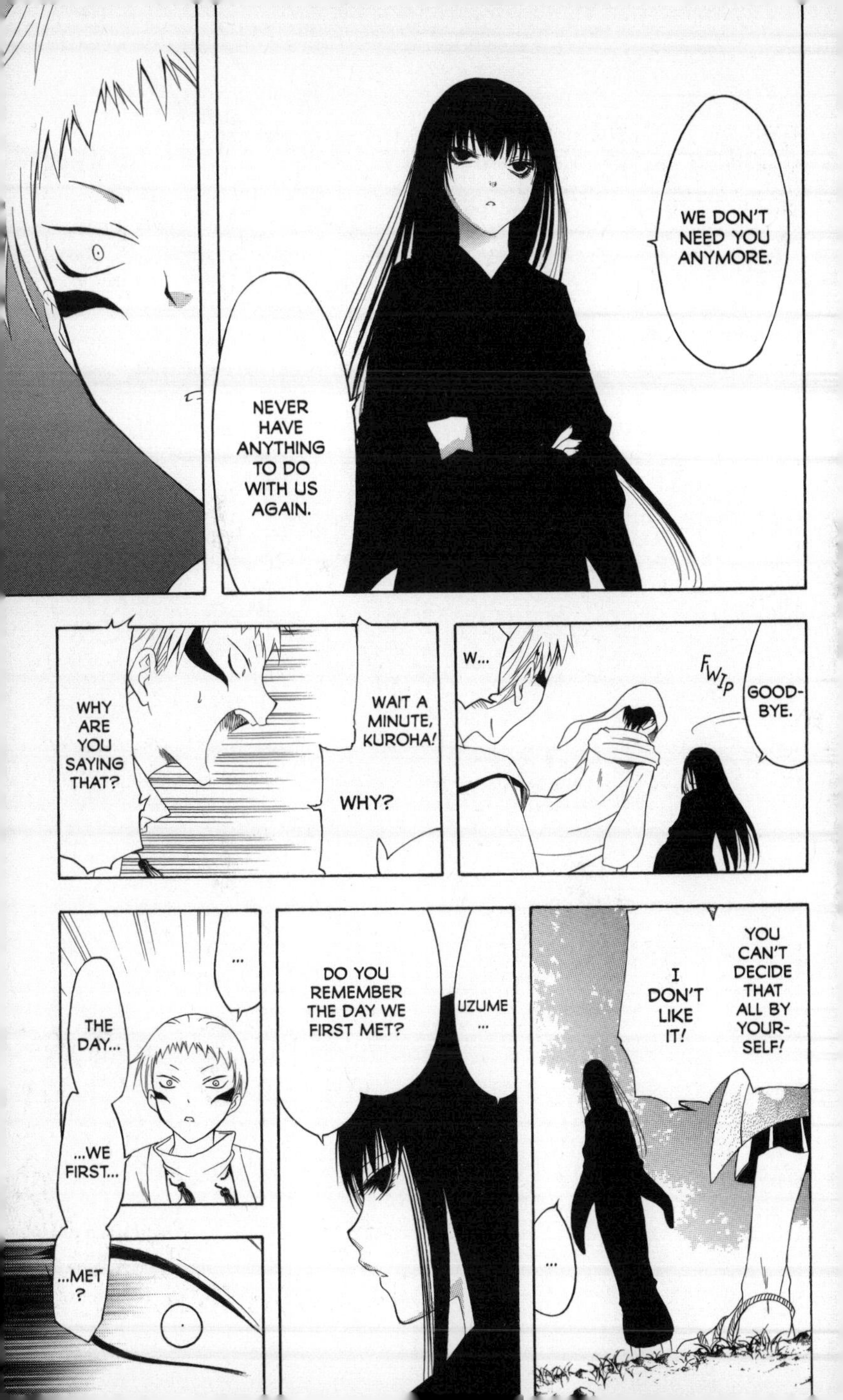
WE DON'T NEED YOU ANYMORE.
NEVER HAVE ANYTHING TO DO WITH US AGAIN.
GOOD-BYE.
FWIP
W...
WAIT A MINUTE, KUROHA!
WHY?
WHY ARE YOU SAYING THAT?
YOU CAN'T DECIDE THAT ALL BY YOURSELF!
I DON'T LIKE IT!
...
UZUME ...
DO YOU REMEMBER THE DAY WE FIRST MET?
...
THE DAY...
...WE FIRST...
...MET?

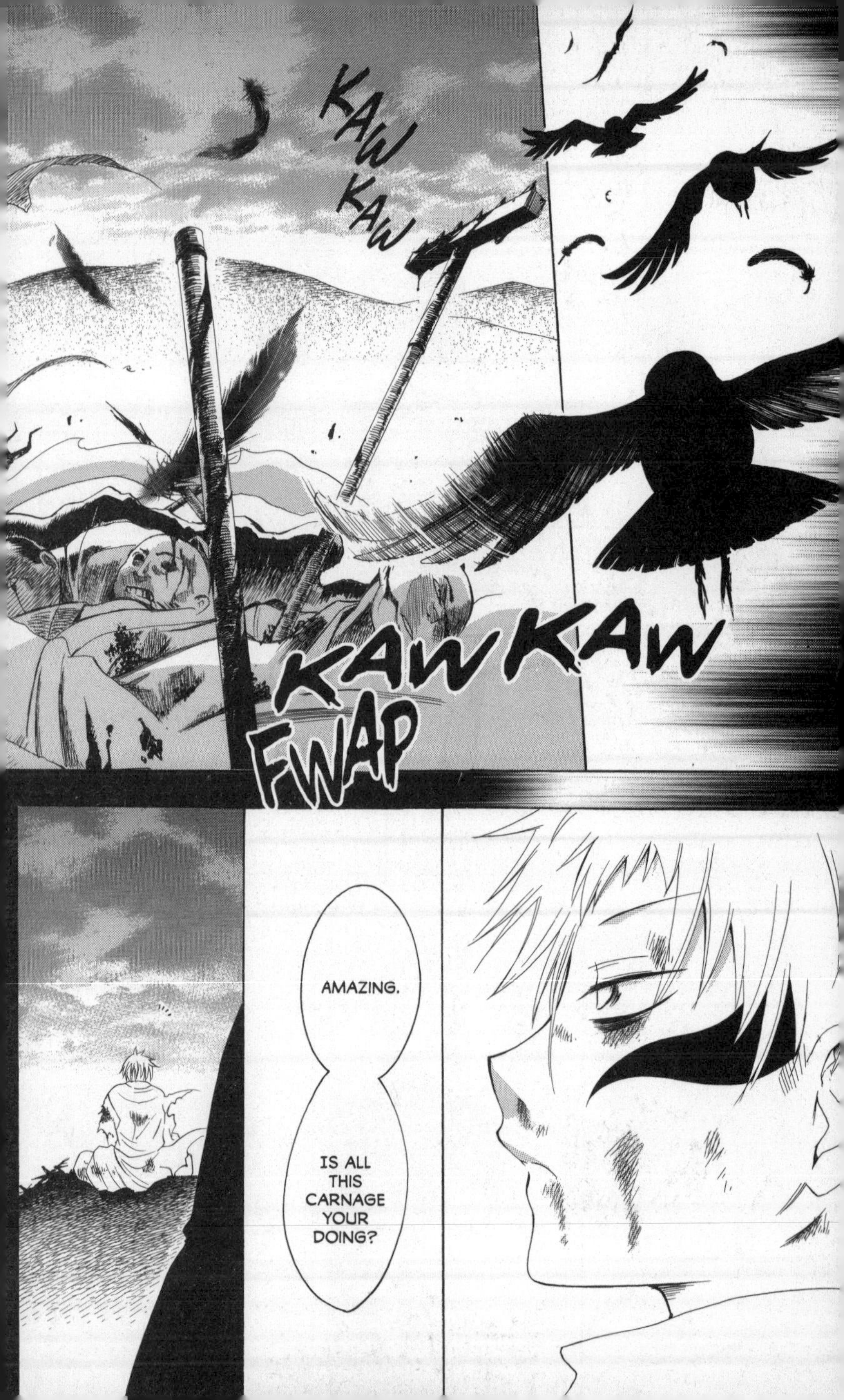
KAW KAW
KAW KAW
FWAP
AMAZING.
IS ALL THIS CARNAGE YOUR DOING?

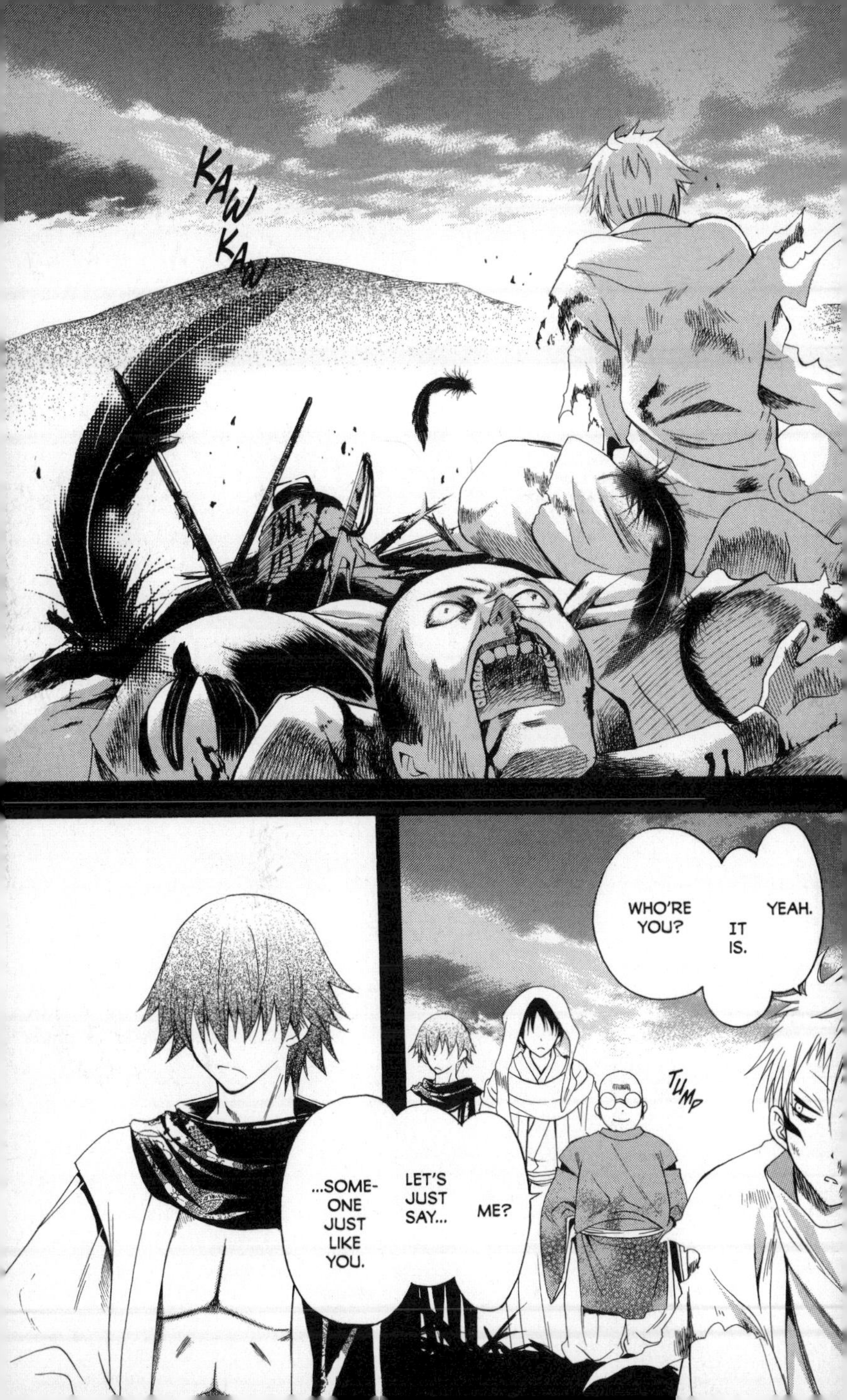
KAW KAW
YEAH.
IT IS.
WHO'RE YOU?
TUMP
ME?
LET'S JUST SAY...
...SOME-ONE JUST LIKE YOU.

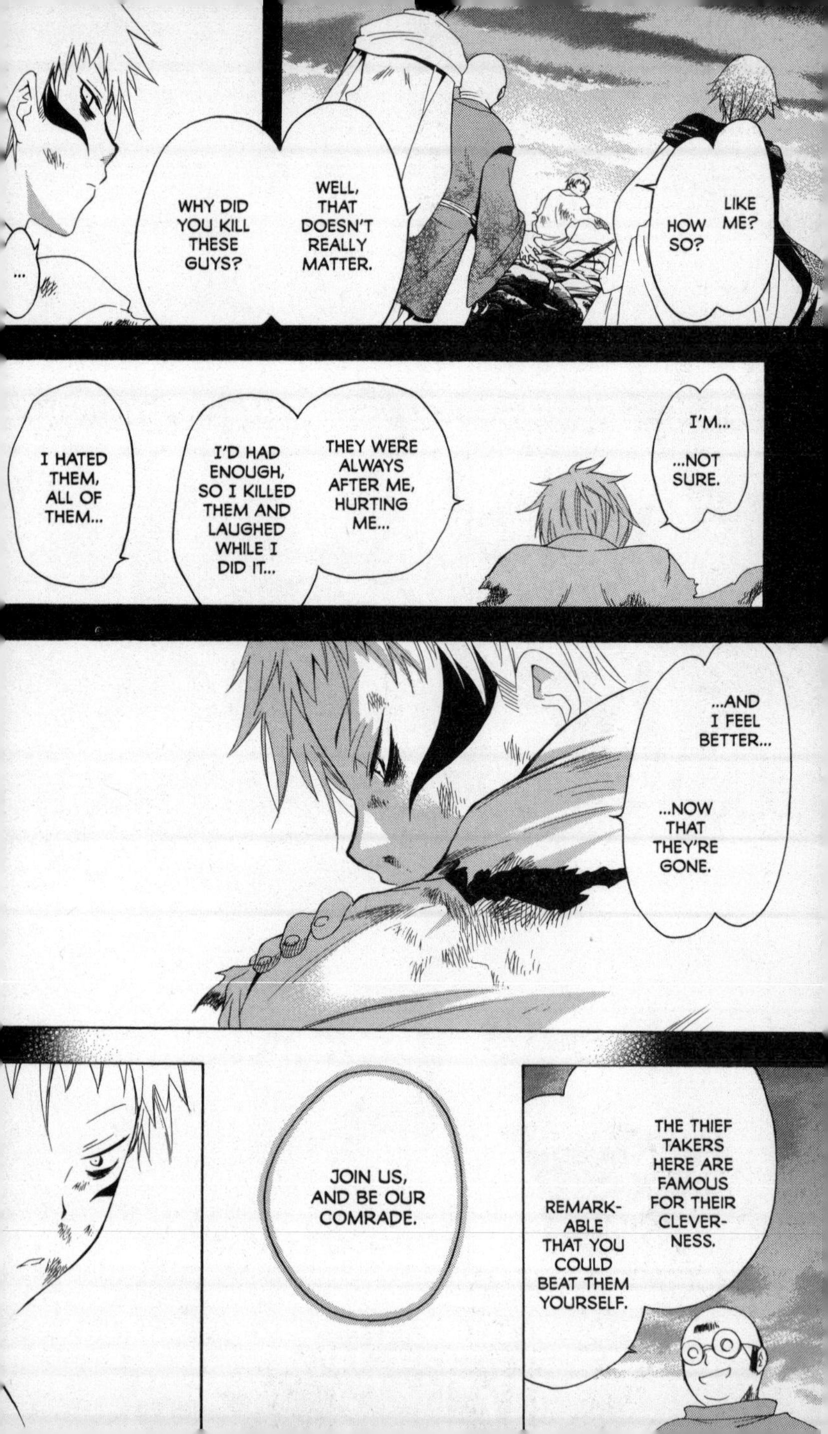
LIKE ME?
HOW SO?
WELL, THAT DOESN'T REALLY MATTER.
WHY DID YOU KILL THESE GUYS?
...
I'M...
...NOT SURE.
THEY WERE ALWAYS AFTER ME, HURTING ME...
I'D HAD ENOUGH, SO I KILLED THEM AND LAUGHED WHILE I DID IT...
I HATED THEM, ALL OF THEM...
...AND I FEEL BETTER...
...NOW THAT THEY'RE GONE.
THE THIEF TAKERS HERE ARE FAMOUS FOR THEIR CLEVER-NESS.
REMARK-ABLE THAT YOU COULD BEAT THEM YOURSELF.
JOIN US, AND BE OUR COMRADE.

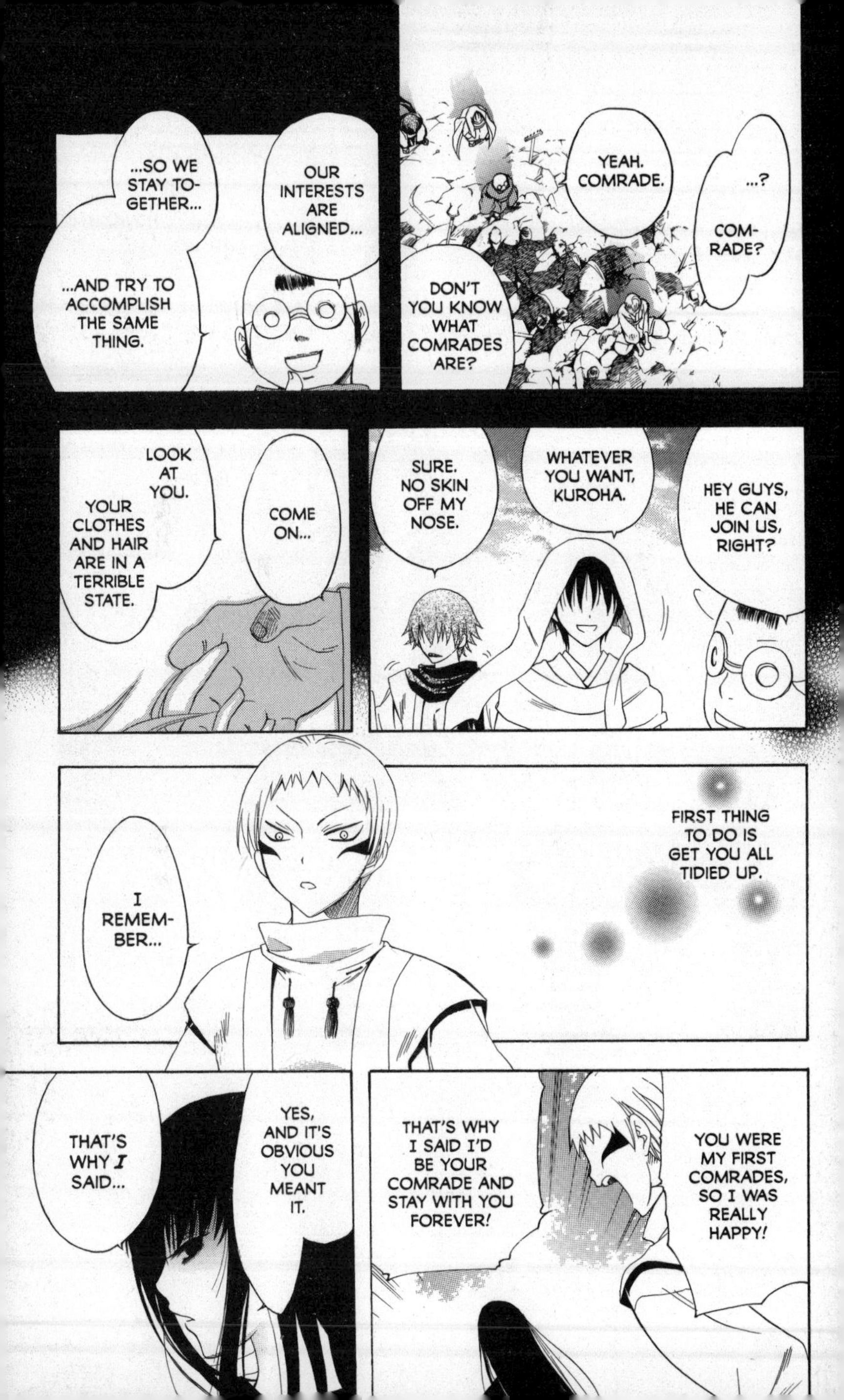
...?
COMRADE?
YEAH. COMRADE.
DON'T YOU KNOW WHAT COMRADES ARE?
OUR INTERESTS ARE ALIGNED...
...SO WE STAY TOGETHER...
...AND TRY TO ACCOMPLISH THE SAME THING.
HEY GUYS, HE CAN JOIN US, RIGHT?
WHATEVER YOU WANT, KUROHA.
SURE. NO SKIN OFF MY NOSE.
COME ON...
LOOK AT YOU.
YOUR CLOTHES AND HAIR ARE IN A TERRIBLE STATE.
FIRST THING TO DO IS GET YOU ALL TIDIED UP.
I REMEMBER...
YOU WERE MY FIRST COMRADES, SO I WAS REALLY HAPPY!
THAT'S WHY I SAID I'D BE YOUR COMRADE AND STAY WITH YOU FOREVER!
YES, AND IT'S OBVIOUS YOU MEANT IT.
THAT'S WHY *I* SAID...

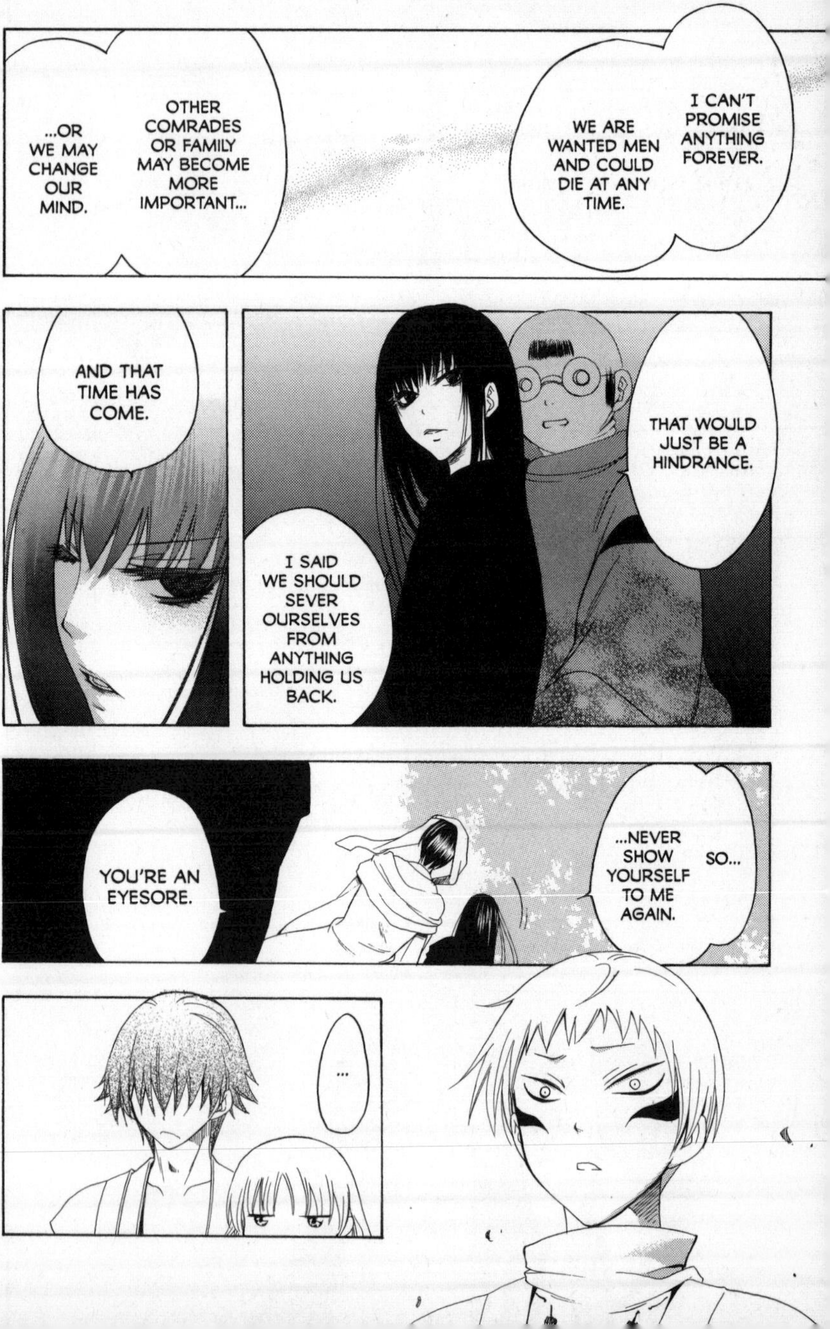
I CAN'T PROMISE ANYTHING FOREVER.
WE ARE WANTED MEN AND COULD DIE AT ANY TIME.
OTHER COMRADES OR FAMILY MAY BECOME MORE IMPORTANT...
...OR WE MAY CHANGE OUR MIND.
THAT WOULD JUST BE A HINDRANCE.
I SAID WE SHOULD SEVER OURSELVES FROM ANYTHING HOLDING US BACK.
AND THAT TIME HAS COME.
SO...
...NEVER SHOW YOURSELF TO ME AGAIN.
YOU'RE AN EYESORE.
...

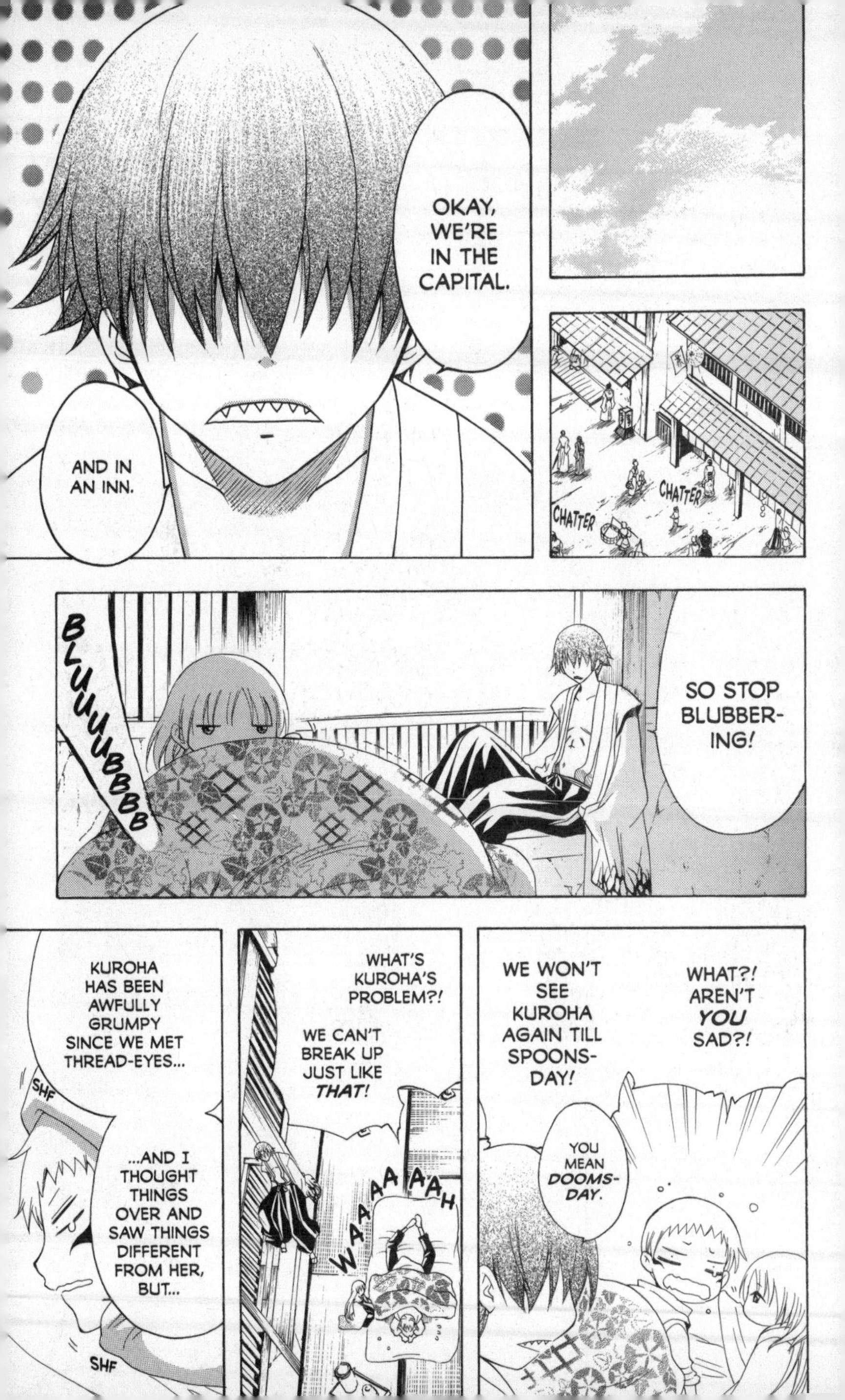
CHATTER
CHATTER
OKAY, WE'RE IN THE CAPITAL.
AND IN AN INN.
SO STOP BLUBBER-ING!
BLUUUUBBBB
WHAT?! AREN'T *YOU* SAD?!
WE WON'T SEE KUROHA AGAIN TILL SPOONS-DAY!
YOU MEAN *DOOMS-DAY*.
WHAT'S KUROHA'S PROBLEM?!
WE CAN'T BREAK UP JUST LIKE *THAT*!
WAAAAAAAH
KUROHA HAS BEEN AWFULLY GRUMPY SINCE WE MET THREAD-EYES...
SHF
...AND I THOUGHT THINGS OVER AND SAW THINGS DIFFERENT FROM HER, BUT...
SHF

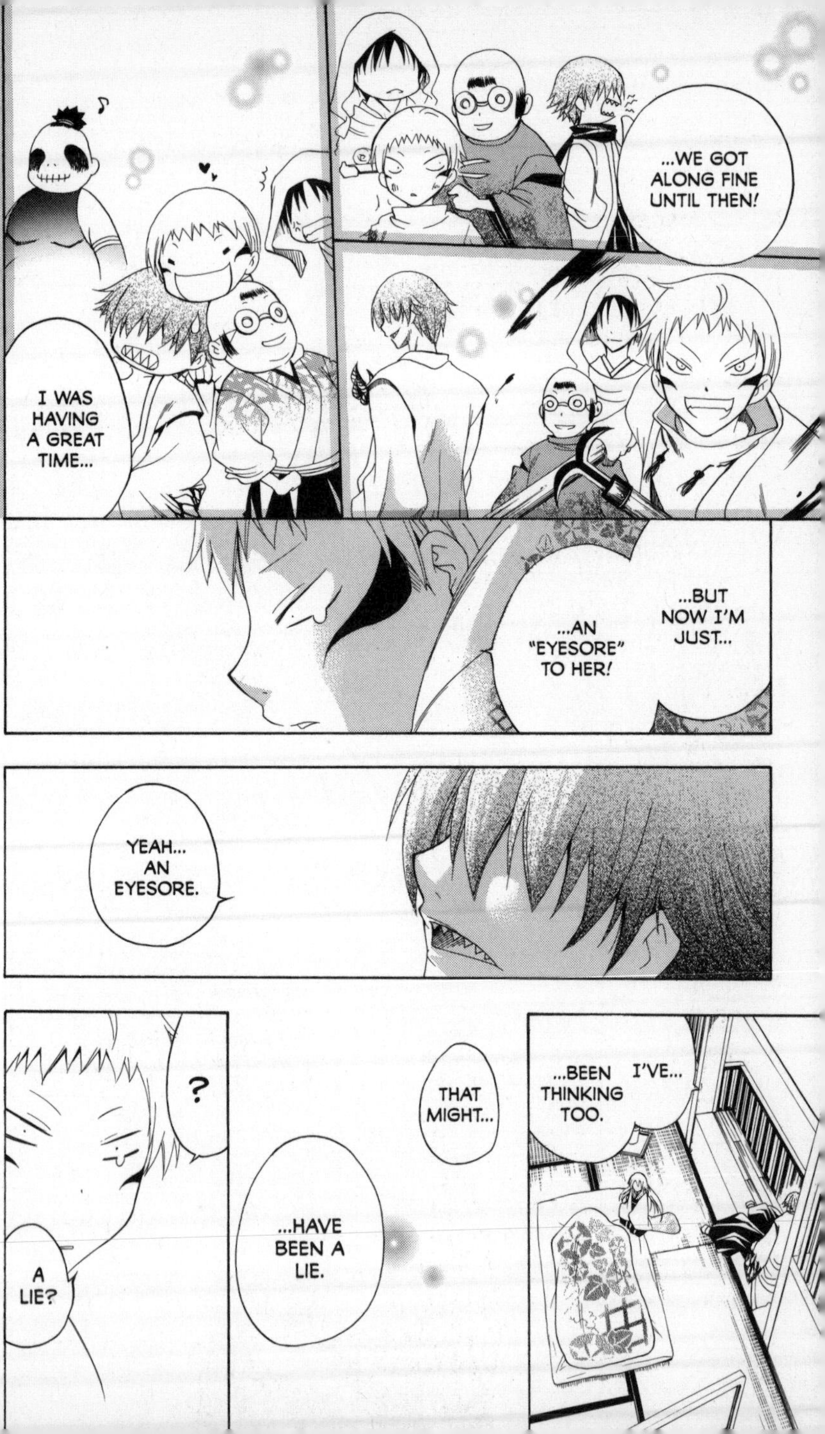
...WE GOT ALONG FINE UNTIL THEN!
I WAS HAVING A GREAT TIME...
...BUT NOW I'M JUST...
...AN "EYESORE" TO HER!
YEAH... AN EYESORE.
I'VE...
...BEEN THINKING TOO.
THAT MIGHT...
...HAVE BEEN A LIE.
?
A LIE?

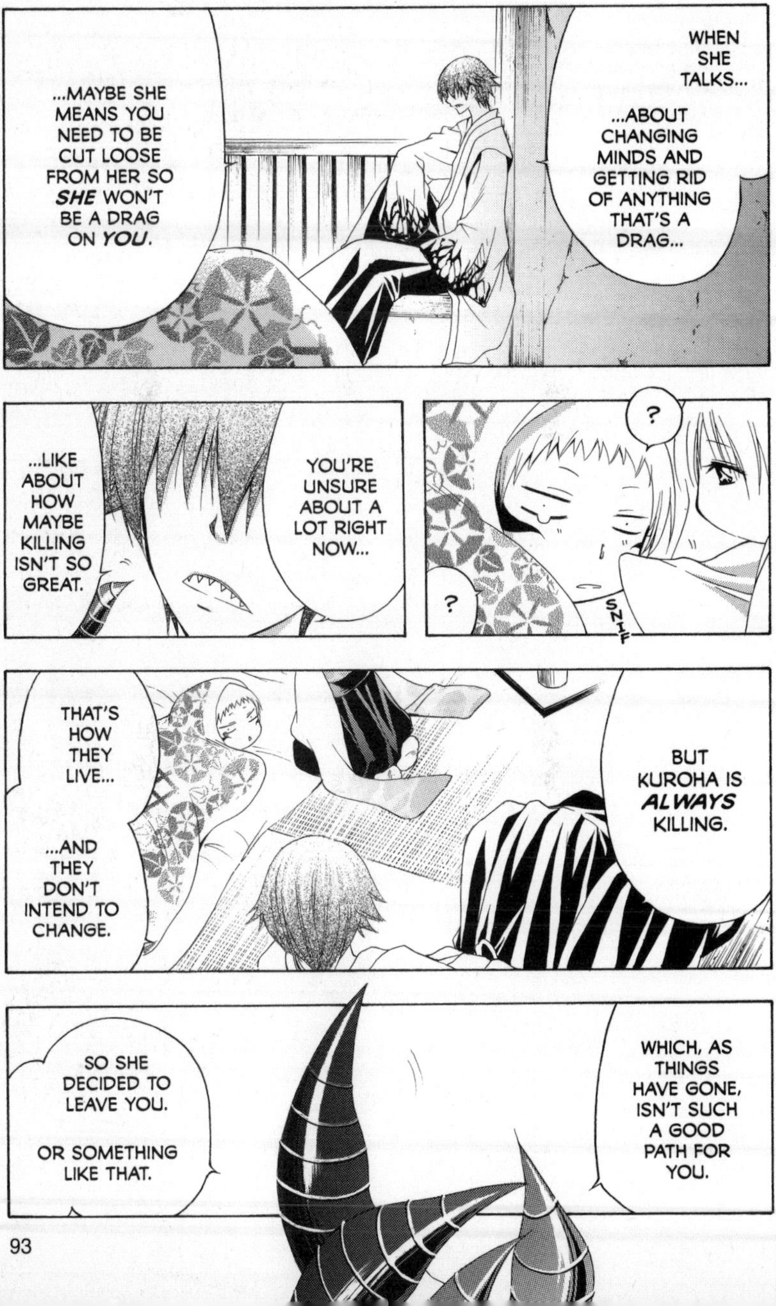
WHEN SHE TALKS...
...ABOUT CHANGING MINDS AND GETTING RID OF ANYTHING THAT'S A DRAG...
...MAYBE SHE MEANS YOU NEED TO BE CUT LOOSE FROM HER SO SHE WON'T BE A DRAG ON YOU.
?
?
SNIF
YOU'RE UNSURE ABOUT A LOT RIGHT NOW...
...LIKE ABOUT HOW MAYBE KILLING ISN'T SO GREAT.
BUT KUROHA IS ALWAYS KILLING.
THAT'S HOW THEY LIVE...
...AND THEY DON'T INTEND TO CHANGE.
WHICH, AS THINGS HAVE GONE, ISN'T SUCH A GOOD PATH FOR YOU.
SO SHE DECIDED TO LEAVE YOU.
OR SOMETHING LIKE THAT.

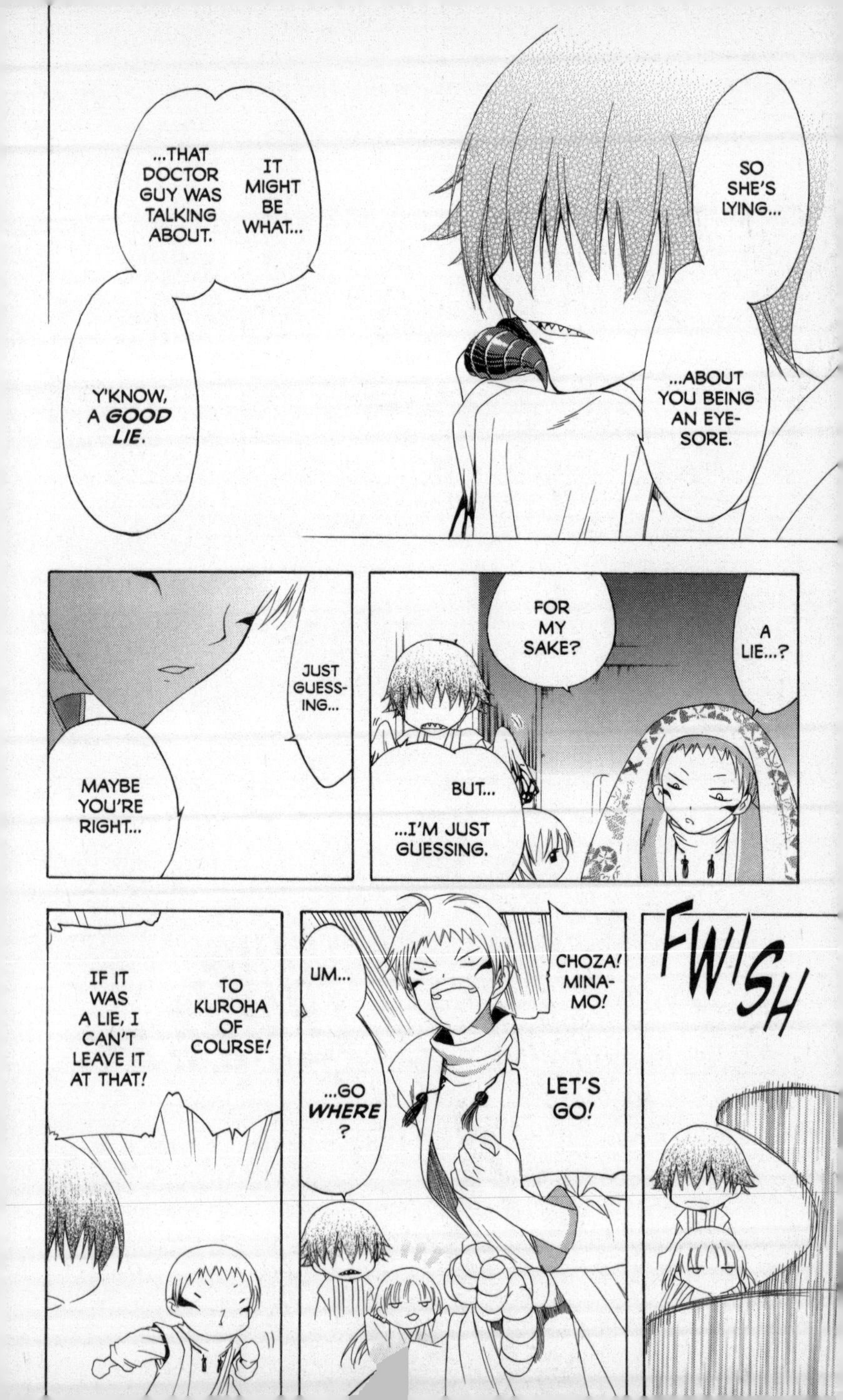
SO SHE'S LYING...
...ABOUT YOU BEING AN EYE-SORE.
IT MIGHT BE WHAT...
...THAT DOCTOR GUY WAS TALKING ABOUT.
Y'KNOW, A *GOOD* *LIE*.
A LIE...?
FOR MY SAKE?
BUT... ...I'M JUST GUESSING.
JUST GUESSING...
MAYBE YOU'RE RIGHT...
FWISH
CHOZA! MINAMO!
LET'S GO!
UM...
...GO *WHERE*?
TO KUROHA OF COURSE!
IF IT WAS A LIE, I CAN'T LEAVE IT AT THAT!

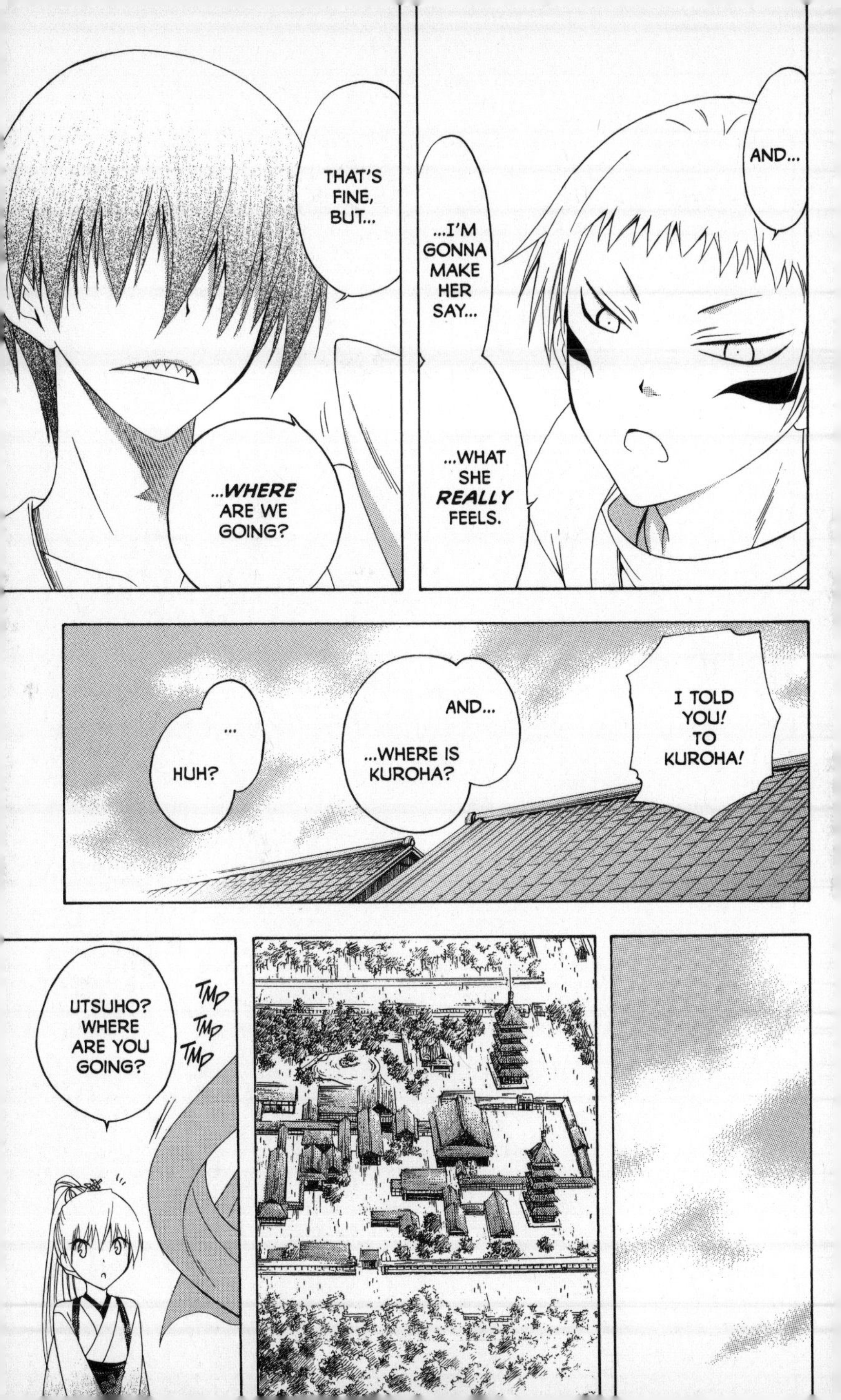
AND...
...I'M GONNA MAKE HER SAY...
...WHAT SHE REALLY FEELS.
THAT'S FINE, BUT...
...WHERE ARE WE GOING?
I TOLD YOU! TO KUROHA!
AND...
...WHERE IS KUROHA?
...
HUH?
UTSUHO? WHERE ARE YOU GOING?
TMP TMP TMP

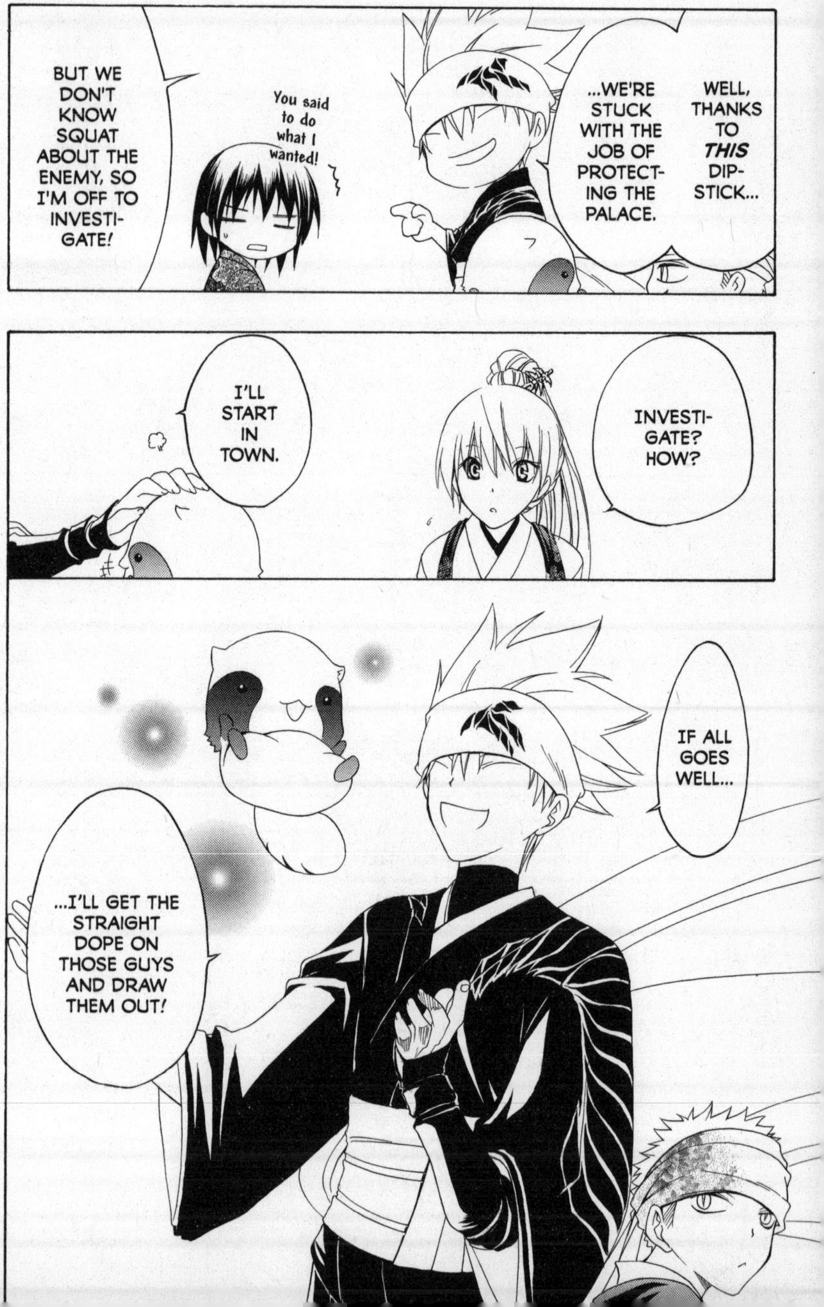
WELL, THANKS TO *THIS* DIPSTICK...
...WE'RE STUCK WITH THE JOB OF PROTECTING THE PALACE.
You said to do what I wanted!
BUT WE DON'T KNOW SQUAT ABOUT THE ENEMY, SO I'M OFF TO INVESTIGATE!
INVESTIGATE? HOW?
I'LL START IN TOWN.
IF ALL GOES WELL...
...I'LL GET THE STRAIGHT DOPE ON THOSE GUYS AND DRAW THEM OUT!

Chapter 93 Utsuho's Plan

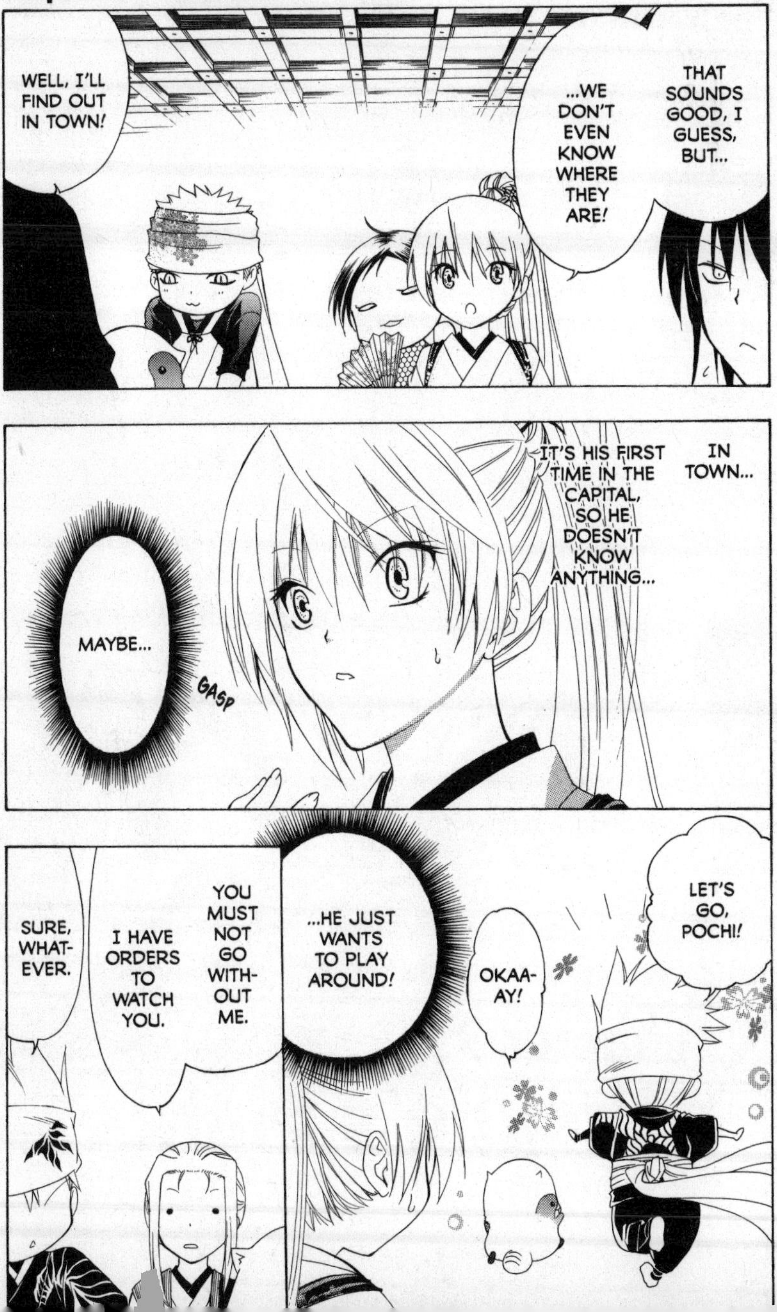
THAT SOUNDS GOOD, I GUESS, BUT...
...WE DON'T EVEN KNOW WHERE THEY ARE!
WELL, I'LL FIND OUT IN TOWN!
IN TOWN...
IT'S HIS FIRST TIME IN THE CAPITAL, SO HE DOESN'T KNOW ANYTHING...
GASP
MAYBE...
LET'S GO, POCHI!
OKAA-AY!
...HE JUST WANTS TO PLAY AROUND!
YOU MUST NOT GO WITH-OUT ME.
I HAVE ORDERS TO WATCH YOU.
SURE, WHAT-EVER.

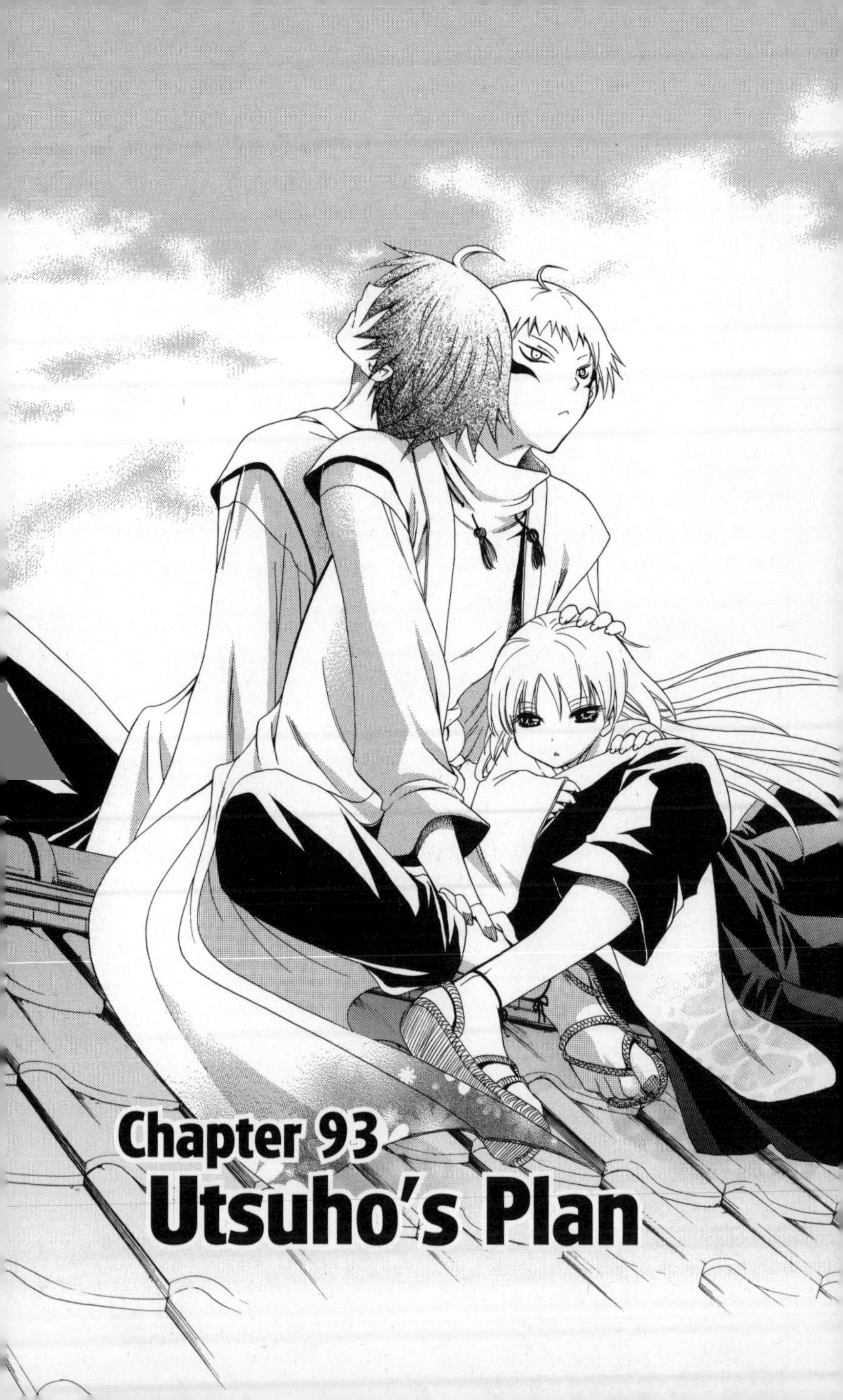
Chapter 93
Utsuho's Plan

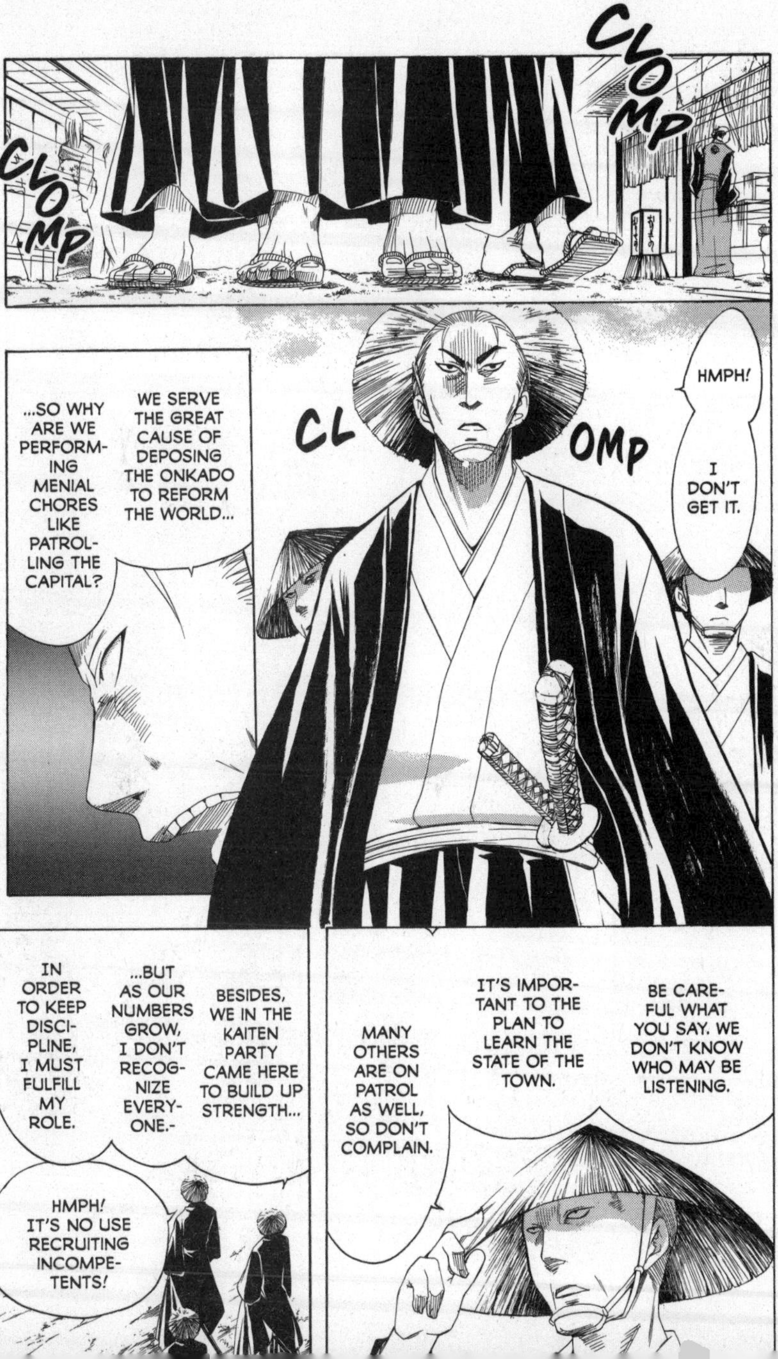
CLOMP
CLOMP
HMPH!
I DON'T GET IT.
CL OMP
WE SERVE THE GREAT CAUSE OF DEPOSING THE ONKADO TO REFORM THE WORLD...
...SO WHY ARE WE PERFORMING MENIAL CHORES LIKE PATROLLING THE CAPITAL?
BE CAREFUL WHAT YOU SAY. WE DON'T KNOW WHO MAY BE LISTENING.
IT'S IMPORTANT TO THE PLAN TO LEARN THE STATE OF THE TOWN.
MANY OTHERS ARE ON PATROL AS WELL, SO DON'T COMPLAIN.
BESIDES, WE IN THE KAITEN PARTY CAME HERE TO BUILD UP STRENGTH...
...BUT AS OUR NUMBERS GROW, I DON'T RECOGNIZE EVERYONE.-
IN ORDER TO KEEP DISCIPLINE, I MUST FULFILL MY ROLE.
HMPH! IT'S NO USE RECRUITING INCOMPETENTS!

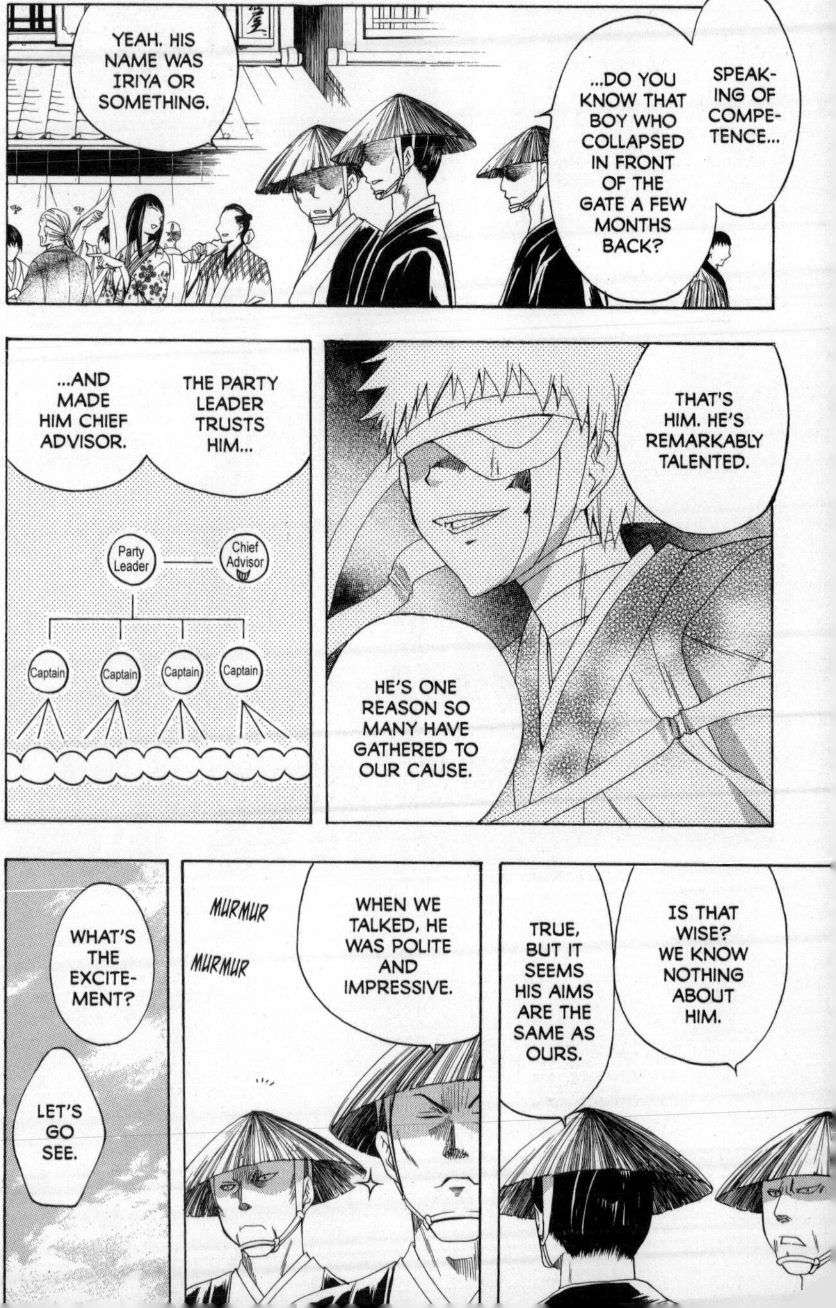
SPEAKING OF COMPETENCE...
...DO YOU KNOW THAT BOY WHO COLLAPSED IN FRONT OF THE GATE A FEW MONTHS BACK?
YEAH. HIS NAME WAS IRIYA OR SOMETHING.
THAT'S HIM. HE'S REMARKABLY TALENTED.
HE'S ONE REASON SO MANY HAVE GATHERED TO OUR CAUSE.
THE PARTY LEADER TRUSTS HIM...
...AND MADE HIM CHIEF ADVISOR.
Party Leader
Chief Advisor
Captain
Captain
Captain
Captain
IS THAT WISE? WE KNOW NOTHING ABOUT HIM.
TRUE, BUT IT SEEMS HIS AIMS ARE THE SAME AS OURS.
WHEN WE TALKED, HE WAS POLITE AND IMPRESSIVE.
MURMUR
MURMUR
WHAT'S THE EXCITEMENT?
LET'S GO SEE.

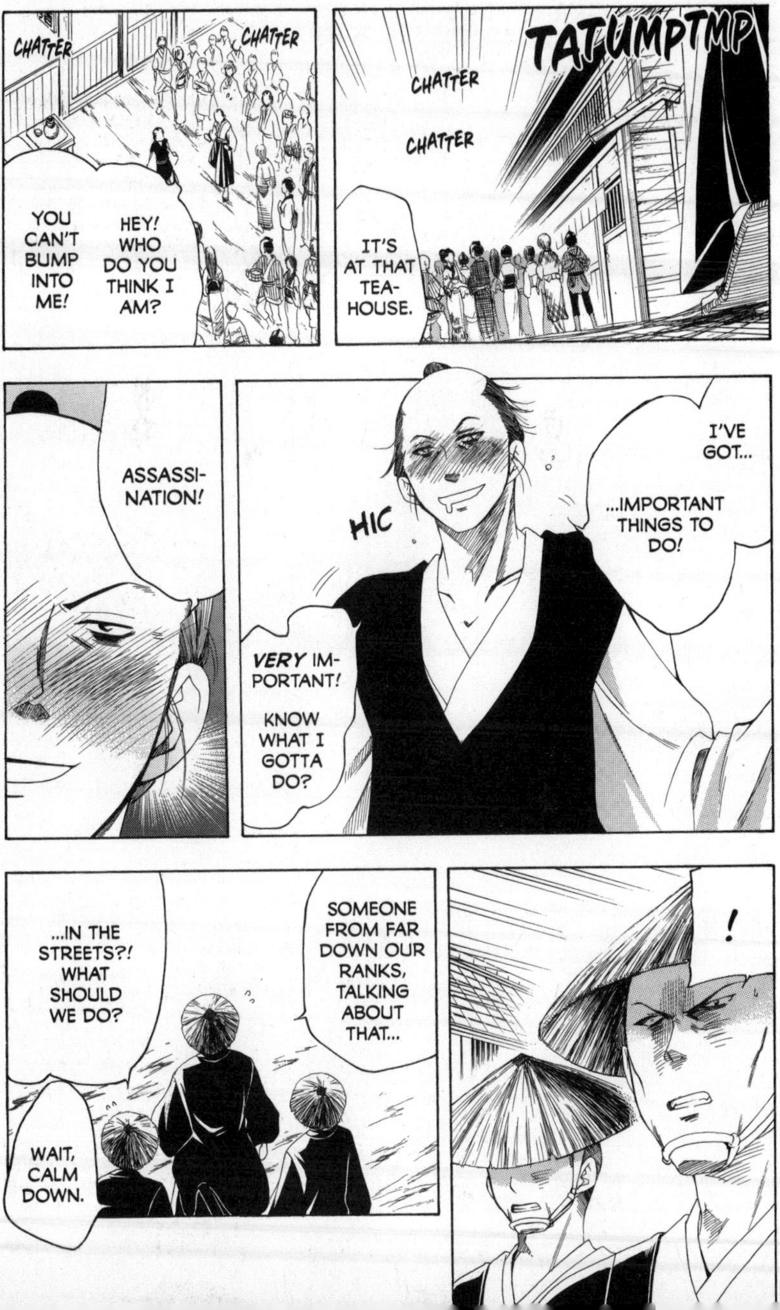
TATUMPTMP
CHATTER
CHATTER
IT'S AT THAT TEA-HOUSE.
CHATTER
CHATTER
HEY! WHO DO YOU THINK I AM?
YOU CAN'T BUMP INTO ME!
I'VE GOT...
...IMPORTANT THINGS TO DO!
HIC
VERY IMPORTANT!
KNOW WHAT I GOTTA DO?
ASSASSINATION!
!
SOMEONE FROM FAR DOWN OUR RANKS, TALKING ABOUT THAT...
...IN THE STREETS?! WHAT SHOULD WE DO?
WAIT, CALM DOWN.

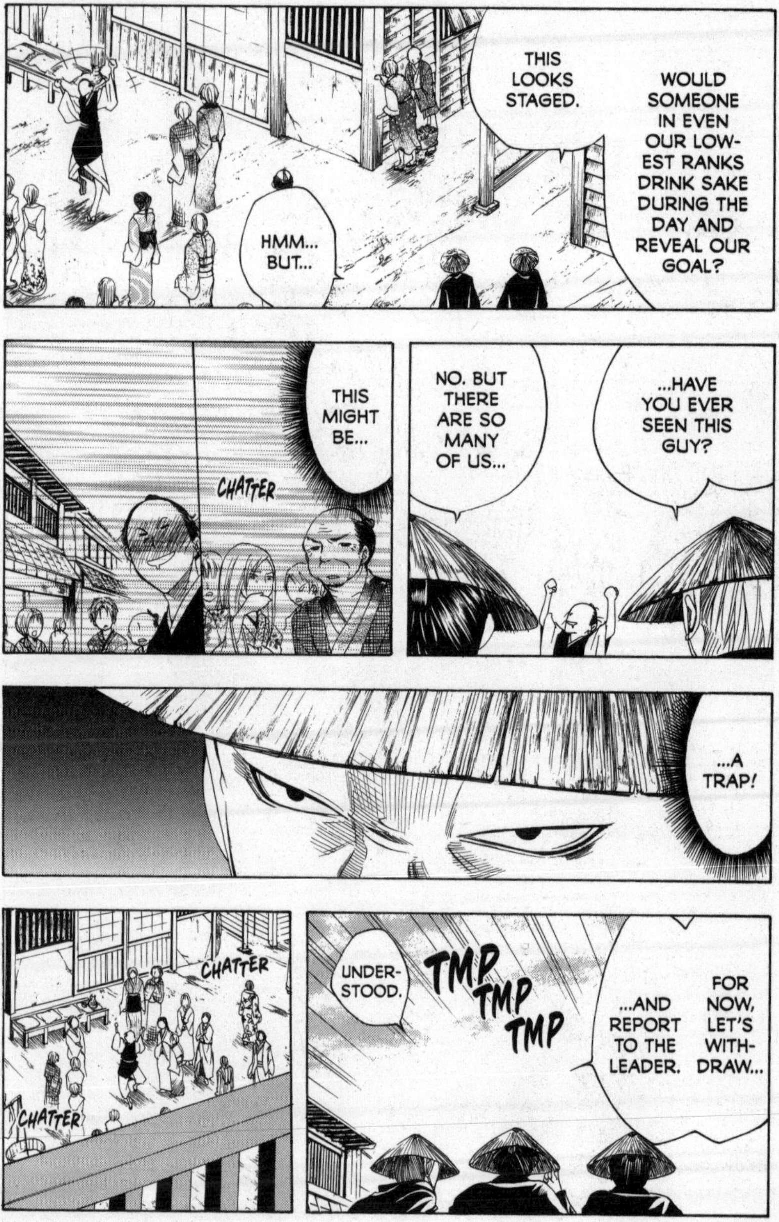
THIS LOOKS STAGED.
WOULD SOMEONE IN EVEN OUR LOW-EST RANKS DRINK SAKE DURING THE DAY AND REVEAL OUR GOAL?
HMM... BUT...
...HAVE YOU EVER SEEN THIS GUY?
NO. BUT THERE ARE SO MANY OF US...
THIS MIGHT BE...
CHATTER
...A TRAP!
FOR NOW, LET'S WITH-DRAW...
...AND REPORT TO THE LEADER.
TMP TMP TMP
UNDER-STOOD.
CHATTER
CHATTER

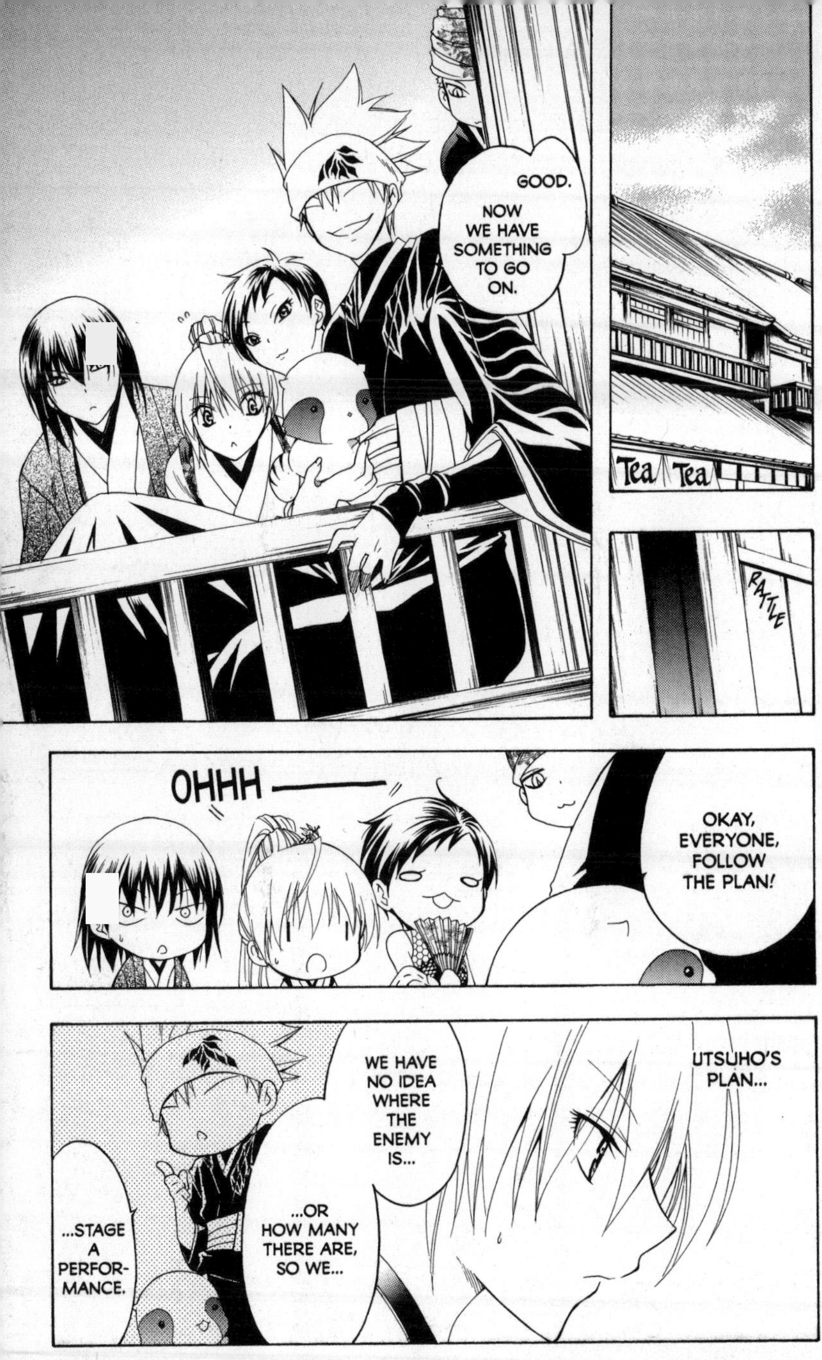
Tea
Tea
RATTLE
GOOD.
NOW WE HAVE SOMETHING TO GO ON.
OKAY, EVERYONE, FOLLOW THE PLAN!
OHHH ——
UTSUHO'S PLAN...
WE HAVE NO IDEA WHERE THE ENEMY IS...
...OR HOW MANY THERE ARE, SO WE...
...STAGE A PERFORMANCE.

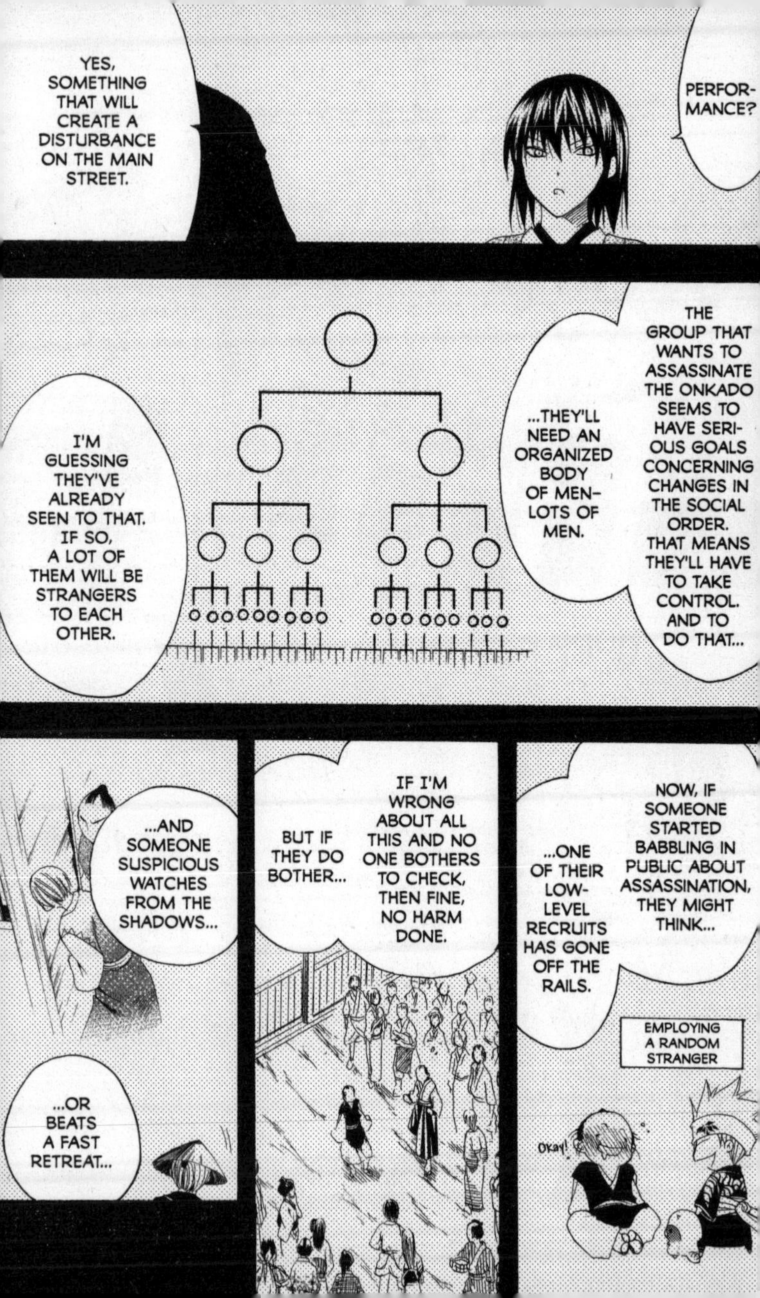
PERFORMANCE?
YES, SOMETHING THAT WILL CREATE A DISTURBANCE ON THE MAIN STREET.
THE GROUP THAT WANTS TO ASSASSINATE THE ONKADO SEEMS TO HAVE SERIOUS GOALS CONCERNING CHANGES IN THE SOCIAL ORDER. THAT MEANS THEY'LL HAVE TO TAKE CONTROL. AND TO DO THAT...
...THEY'LL NEED AN ORGANIZED BODY OF MEN–LOTS OF MEN.
I'M GUESSING THEY'VE ALREADY SEEN TO THAT. IF SO, A LOT OF THEM WILL BE STRANGERS TO EACH OTHER.
NOW, IF SOMEONE STARTED BABBLING IN PUBLIC ABOUT ASSASSINATION, THEY MIGHT THINK...
...ONE OF THEIR LOW-LEVEL RECRUITS HAS GONE OFF THE RAILS.
EMPLOYING A RANDOM STRANGER
Okay!
IF I'M WRONG ABOUT ALL THIS AND NO ONE BOTHERS TO CHECK, THEN FINE, NO HARM DONE.
BUT IF THEY DO BOTHER...
...AND SOMEONE SUSPICIOUS WATCHES FROM THE SHADOWS...
...OR BEATS A FAST RETREAT...

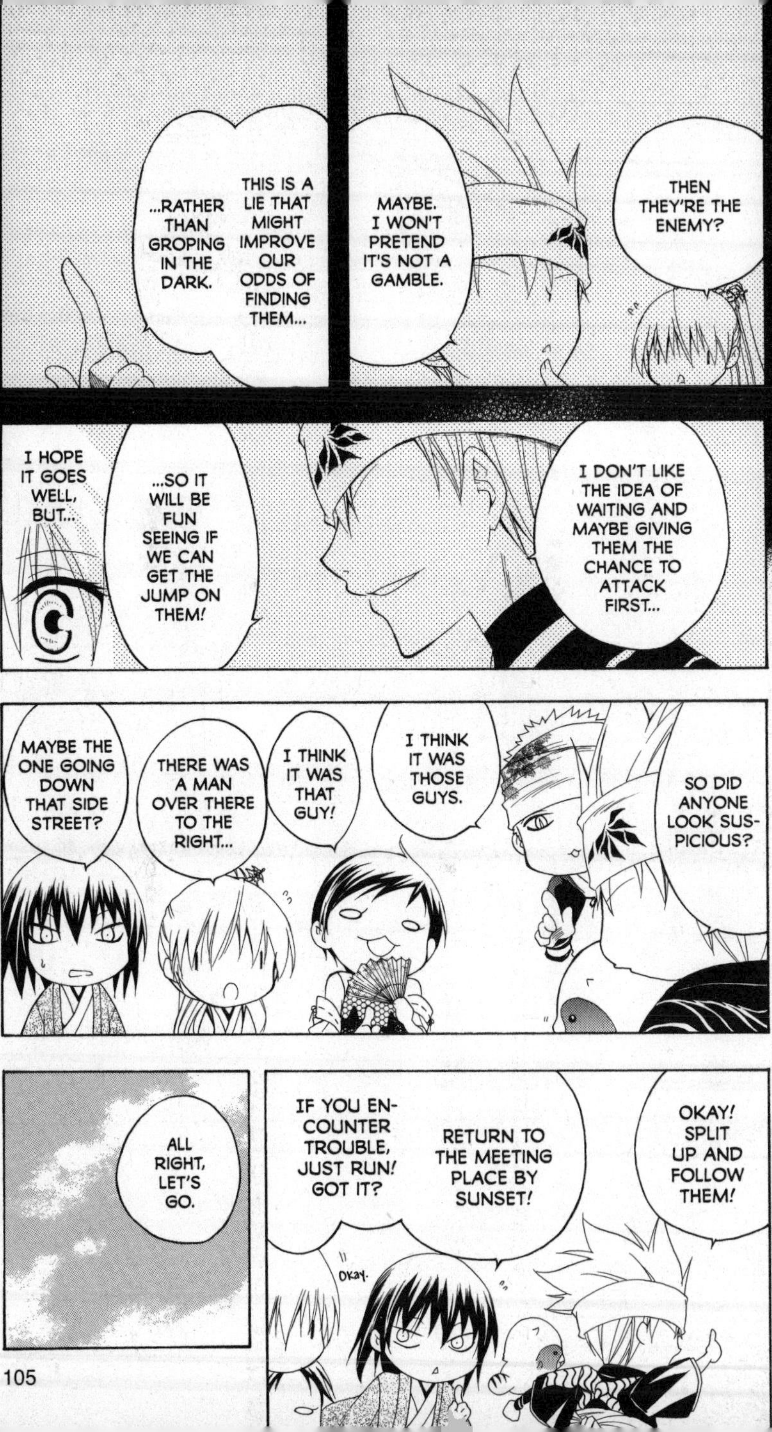
THEN THEY'RE THE ENEMY?
MAYBE. I WON'T PRETEND IT'S NOT A GAMBLE.
THIS IS A LIE THAT MIGHT IMPROVE OUR ODDS OF FINDING THEM...
...RATHER THAN GROPING IN THE DARK.
I DON'T LIKE THE IDEA OF WAITING AND MAYBE GIVING THEM THE CHANCE TO ATTACK FIRST...
...SO IT WILL BE FUN SEEING IF WE CAN GET THE JUMP ON THEM!
I HOPE IT GOES WELL, BUT...
SO DID ANYONE LOOK SUS-PICIOUS?
I THINK IT WAS THOSE GUYS.
I THINK IT WAS THAT GUY!
THERE WAS A MAN OVER THERE TO THE RIGHT...
MAYBE THE ONE GOING DOWN THAT SIDE STREET?
OKAY! SPLIT UP AND FOLLOW THEM!
RETURN TO THE MEETING PLACE BY SUNSET!
IF YOU EN-COUNTER TROUBLE, JUST RUN! GOT IT?
Okay.
ALL RIGHT, LET'S GO.

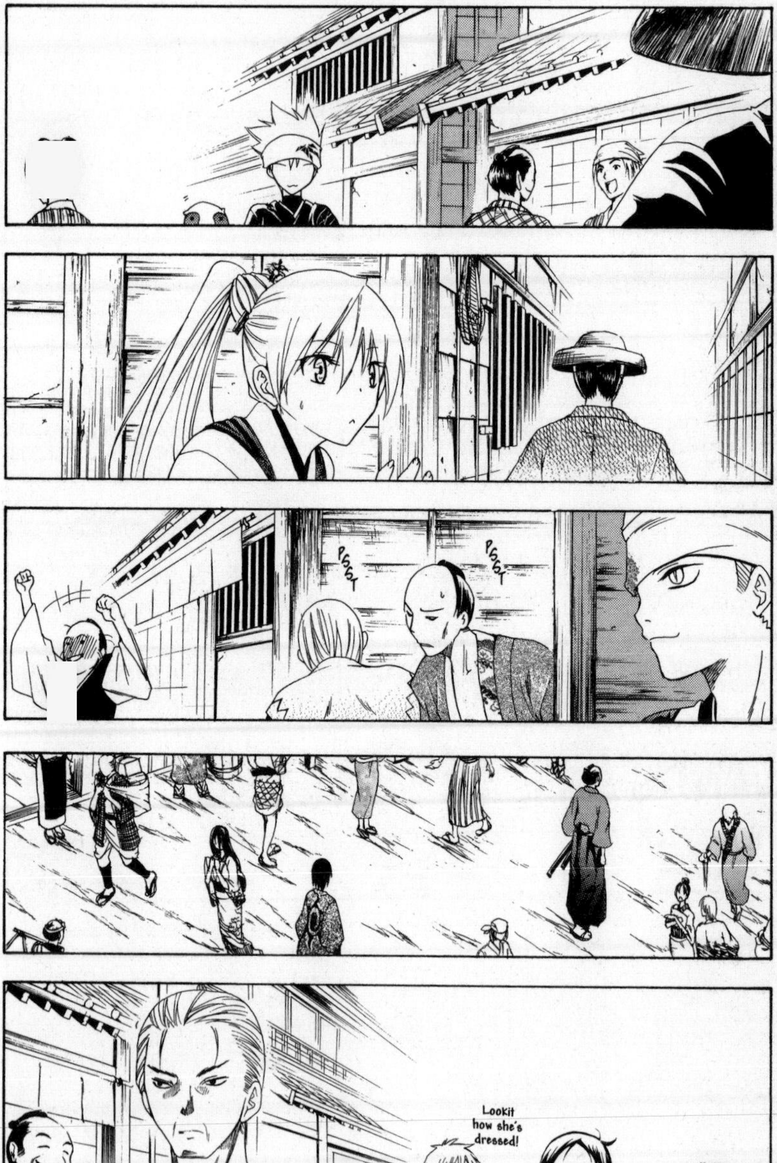
PSSST
PSSST
Lookit how she's dressed!

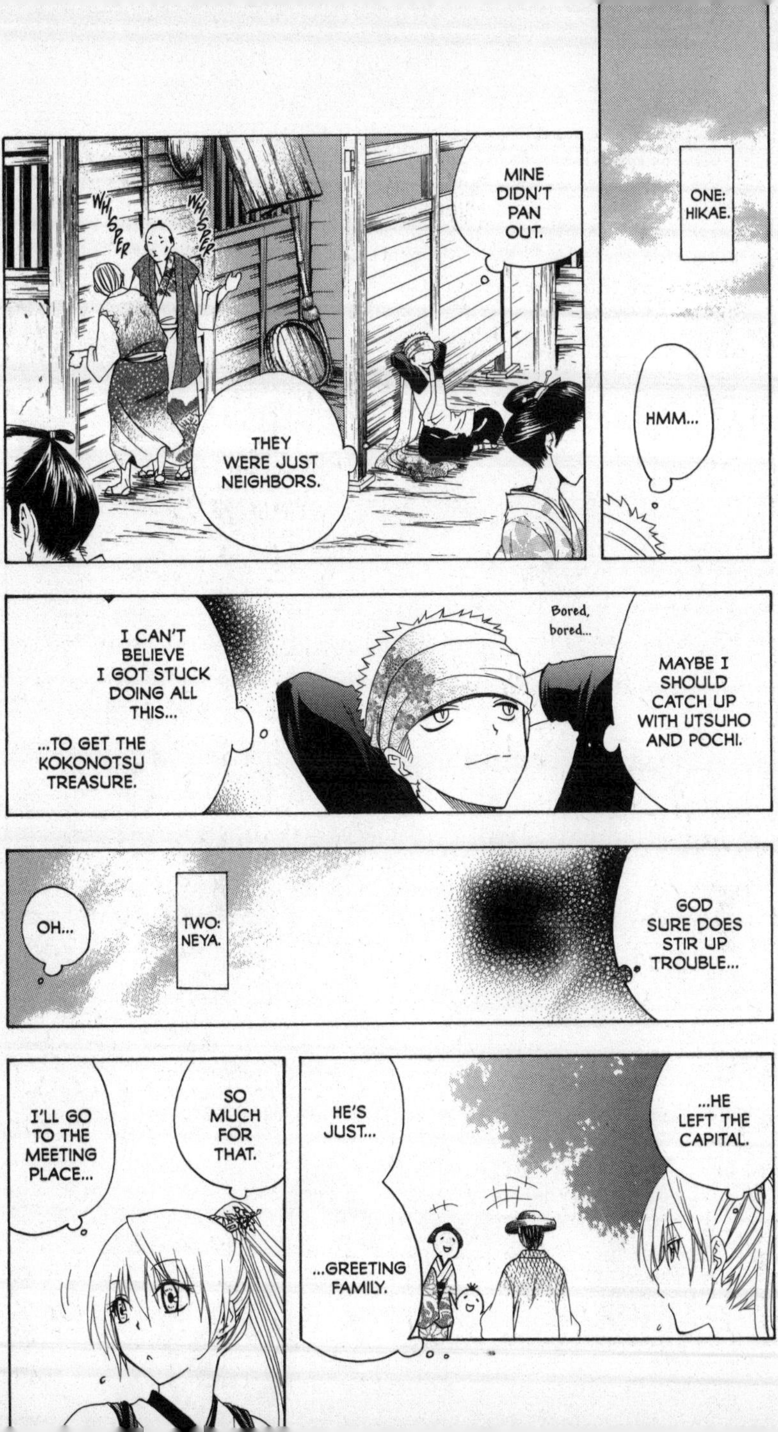
ONE: HIKAE.
HMM...
MINE DIDN'T PAN OUT.
WHISPER
WHISPER
THEY WERE JUST NEIGHBORS.
Bored, bored...
MAYBE I SHOULD CATCH UP WITH UTSUHO AND POCHI.
I CAN'T BELIEVE I GOT STUCK DOING ALL THIS...
...TO GET THE KOKONOTSU TREASURE.
GOD SURE DOES STIR UP TROUBLE...
TWO: NEYA.
OH...
...HE LEFT THE CAPITAL.
HE'S JUST...
...GREETING FAMILY.
SO MUCH FOR THAT.
I'LL GO TO THE MEETING PLACE...

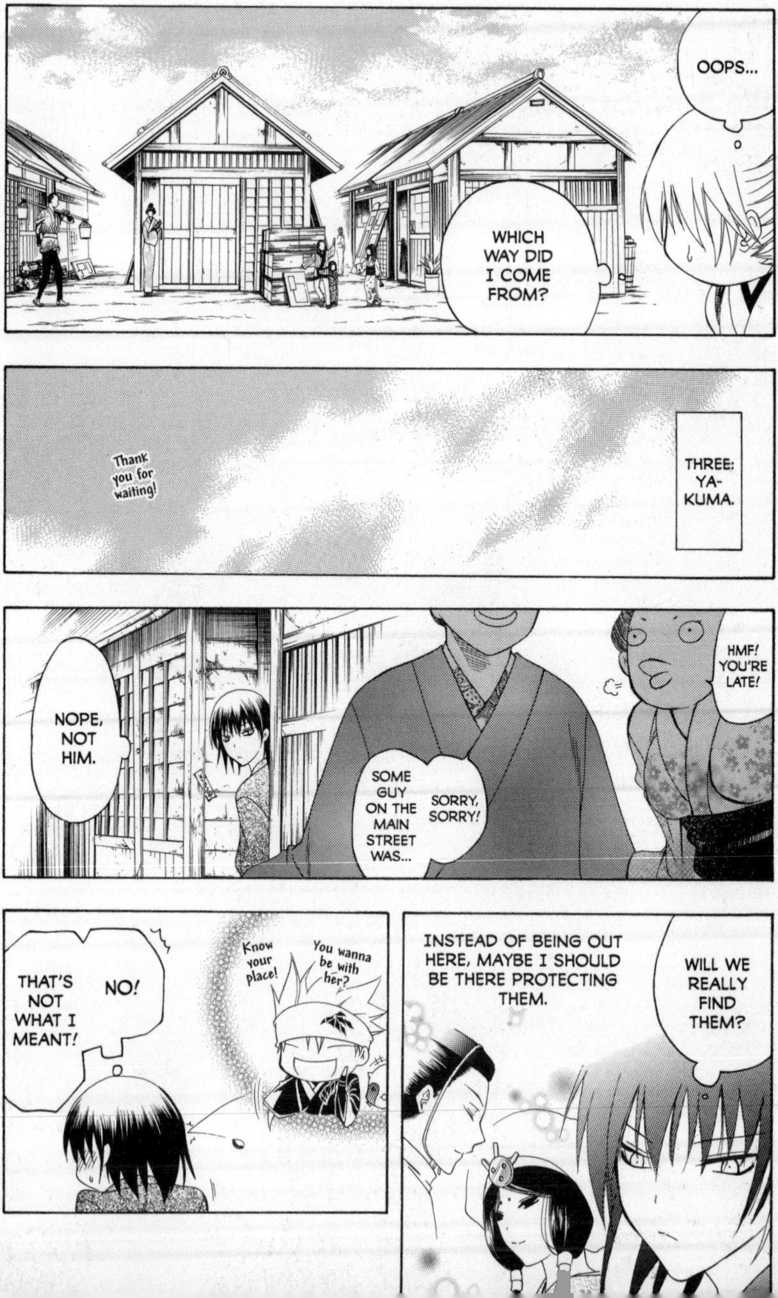
OOPS...
WHICH WAY DID I COME FROM?
THREE: YA-KUMA.
Thank you for waiting!
HMF! YOU'RE LATE!
SORRY, SORRY!
SOME GUY ON THE MAIN STREET WAS...
NOPE, NOT HIM.
WILL WE REALLY FIND THEM?
INSTEAD OF BEING OUT HERE, MAYBE I SHOULD BE THERE PROTECTING THEM.
You wanna be with her?
Know your place!
NO!
THAT'S NOT WHAT I MEANT!

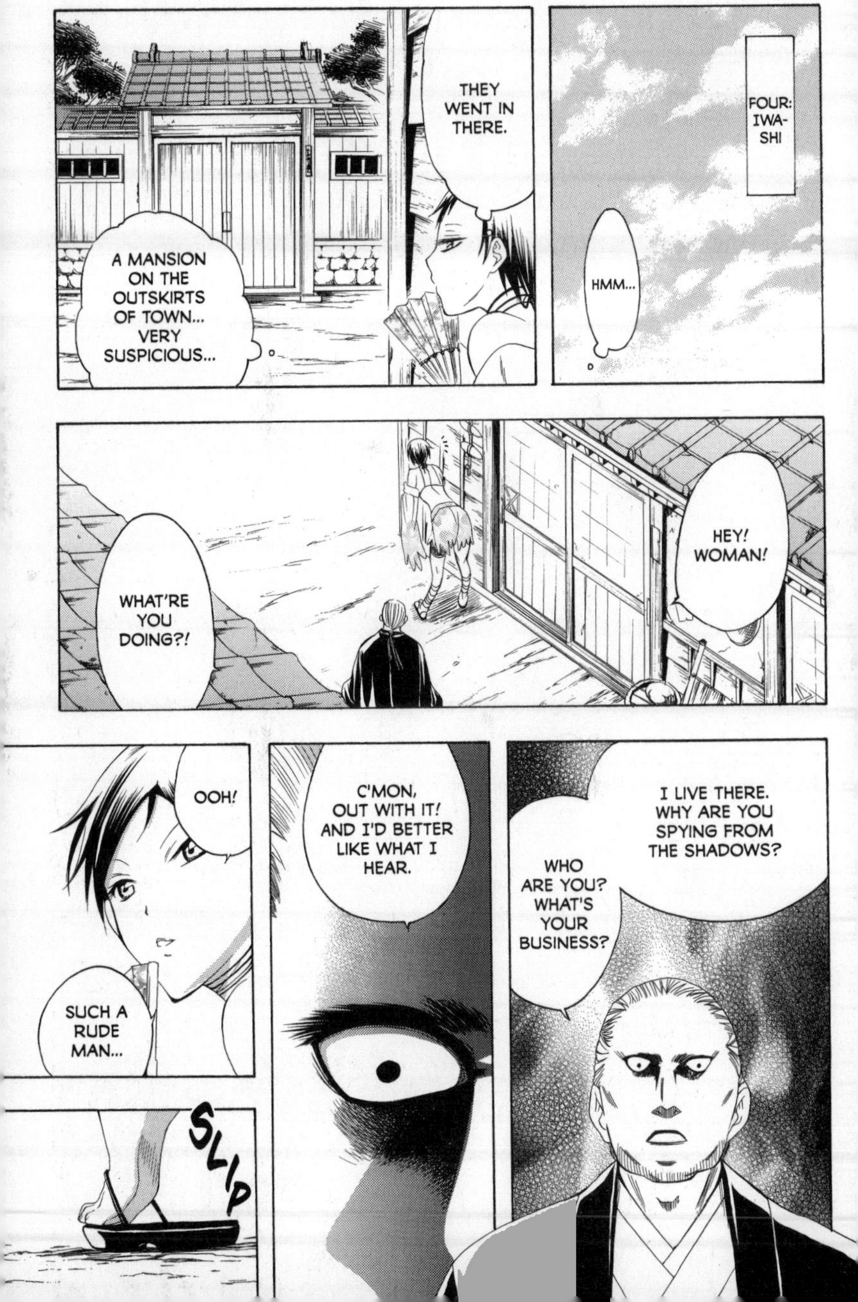
FOUR: IWA-SHI
HMM...
THEY WENT IN THERE.
A MANSION ON THE OUTSKIRTS OF TOWN... VERY SUSPICIOUS...
HEY! WOMAN!
WHAT'RE YOU DOING?!
I LIVE THERE. WHY ARE YOU SPYING FROM THE SHADOWS?
WHO ARE YOU? WHAT'S YOUR BUSINESS?
C'MON, OUT WITH IT! AND I'D BETTER LIKE WHAT I HEAR.
OOH!
SUCH A RUDE MAN...
SLIP

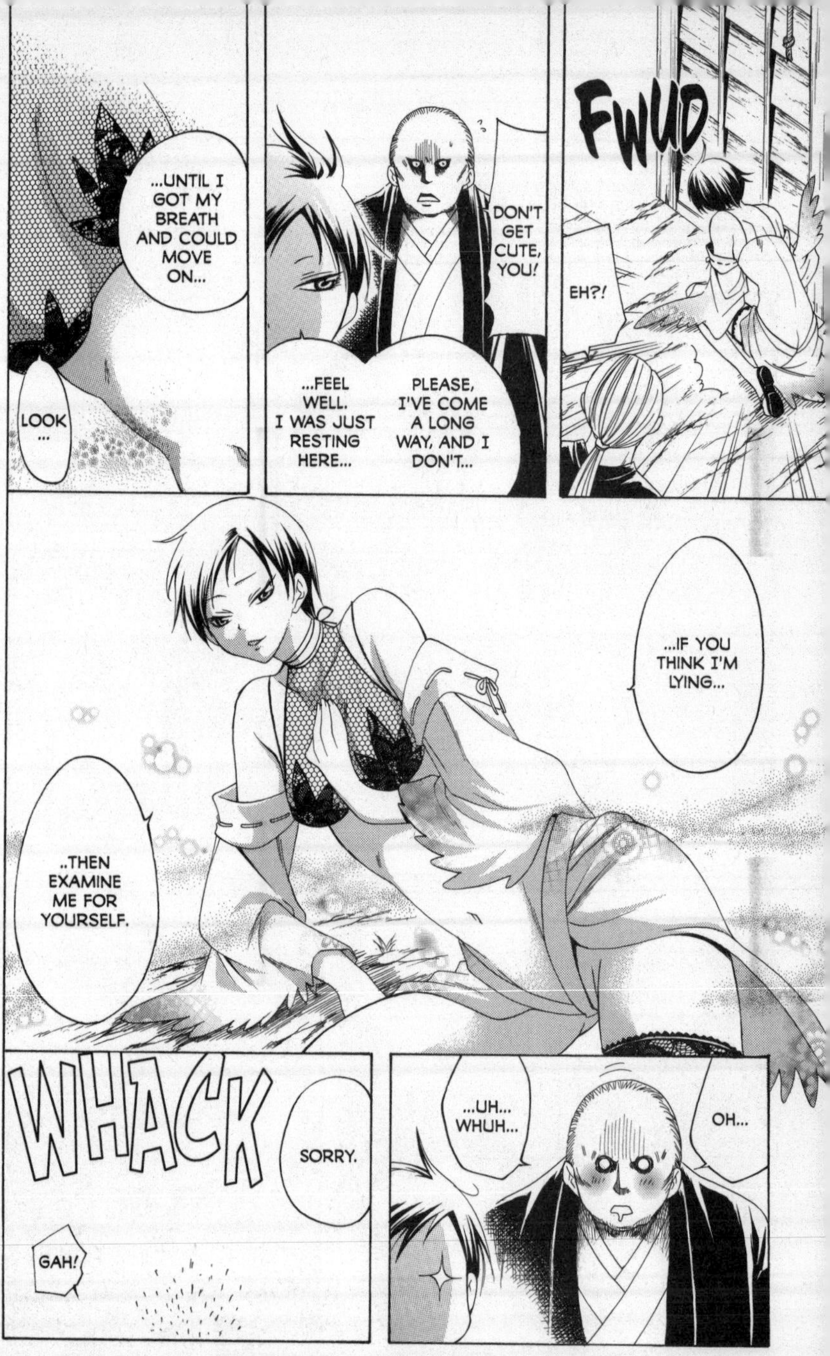
FWUD
EH?!
DON'T GET CUTE, YOU!
PLEASE, I'VE COME A LONG WAY, AND I DON'T...
...FEEL WELL. I WAS JUST RESTING HERE...
...UNTIL I GOT MY BREATH AND COULD MOVE ON...
LOOK...
...IF YOU THINK I'M LYING...
..THEN EXAMINE ME FOR YOURSELF.
OH...
...UH... WHUH...
SORRY.
WHACK
GAH!

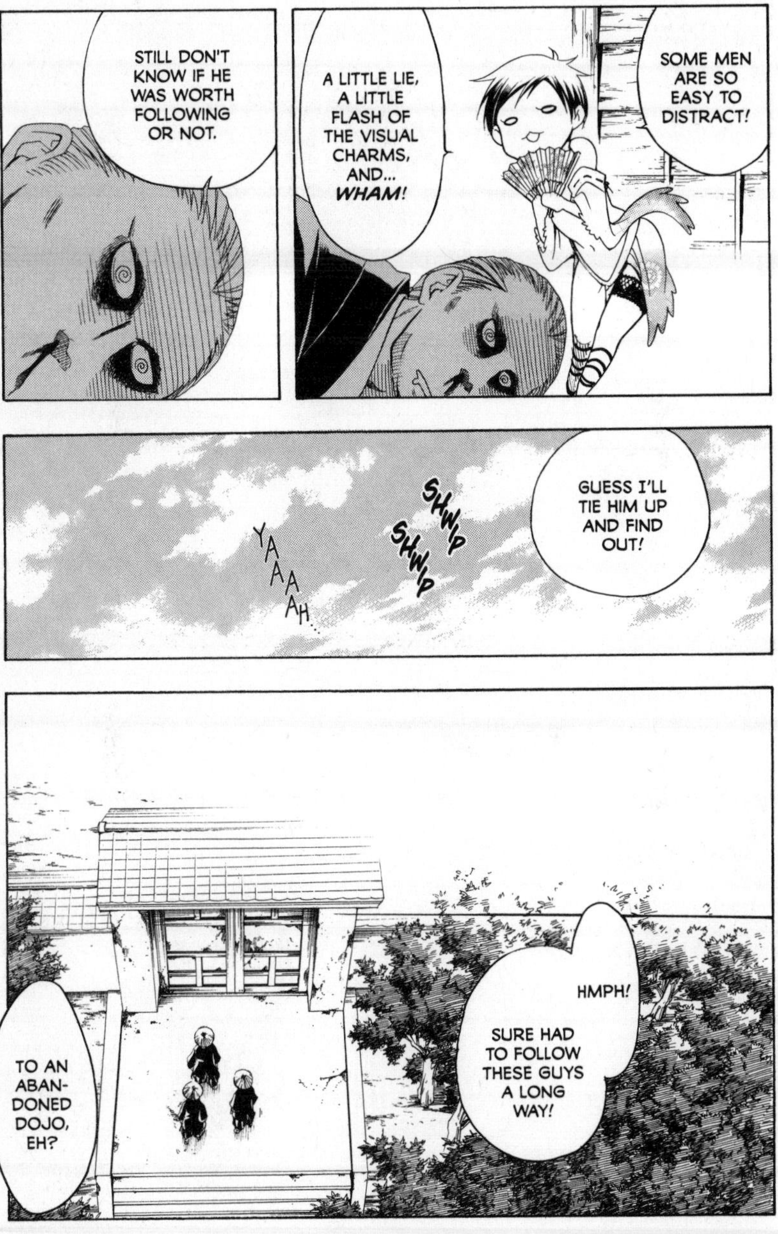
SOME MEN ARE SO EASY TO DISTRACT!
A LITTLE LIE, A LITTLE FLASH OF THE VISUAL CHARMS, AND... *WHAM!*
STILL DON'T KNOW IF HE WAS WORTH FOLLOWING OR NOT.
GUESS I'LL TIE HIM UP AND FIND OUT!
SHWIP SHWIP
YAAAAH...
HMPH!
SURE HAD TO FOLLOW THESE GUYS A LONG WAY!
TO AN ABAN-DONED DOJO, EH?

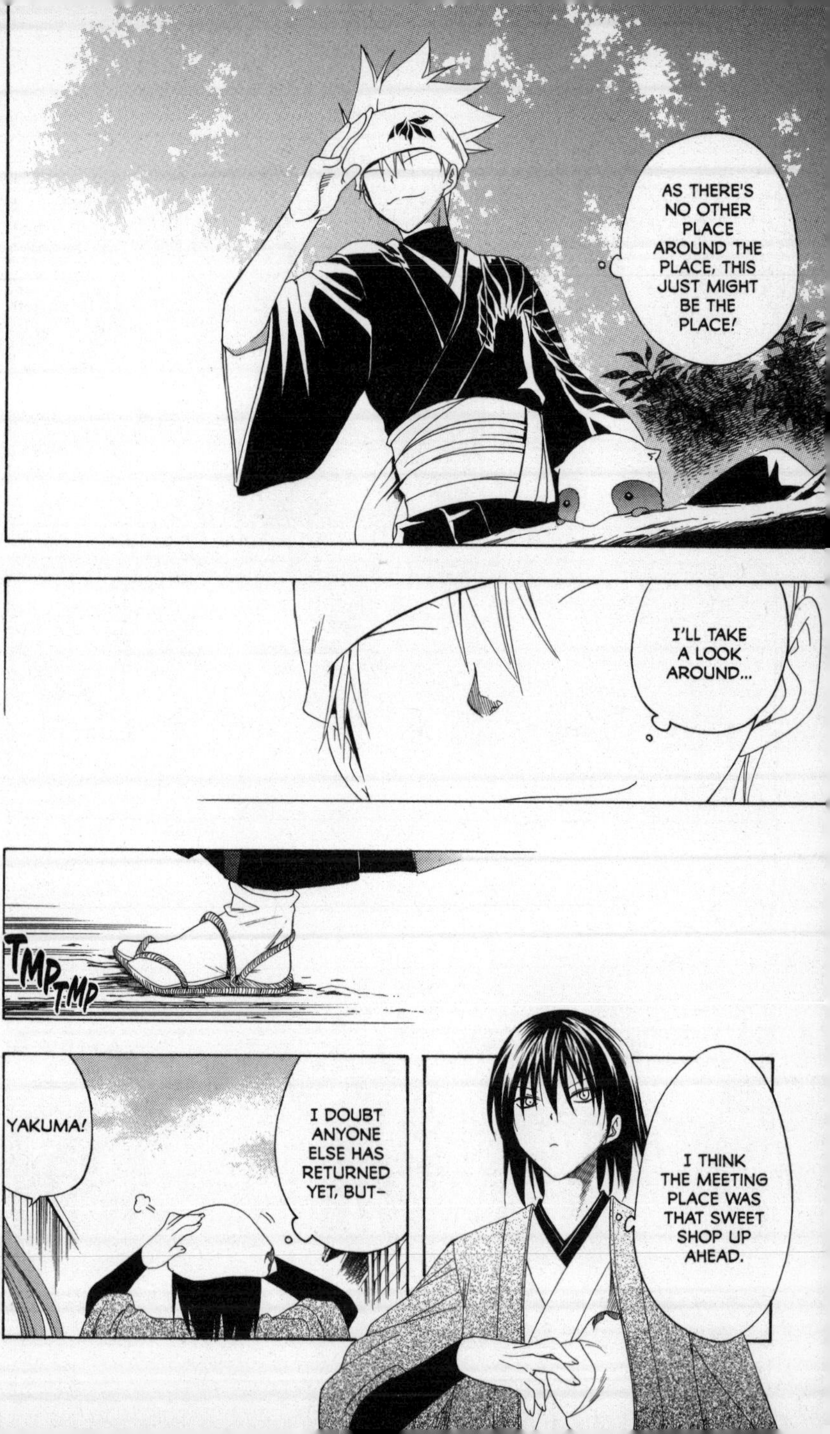
AS THERE'S NO OTHER PLACE AROUND THE PLACE, THIS JUST MIGHT BE THE PLACE!
I'LL TAKE A LOOK AROUND...
TMP TMP
I THINK THE MEETING PLACE WAS THAT SWEET SHOP UP AHEAD.
I DOUBT ANYONE ELSE HAS RETURNED YET, BUT-
YAKUMA!

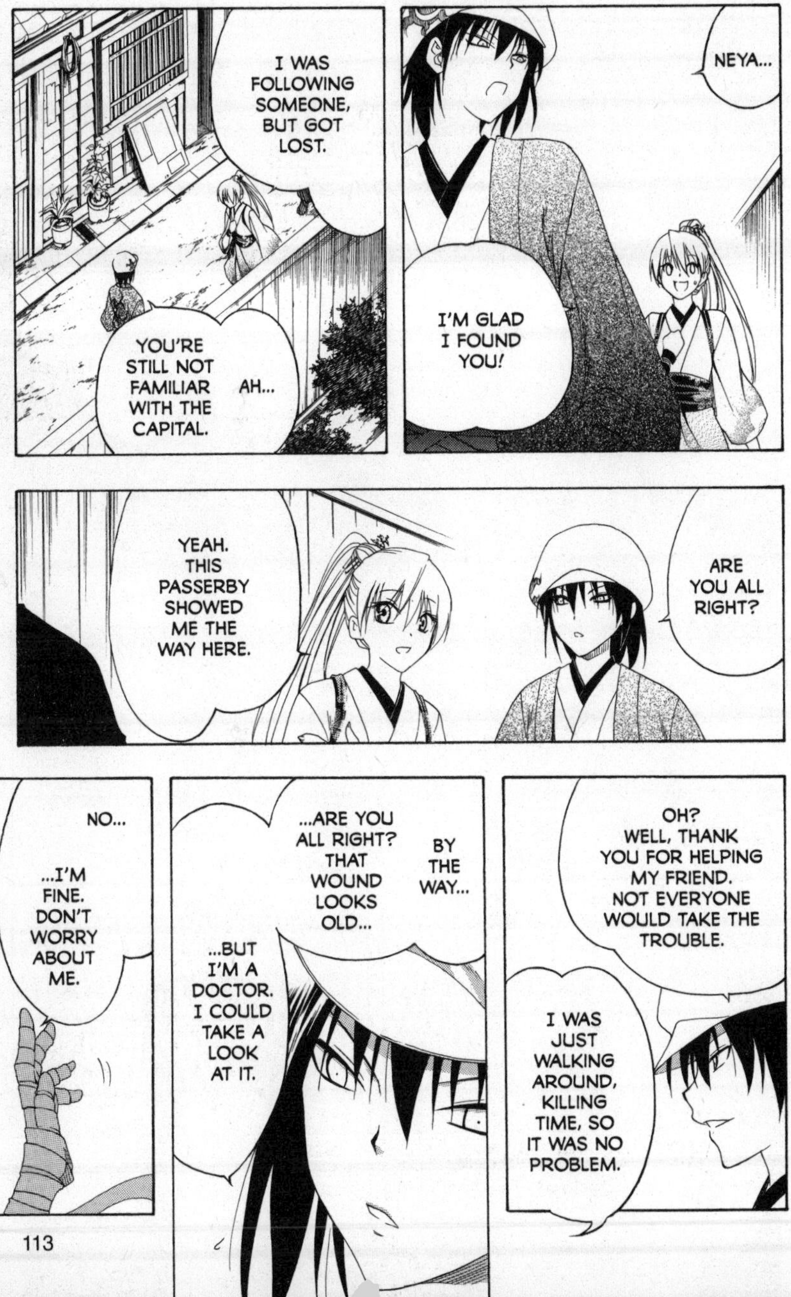
NEYA...
I'M GLAD I FOUND YOU!
I WAS FOLLOWING SOMEONE, BUT GOT LOST.
AH...
YOU'RE STILL NOT FAMILIAR WITH THE CAPITAL.
ARE YOU ALL RIGHT?
YEAH. THIS PASSERBY SHOWED ME THE WAY HERE.
OH? WELL, THANK YOU FOR HELPING MY FRIEND. NOT EVERYONE WOULD TAKE THE TROUBLE.
I WAS JUST WALKING AROUND, KILLING TIME, SO IT WAS NO PROBLEM.
BY THE WAY...
...ARE YOU ALL RIGHT? THAT WOUND LOOKS OLD...
...BUT I'M A DOCTOR. I COULD TAKE A LOOK AT IT.
NO...
...I'M FINE. DON'T WORRY ABOUT ME.

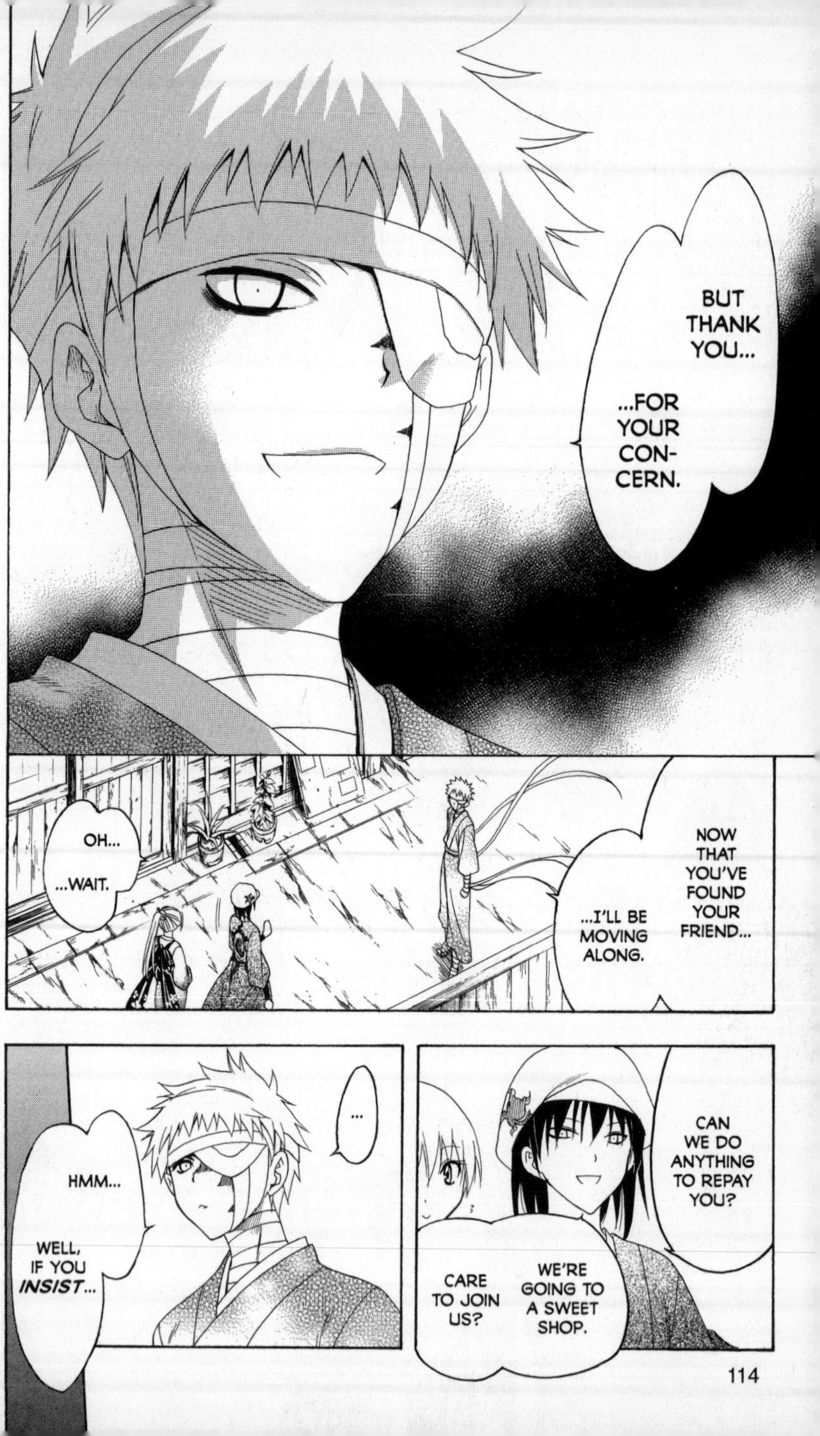
BUT THANK YOU...
...FOR YOUR CON-CERN.
NOW THAT YOU'VE FOUND YOUR FRIEND...
...I'LL BE MOVING ALONG.
OH...
...WAIT.
CAN WE DO ANYTHING TO REPAY YOU?
WE'RE GOING TO A SWEET SHOP.
CARE TO JOIN US?
...
HMM...
WELL, IF YOU *INSIST*...

Chapter 94 Friends

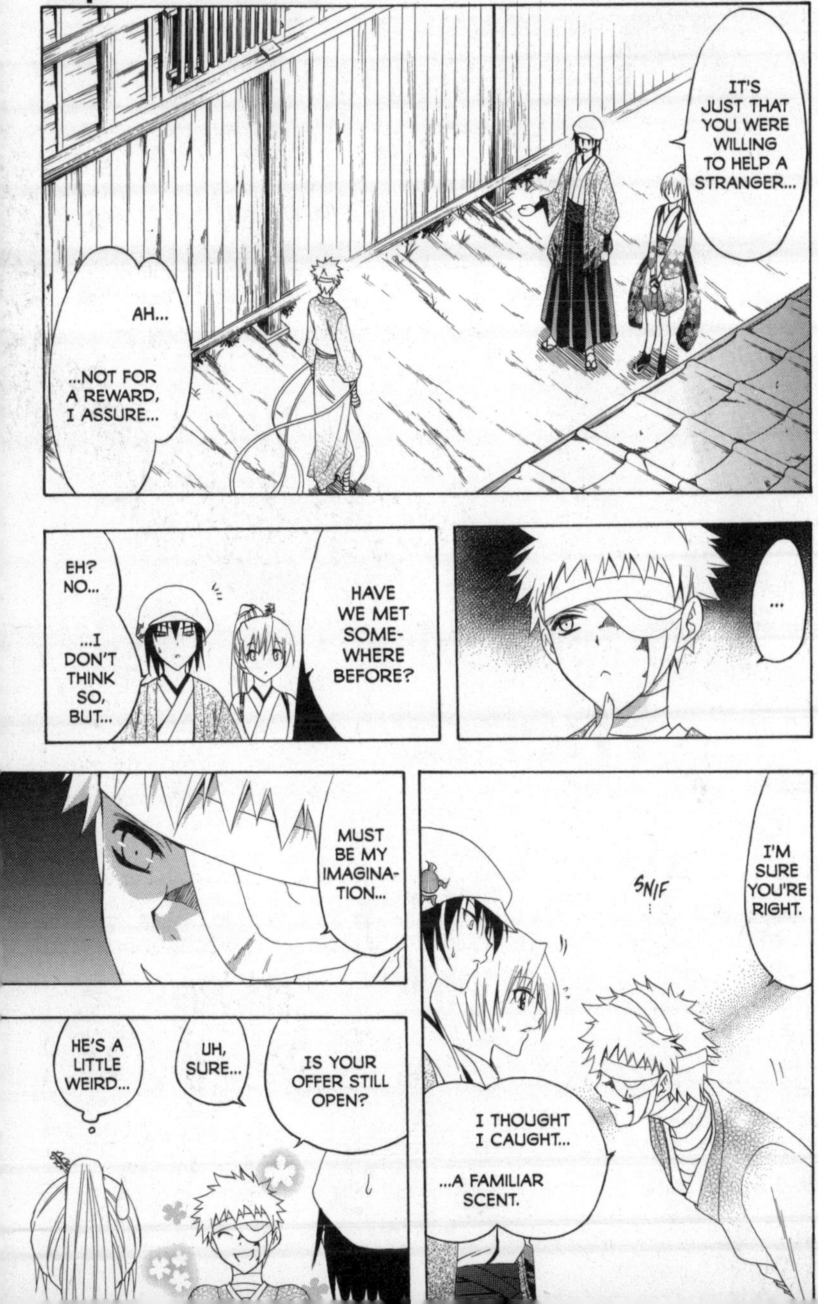
IT'S JUST THAT YOU WERE WILLING TO HELP A STRANGER...
AH...
...NOT FOR A REWARD, I ASSURE...
...
HAVE WE MET SOME-WHERE BEFORE?
EH? NO...
...I DON'T THINK SO, BUT...
I'M SURE YOU'RE RIGHT.
SNIF
I THOUGHT I CAUGHT...
...A FAMILIAR SCENT.
MUST BE MY IMAGINA-TION...
IS YOUR OFFER STILL OPEN?
UH, SURE...
HE'S A LITTLE WEIRD...

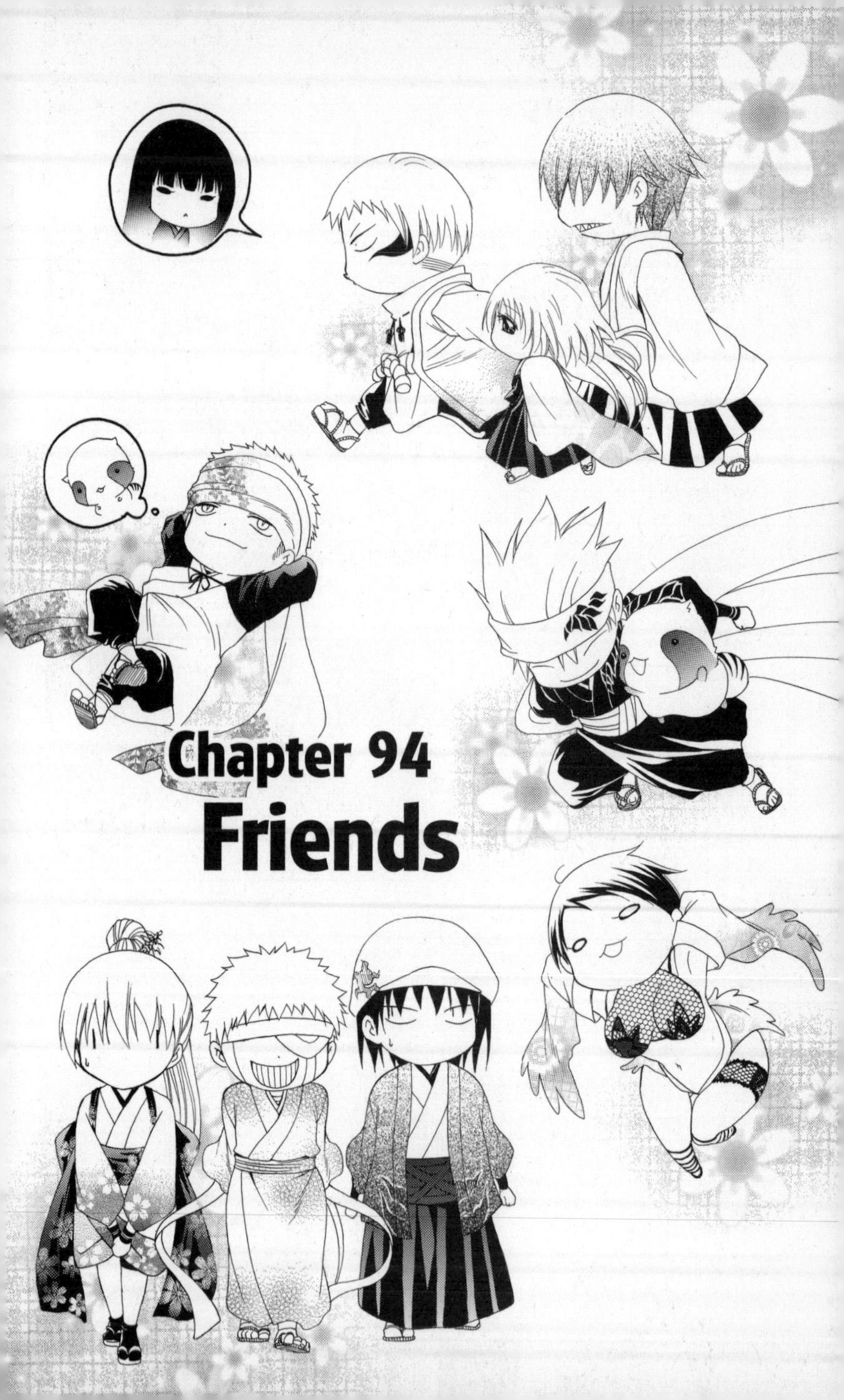
Chapter 94
Friends

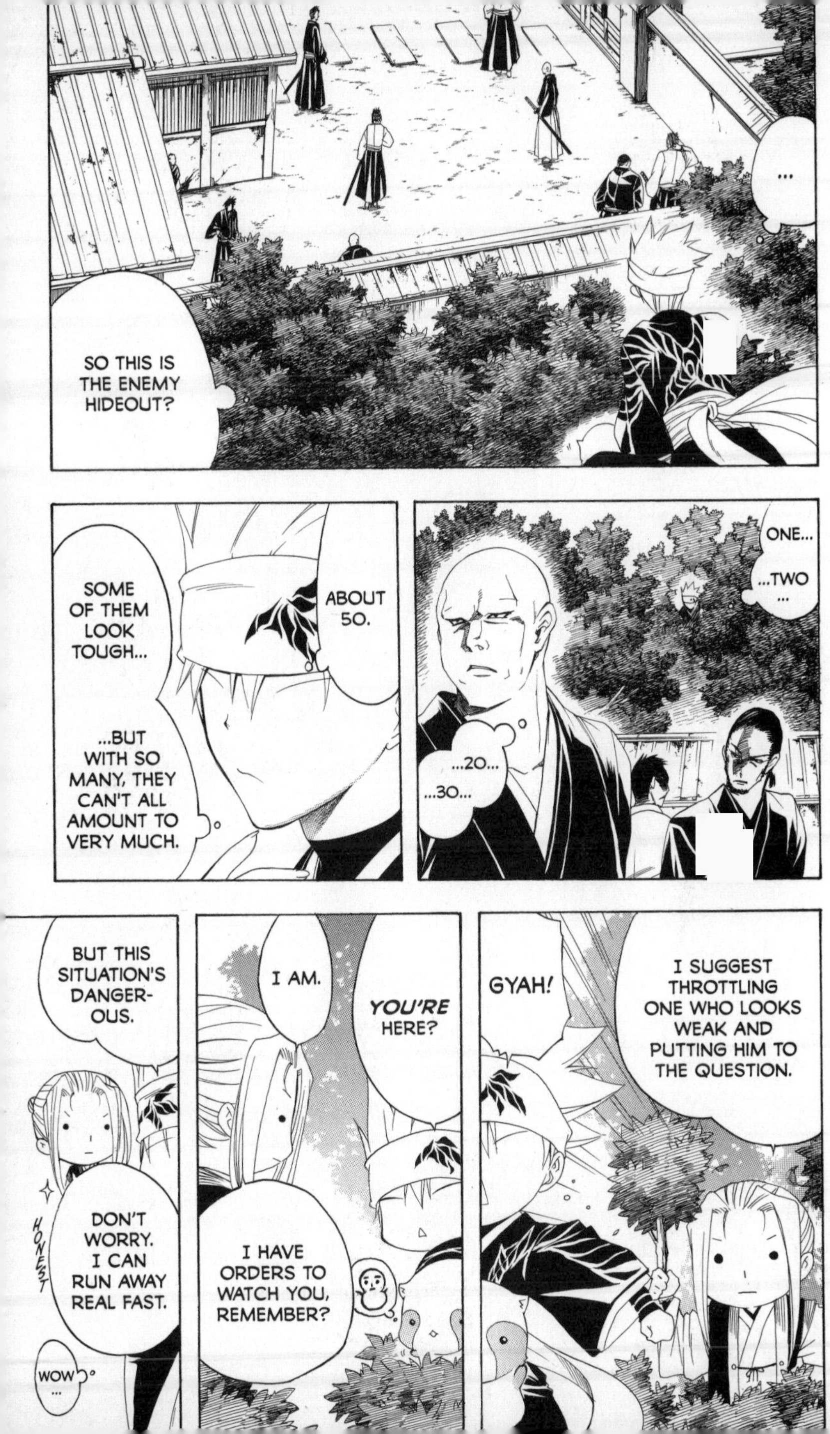
...
SO THIS IS THE ENEMY HIDEOUT?
ONE...
...TWO ...
...20... ...30...
ABOUT 50.
SOME OF THEM LOOK TOUGH...
...BUT WITH SO MANY, THEY CAN'T ALL AMOUNT TO VERY MUCH.
I SUGGEST THROTTLING ONE WHO LOOKS WEAK AND PUTTING HIM TO THE QUESTION.
GYAH!
YOU'RE HERE?
I AM.
I HAVE ORDERS TO WATCH YOU, REMEMBER?
BUT THIS SITUATION'S DANGER-OUS.
DON'T WORRY. I CAN RUN AWAY REAL FAST.
HONEST
WOW ...

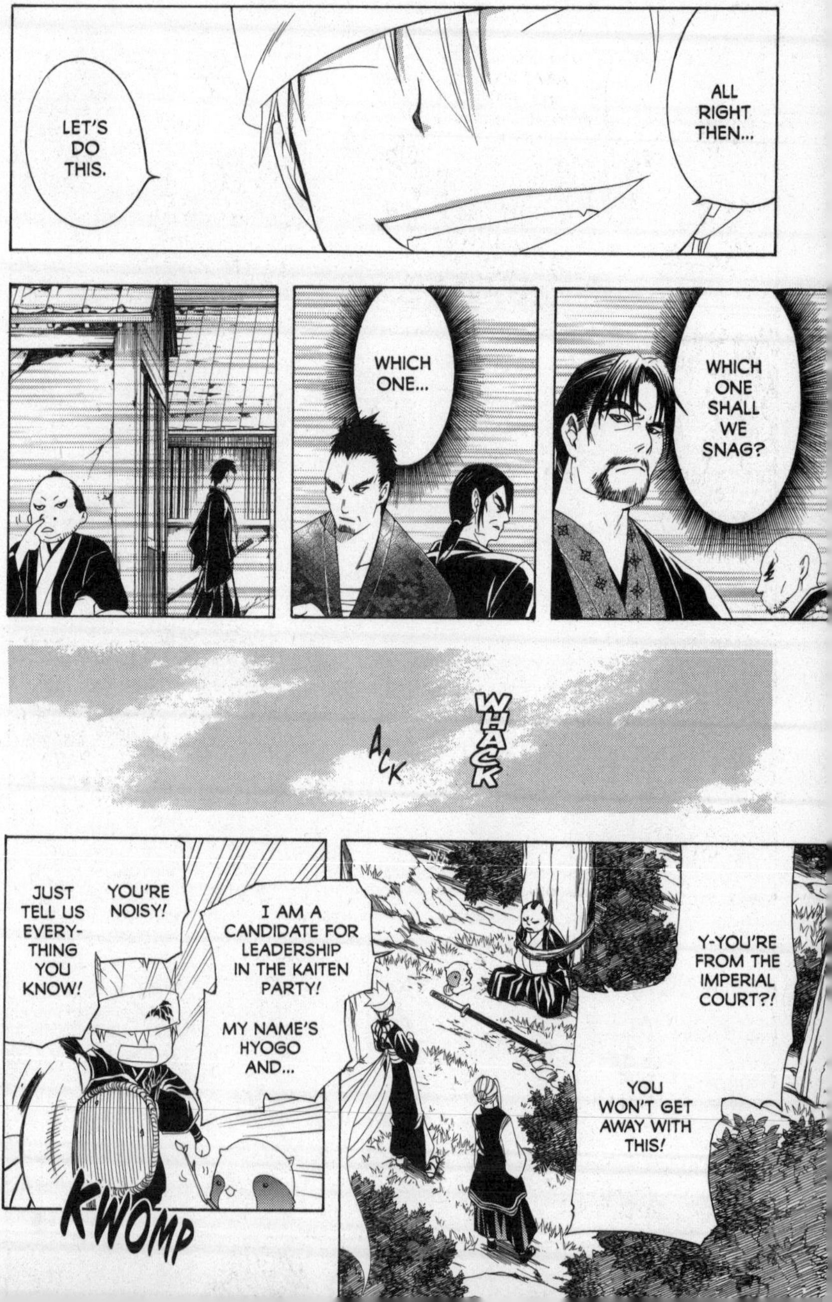

ALL RIGHT THEN...
LET'S DO THIS.
WHICH ONE SHALL WE SNAG?
WHICH ONE...
WHACK
ACK
Y-YOU'RE FROM THE IMPERIAL COURT?!
YOU WON'T GET AWAY WITH THIS!
I AM A CANDIDATE FOR LEADERSHIP IN THE KAITEN PARTY!
MY NAME'S HYOGO AND...
YOU'RE NOISY!
JUST TELL US EVERY-THING YOU KNOW!
KWOMP

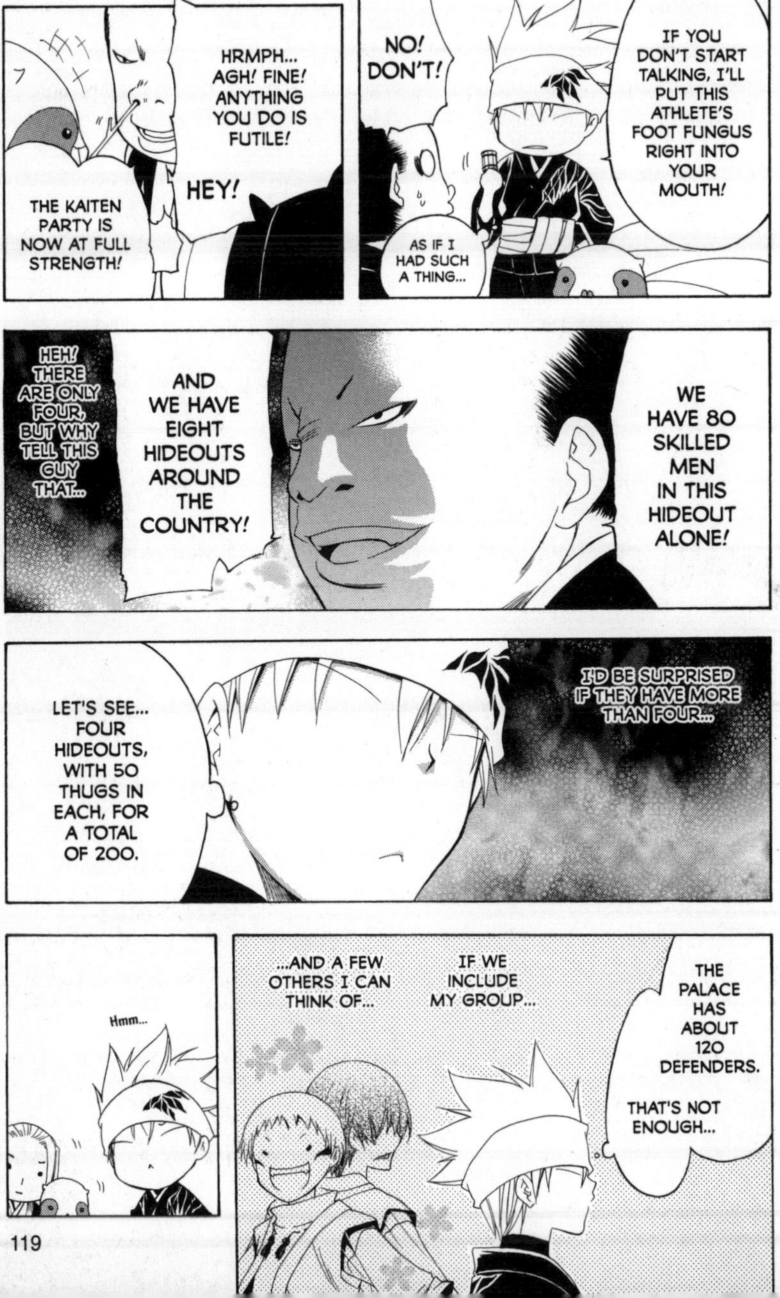
IF YOU DON'T START TALKING, I'LL PUT THIS ATHLETE'S FOOT FUNGUS RIGHT INTO YOUR MOUTH!
NO! DON'T!
AS IF I HAD SUCH A THING...
HRMPH... AGH! FINE! ANYTHING YOU DO IS FUTILE!
HEY!
THE KAITEN PARTY IS NOW AT FULL STRENGTH!
WE HAVE 80 SKILLED MEN IN THIS HIDEOUT ALONE!
AND WE HAVE EIGHT HIDEOUTS AROUND THE COUNTRY!
HEH! THERE ARE ONLY FOUR, BUT WHY TELL THIS GUY THAT...
I'D BE SURPRISED IF THEY HAVE MORE THAN FOUR...
LET'S SEE... FOUR HIDEOUTS, WITH 50 THUGS IN EACH, FOR A TOTAL OF 200.
THE PALACE HAS ABOUT 120 DEFENDERS.
THAT'S NOT ENOUGH...
IF WE INCLUDE MY GROUP...
...AND A FEW OTHERS I CAN THINK OF...
Hmm...

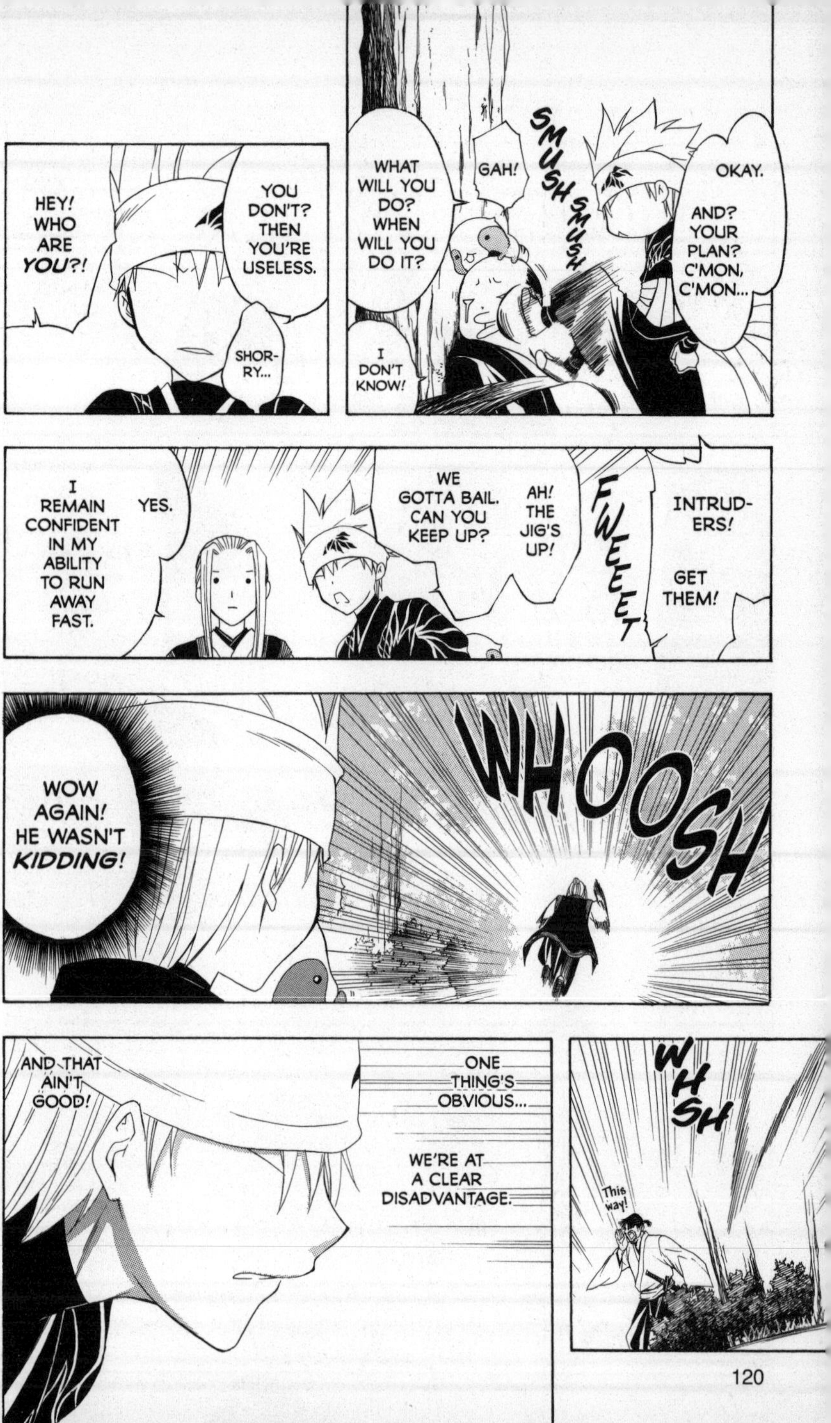

OKAY.
AND? YOUR PLAN? C'MON, C'MON...
SMUSH SMUSH
GAH!
WHAT WILL YOU DO? WHEN WILL YOU DO IT?
I DON'T KNOW!
YOU DON'T? THEN YOU'RE USELESS.
HEY! WHO ARE *YOU*?!
SHORRY...
INTRUDERS!
GET THEM!
FWEEEET
AH! THE JIG'S UP!
WE GOTTA BAIL. CAN YOU KEEP UP?
YES.
I REMAIN CONFIDENT IN MY ABILITY TO RUN AWAY FAST.
WHOOSH
WOW AGAIN! HE WASN'T *KIDDING*!
WHSH
This way!
ONE THING'S OBVIOUS...
WE'RE AT A CLEAR DISADVANTAGE.
AND THAT AIN'T GOOD!

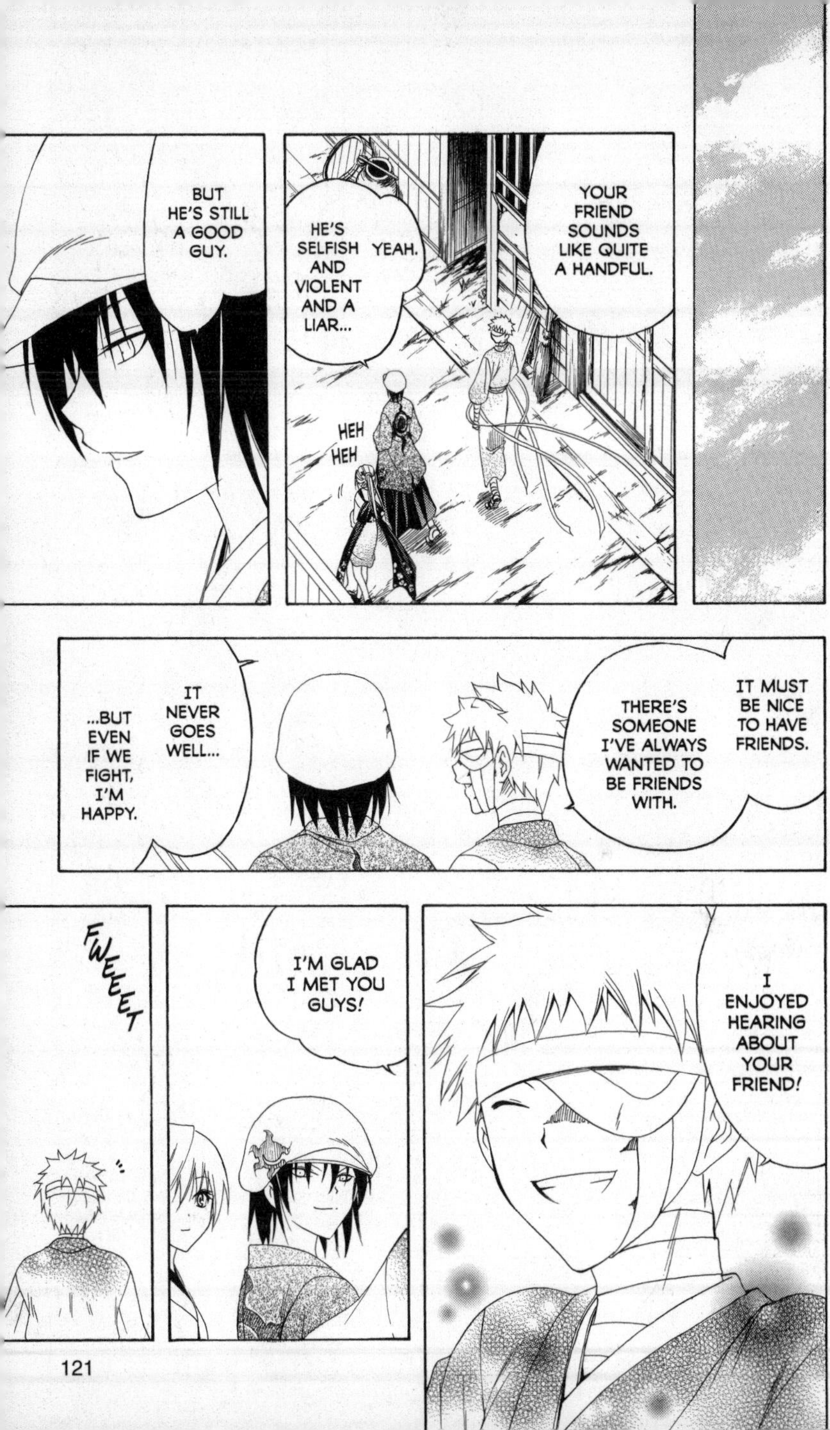
YOUR FRIEND SOUNDS LIKE QUITE A HANDFUL.
YEAH.
HE'S SELFISH AND VIOLENT AND A LIAR...
HEH HEH
BUT HE'S STILL A GOOD GUY.
IT MUST BE NICE TO HAVE FRIENDS.
THERE'S SOMEONE I'VE ALWAYS WANTED TO BE FRIENDS WITH.
IT NEVER GOES WELL...
...BUT EVEN IF WE FIGHT, I'M HAPPY.
I ENJOYED HEARING ABOUT YOUR FRIEND!
I'M GLAD I MET YOU GUYS!
FWEEET

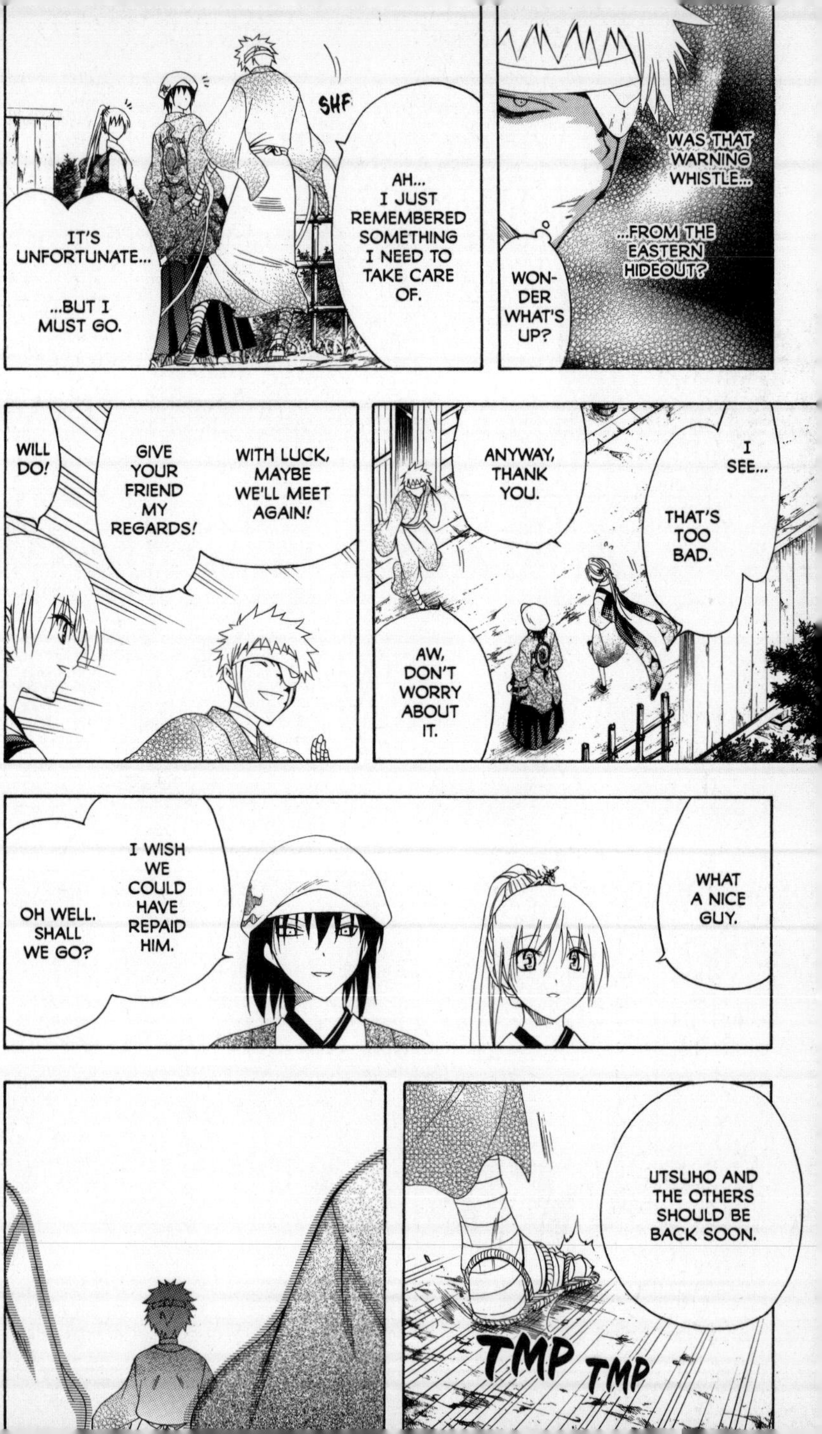
WAS THAT WARNING WHISTLE...
...FROM THE EASTERN HIDEOUT?
WONDER WHAT'S UP?
SHF
AH... I JUST REMEMBERED SOMETHING I NEED TO TAKE CARE OF.
IT'S UNFORTUNATE...
...BUT I MUST GO.
I SEE...
THAT'S TOO BAD.
ANYWAY, THANK YOU.
AW, DON'T WORRY ABOUT IT.
WITH LUCK, MAYBE WE'LL MEET AGAIN!
GIVE YOUR FRIEND MY REGARDS!
WILL DO!
WHAT A NICE GUY.
I WISH WE COULD HAVE REPAID HIM.
OH WELL. SHALL WE GO?
UTSUHO AND THE OTHERS SHOULD BE BACK SOON.
TMP TMP

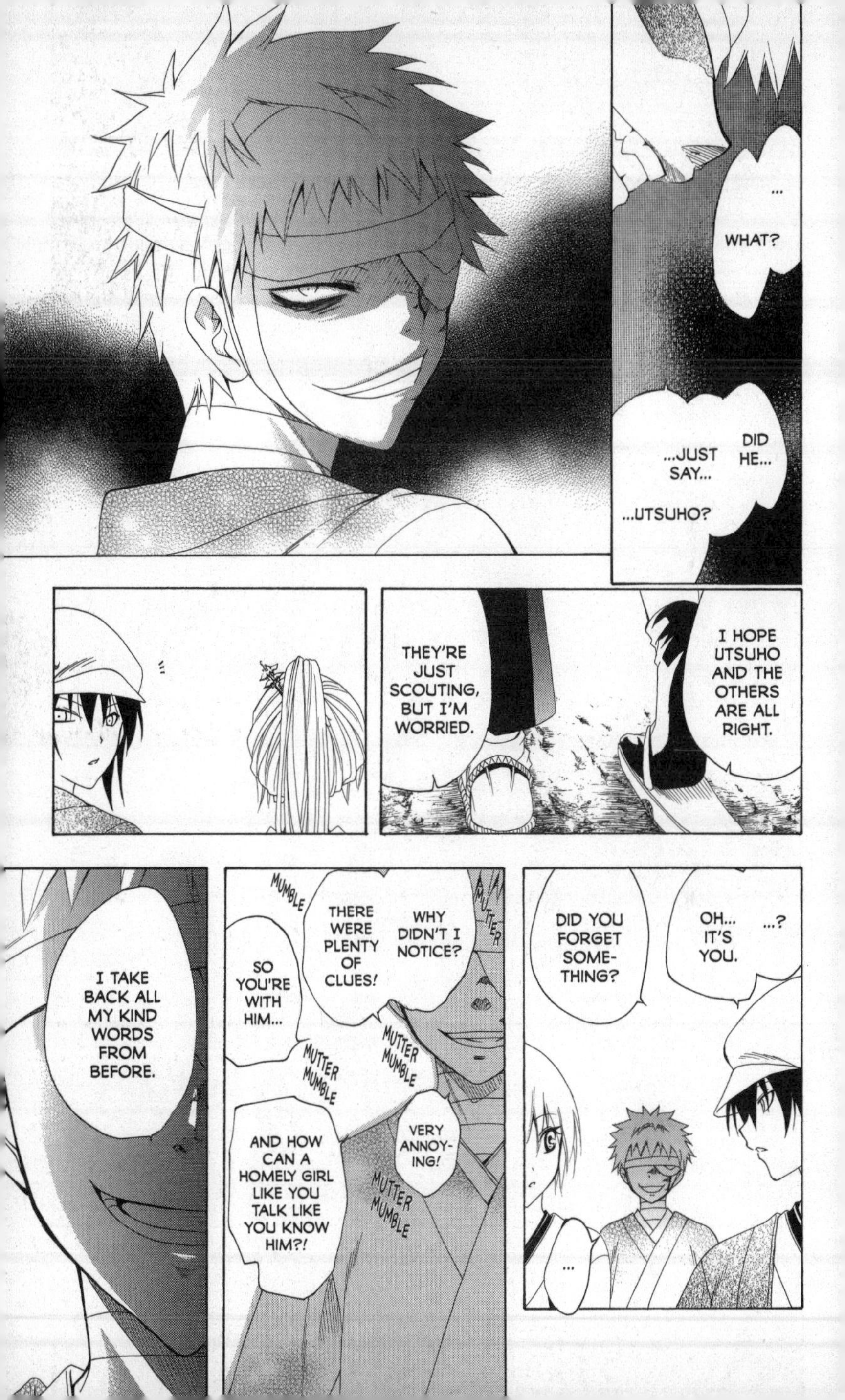
...
WHAT?
DID HE... ...JUST SAY...
...UTSUHO?
I HOPE UTSUHO AND THE OTHERS ARE ALL RIGHT.
THEY'RE JUST SCOUTING, BUT I'M WORRIED.
...?
OH... IT'S YOU.
DID YOU FORGET SOMETHING?
...
MUTTER
WHY DIDN'T I NOTICE?
THERE WERE PLENTY OF CLUES!
MUMBLE
SO YOU'RE WITH HIM...
MUTTER MUMBLE
MUTTER MUMBLE
VERY ANNOY-ING!
AND HOW CAN A HOMELY GIRL LIKE YOU TALK LIKE YOU KNOW HIM?!
MUTTER MUMBLE
I TAKE BACK ALL MY KIND WORDS FROM BEFORE.

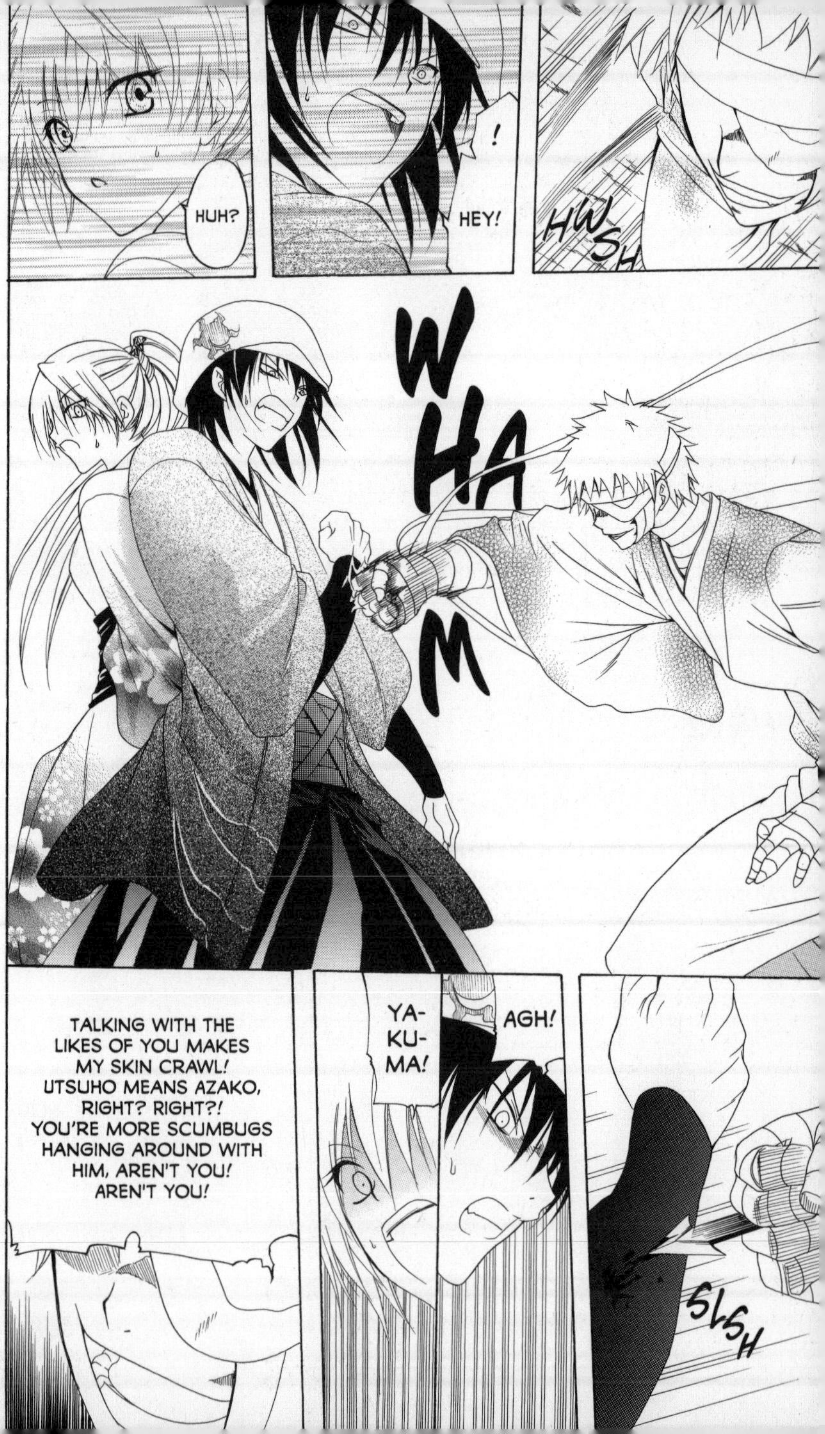
HWSH
!
HEY!
HUH?
WHAM
SLSH
AGH!
YA-KU-MA!
TALKING WITH THE LIKES OF YOU MAKES MY SKIN CRAWL! UTSUHO MEANS AZAKO, RIGHT? RIGHT?! YOU'RE MORE SCUMBUGS HANGING AROUND WITH HIM, AREN'T YOU! AREN'T YOU!

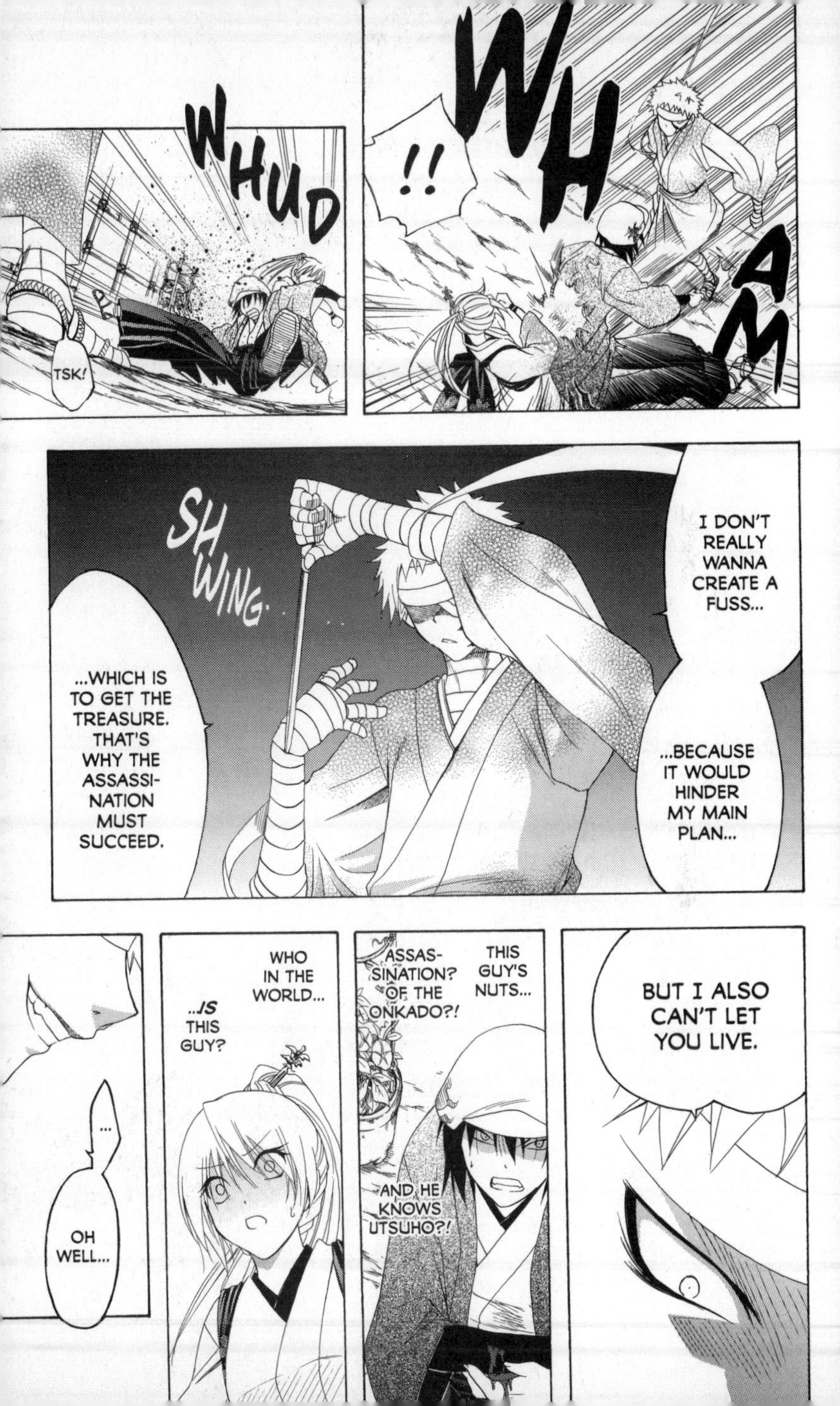
WHAM
!!
WHUD
TSK!
I DON'T REALLY WANNA CREATE A FUSS...
...BECAUSE IT WOULD HINDER MY MAIN PLAN...
SHWING
...WHICH IS TO GET THE TREASURE. THAT'S WHY THE ASSASSINATION MUST SUCCEED.
BUT I ALSO CAN'T LET YOU LIVE.
THIS GUY'S NUTS...
ASSASSINATION? OF THE ONKADO?!
AND HE KNOWS UTSUHO?!
WHO IN THE WORLD...
...IS THIS GUY?
...
OH WELL...

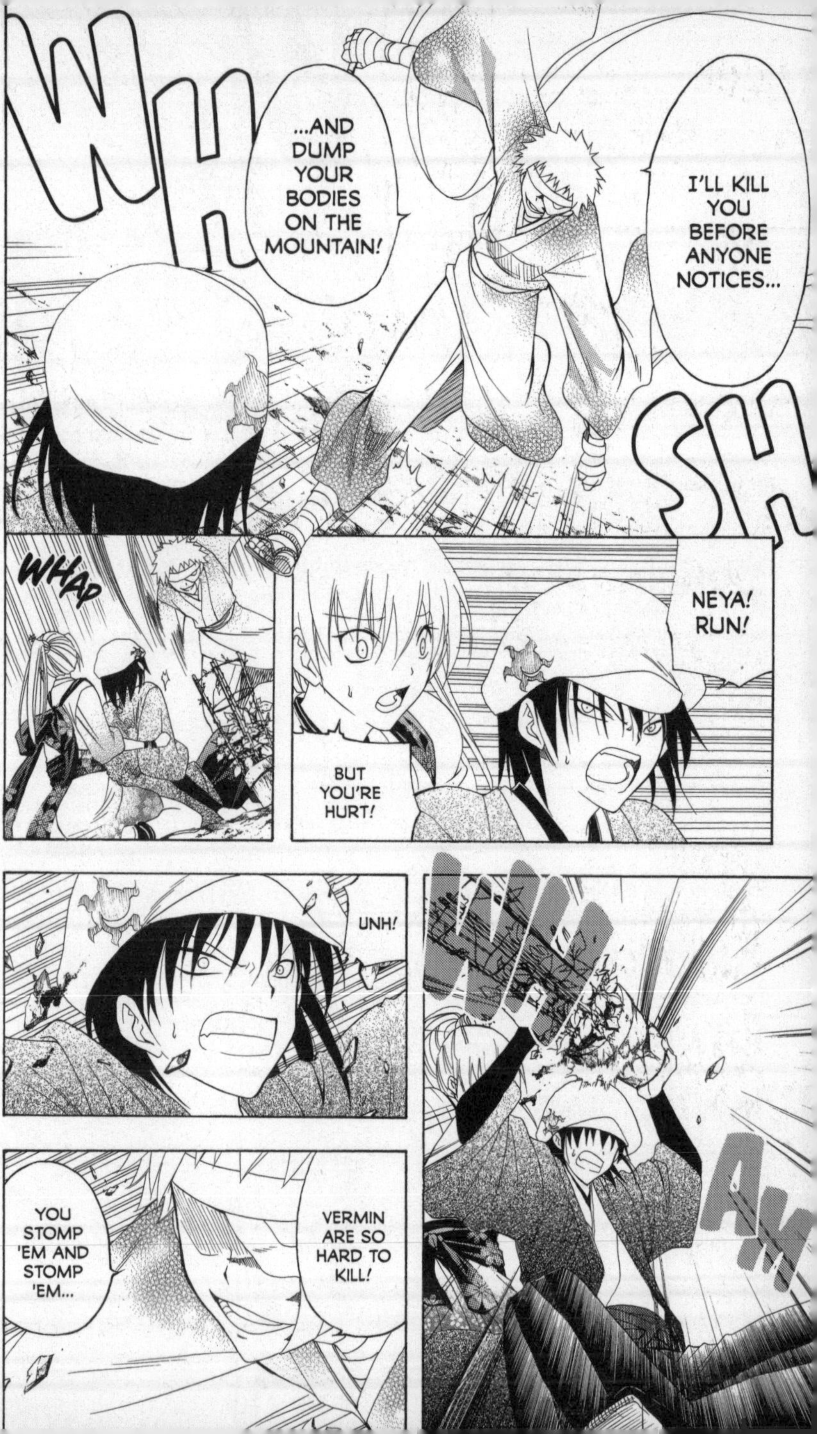
I'LL KILL YOU BEFORE ANYONE NOTICES...
WH
...AND DUMP YOUR BODIES ON THE MOUNTAIN!
SH
NEYA! RUN!
BUT YOU'RE HURT!
WHAP
WH
AM
UNH!
VERMIN ARE SO HARD TO KILL!
YOU STOMP 'EM AND STOMP 'EM...

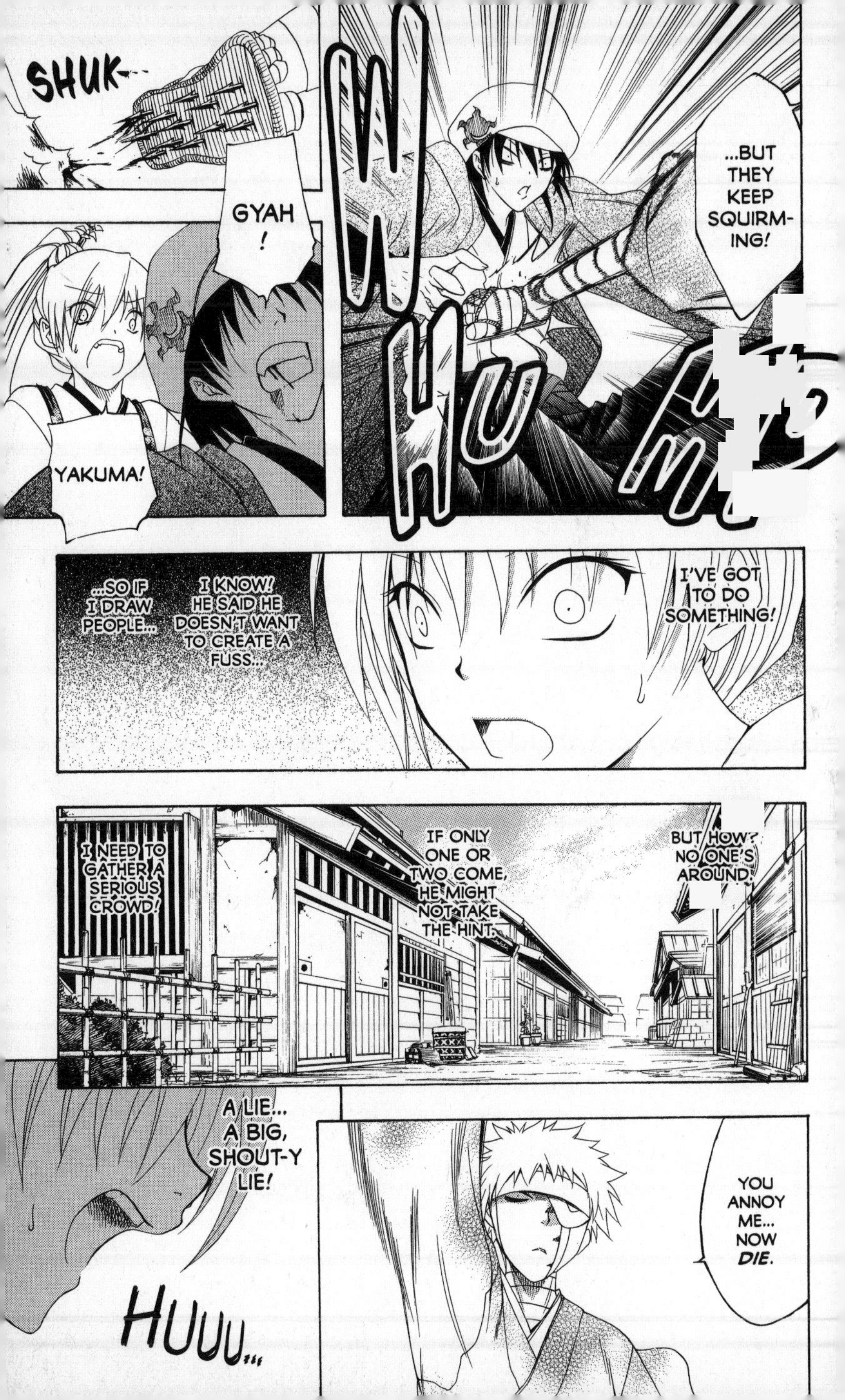
WHUM
...BUT THEY KEEP SQUIRMING!
SHUK
GYAH!
YAKUMA!
I'VE GOT TO DO SOMETHING!
I KNOW! HE SAID HE DOESN'T WANT TO CREATE A FUSS...
...SO IF I DRAW PEOPLE...
BUT HOW? NO ONE'S AROUND.
IF ONLY ONE OR TWO COME, HE MIGHT NOT TAKE THE HINT.
I NEED TO GATHER A SERIOUS CROWD!
YOU ANNOY ME... NOW *DIE*.
A LIE... A BIG, SHOUT-Y LIE!
HUUU...

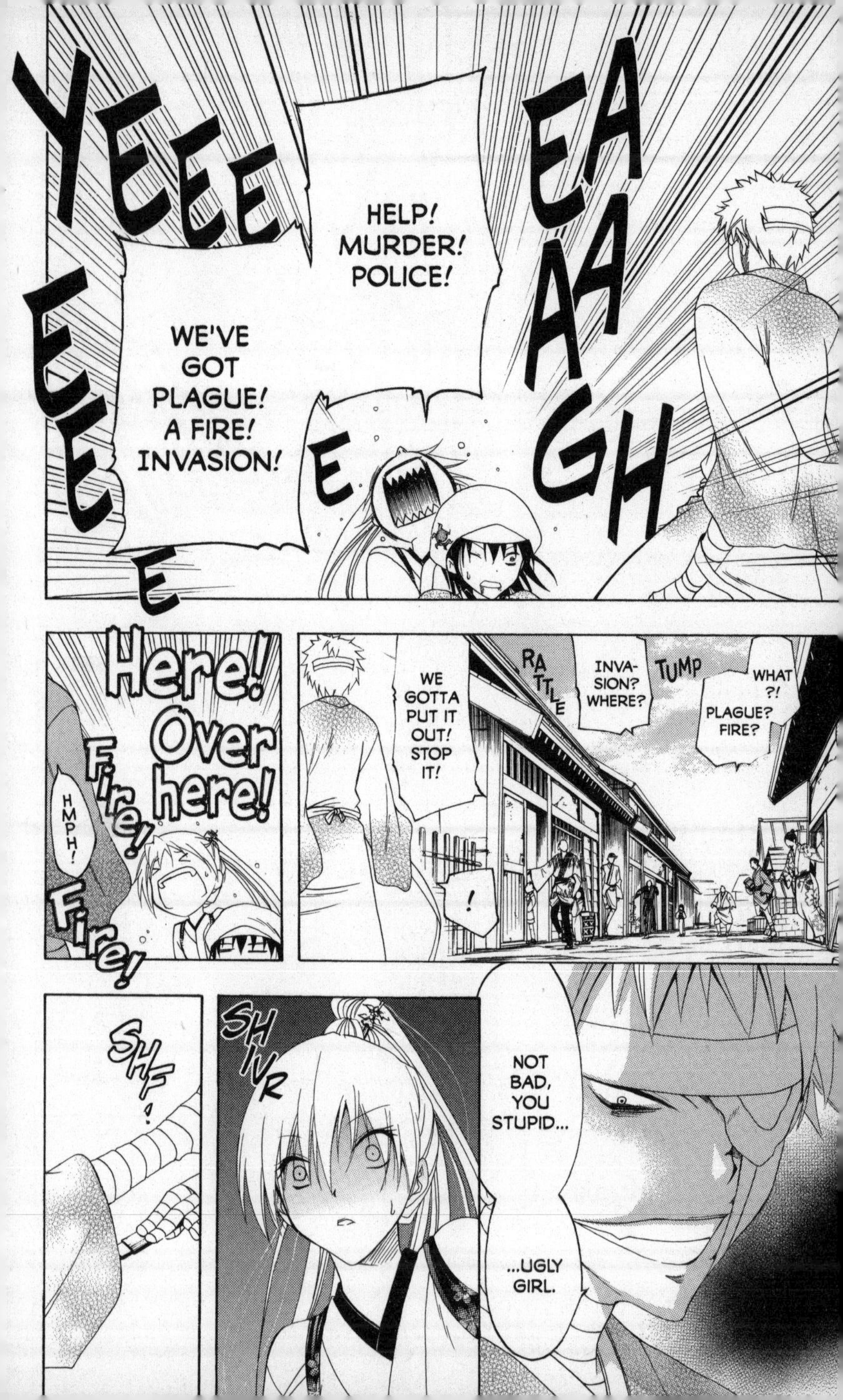

HELP! MURDER! POLICE!
WE'VE GOT PLAGUE! A FIRE! INVASION!
YEEEEEEEEEAAAGH
WHAT?!
PLAGUE? FIRE?
TUMP
INVA-SION? WHERE?
RATTLE
WE GOTTA PUT IT OUT! STOP IT!
!
Here! Over here!
Fire! Fire!
HMPH!
NOT BAD, YOU STUPID...
...UGLY GIRL.
SHIVR
SHF!

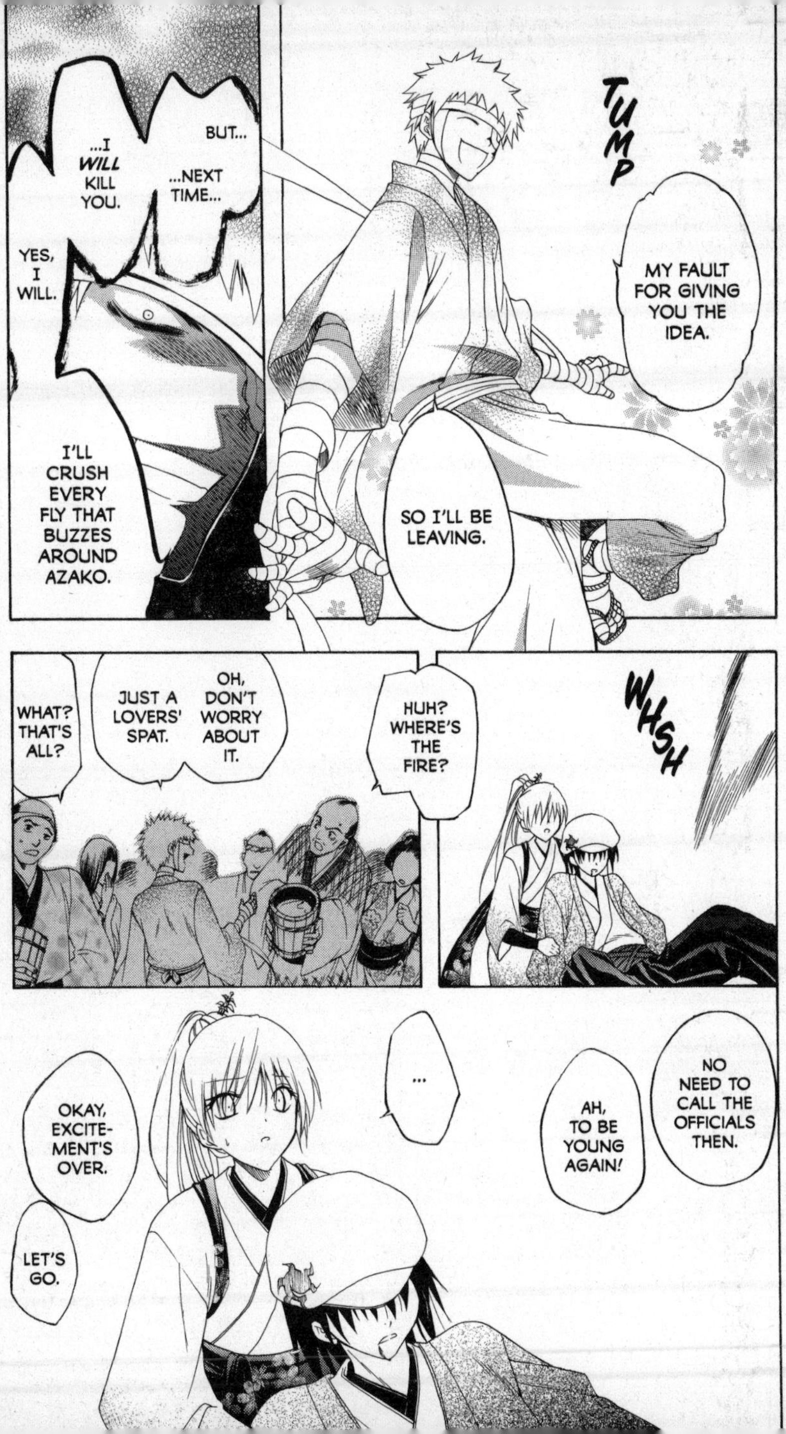
TUMP
MY FAULT FOR GIVING YOU THE IDEA.
SO I'LL BE LEAVING.
BUT...
...NEXT TIME...
...I WILL KILL YOU.
YES, I WILL.
I'LL CRUSH EVERY FLY THAT BUZZES AROUND AZAKO.
WHSH
HUH? WHERE'S THE FIRE?
OH, DON'T WORRY ABOUT IT.
JUST A LOVERS' SPAT.
WHAT? THAT'S ALL?
NO NEED TO CALL THE OFFICIALS THEN.
AH, TO BE YOUNG AGAIN!
...
OKAY, EXCITE-MENT'S OVER.
LET'S GO.

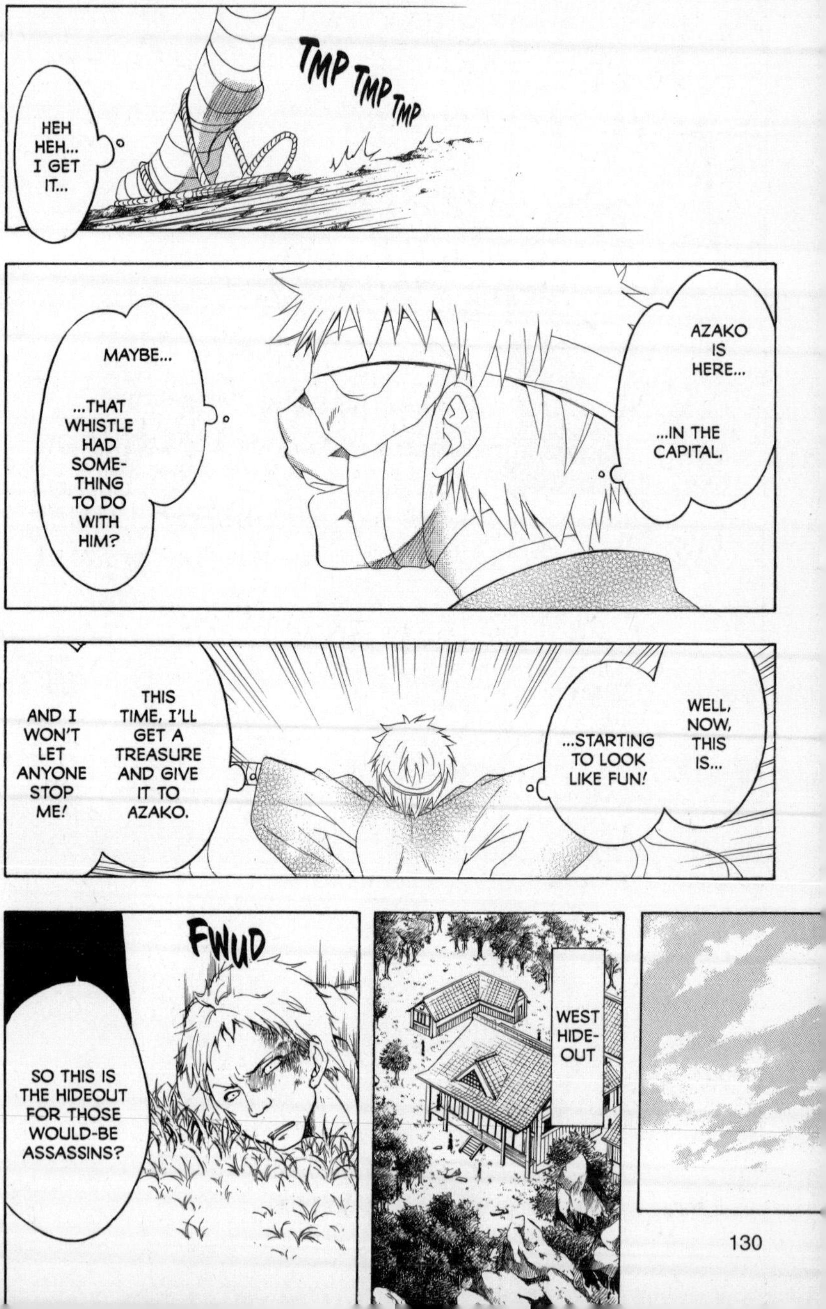

TMP TMP TMP
HEH HEH... I GET IT...
AZAKO IS HERE...
...IN THE CAPITAL.
MAYBE...
...THAT WHISTLE HAD SOMETHING TO DO WITH HIM?
WELL, NOW, THIS IS...
...STARTING TO LOOK LIKE FUN!
THIS TIME, I'LL GET A TREASURE AND GIVE IT TO AZAKO.
AND I WON'T LET ANYONE STOP ME!
WEST HIDEOUT
FWUD
SO THIS IS THE HIDEOUT FOR THOSE WOULD-BE ASSASSINS?

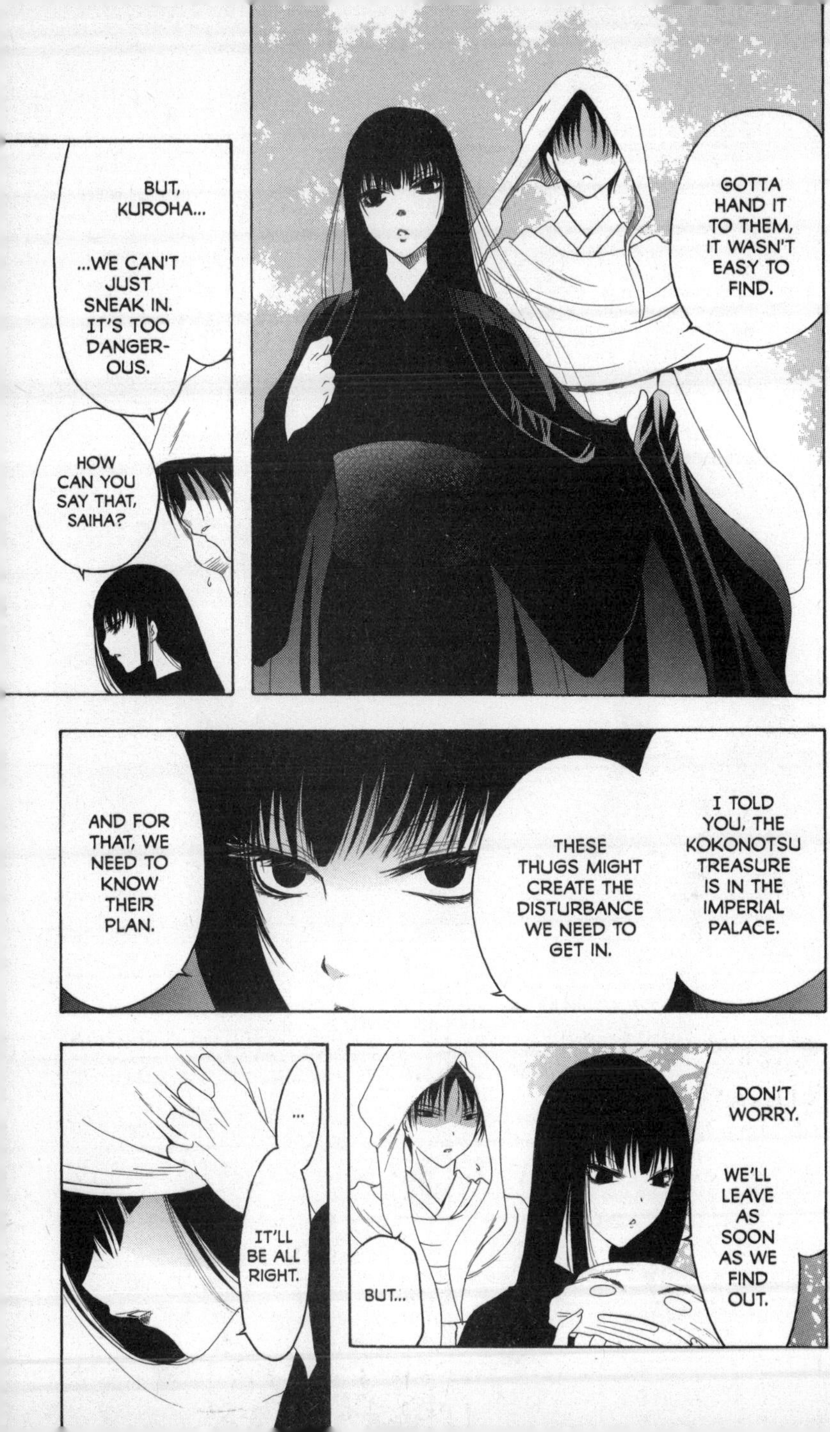
GOTTA HAND IT TO THEM, IT WASN'T EASY TO FIND.
BUT, KUROHA...
...WE CAN'T JUST SNEAK IN. IT'S TOO DANGER-OUS.
HOW CAN YOU SAY THAT, SAIHA?
I TOLD YOU, THE KOKONOTSU TREASURE IS IN THE IMPERIAL PALACE.
THESE THUGS MIGHT CREATE THE DISTURBANCE WE NEED TO GET IN.
AND FOR THAT, WE NEED TO KNOW THEIR PLAN.
DON'T WORRY.
WE'LL LEAVE AS SOON AS WE FIND OUT.
BUT...
...
IT'LL BE ALL RIGHT.

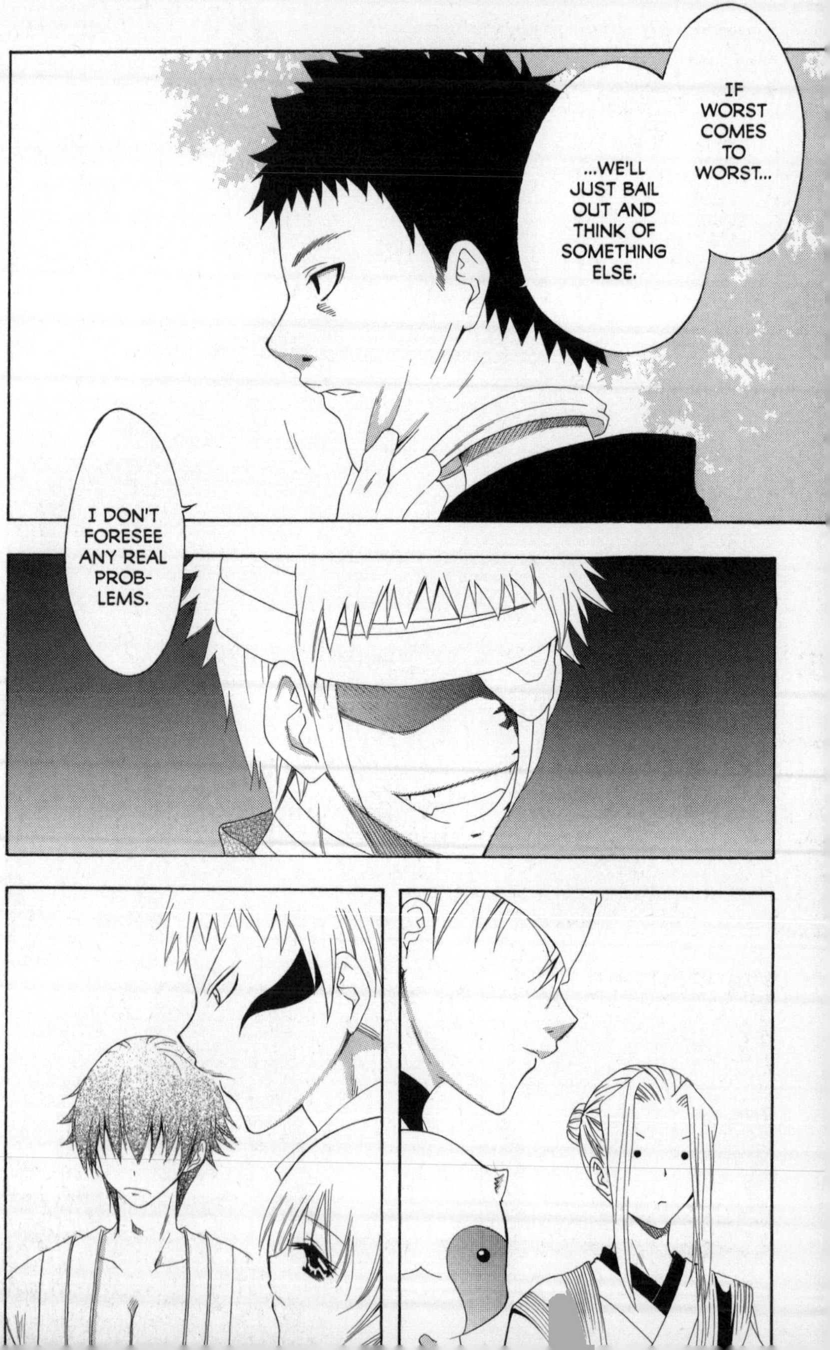
IF WORST COMES TO WORST...
...WE'LL JUST BAIL OUT AND THINK OF SOMETHING ELSE.
I DON'T FORESEE ANY REAL PROB-LEMS.

Chapter 95 Infiltration

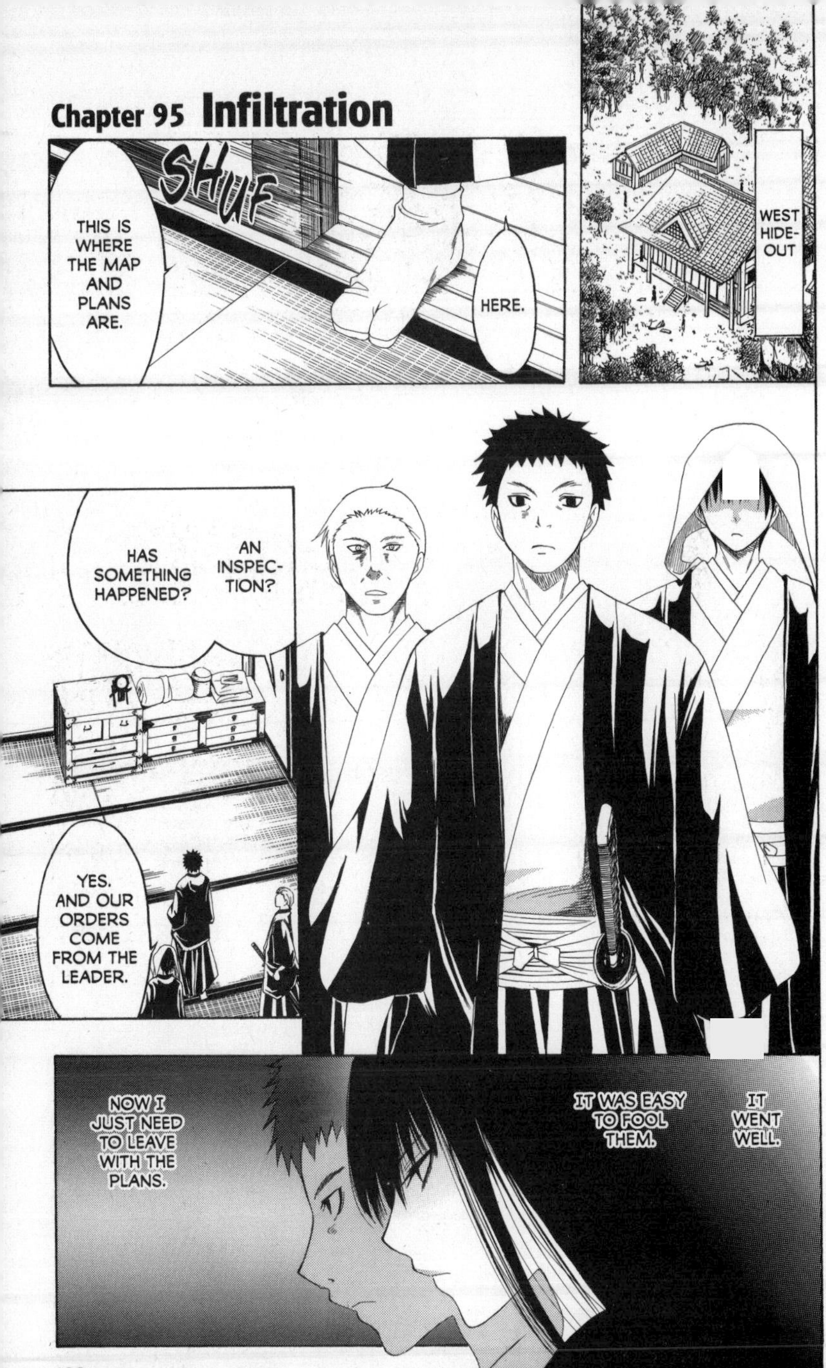
WEST HIDE-OUT
SHUF
HERE.
THIS IS WHERE THE MAP AND PLANS ARE.
AN INSPECTION?
HAS SOMETHING HAPPENED?
YES. AND OUR ORDERS COME FROM THE LEADER.
IT WENT WELL.
IT WAS EASY TO FOOL THEM.
NOW I JUST NEED TO LEAVE WITH THE PLANS.

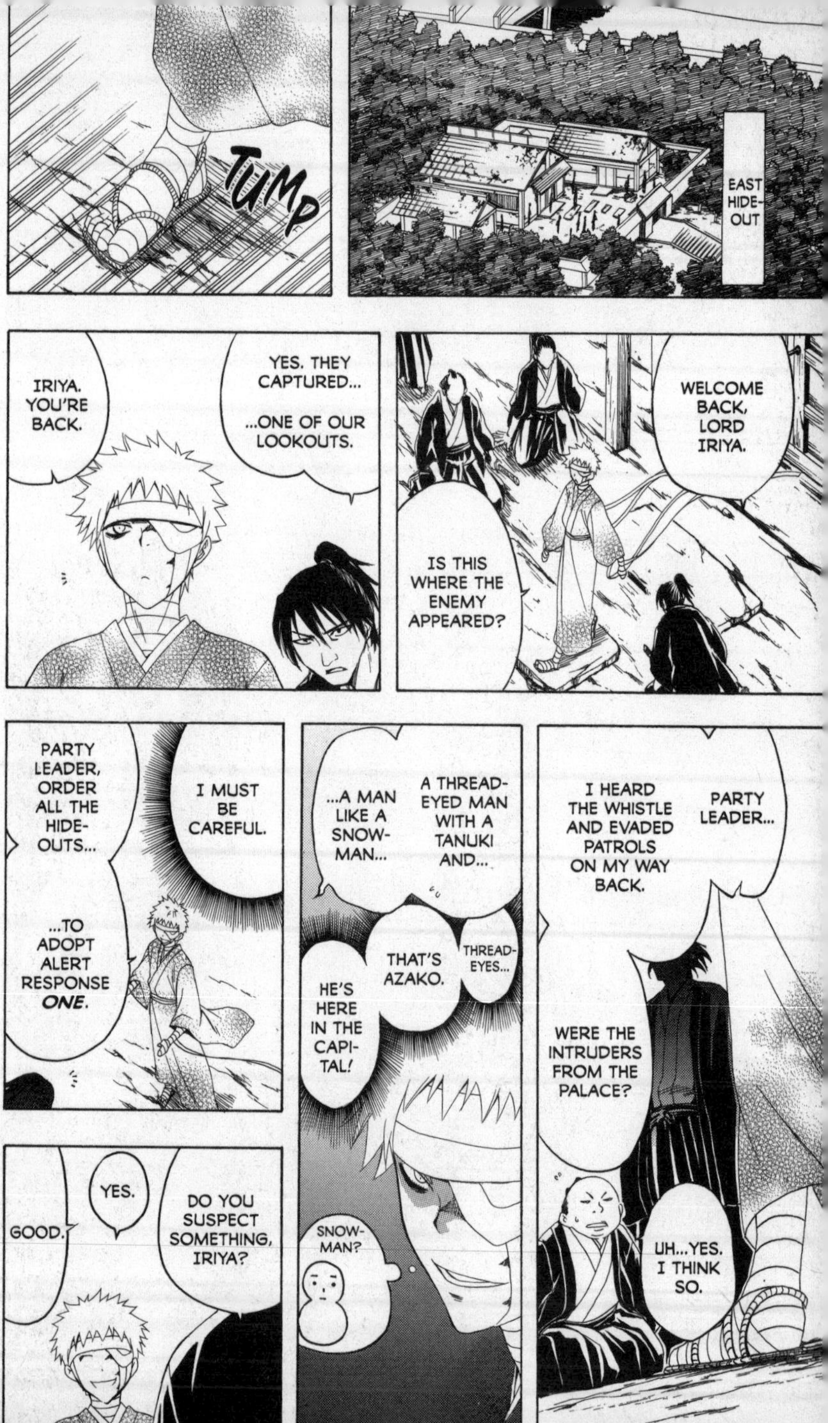
EAST HIDE-OUT
TUMP
WELCOME BACK, LORD IRIYA.
IS THIS WHERE THE ENEMY APPEARED?
YES. THEY CAPTURED...
...ONE OF OUR LOOKOUTS.
IRIYA. YOU'RE BACK.
PARTY LEADER...
I HEARD THE WHISTLE AND EVADED PATROLS ON MY WAY BACK.
WERE THE INTRUDERS FROM THE PALACE?
UH...YES. I THINK SO.
A THREAD-EYED MAN WITH A TANUKI AND...
...A MAN LIKE A SNOW-MAN...
THREAD-EYES...
THAT'S AZAKO.
HE'S HERE IN THE CAPI-TAL!
SNOW-MAN?
I MUST BE CAREFUL.
PARTY LEADER, ORDER ALL THE HIDE-OUTS...
...TO ADOPT ALERT RESPONSE *ONE*.
DO YOU SUSPECT SOMETHING, IRIYA?
YES.
GOOD.

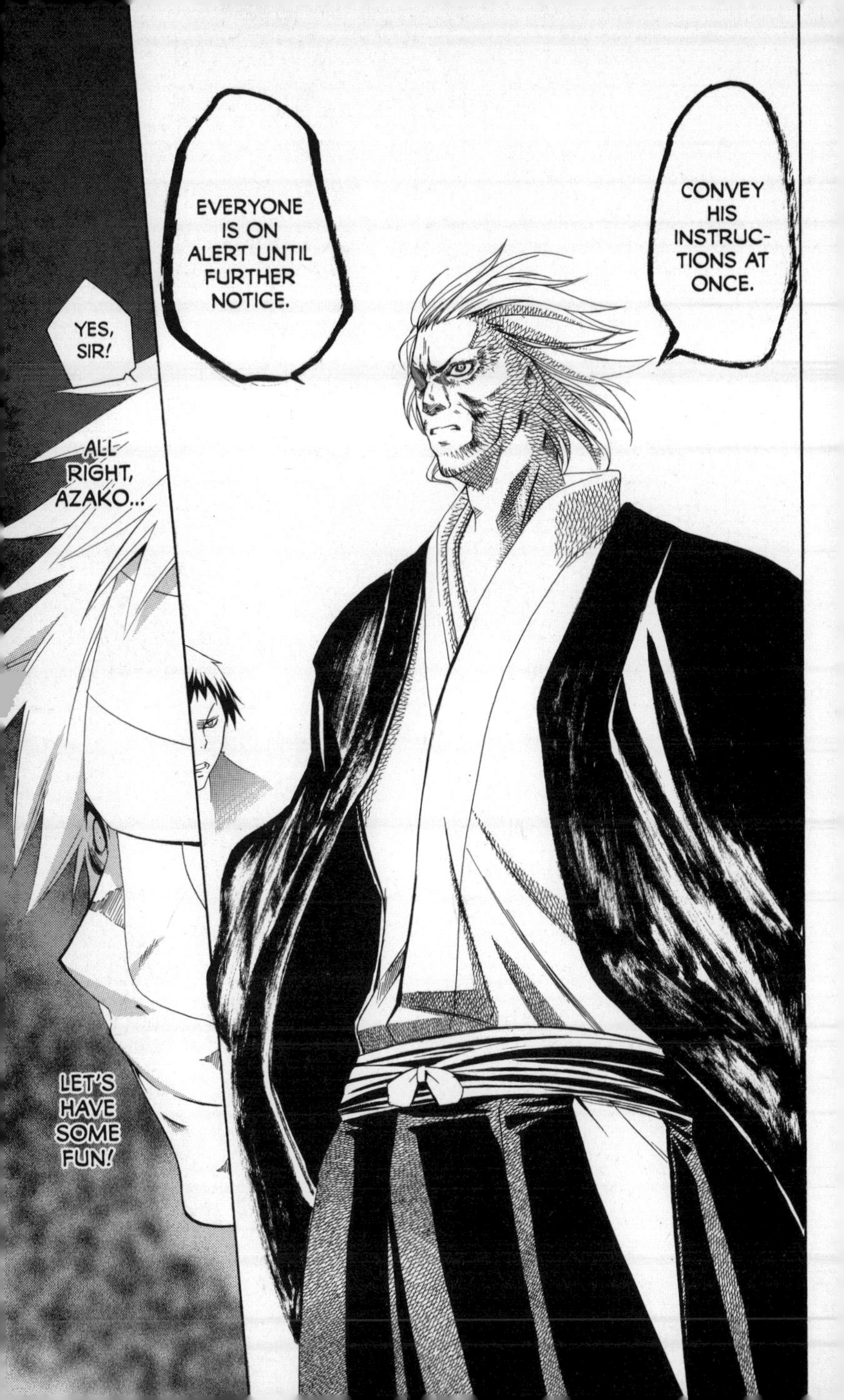
CONVEY HIS INSTRUCTIONS AT ONCE.
EVERYONE IS ON ALERT UNTIL FURTHER NOTICE.
YES, SIR!
ALL RIGHT, AZAKO...
LET'S HAVE SOME FUN!

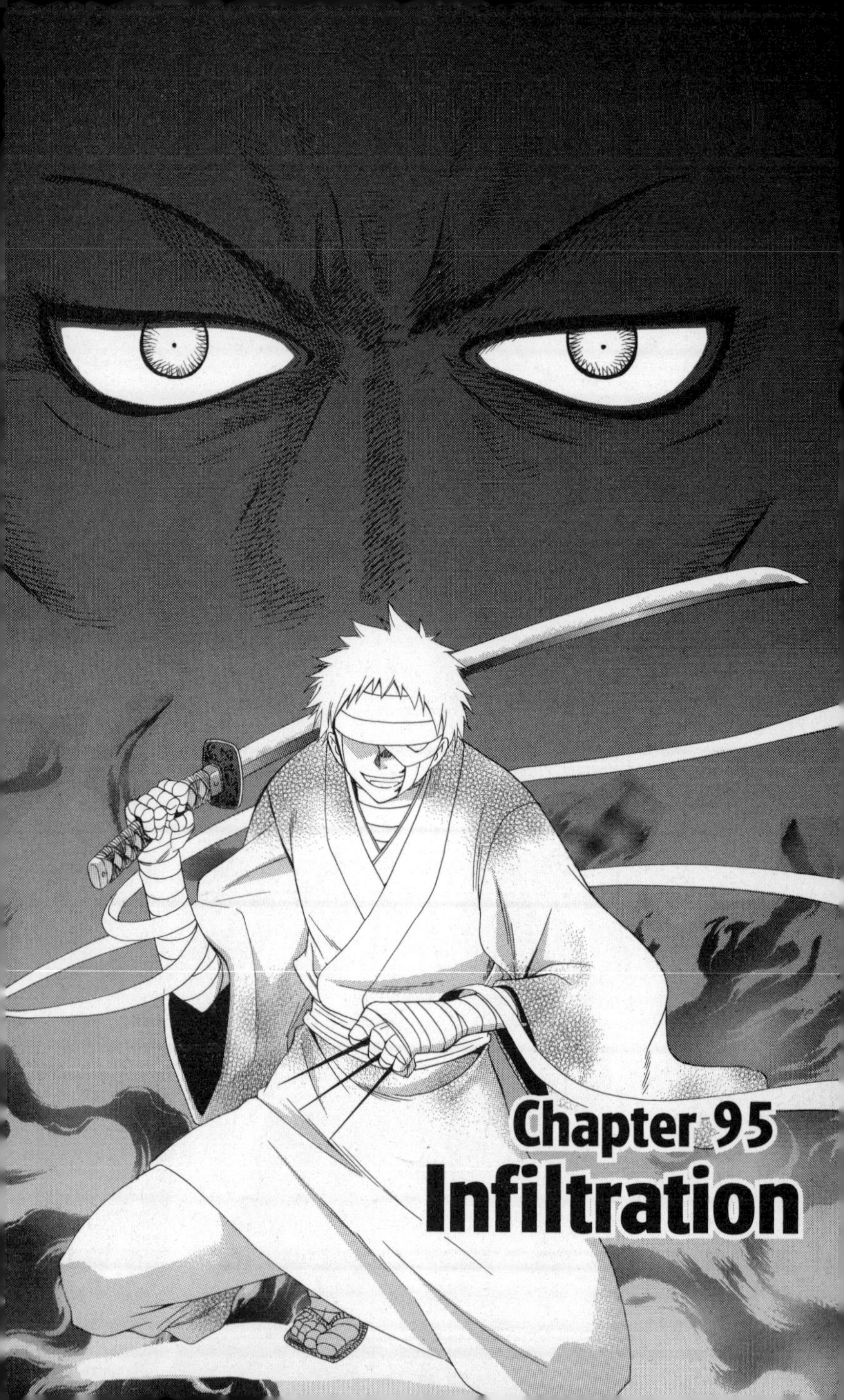
Chapter 95
Infiltration

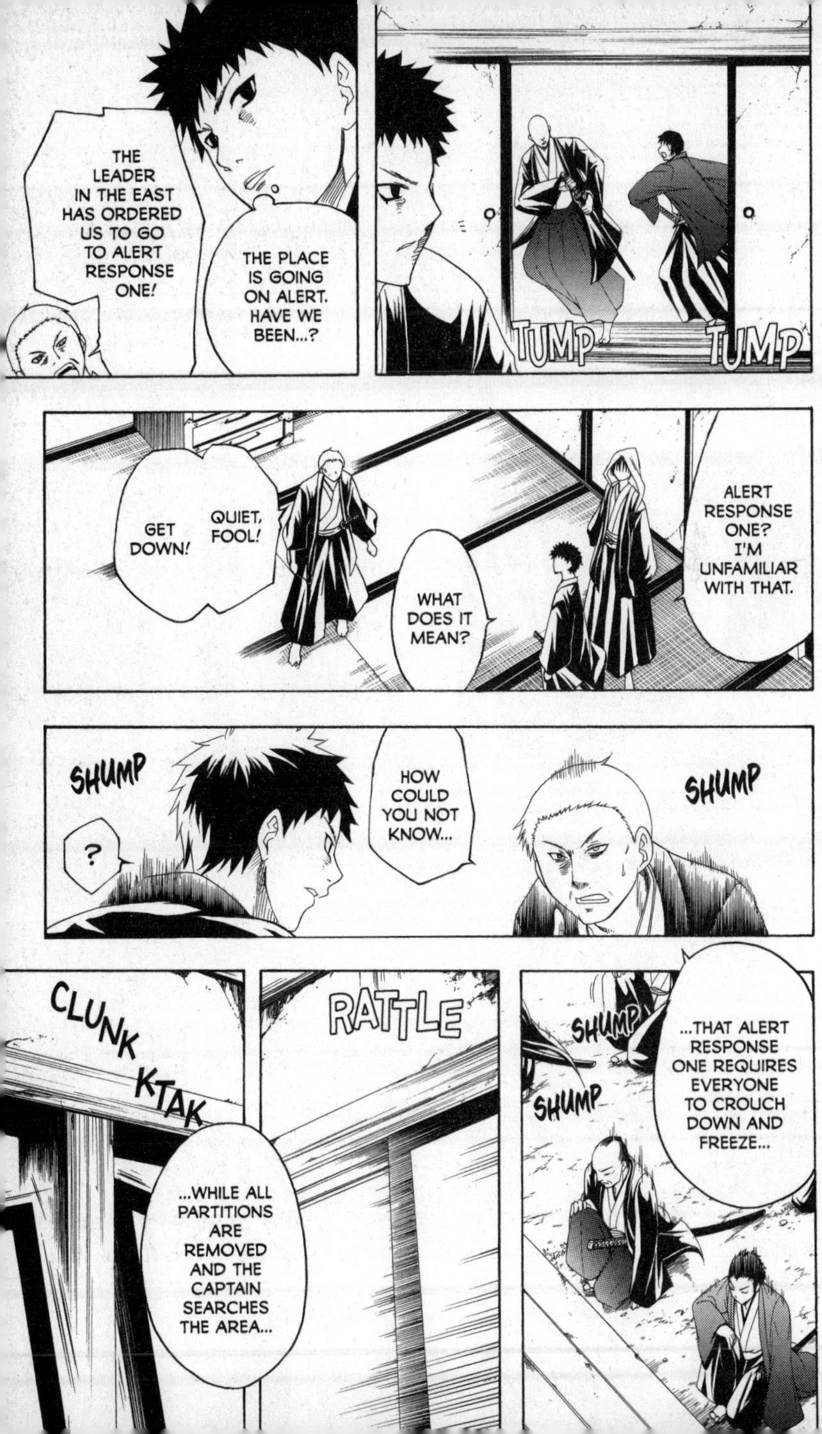
TUMP
TUMP
THE PLACE IS GOING ON ALERT. HAVE WE BEEN...?
THE LEADER IN THE EAST HAS ORDERED US TO GO TO ALERT RESPONSE ONE!
ALERT RESPONSE ONE? I'M UNFAMILIAR WITH THAT.
WHAT DOES IT MEAN?
QUIET, FOOL!
GET DOWN!
SHUMP
HOW COULD YOU NOT KNOW...
?
SHUMP
...THAT ALERT RESPONSE ONE REQUIRES EVERYONE TO CROUCH DOWN AND FREEZE...
SHUMP
SHUMP
RATTLE
CLUNK
KTAK
...WHILE ALL PARTITIONS ARE REMOVED AND THE CAPTAIN SEARCHES THE AREA...

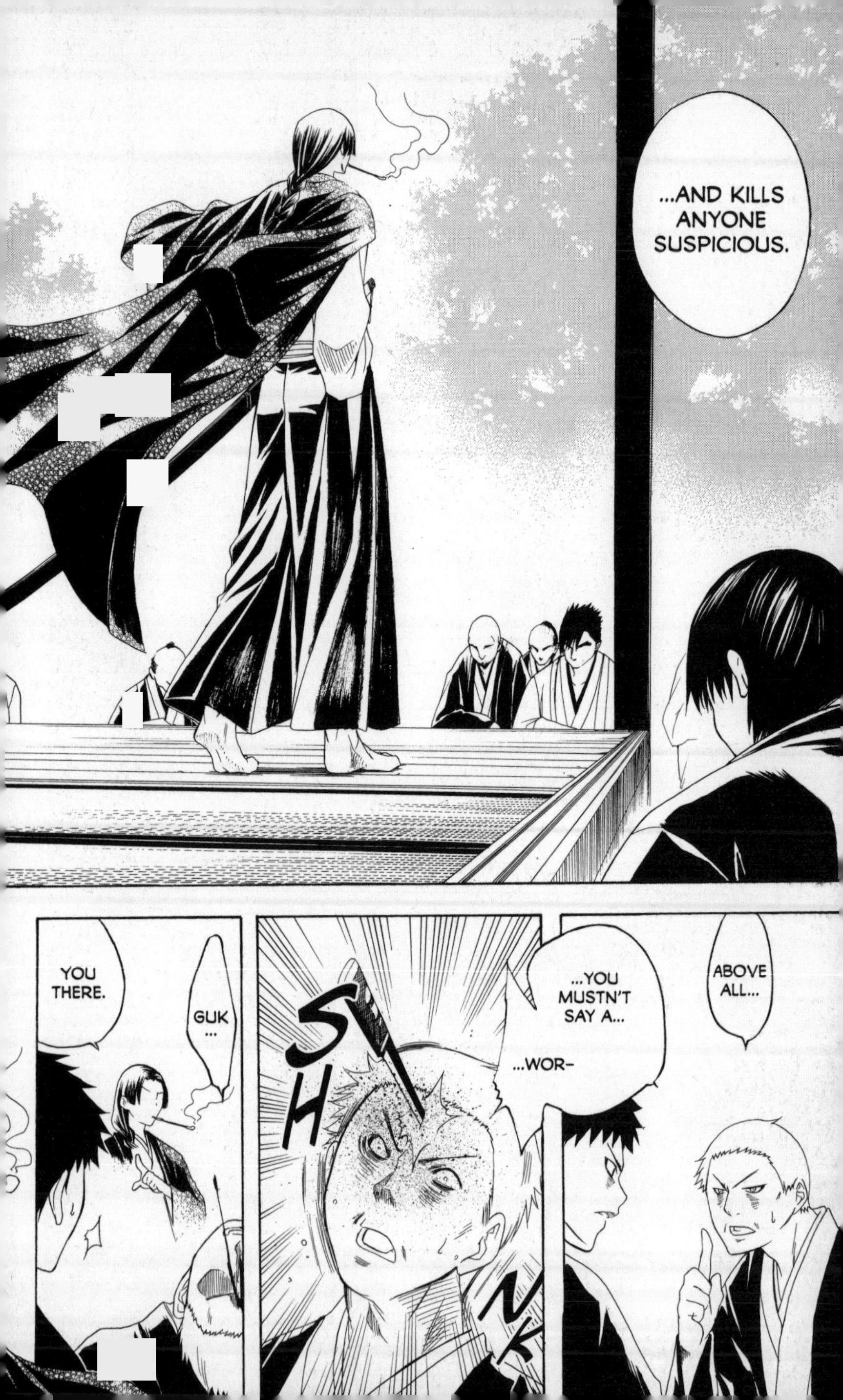
...AND KILLS ANYONE SUSPICIOUS.
ABOVE ALL...
...YOU MUSTN'T SAY A...
...WOR-
SHNK
GUK ...
YOU THERE.

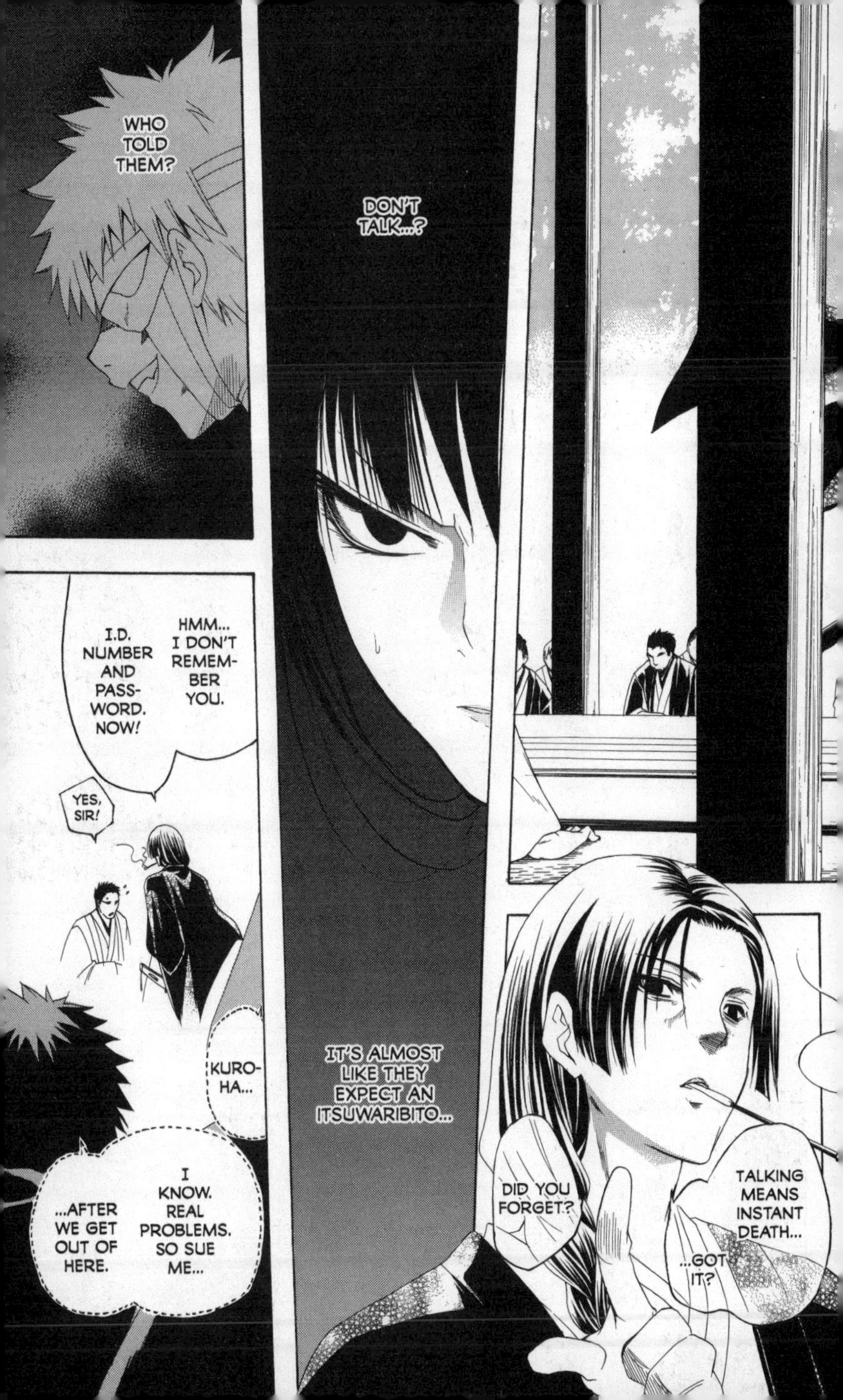

TALKING MEANS INSTANT DEATH...
...GOT IT?
DID YOU FORGET?
DON'T TALK...?
IT'S ALMOST LIKE THEY EXPECT AN ITSUWARIBITO...
WHO TOLD THEM?
HMM... I DON'T REMEM-BER YOU.
I.D. NUMBER AND PASS-WORD. NOW!
YES, SIR!
KURO-HA...
I KNOW. REAL PROBLEMS. SO SUE ME...
...AFTER WE GET OUT OF HERE.

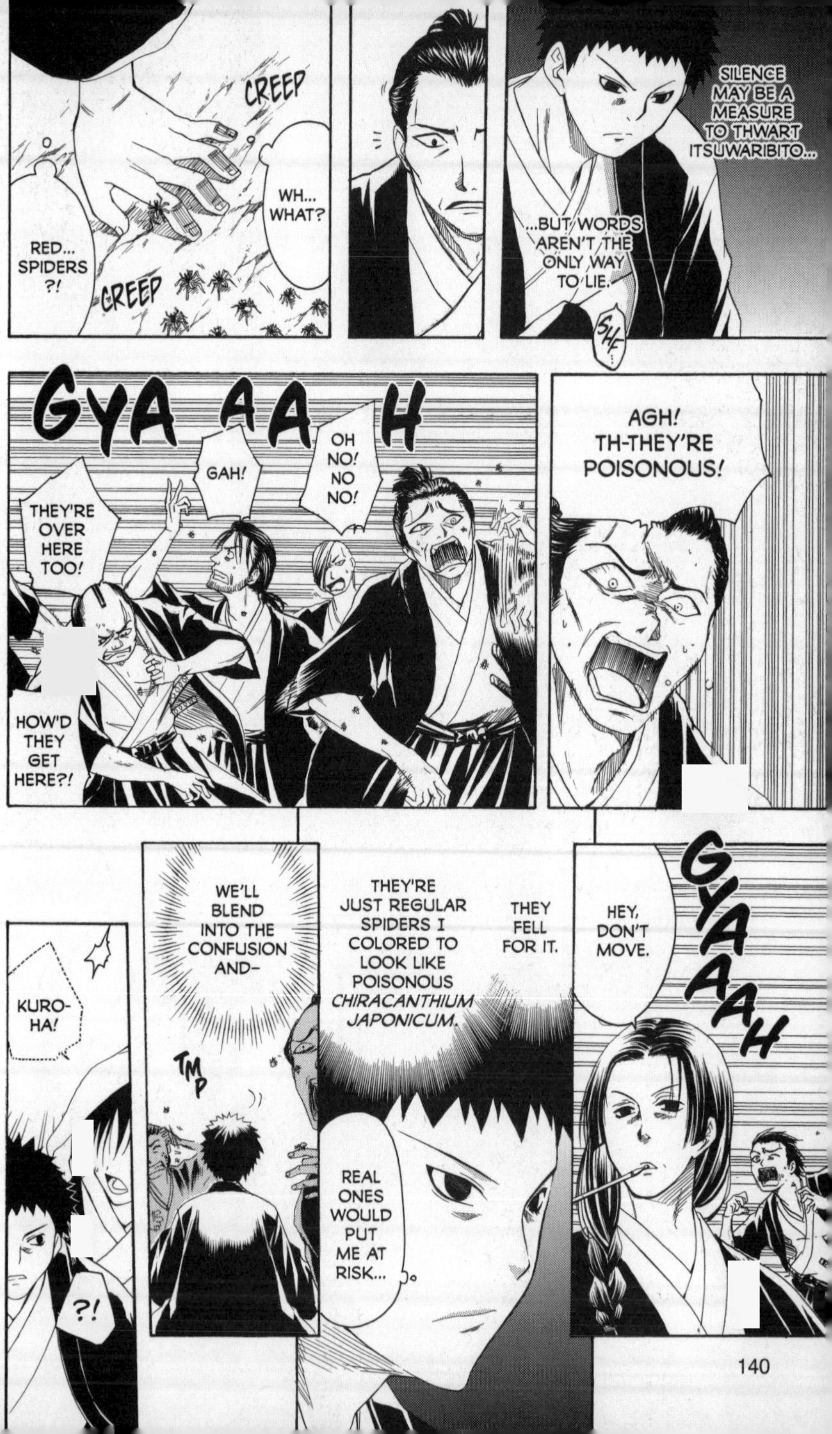
SILENCE MAY BE A MEASURE TO THWART ITSUWARIBITO...
...BUT WORDS AREN'T THE ONLY WAY TO LIE.
SHF
CREEP
WH... WHAT?
RED... SPIDERS ?!
CREEP
AGH! TH-THEY'RE POISONOUS!
GYA AA H
OH NO! NO NO!
GAH!
THEY'RE OVER HERE TOO!
HOW'D THEY GET HERE?!
GYAAAH
HEY, DON'T MOVE.
THEY FELL FOR IT.
THEY'RE JUST REGULAR SPIDERS I COLORED TO LOOK LIKE POISONOUS *CHIRACANTHIUM JAPONICUM*.
REAL ONES WOULD PUT ME AT RISK...
WE'LL BLEND INTO THE CONFUSION AND–
TMP
KURO-HA!
?!

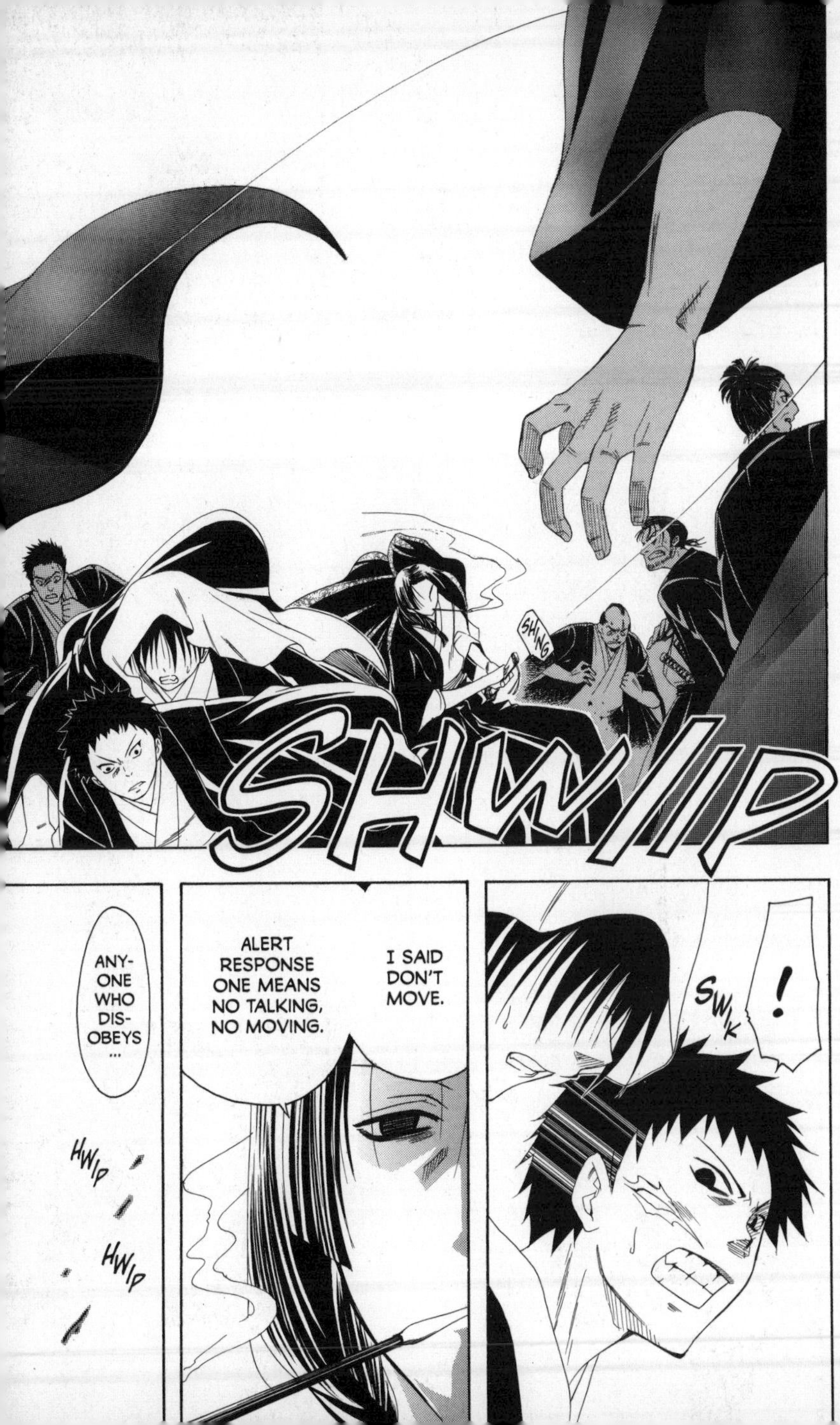
SHING
SHWIP
SWIK
!
I SAID DON'T MOVE.
ALERT RESPONSE ONE MEANS NO TALKING, NO MOVING.
ANY-ONE WHO DIS-OBEYS ...
HWIP
HWIP

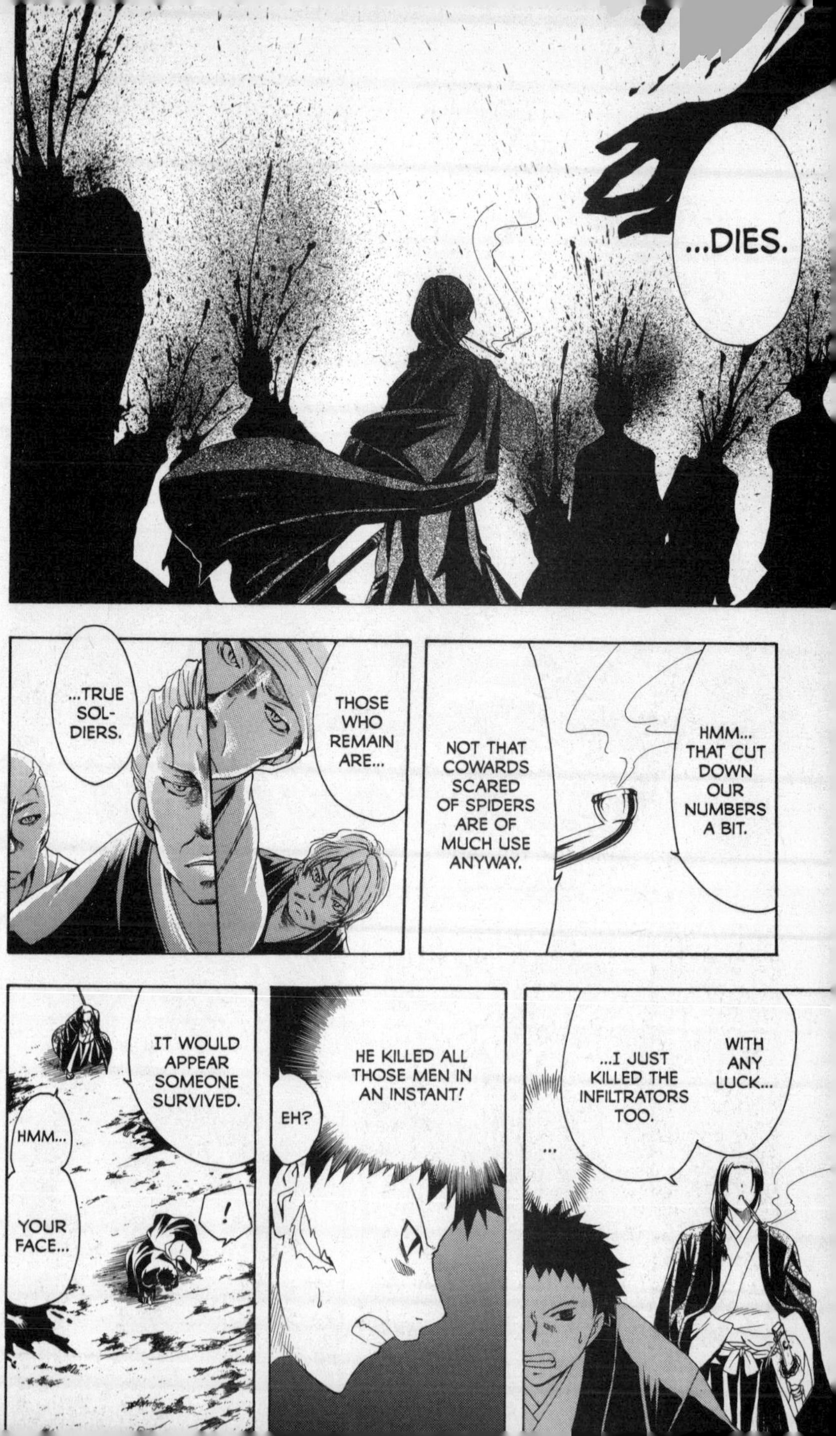
...DIES.
HMM... THAT CUT DOWN OUR NUMBERS A BIT.
NOT THAT COWARDS SCARED OF SPIDERS ARE OF MUCH USE ANYWAY.
THOSE WHO REMAIN ARE...
...TRUE SOL-DIERS.
WITH ANY LUCK...
...I JUST KILLED THE INFILTRATORS TOO.
...
HE KILLED ALL THOSE MEN IN AN INSTANT!
EH?
IT WOULD APPEAR SOMEONE SURVIVED.
HMM...
!
YOUR FACE...

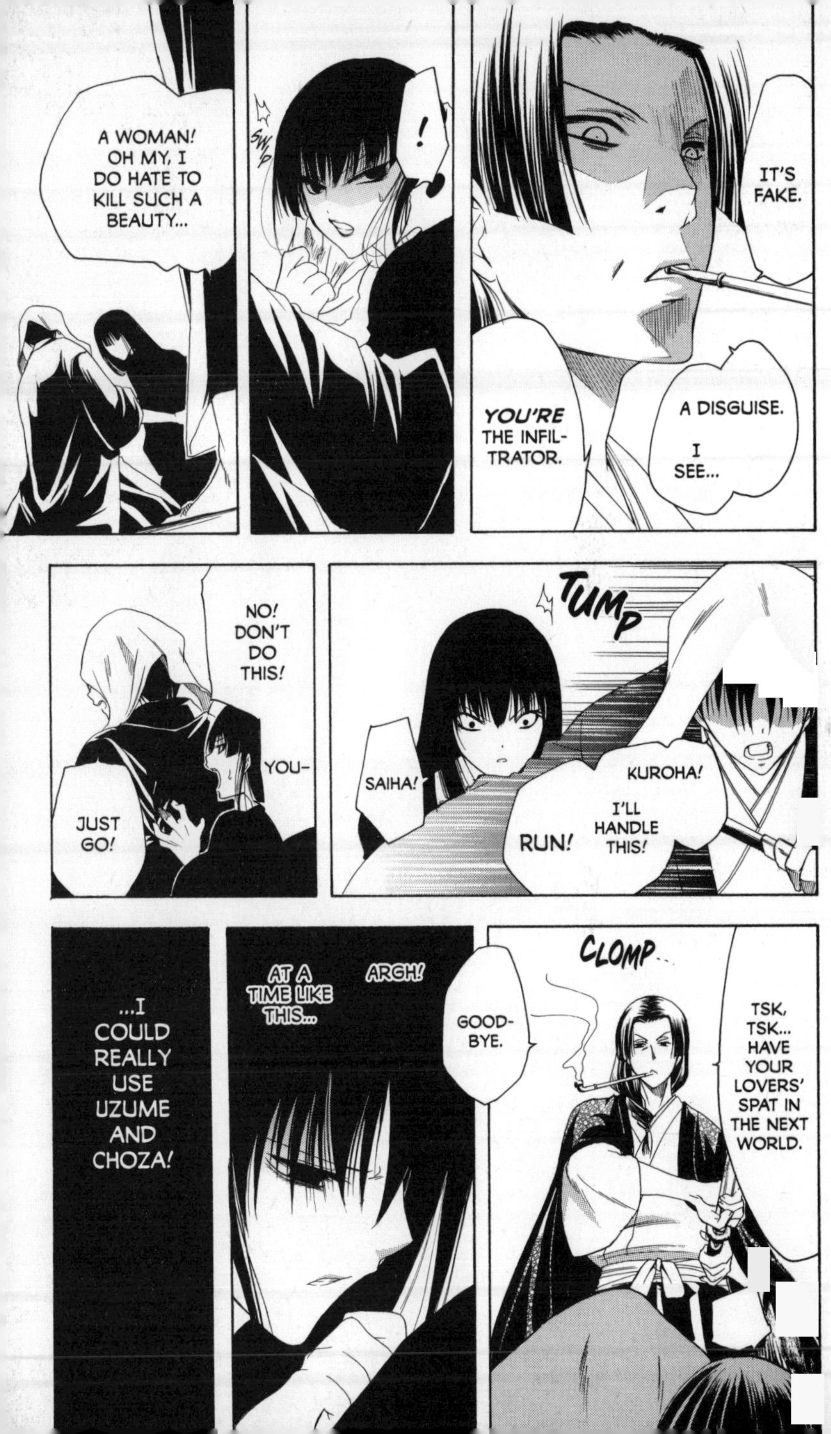
IT'S FAKE.
A DISGUISE. I SEE...
YOU'RE THE INFILTRATOR.
!
A WOMAN! OH MY, I DO HATE TO KILL SUCH A BEAUTY...
TUMP
KUROHA! I'LL HANDLE THIS!
RUN!
SAIHA!
NO! DON'T DO THIS!
YOU-
JUST GO!
CLOMP...
TSK, TSK... HAVE YOUR LOVERS' SPAT IN THE NEXT WORLD.
GOOD-BYE.
ARGH!
AT A TIME LIKE THIS...
...I COULD REALLY USE UZUME AND CHOZA!

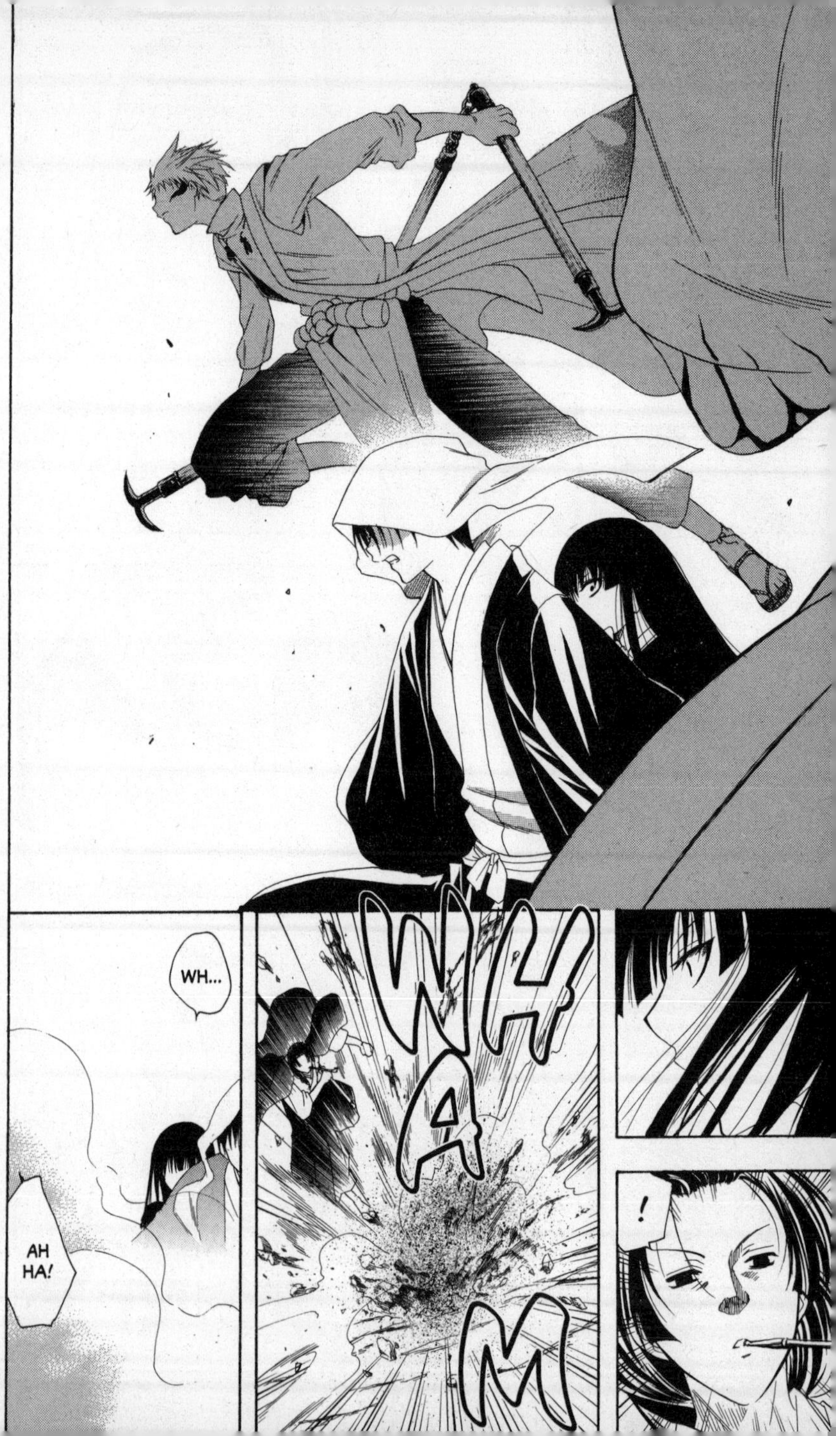
!
WHAM
WH...
AH HA!

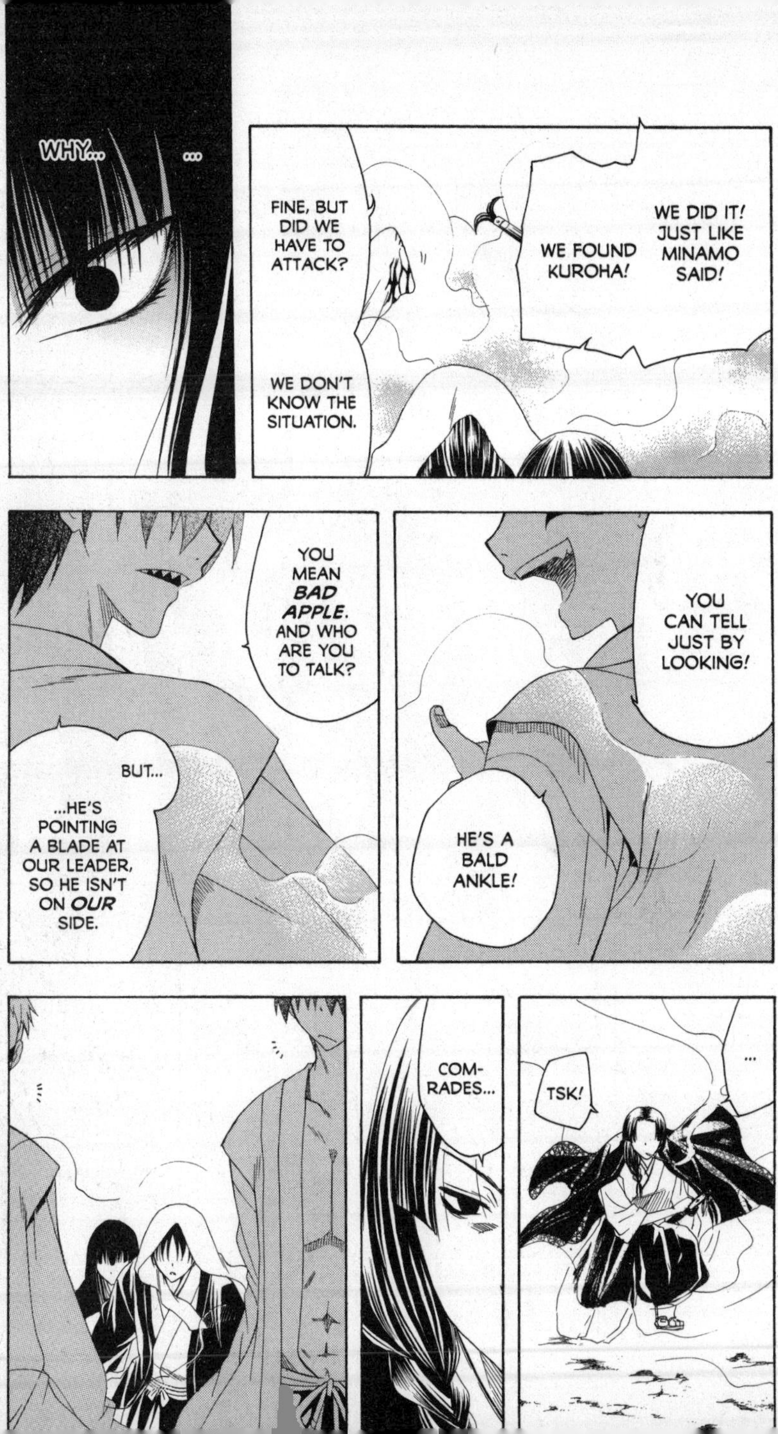
WE DID IT! JUST LIKE MINAMO SAID!
WE FOUND KUROHA!
FINE, BUT DID WE HAVE TO ATTACK?
WE DON'T KNOW THE SITUATION.
...
WHY...
YOU CAN TELL JUST BY LOOKING!
HE'S A BALD ANKLE!
YOU MEAN *BAD APPLE*. AND WHO ARE YOU TO TALK?
BUT...
...HE'S POINTING A BLADE AT OUR LEADER, SO HE ISN'T ON *OUR* SIDE.
...
TSK!
COM-RADES...

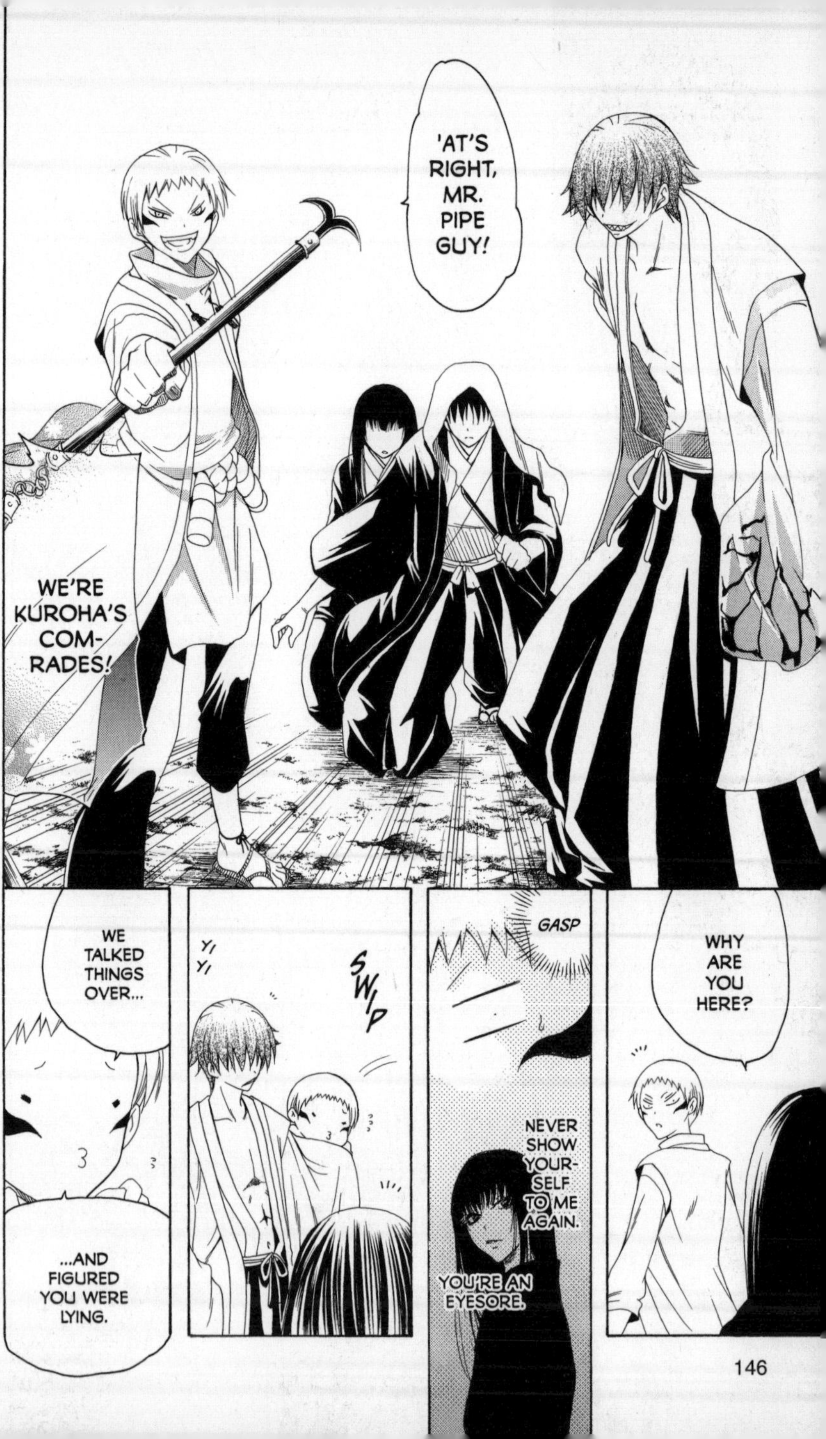
'AT'S RIGHT, MR. PIPE GUY!
WE'RE KUROHA'S COM-RADES!
WHY ARE YOU HERE?
GASP
NEVER SHOW YOUR-SELF TO ME AGAIN.
YOU'RE AN EYESORE.
SWIP
YI YI
WE TALKED THINGS OVER...
...AND FIGURED YOU WERE LYING.

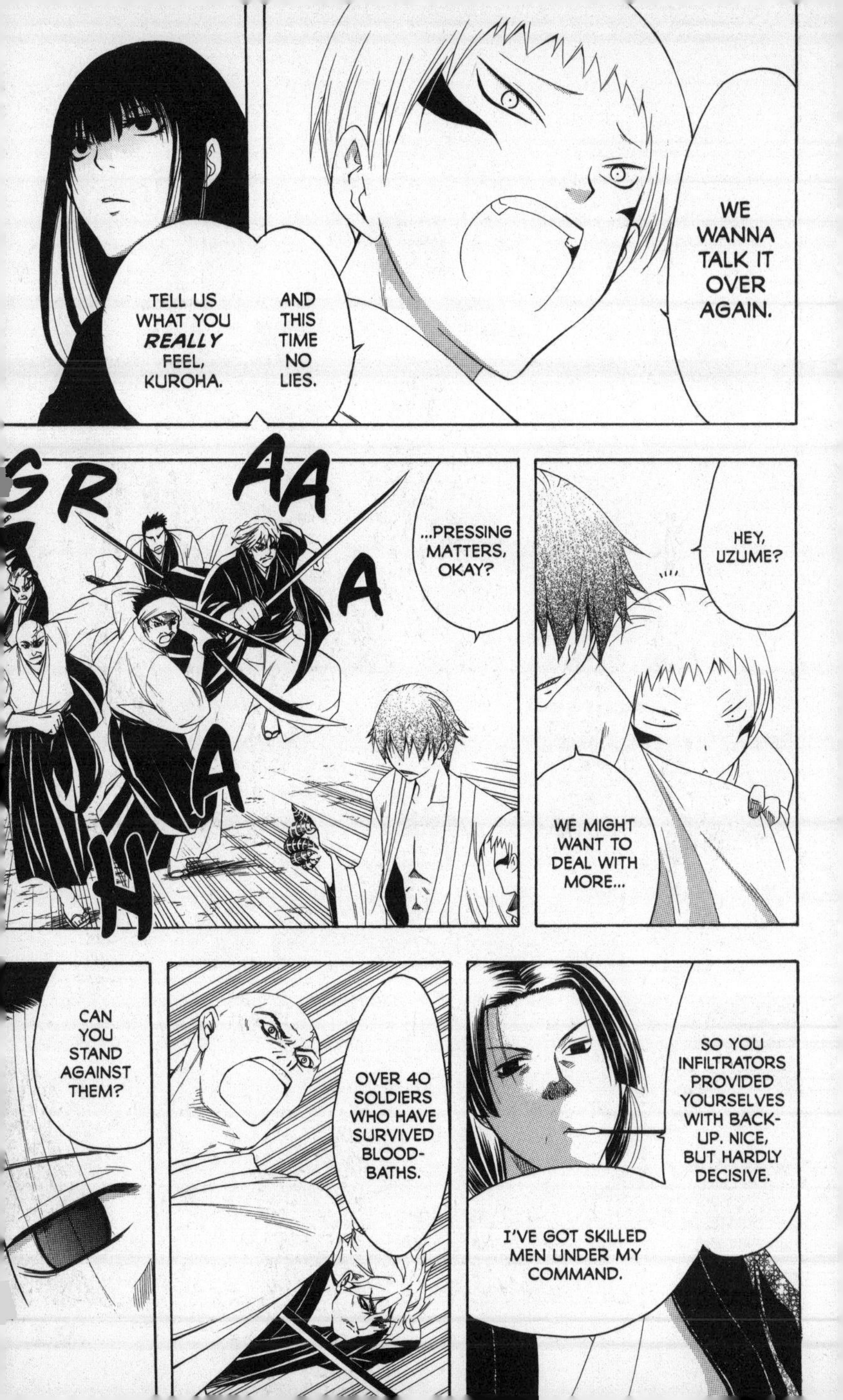
WE WANNA TALK IT OVER AGAIN.
AND THIS TIME NO LIES.
TELL US WHAT YOU *REALLY* FEEL, KUROHA.
HEY, UZUME?
WE MIGHT WANT TO DEAL WITH MORE...
...PRESSING MATTERS, OKAY?
SRAAAAH
SO YOU INFILTRATORS PROVIDED YOURSELVES WITH BACK-UP. NICE, BUT HARDLY DECISIVE.
I'VE GOT SKILLED MEN UNDER MY COMMAND.
OVER 40 SOLDIERS WHO HAVE SURVIVED BLOOD-BATHS.
CAN YOU STAND AGAINST THEM?

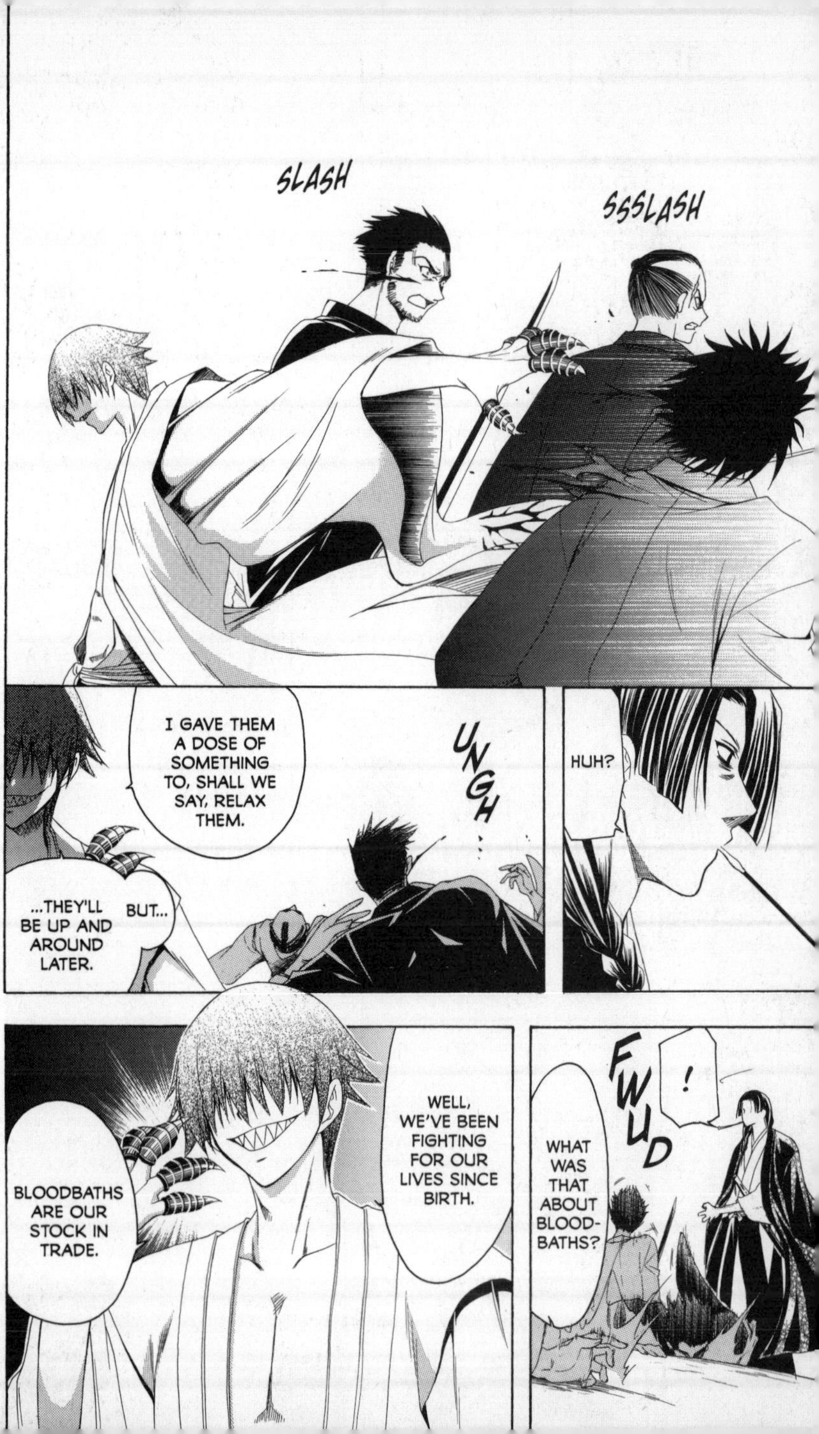
SSSLASH
SLASH
HUH?
UNGH...
I GAVE THEM A DOSE OF SOMETHING TO, SHALL WE SAY, RELAX THEM.
BUT...
...THEY'LL BE UP AND AROUND LATER.
!
FWUD
WHAT WAS THAT ABOUT BLOOD-BATHS?
WELL, WE'VE BEEN FIGHTING FOR OUR LIVES SINCE BIRTH.
BLOODBATHS ARE OUR STOCK IN TRADE.

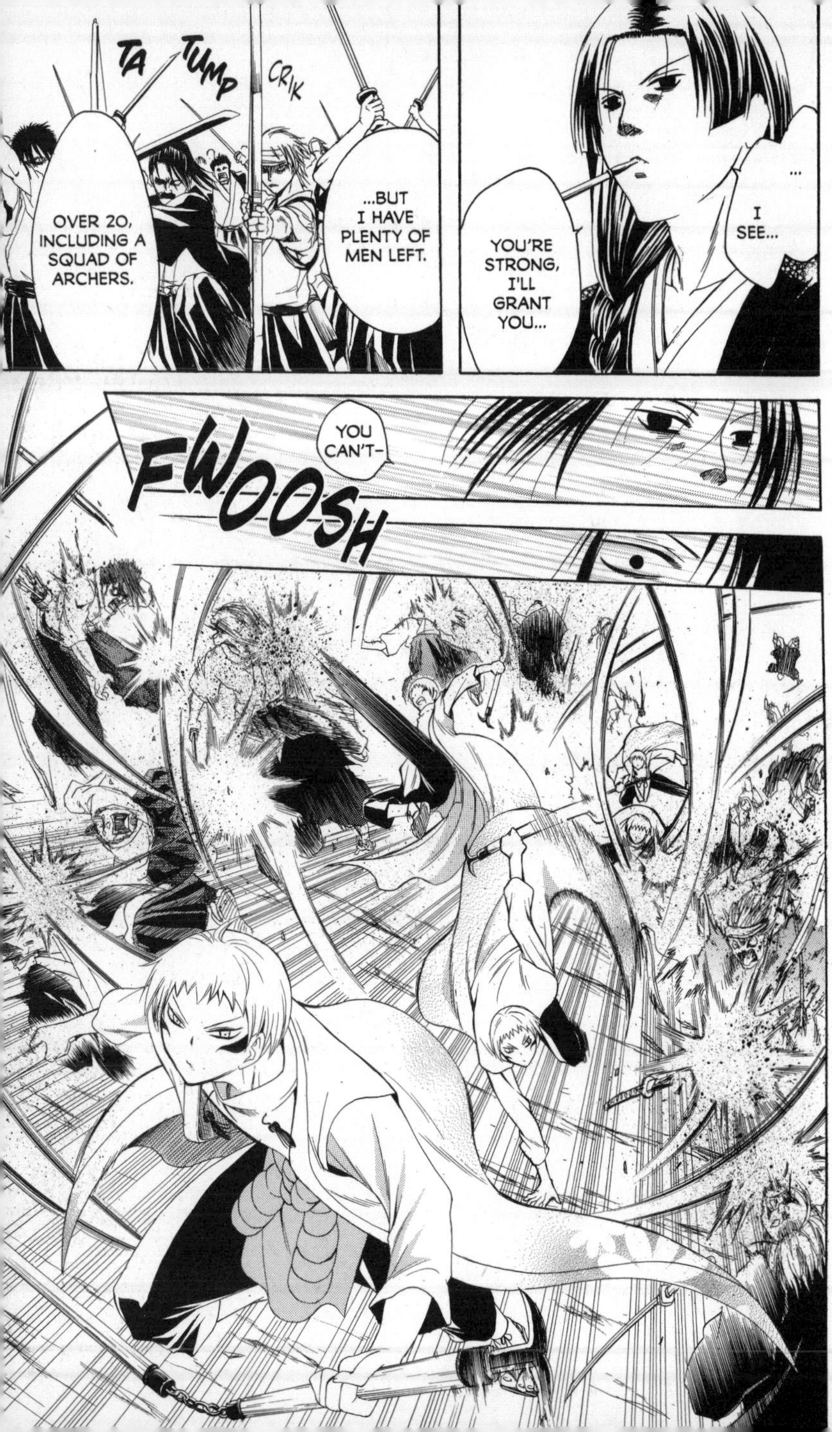
...
I SEE...
YOU'RE STRONG, I'LL GRANT YOU...
CRIK
TA TUMP
...BUT I HAVE PLENTY OF MEN LEFT.
OVER 20, INCLUDING A SQUAD OF ARCHERS.
YOU CAN'T-
FWOOSH

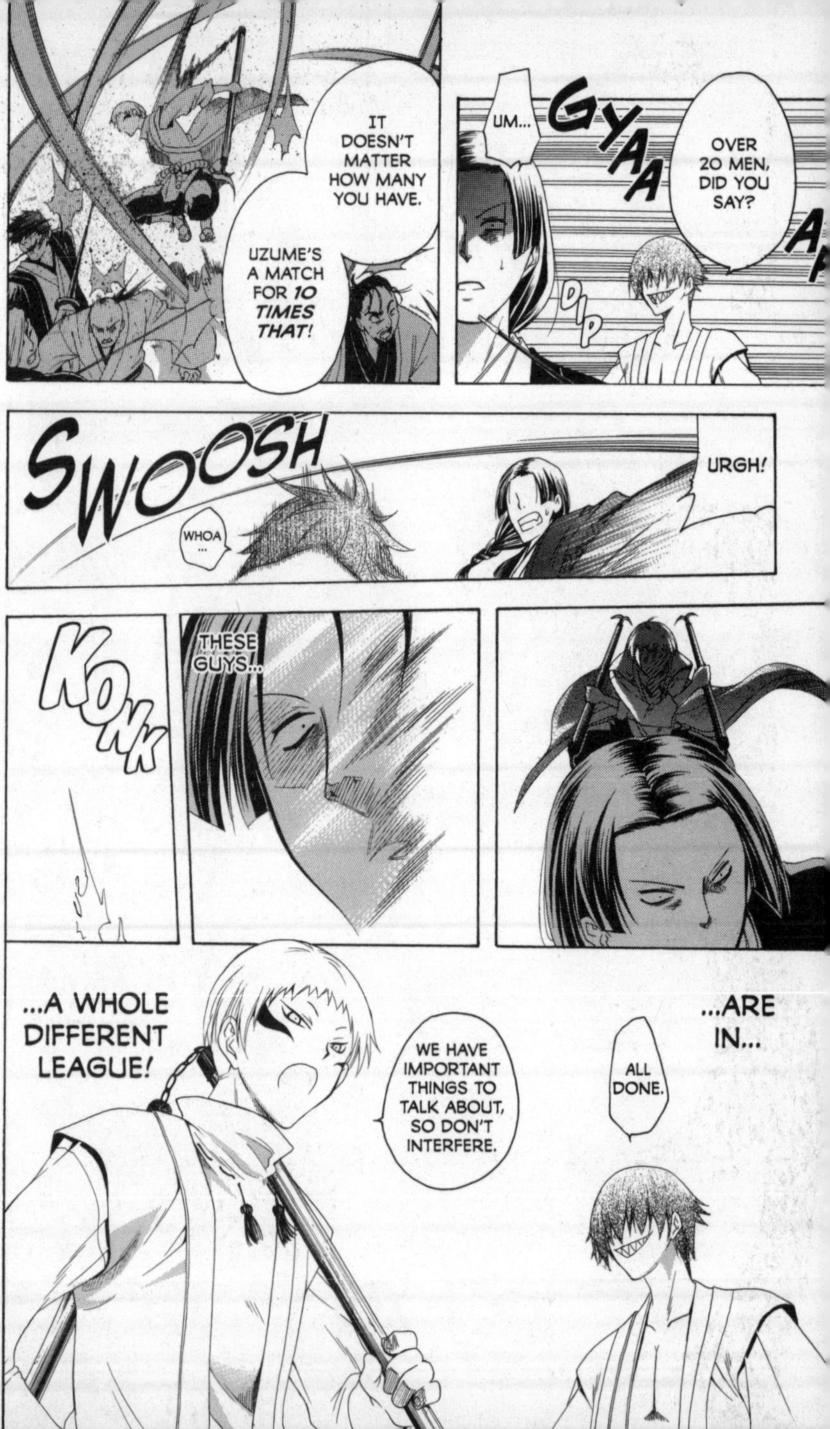
OVER 20 MEN, DID YOU SAY?
GYAA
UM...
DIP
IT DOESN'T MATTER HOW MANY YOU HAVE.
UZUME'S A MATCH FOR *10 TIMES THAT!*
URGH!
SWOOSH
WHOA ...
THESE GUYS...
KONK
...ARE IN...
ALL DONE.
WE HAVE IMPORTANT THINGS TO TALK ABOUT, SO DON'T INTERFERE.
...A WHOLE DIFFERENT LEAGUE!

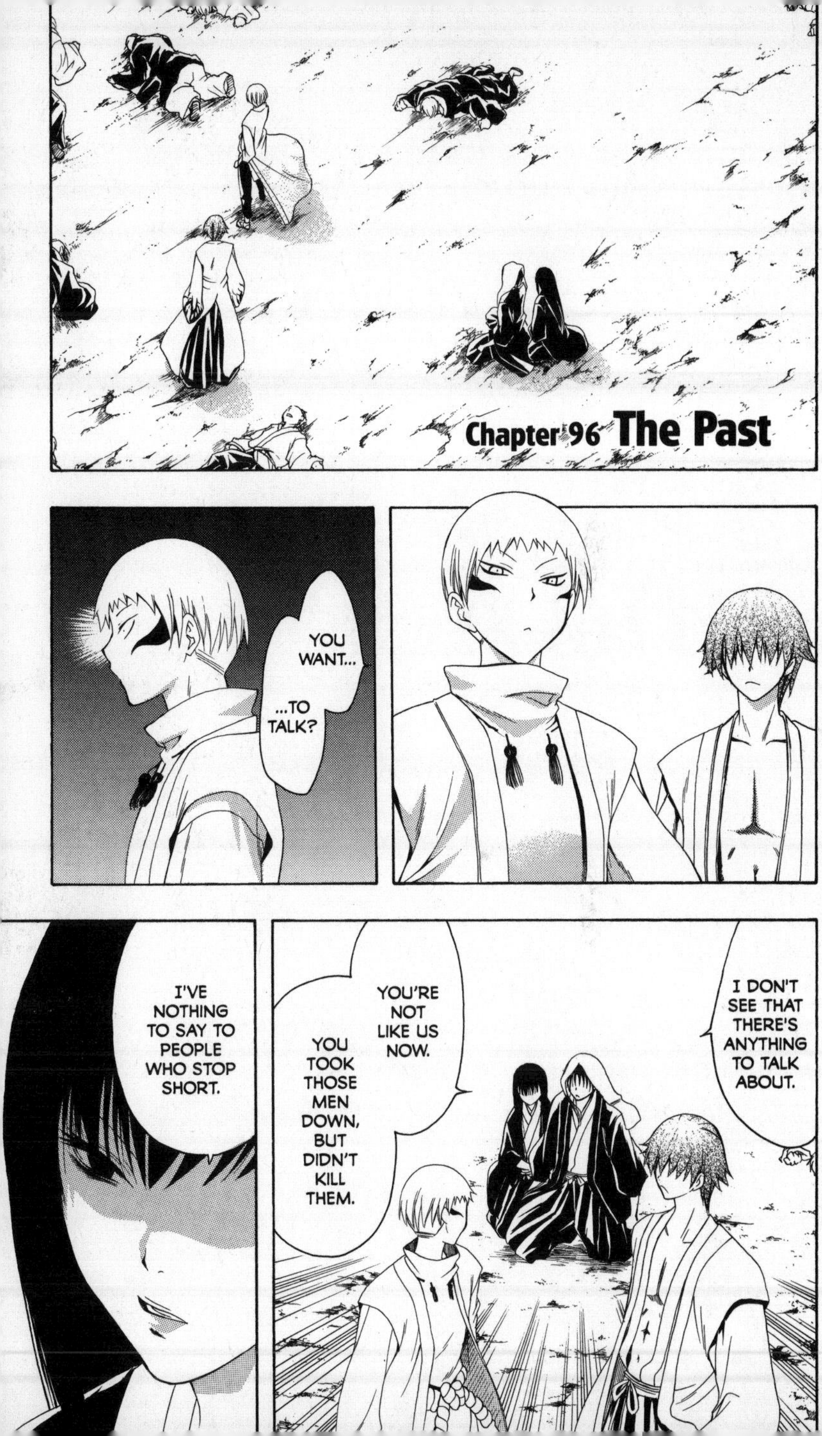
Chapter 96 The Past
YOU WANT...
...TO TALK?
I DON'T SEE THAT THERE'S ANYTHING TO TALK ABOUT.
YOU'RE NOT LIKE US NOW.
YOU TOOK THOSE MEN DOWN, BUT DIDN'T KILL THEM.
I'VE NOTHING TO SAY TO PEOPLE WHO STOP SHORT.

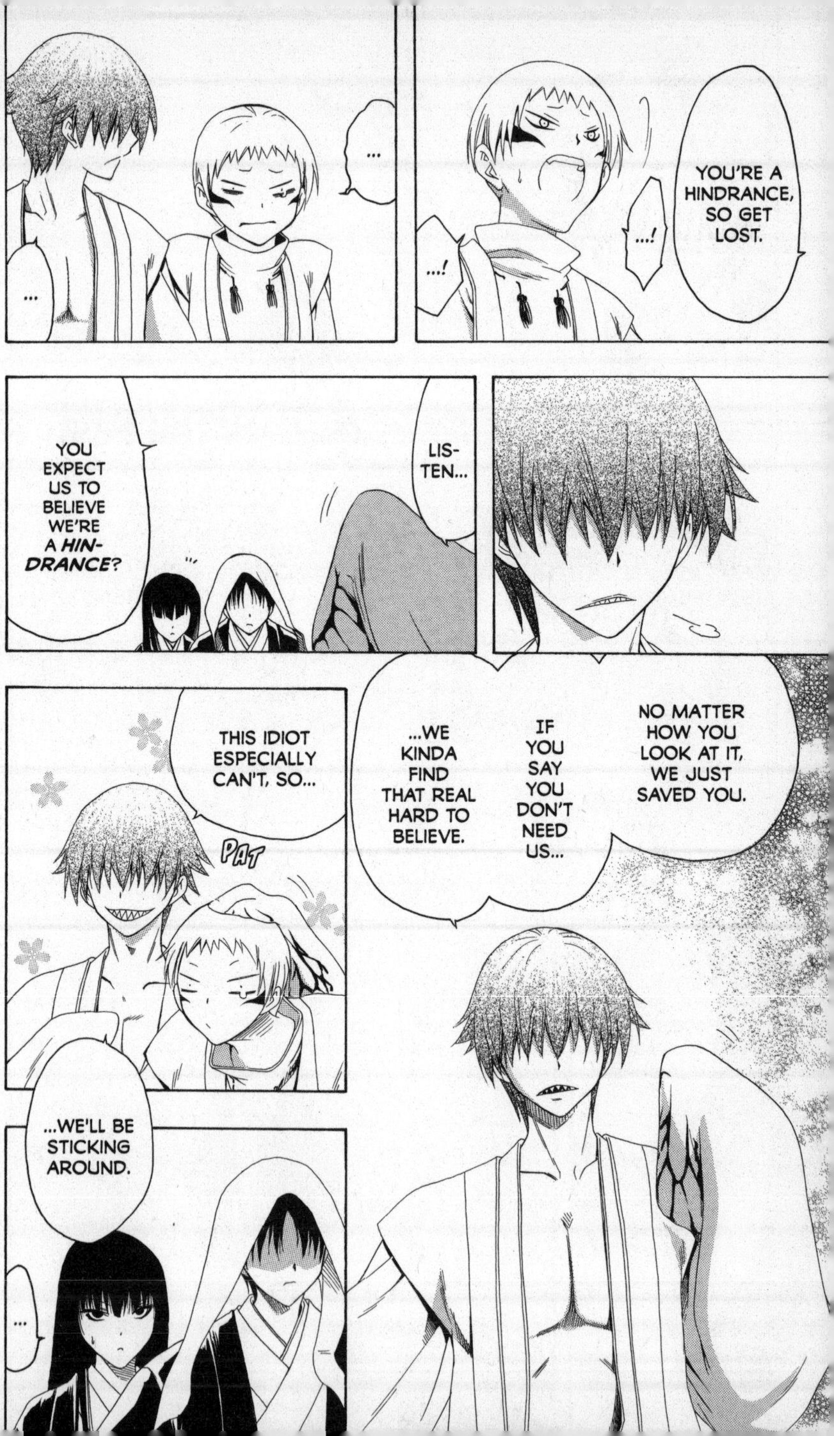
YOU'RE A HINDRANCE, SO GET LOST.
...!
...!
...
...
LIS-TEN...
YOU EXPECT US TO BELIEVE WE'RE A *HIN-DRANCE*?
NO MATTER HOW YOU LOOK AT IT, WE JUST SAVED YOU.
IF YOU SAY YOU DON'T NEED US...
...WE KINDA FIND THAT REAL HARD TO BELIEVE.
THIS IDIOT ESPECIALLY CAN'T, SO...
PAT
...WE'LL BE STICKING AROUND.
...

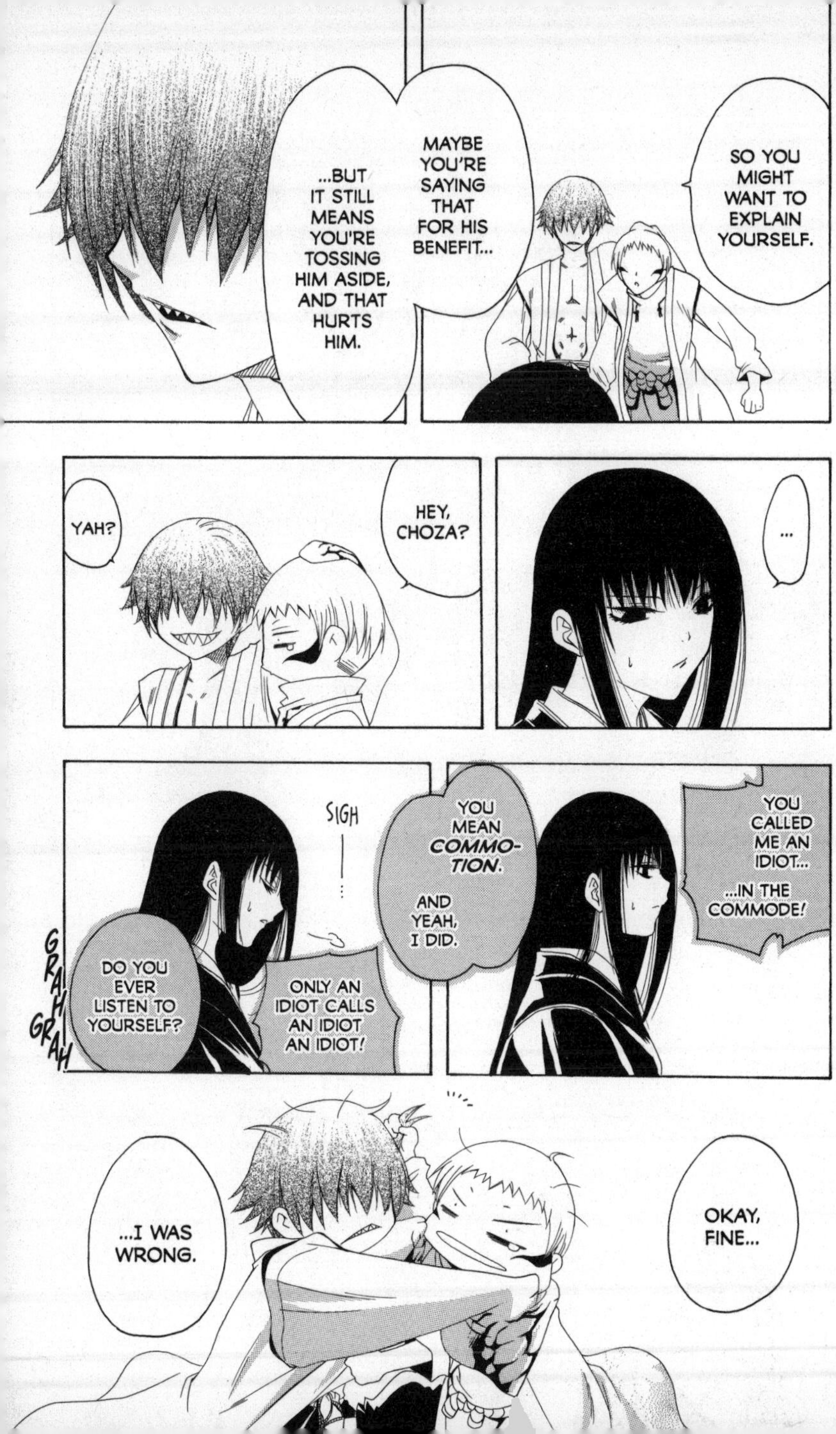
SO YOU MIGHT WANT TO EXPLAIN YOURSELF.
MAYBE YOU'RE SAYING THAT FOR HIS BENEFIT...
...BUT IT STILL MEANS YOU'RE TOSSING HIM ASIDE, AND THAT HURTS HIM.
...
HEY, CHOZA?
YAH?
YOU CALLED ME AN IDIOT...
...IN THE COMMODE!
YOU MEAN *COMMOTION*.
AND YEAH, I DID.
SIGH
ONLY AN IDIOT CALLS AN IDIOT AN IDIOT!
DO YOU EVER LISTEN TO YOURSELF?
GRAH GRAH
OKAY, FINE...
...I WAS WRONG.

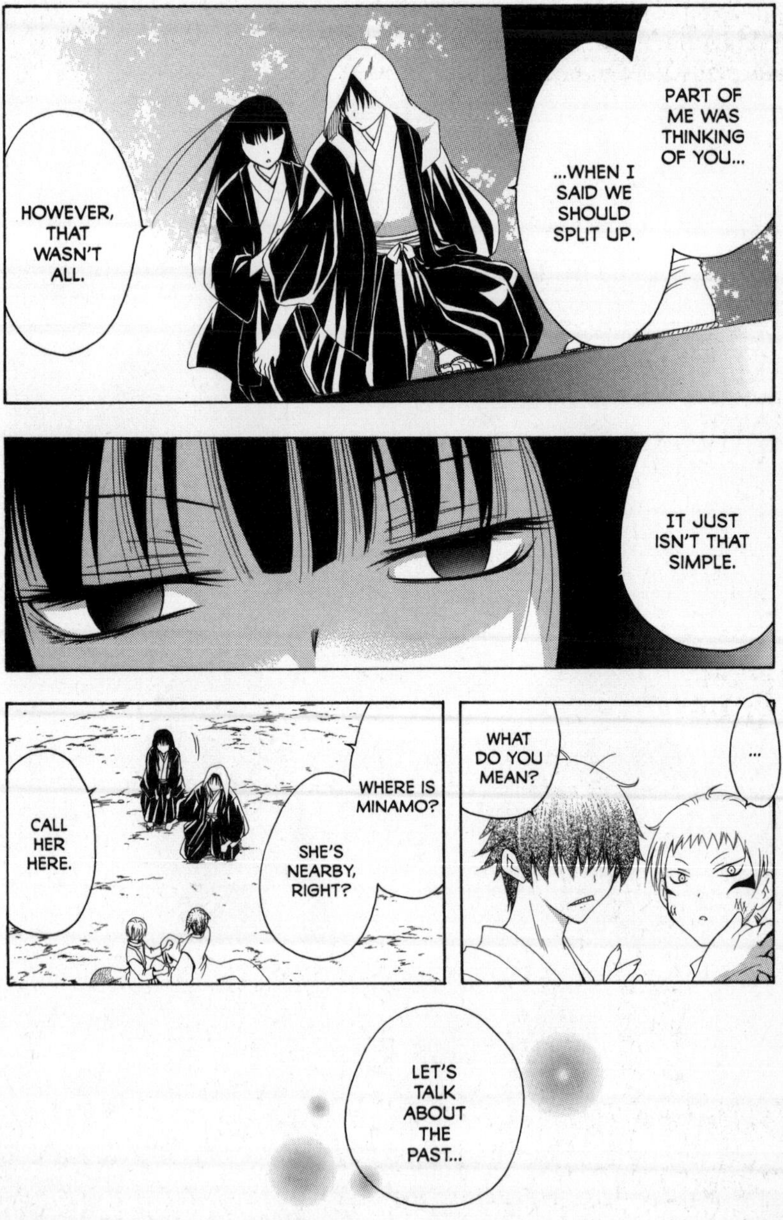
PART OF ME WAS THINKING OF YOU...
...WHEN I SAID WE SHOULD SPLIT UP.
HOWEVER, THAT WASN'T ALL.
IT JUST ISN'T THAT SIMPLE.
...
WHAT DO YOU MEAN?
WHERE IS MINAMO?
SHE'S NEARBY, RIGHT?
CALL HER HERE.
LET'S TALK ABOUT THE PAST...

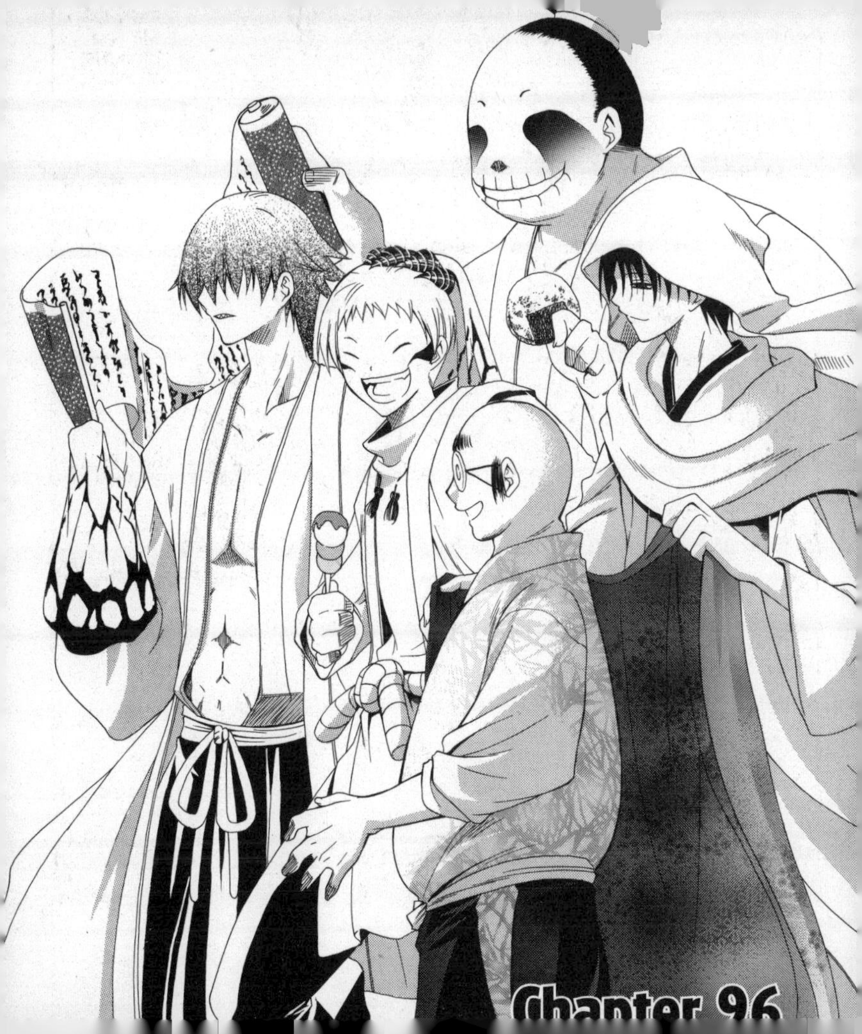
Chapter 96

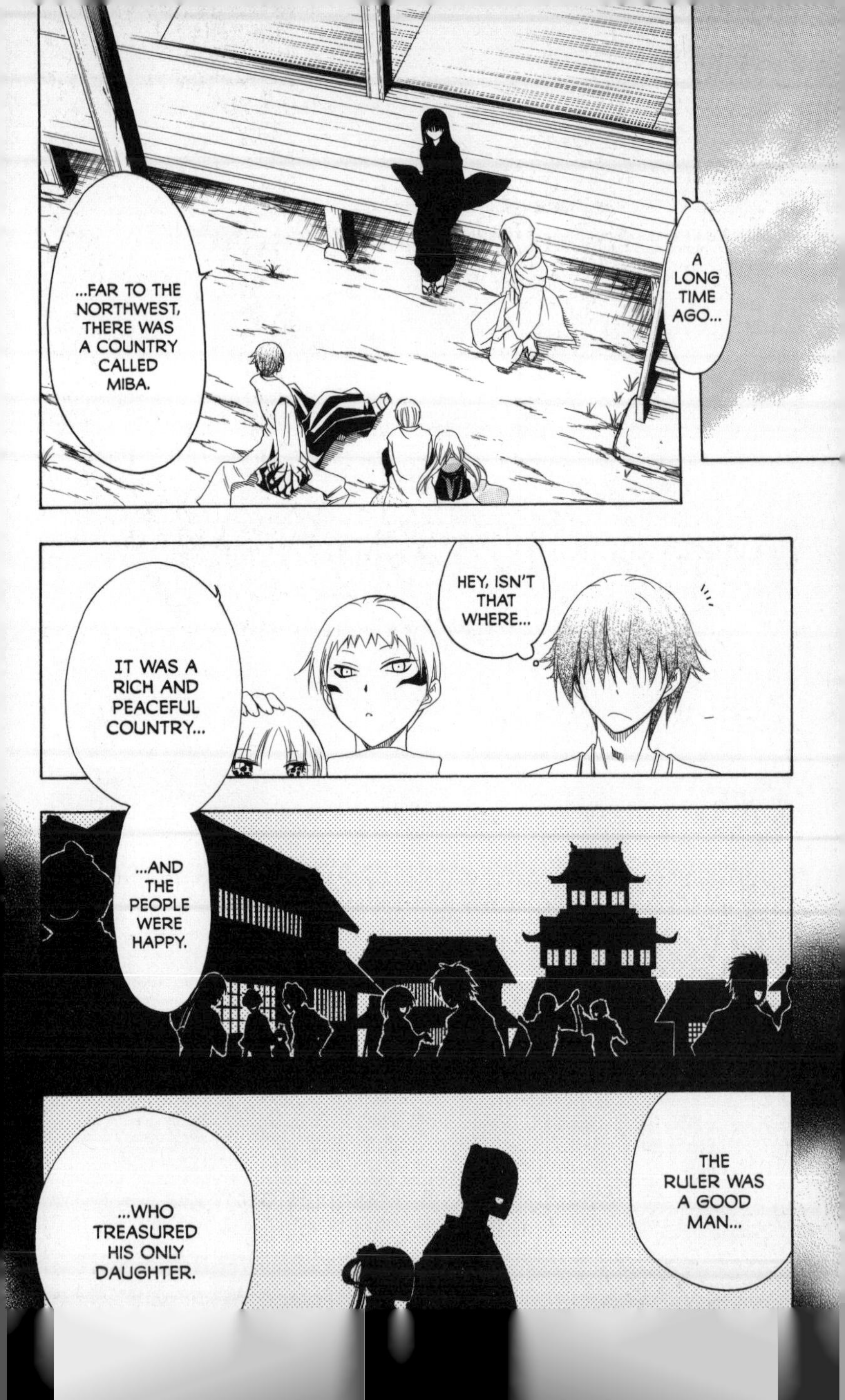
A LONG TIME AGO...
...FAR TO THE NORTHWEST, THERE WAS A COUNTRY CALLED MIBA.
HEY, ISN'T THAT WHERE...
IT WAS A RICH AND PEACEFUL COUNTRY...
...AND THE PEOPLE WERE HAPPY.
THE RULER WAS A GOOD MAN...
...WHO TREASURED HIS ONLY DAUGHTER.

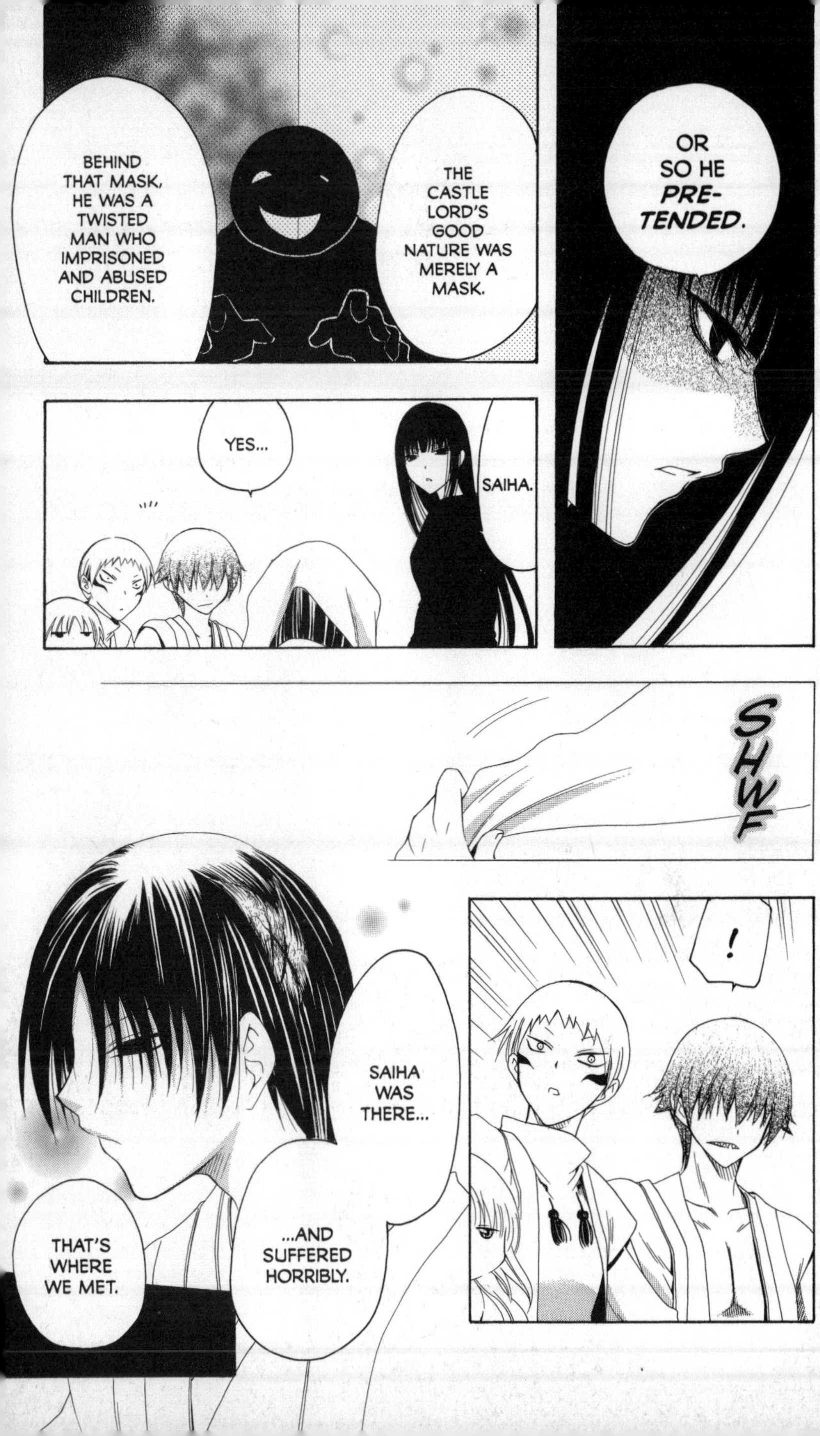

OR SO HE *PRETENDED*.
THE CASTLE LORD'S GOOD NATURE WAS MERELY A MASK.
BEHIND THAT MASK, HE WAS A TWISTED MAN WHO IMPRISONED AND ABUSED CHILDREN.
SAIHA.
YES...
SHWF
!
SAIHA WAS THERE...
...AND SUFFERED HORRIBLY.
THAT'S WHERE WE MET.

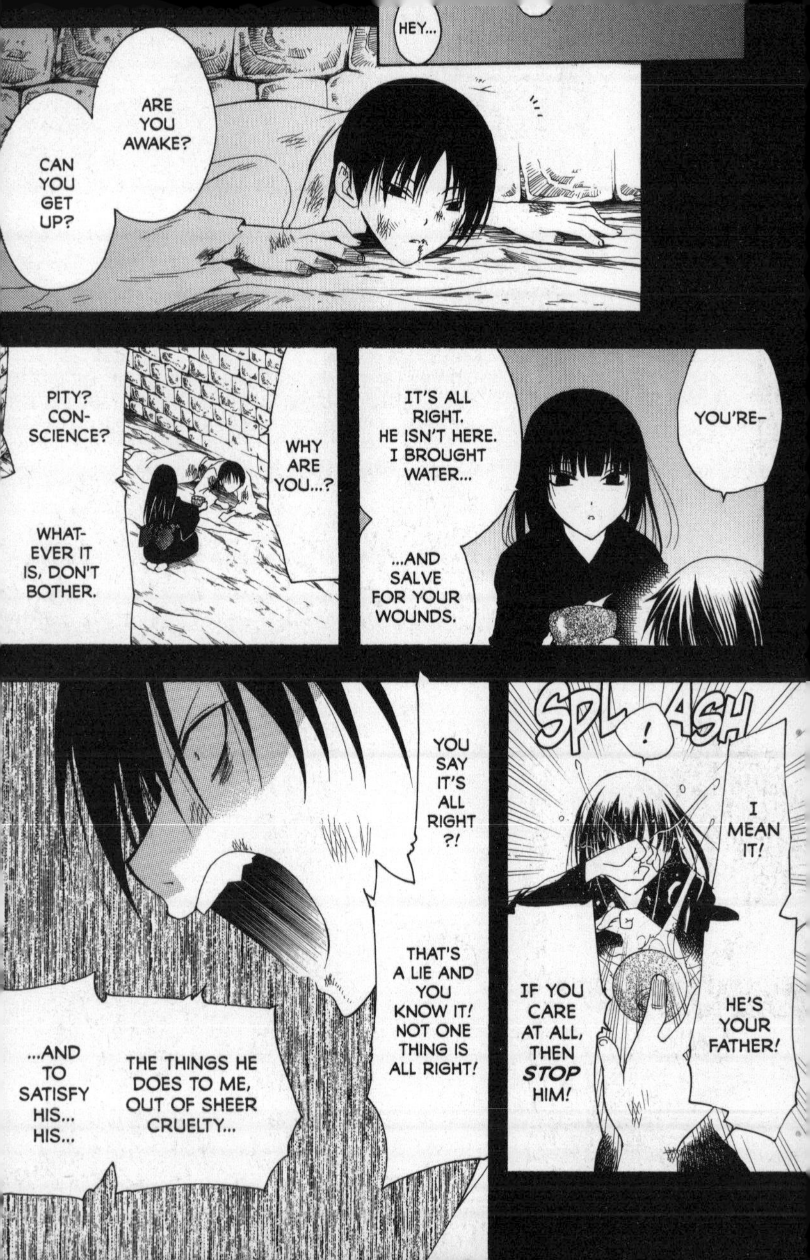
HEY...
ARE YOU AWAKE?
CAN YOU GET UP?
YOU'RE-
IT'S ALL RIGHT. HE ISN'T HERE. I BROUGHT WATER...
...AND SALVE FOR YOUR WOUNDS.
WHY ARE YOU...?
PITY? CON-SCIENCE?
WHATEVER IT IS, DON'T BOTHER.
SPLASH
!
I MEAN IT!
HE'S YOUR FATHER!
IF YOU CARE AT ALL, THEN *STOP* HIM!
YOU SAY IT'S ALL RIGHT?!
THAT'S A LIE AND YOU KNOW IT! NOT ONE THING IS ALL RIGHT!
THE THINGS HE DOES TO ME, OUT OF SHEER CRUELTY...
...AND TO SATISFY HIS... HIS...

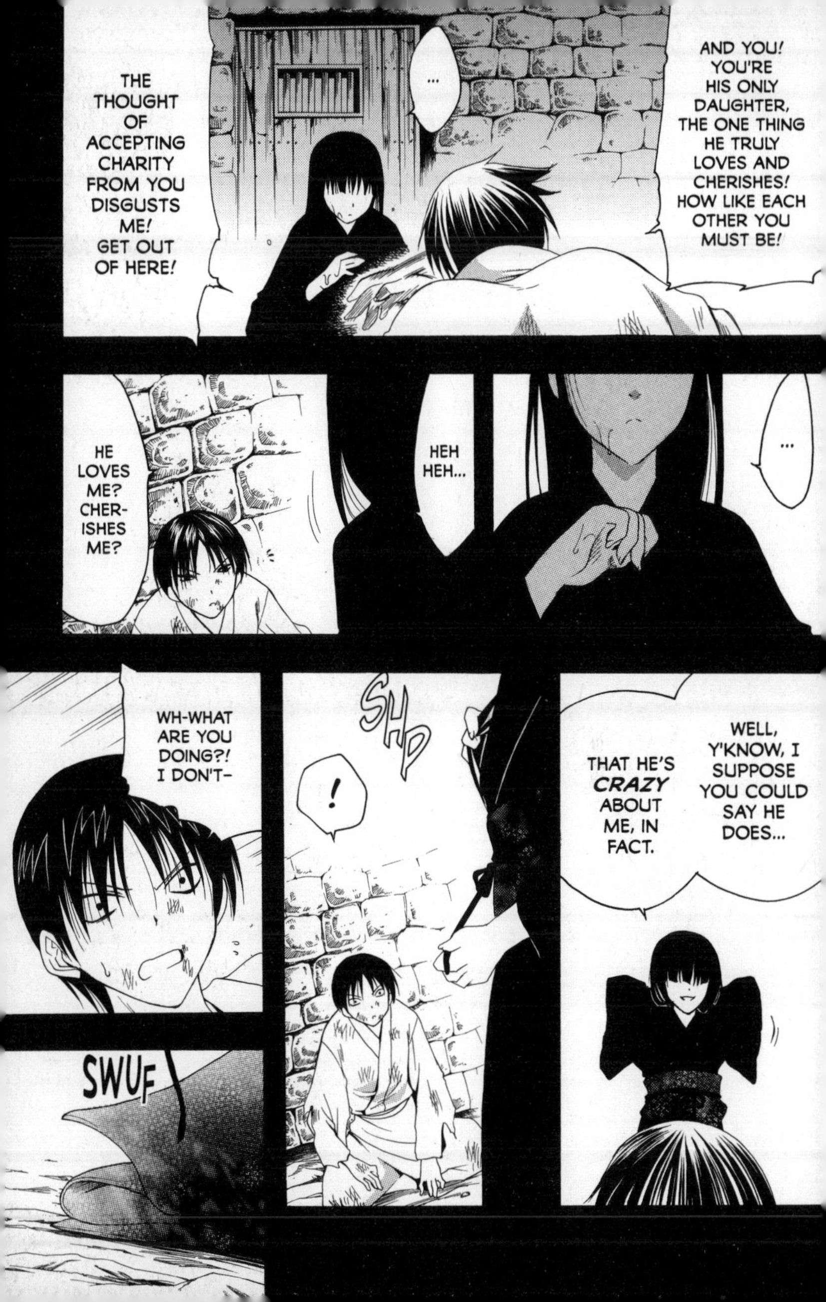
AND YOU! YOU'RE HIS ONLY DAUGHTER, THE ONE THING HE TRULY LOVES AND CHERISHES! HOW LIKE EACH OTHER YOU MUST BE!
...
THE THOUGHT OF ACCEPTING CHARITY FROM YOU DISGUSTS ME! GET OUT OF HERE!
...
HEH HEH...
HE LOVES ME? CHER-ISHES ME?
WELL, Y'KNOW, I SUPPOSE YOU COULD SAY HE DOES...
THAT HE'S *CRAZY* ABOUT ME, IN FACT.
SHP
!
WH-WHAT ARE YOU DOING?! I DON'T-
SWUF

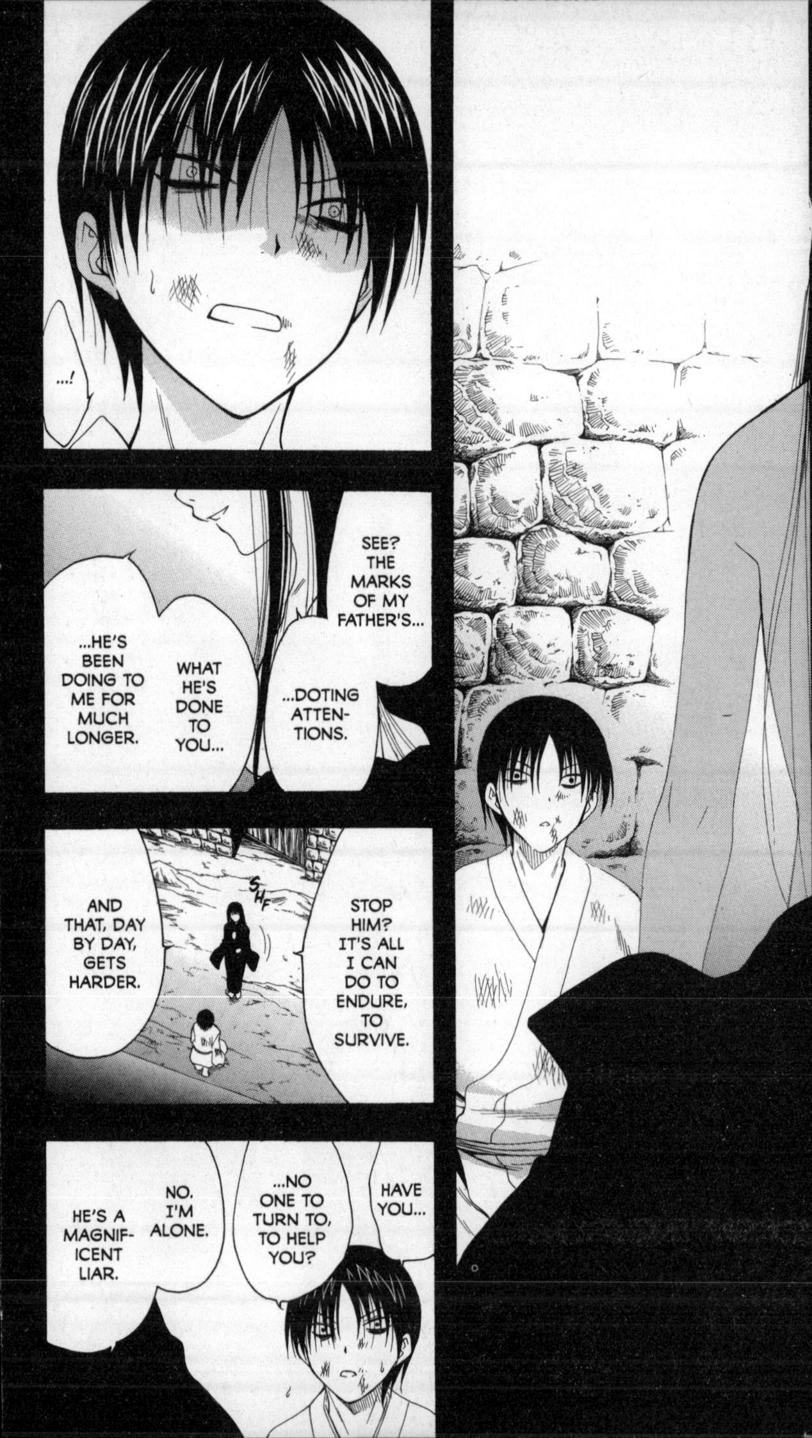
...!
SEE? THE MARKS OF MY FATHER'S...
...DOTING ATTENTIONS.
WHAT HE'S DONE TO YOU...
...HE'S BEEN DOING TO ME FOR MUCH LONGER.
STOP HIM? IT'S ALL I CAN DO TO ENDURE, TO SURVIVE.
SHF
AND THAT, DAY BY DAY, GETS HARDER.
HAVE YOU...
...NO ONE TO TURN TO, TO HELP YOU?
NO. I'M ALONE.
HE'S A MAGNIFICENT LIAR.

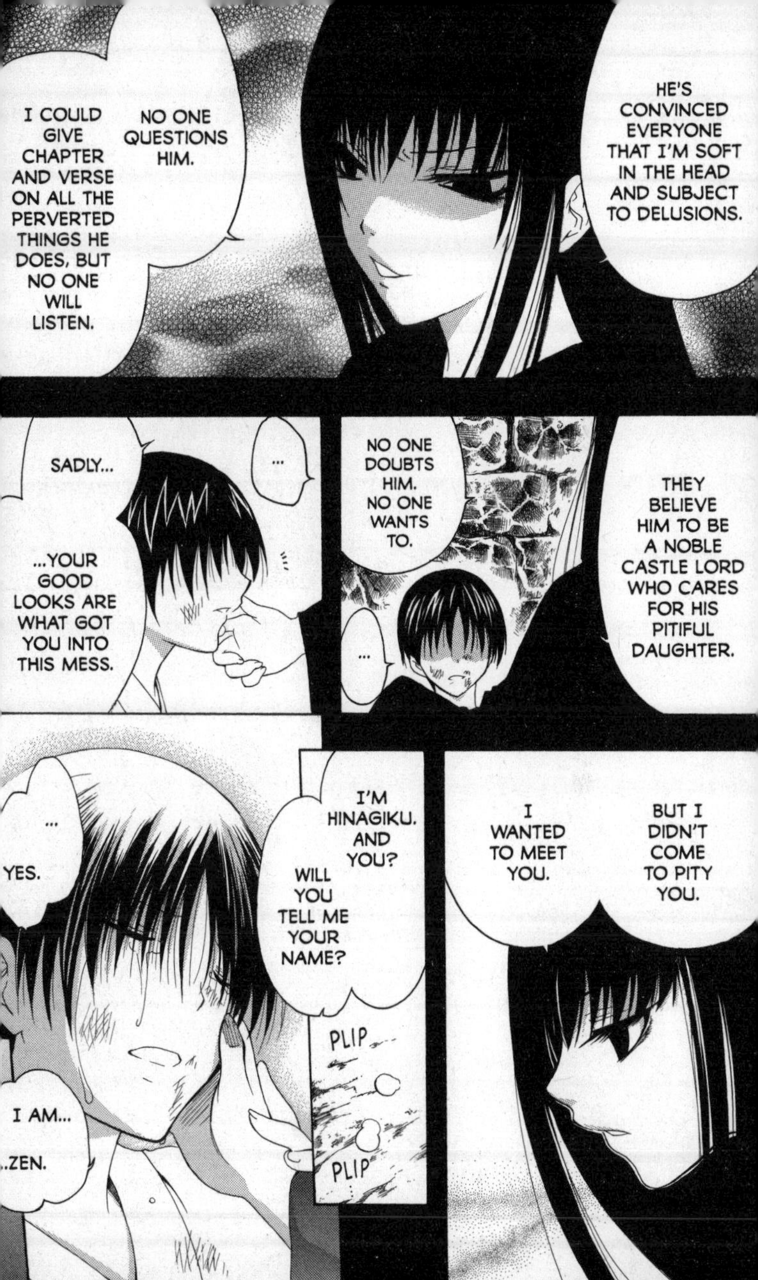
HE'S CONVINCED EVERYONE THAT I'M SOFT IN THE HEAD AND SUBJECT TO DELUSIONS.
NO ONE QUESTIONS HIM.
I COULD GIVE CHAPTER AND VERSE ON ALL THE PERVERTED THINGS HE DOES, BUT NO ONE WILL LISTEN.
THEY BELIEVE HIM TO BE A NOBLE CASTLE LORD WHO CARES FOR HIS PITIFUL DAUGHTER.
NO ONE DOUBTS HIM. NO ONE WANTS TO.
...
...
SADLY...
...YOUR GOOD LOOKS ARE WHAT GOT YOU INTO THIS MESS.
BUT I DIDN'T COME TO PITY YOU.
I WANTED TO MEET YOU.
I'M HINAGIKU. AND YOU?
WILL YOU TELL ME YOUR NAME?
PLIP
PLIP
... YES.
I AM...
..ZEN.

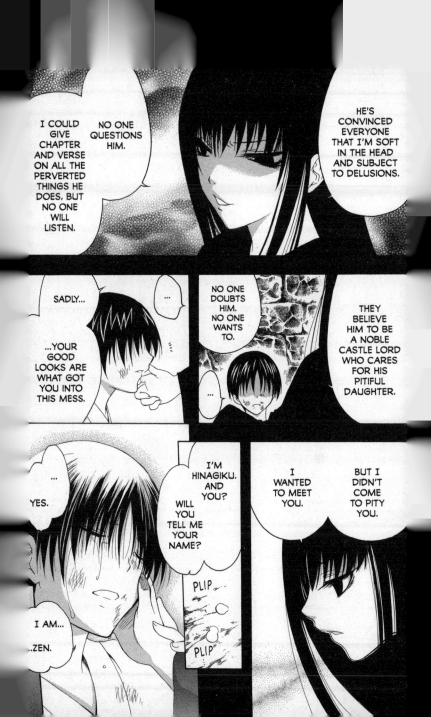

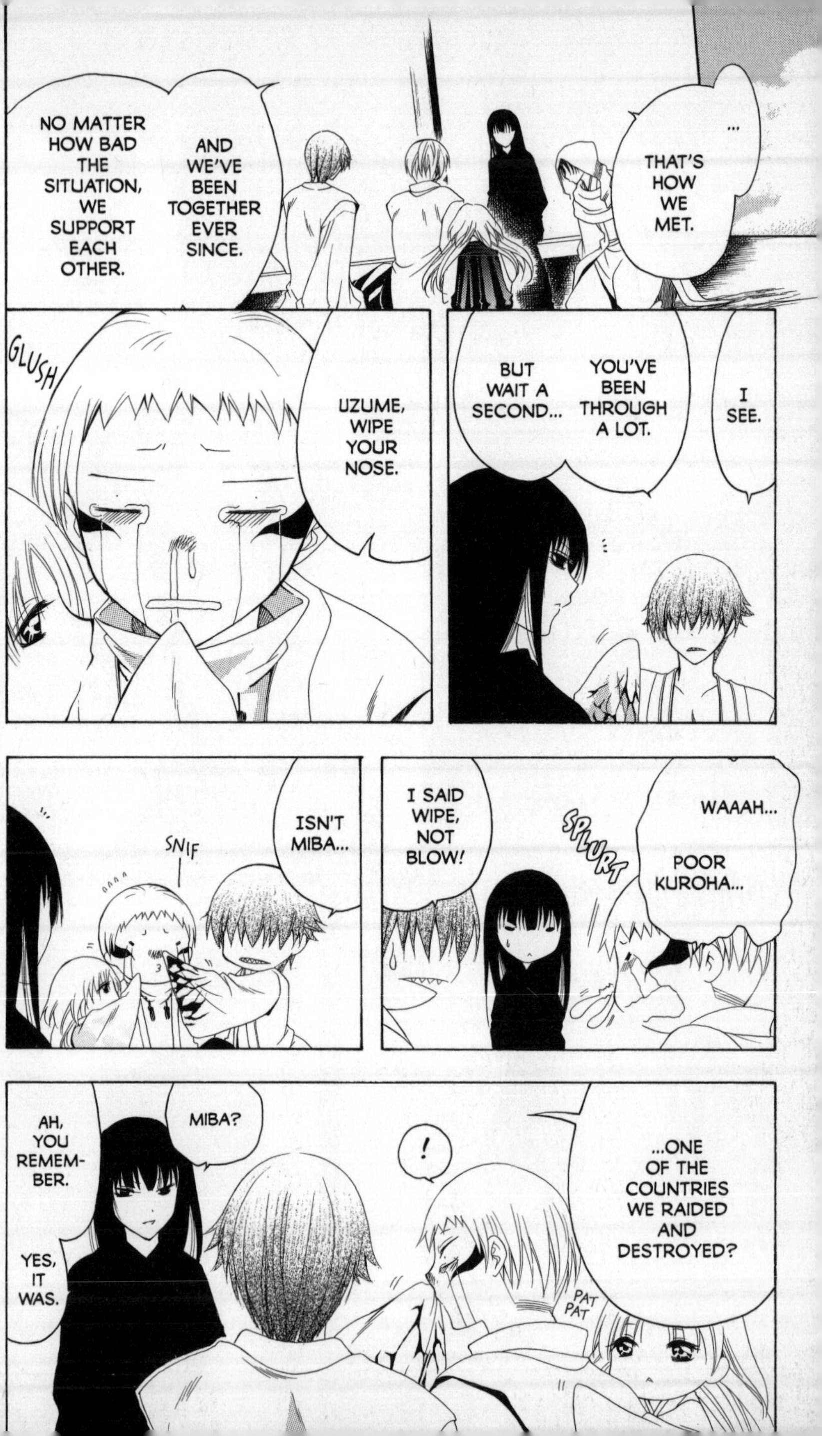
...
THAT'S HOW WE MET.
AND WE'VE BEEN TOGETHER EVER SINCE.
NO MATTER HOW BAD THE SITUATION, WE SUPPORT EACH OTHER.
I SEE.
YOU'VE BEEN THROUGH A LOT.
BUT WAIT A SECOND...
UZUME, WIPE YOUR NOSE.
GLUSH
WAAAH...
POOR KUROHA...
SPLURT
I SAID WIPE, NOT BLOW!
ISN'T MIBA...
SNIF
...ONE OF THE COUNTRIES WE RAIDED AND DESTROYED?
!
PAT PAT
MIBA?
AH, YOU REMEMBER.
YES, IT WAS.

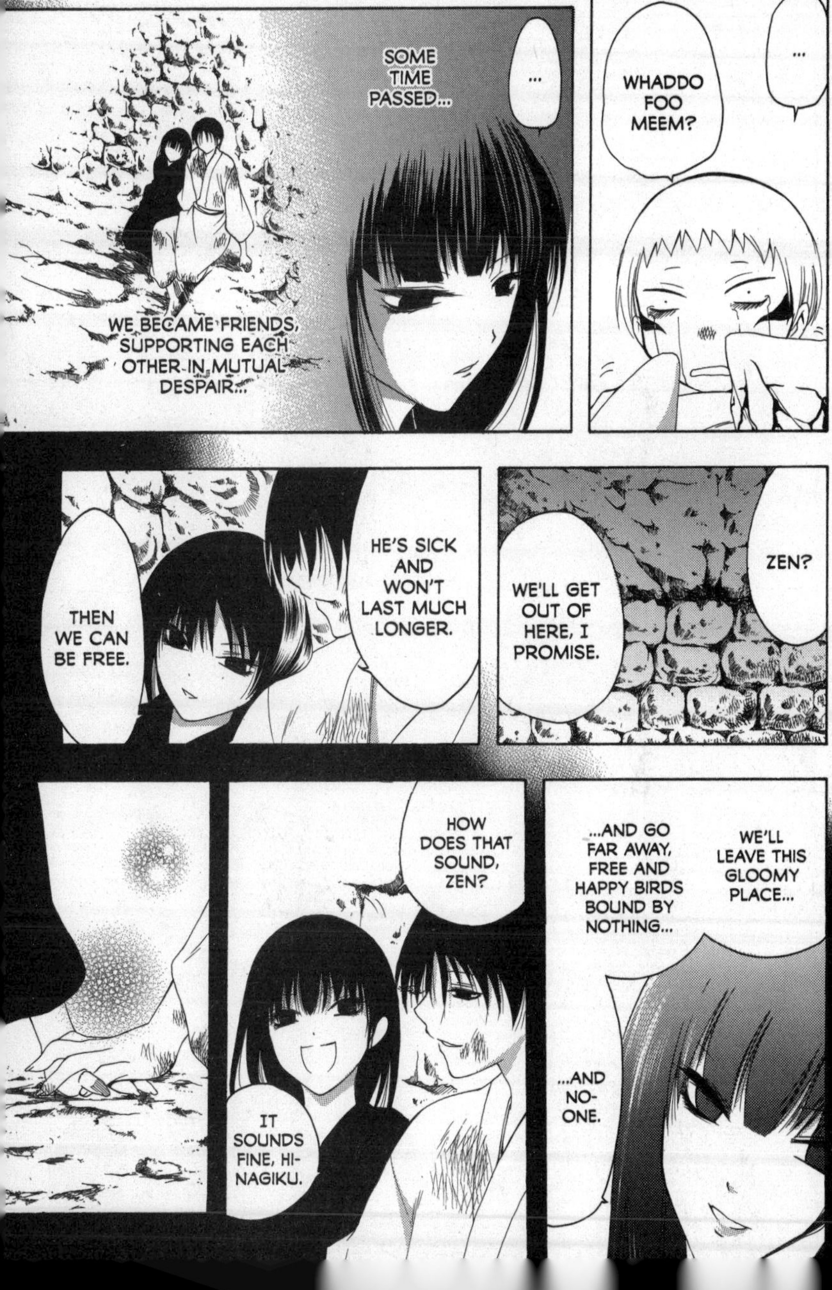
...
WHADDO FOO MEEM?
...
SOME TIME PASSED...
WE BECAME FRIENDS, SUPPORTING EACH OTHER IN MUTUAL DESPAIR...
ZEN?
WE'LL GET OUT OF HERE, I PROMISE.
HE'S SICK AND WON'T LAST MUCH LONGER.
THEN WE CAN BE FREE.
WE'LL LEAVE THIS GLOOMY PLACE...
...AND GO FAR AWAY, FREE AND HAPPY BIRDS BOUND BY NOTHING...
...AND NO-ONE.
HOW DOES THAT SOUND, ZEN?
IT SOUNDS FINE, HI-NAGIKU.

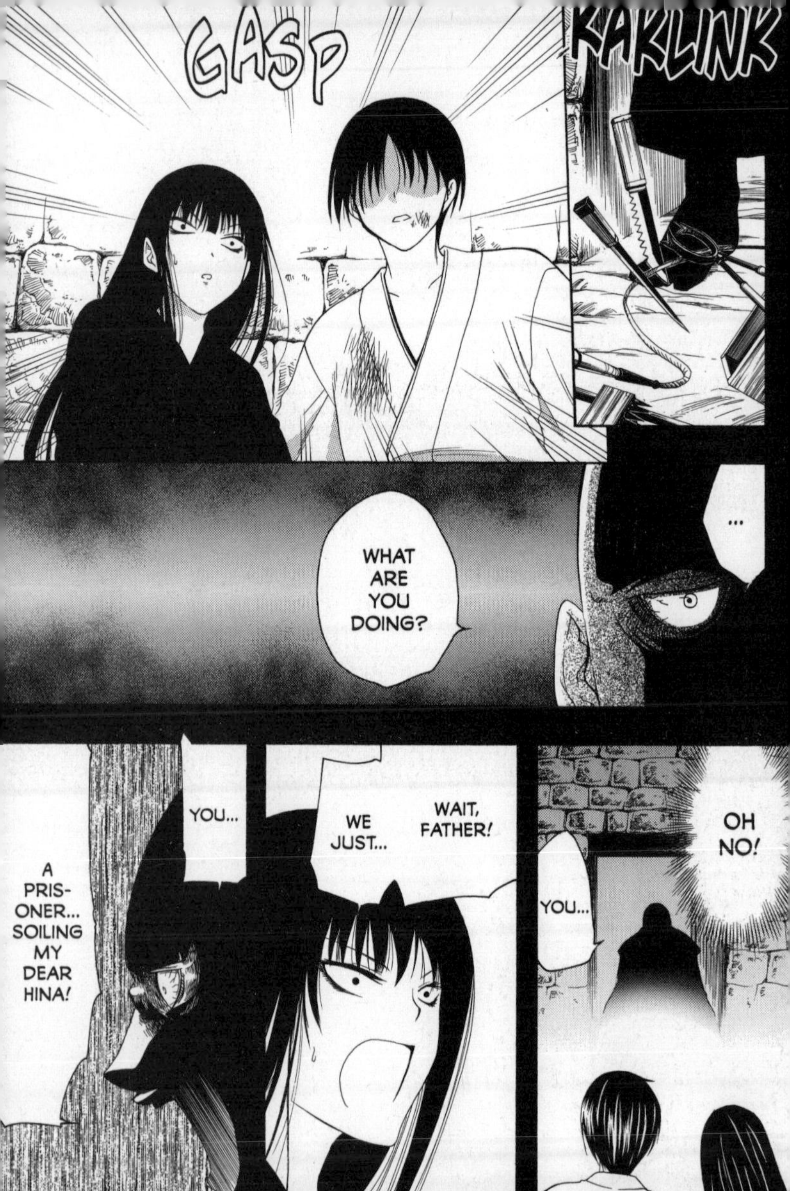

KAKLINK
GASP
...
WHAT ARE YOU DOING?
OH NO!
YOU...
WAIT, FATHER!
WE JUST...
YOU...
A PRISONER... SOILING MY DEAR HINA!

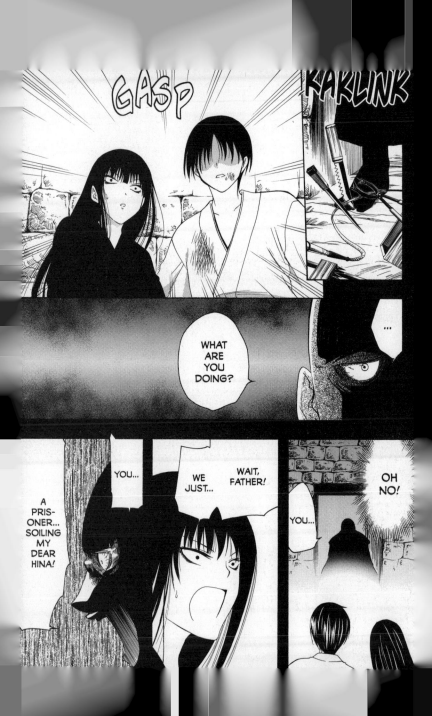

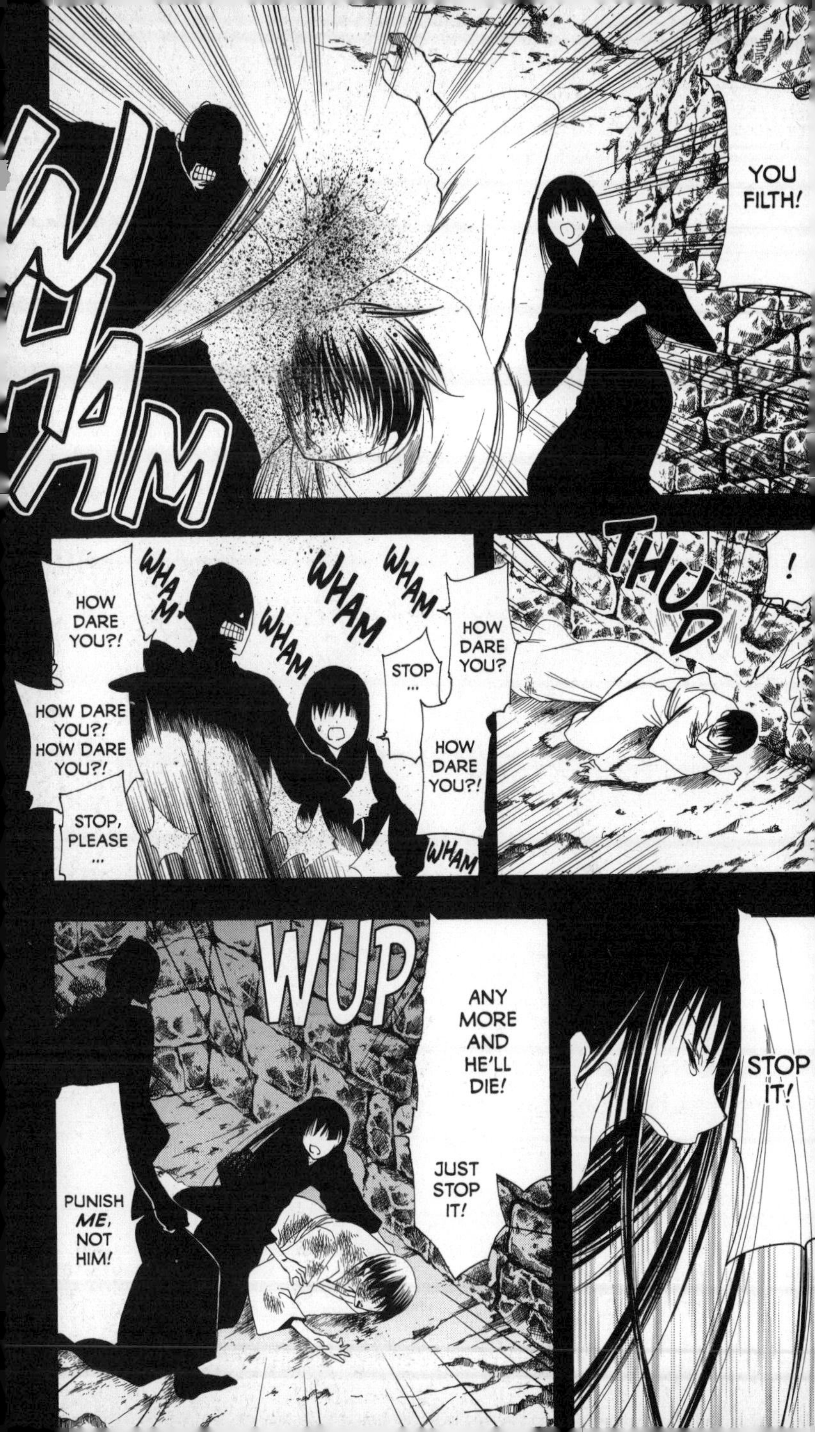
YOU FILTH!
WHAM
!
THUD
HOW DARE YOU?
STOP ...
WHAM
WHAM
HOW DARE YOU?!
WHAM
WHAM
HOW DARE YOU?!
HOW DARE YOU?! HOW DARE YOU?!
STOP, PLEASE ...
WHAM
STOP IT!
WUP
ANY MORE AND HE'LL DIE!
JUST STOP IT!
PUNISH *ME*, NOT HIM!

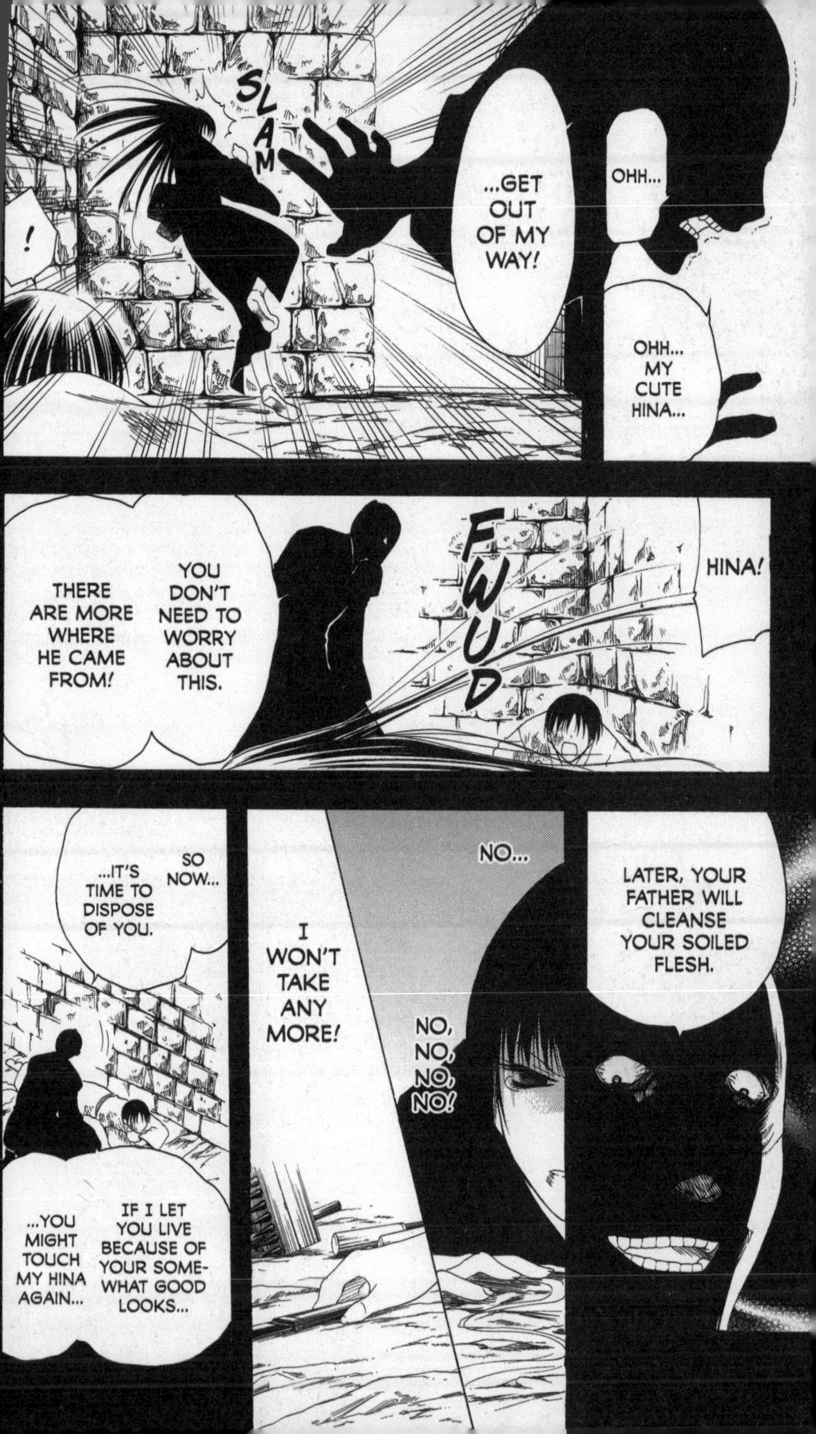
OHH...
OHH... MY CUTE HINA...
...GET OUT OF MY WAY!
SLAM
!
HINA!
FWUD
YOU DON'T NEED TO WORRY ABOUT THIS.
THERE ARE MORE WHERE HE CAME FROM!
LATER, YOUR FATHER WILL CLEANSE YOUR SOILED FLESH.
NO...
I WON'T TAKE ANY MORE!
NO, NO, NO, NO!
SO NOW...
...IT'S TIME TO DISPOSE OF YOU.
IF I LET YOU LIVE BECAUSE OF YOUR SOME-WHAT GOOD LOOKS...
...YOU MIGHT TOUCH MY HINA AGAIN...

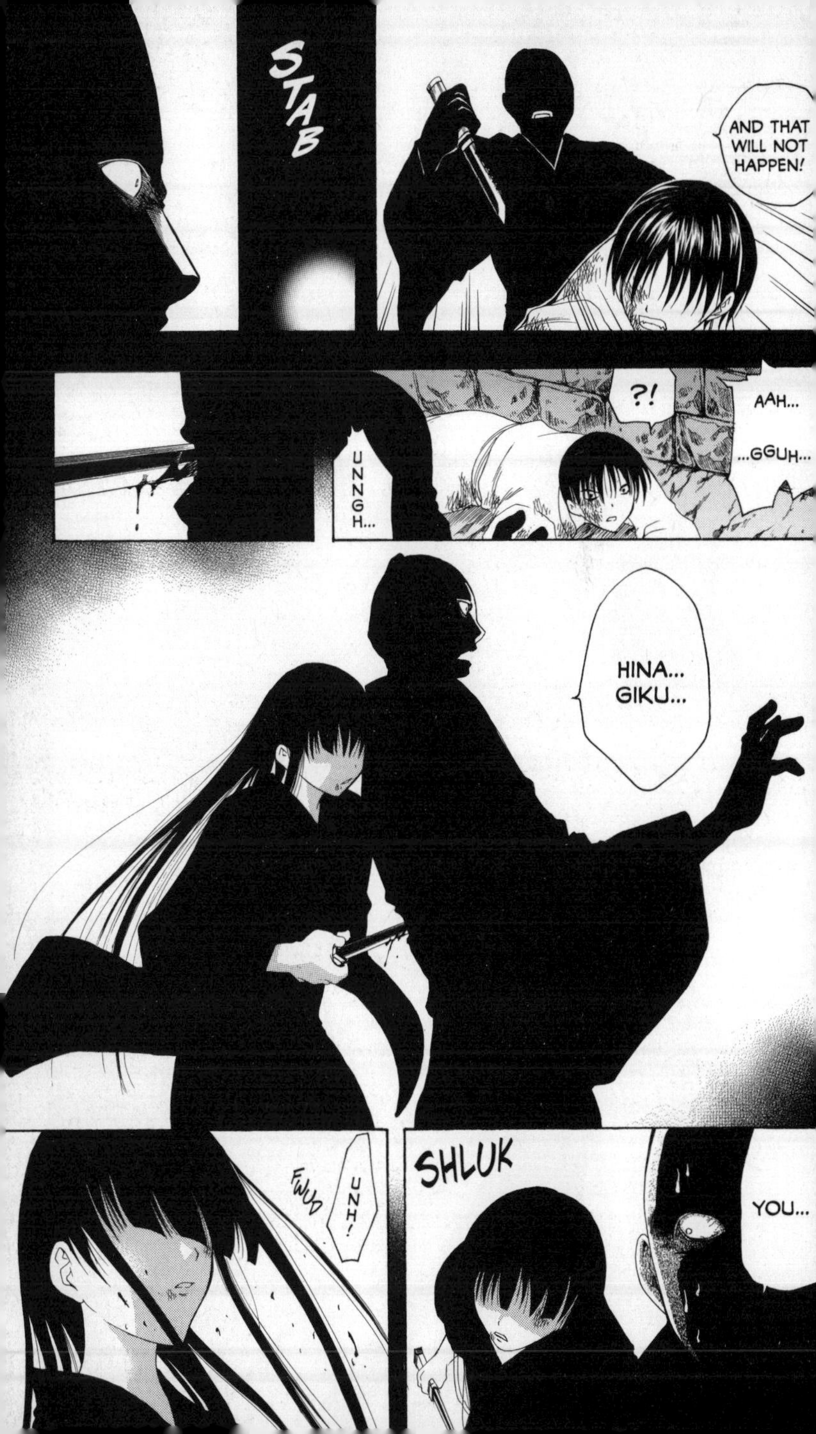
AND THAT WILL NOT HAPPEN!
STAB
AAH...
...GGUH...
?!
UNNGH...
HINA... GIKU...
SHLUK
YOU...
UNH!
FWUD

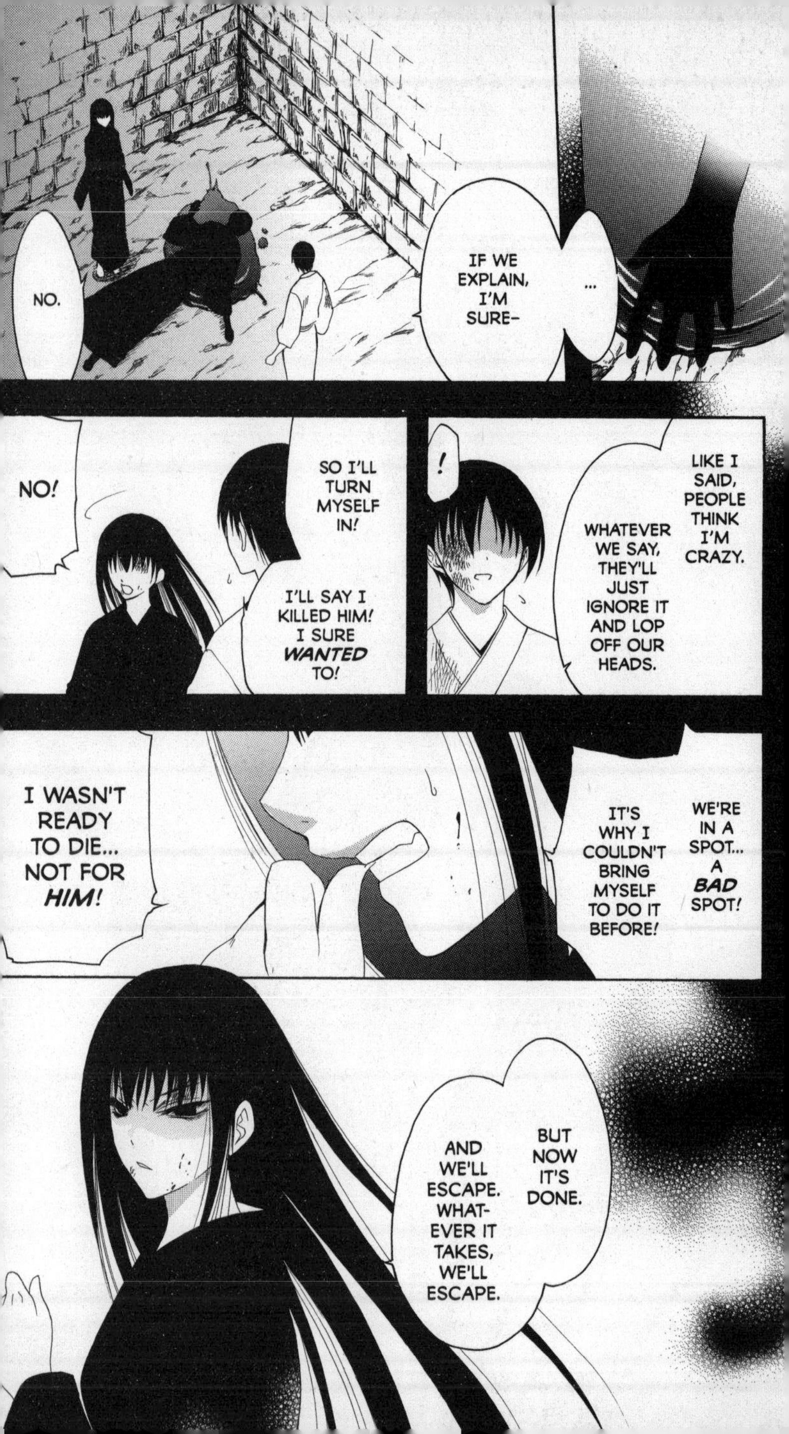
...
IF WE EXPLAIN, I'M SURE–
NO.
LIKE I SAID, PEOPLE THINK I'M CRAZY.
WHATEVER WE SAY, THEY'LL JUST IGNORE IT AND LOP OFF OUR HEADS.
!
SO I'LL TURN MYSELF IN!
I'LL SAY I KILLED HIM! I SURE *WANTED* TO!
NO!
WE'RE IN A SPOT... A *BAD* SPOT!
IT'S WHY I COULDN'T BRING MYSELF TO DO IT BEFORE!
!
I WASN'T READY TO DIE... NOT FOR *HIM*!
BUT NOW IT'S DONE.
AND WE'LL ESCAPE. WHAT-EVER IT TAKES, WE'LL ESCAPE.

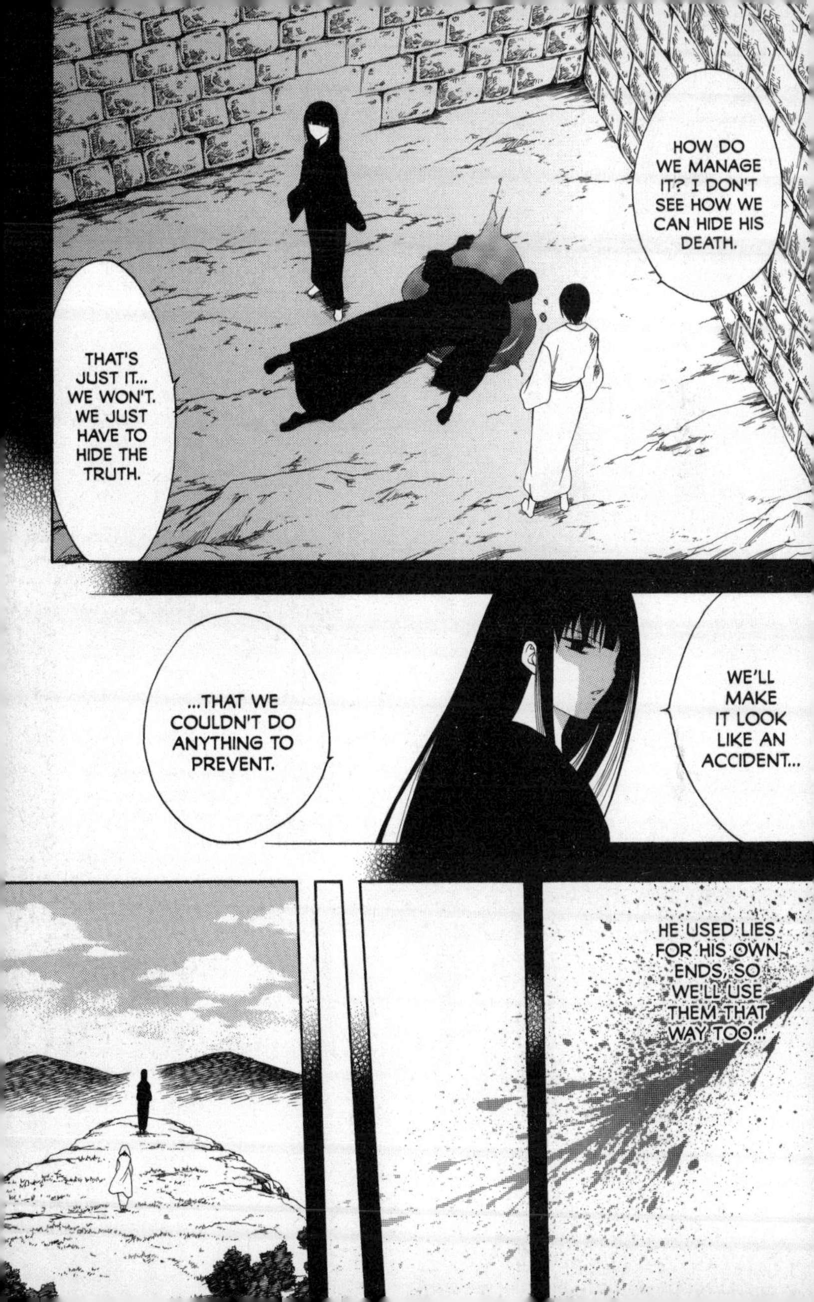
HOW DO WE MANAGE IT? I DON'T SEE HOW WE CAN HIDE HIS DEATH.
THAT'S JUST IT... WE WON'T. WE JUST HAVE TO HIDE THE TRUTH.
WE'LL MAKE IT LOOK LIKE AN ACCIDENT...
...THAT WE COULDN'T DO ANYTHING TO PREVENT.
HE USED LIES FOR HIS OWN ENDS, SO WE'LL USE THEM THAT WAY TOO...

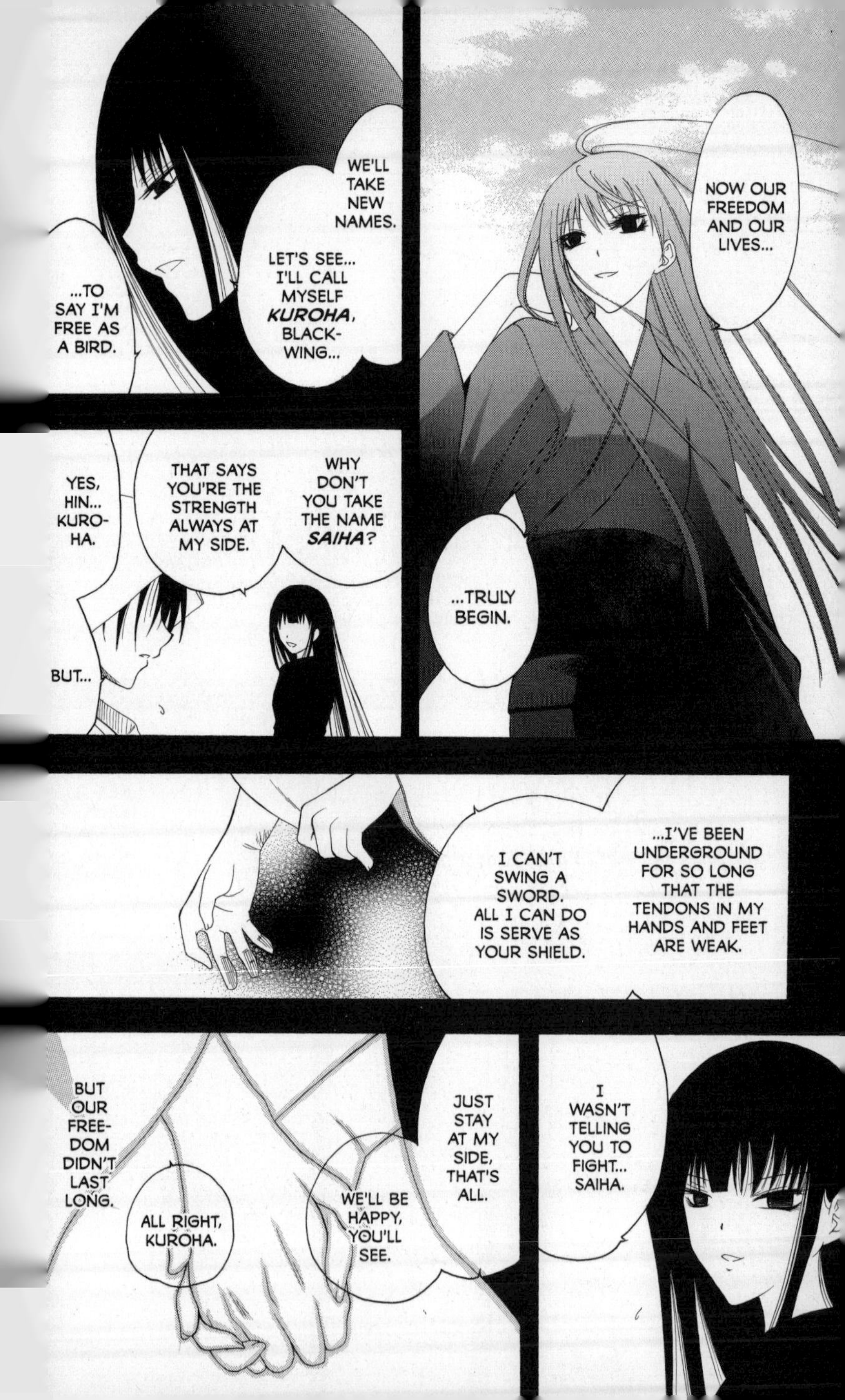
NOW OUR FREEDOM AND OUR LIVES...
...TRULY BEGIN.
WE'LL TAKE NEW NAMES.
LET'S SEE... I'LL CALL MYSELF *KUROHA*, BLACK-WING...
...TO SAY I'M FREE AS A BIRD.
WHY DON'T YOU TAKE THE NAME *SAIHA*?
THAT SAYS YOU'RE THE STRENGTH ALWAYS AT MY SIDE.
YES, HIN... KURO-HA.
BUT...
...I'VE BEEN UNDERGROUND FOR SO LONG THAT THE TENDONS IN MY HANDS AND FEET ARE WEAK.
I CAN'T SWING A SWORD. ALL I CAN DO IS SERVE AS YOUR SHIELD.
I WASN'T TELLING YOU TO FIGHT... SAIHA.
JUST STAY AT MY SIDE, THAT'S ALL.
WE'LL BE HAPPY, YOU'LL SEE.
ALL RIGHT, KUROHA.
BUT OUR FREE-DOM DIDN'T LAST LONG.

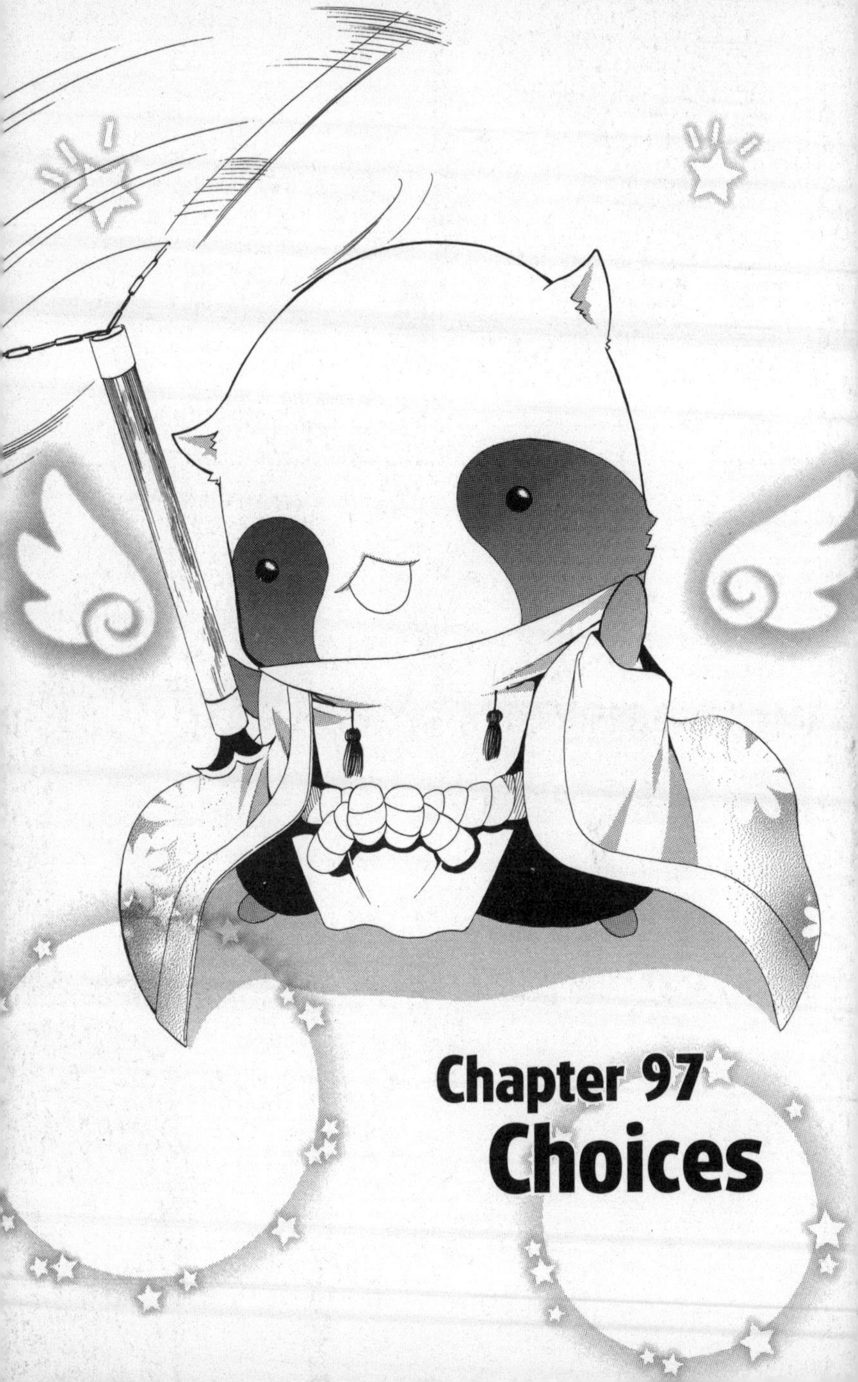

Chapter 97
Choices

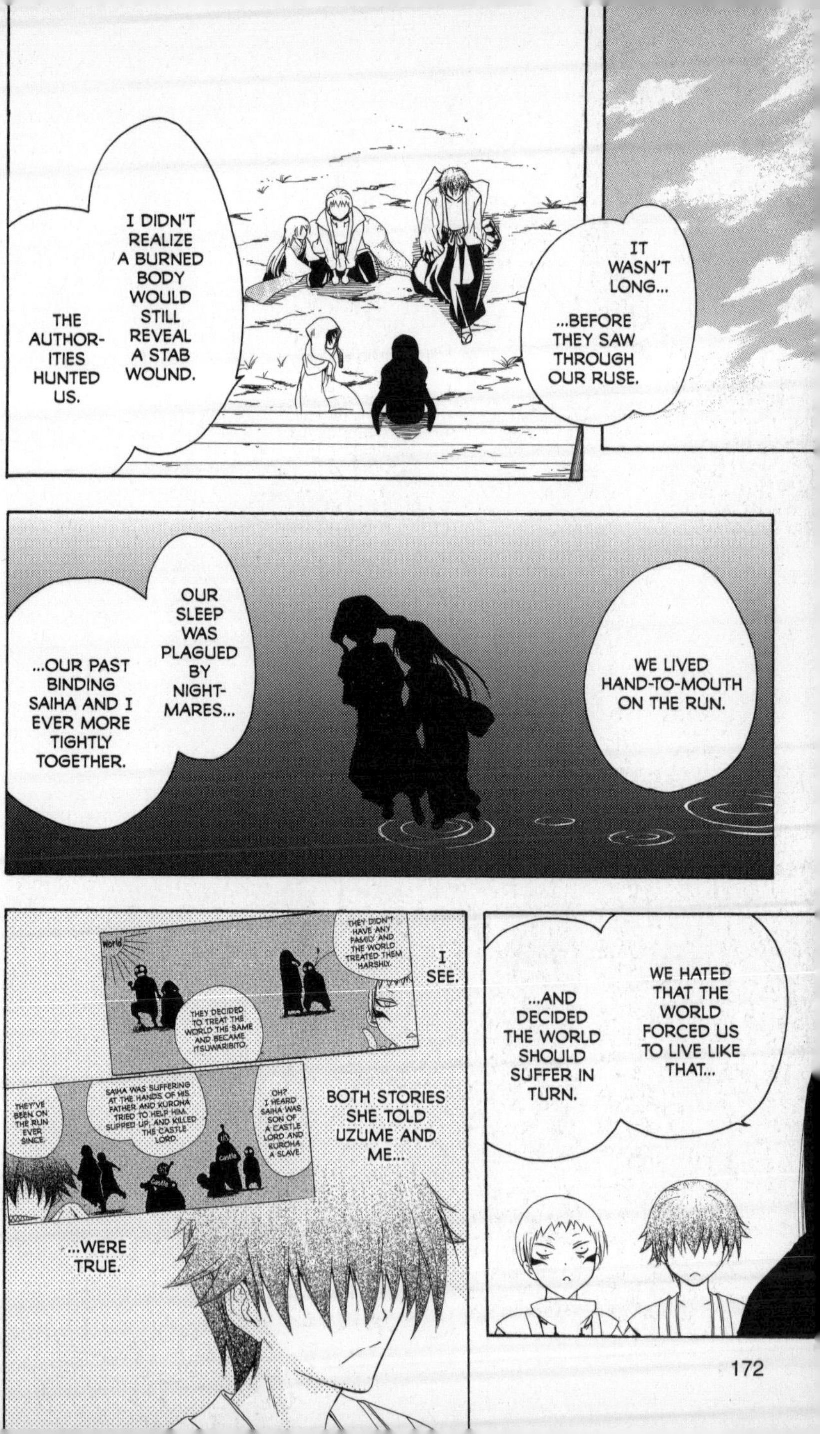
IT WASN'T LONG...
...BEFORE THEY SAW THROUGH OUR RUSE.
I DIDN'T REALIZE A BURNED BODY WOULD STILL REVEAL A STAB WOUND.
THE AUTHOR-ITIES HUNTED US.
WE LIVED HAND-TO-MOUTH ON THE RUN.
OUR SLEEP WAS PLAGUED BY NIGHT-MARES...
...OUR PAST BINDING SAIHA AND I EVER MORE TIGHTLY TOGETHER.
WE HATED THAT THE WORLD FORCED US TO LIVE LIKE THAT...
...AND DECIDED THE WORLD SHOULD SUFFER IN TURN.
I SEE.
THEY DIDN'T HAVE ANY FAMILY AND THE WORLD TREATED THEM HARSHLY.
World
THEY DECIDED TO TREAT THE WORLD THE SAME AND BECAME ITSUWARIBITO.
BOTH STORIES SHE TOLD UZUME AND ME...
OH? I HEARD SAIHA WAS SON OF A CASTLE LORD AND KUROHA A SLAVE.
SAIHA WAS SUFFERING AT THE HANDS OF HIS FATHER AND KUROHA TRIED TO HELP HIM, SLIPPED UP, AND KILLED THE CASTLE LORD.
THEY'VE BEEN ON THE RUN EVER SINCE.
Castle
Castle
...WERE TRUE.

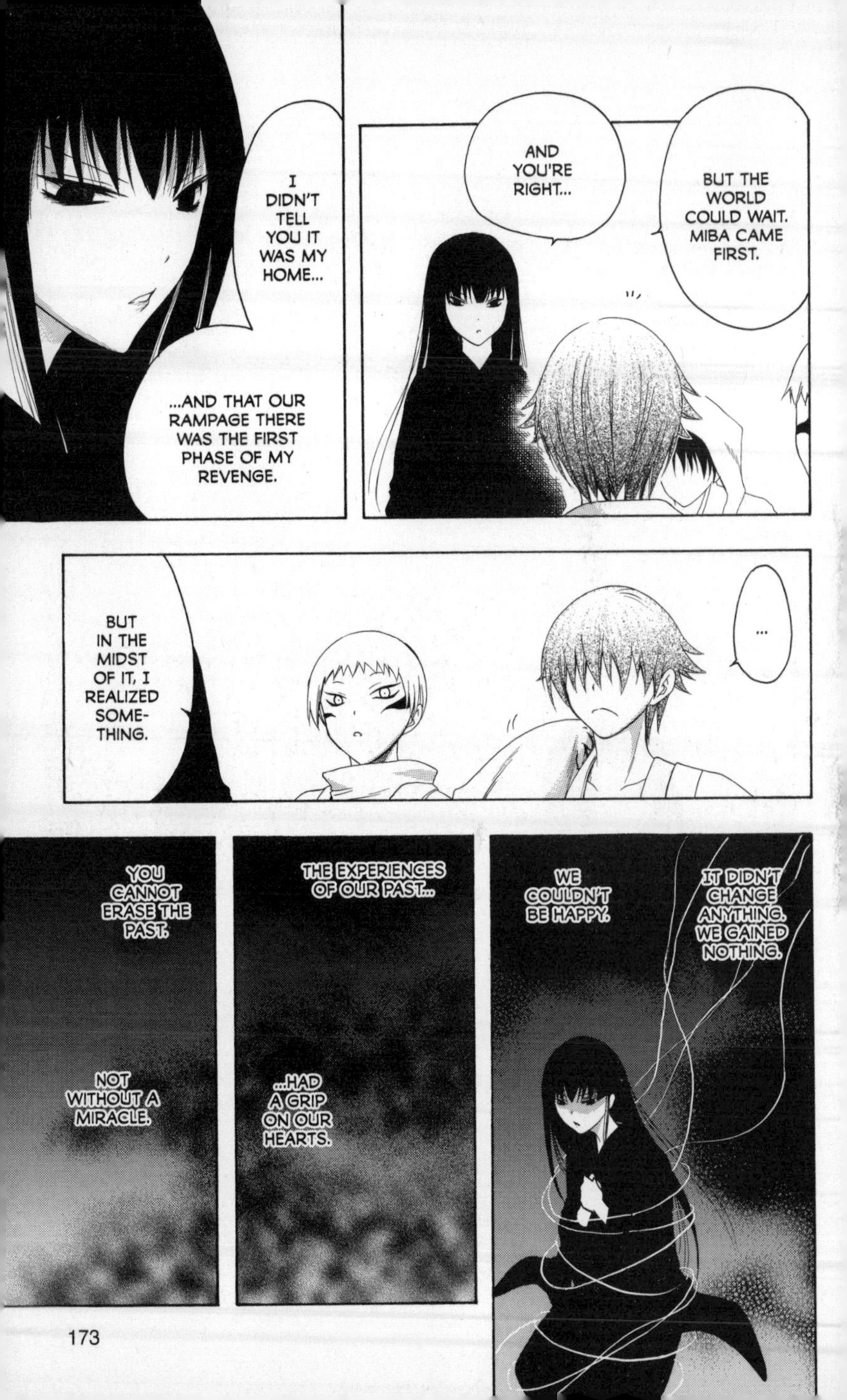
BUT THE WORLD COULD WAIT. MIBA CAME FIRST.
AND YOU'RE RIGHT...
I DIDN'T TELL YOU IT WAS MY HOME...
...AND THAT OUR RAMPAGE THERE WAS THE FIRST PHASE OF MY REVENGE.
...
BUT IN THE MIDST OF IT, I REALIZED SOME-THING.
IT DIDN'T CHANGE ANYTHING. WE GAINED NOTHING.
WE COULDN'T BE HAPPY.
THE EXPERIENCES OF OUR PAST...
...HAD A GRIP ON OUR HEARTS.
YOU CANNOT ERASE THE PAST.
NOT WITHOUT A MIRACLE.

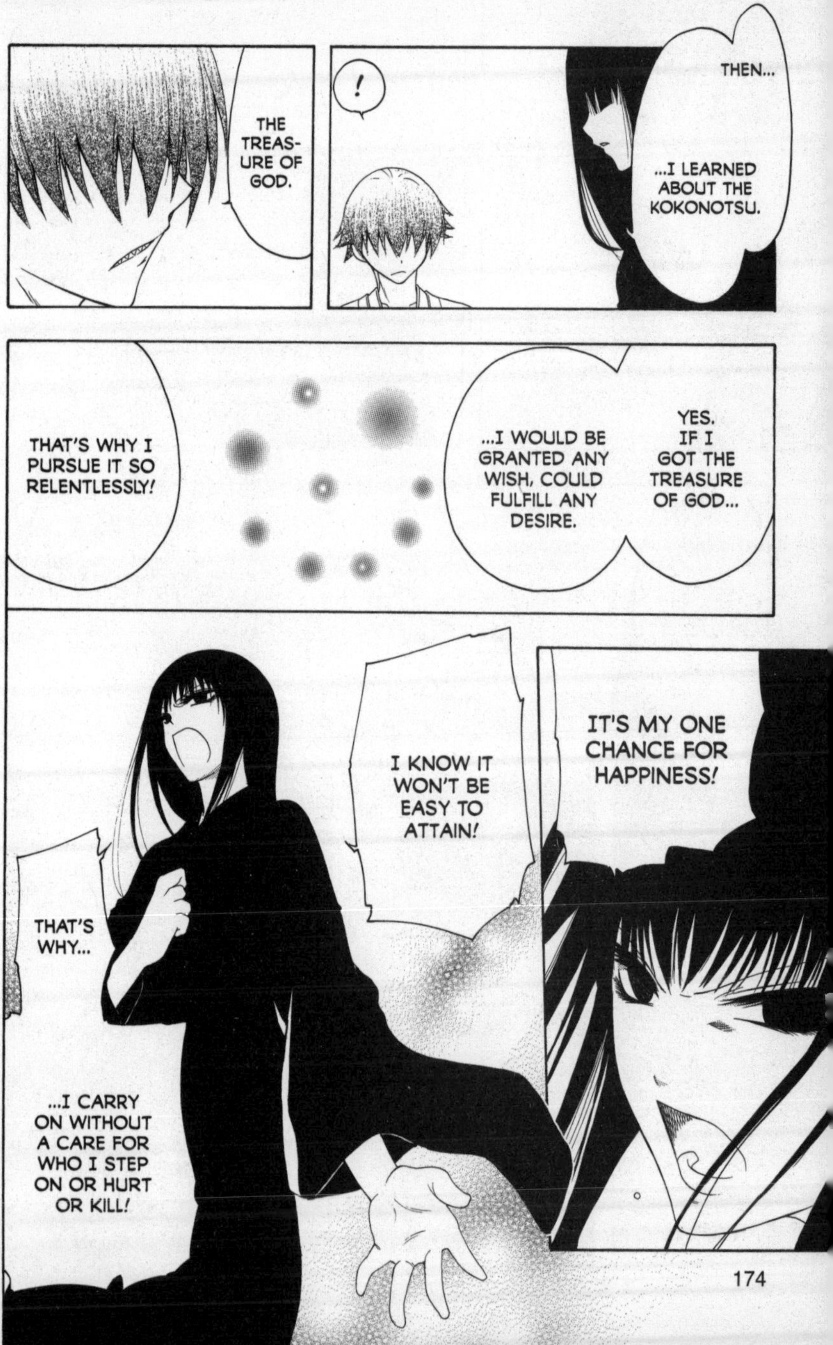
THEN...
...I LEARNED ABOUT THE KOKONOTSU.
!
THE TREAS-URE OF GOD.
YES. IF I GOT THE TREASURE OF GOD...
...I WOULD BE GRANTED ANY WISH, COULD FULFILL ANY DESIRE.
THAT'S WHY I PURSUE IT SO RELENTLESSLY!
IT'S MY ONE CHANCE FOR HAPPINESS!
I KNOW IT WON'T BE EASY TO ATTAIN!
THAT'S WHY...
...I CARRY ON WITHOUT A CARE FOR WHO I STEP ON OR HURT OR KILL!

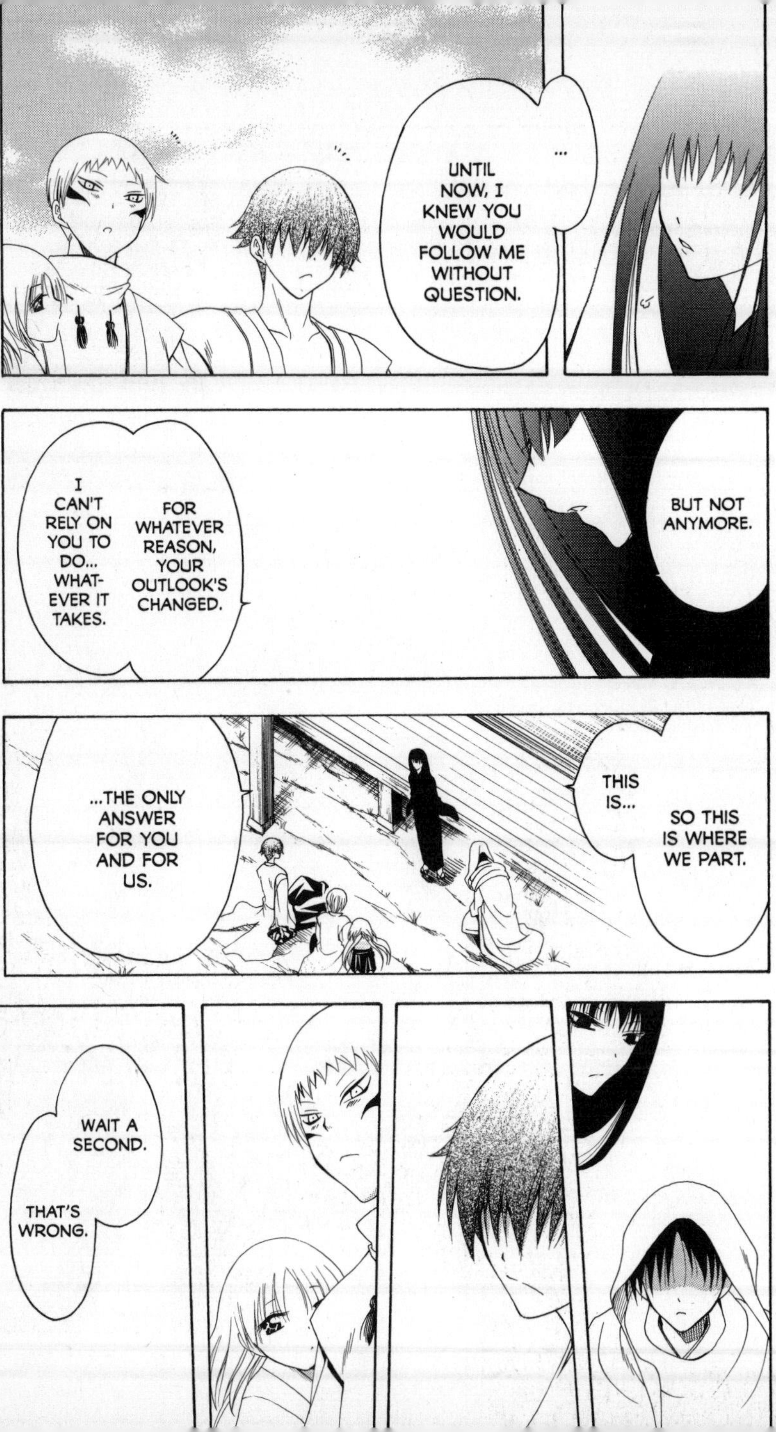
...
UNTIL NOW, I KNEW YOU WOULD FOLLOW ME WITHOUT QUESTION.
BUT NOT ANYMORE.
FOR WHATEVER REASON, YOUR OUTLOOK'S CHANGED.
I CAN'T RELY ON YOU TO DO... WHAT-EVER IT TAKES.
THIS IS...
SO THIS IS WHERE WE PART.
...THE ONLY ANSWER FOR YOU AND FOR US.
WAIT A SECOND.
THAT'S WRONG.

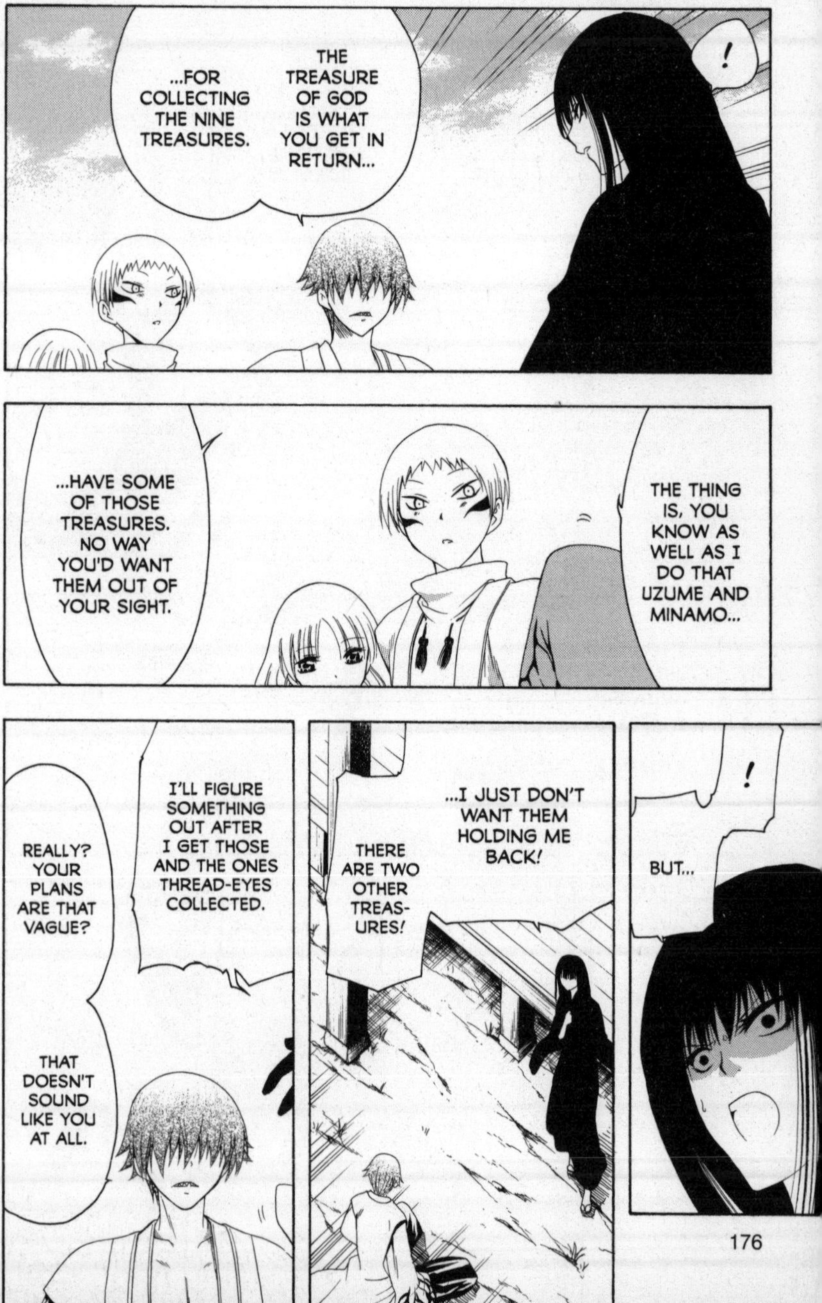
!
THE TREASURE OF GOD IS WHAT YOU GET IN RETURN...
...FOR COLLECTING THE NINE TREASURES.
THE THING IS, YOU KNOW AS WELL AS I DO THAT UZUME AND MINAMO...
...HAVE SOME OF THOSE TREASURES. NO WAY YOU'D WANT THEM OUT OF YOUR SIGHT.
!
BUT...
...I JUST DON'T WANT THEM HOLDING ME BACK!
THERE ARE TWO OTHER TREASURES!
I'LL FIGURE SOMETHING OUT AFTER I GET THOSE AND THE ONES THREAD-EYES COLLECTED.
REALLY? YOUR PLANS ARE THAT VAGUE?
THAT DOESN'T SOUND LIKE YOU AT ALL.

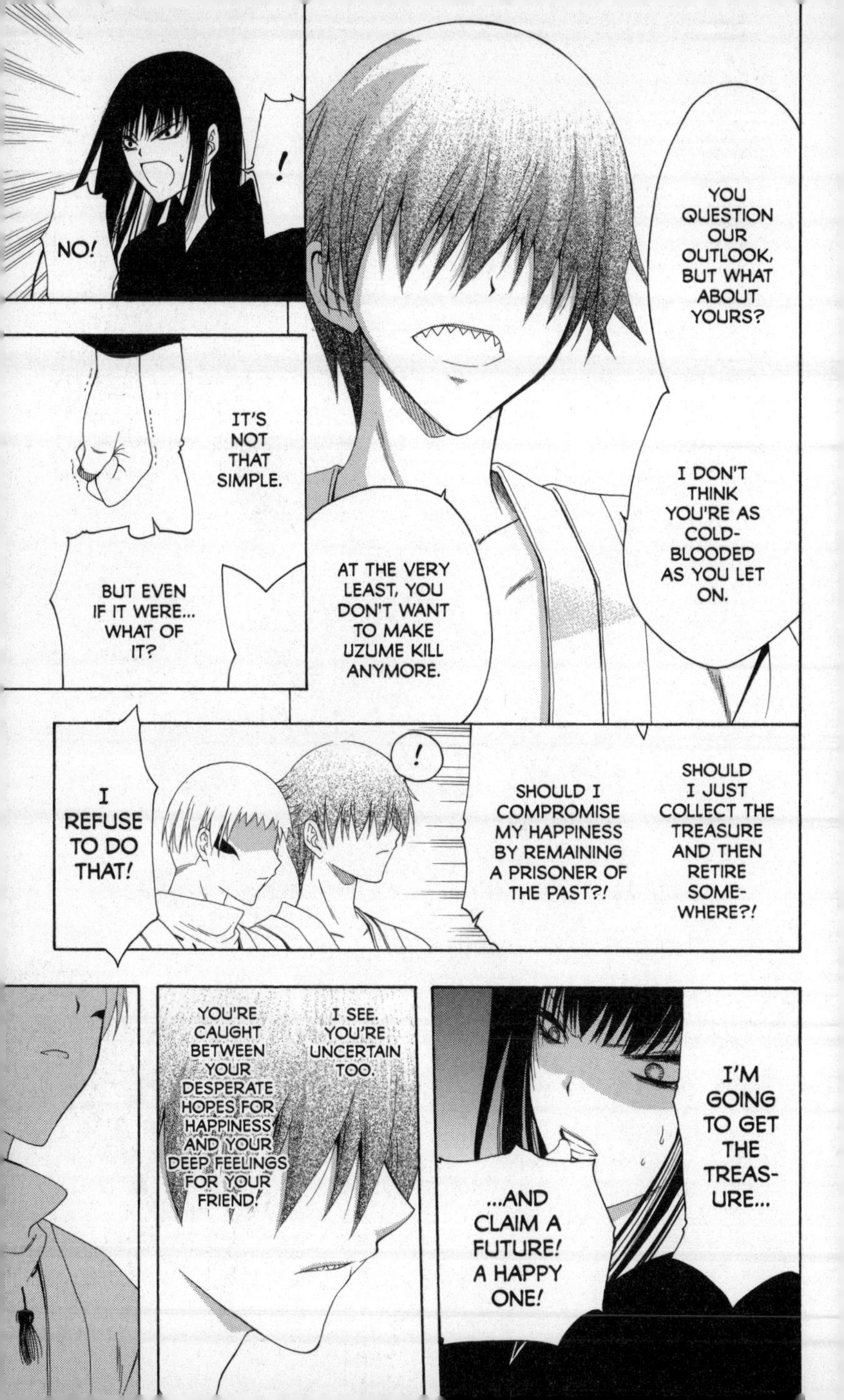

YOU QUESTION OUR OUTLOOK, BUT WHAT ABOUT YOURS?
I DON'T THINK YOU'RE AS COLD-BLOODED AS YOU LET ON.
AT THE VERY LEAST, YOU DON'T WANT TO MAKE UZUME KILL ANYMORE.
!
NO!
IT'S NOT THAT SIMPLE.
BUT EVEN IF IT WERE... WHAT OF IT?
SHOULD I JUST COLLECT THE TREASURE AND THEN RETIRE SOMEWHERE?!
SHOULD I COMPROMISE MY HAPPINESS BY REMAINING A PRISONER OF THE PAST?!
!
I REFUSE TO DO THAT!
I'M GOING TO GET THE TREASURE...
...AND CLAIM A FUTURE! A HAPPY ONE!
I SEE. YOU'RE UNCERTAIN TOO.
YOU'RE CAUGHT BETWEEN YOUR DESPERATE HOPES FOR HAPPINESS AND YOUR DEEP FEELINGS FOR YOUR FRIEND.

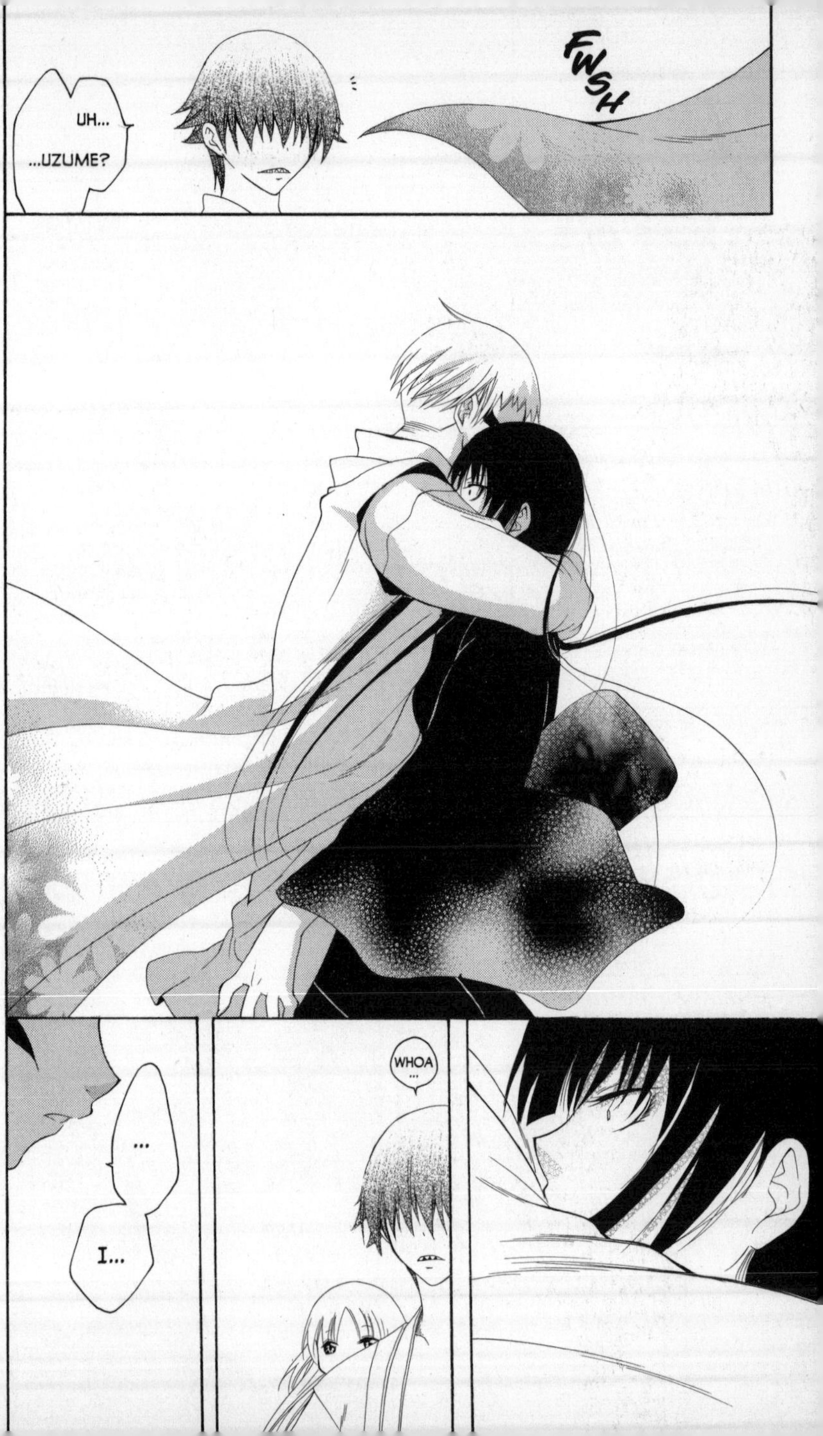
FWSH
UH... ...UZUME?
WHOA...
...
I...

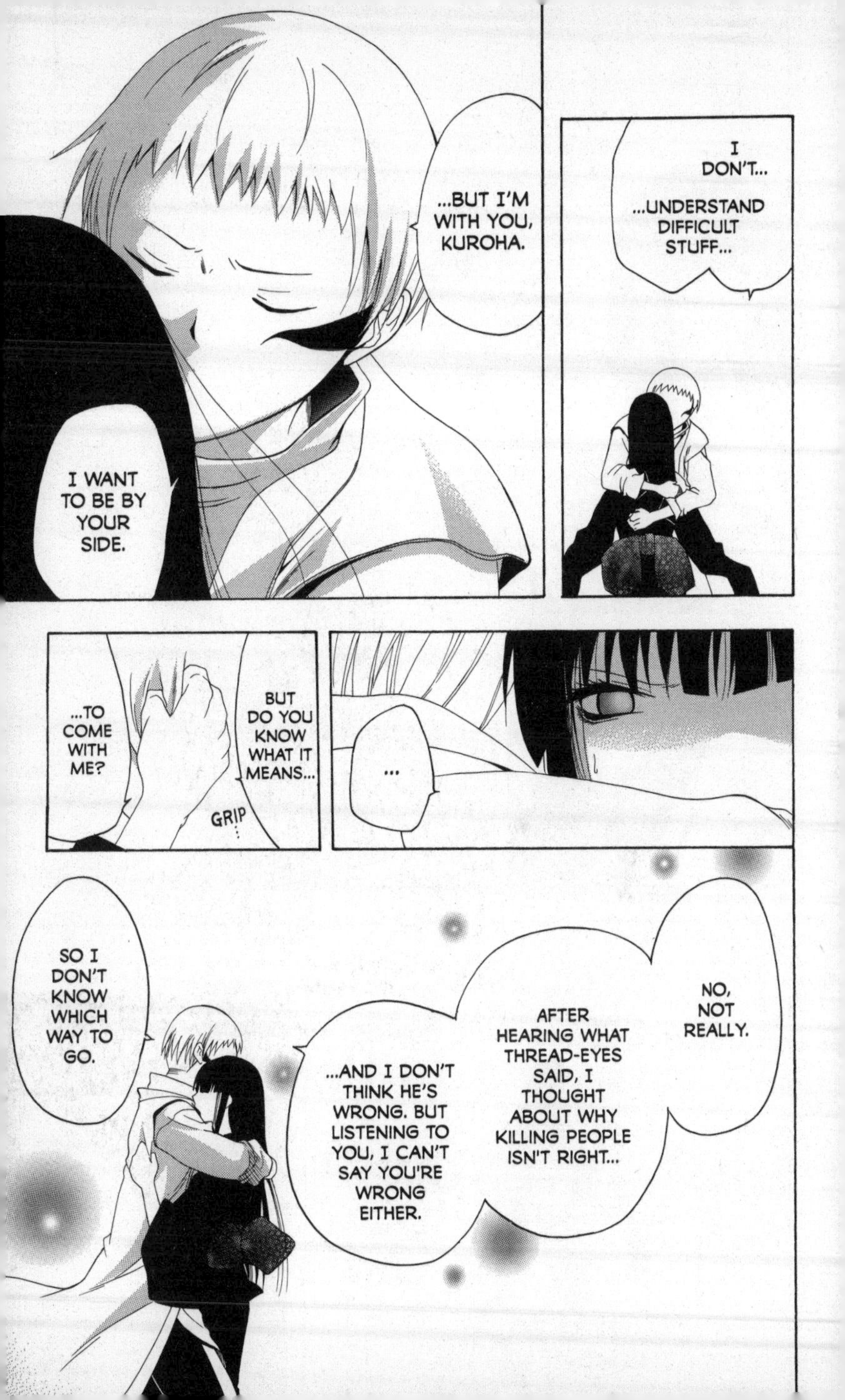
I DON'T... ...UNDERSTAND DIFFICULT STUFF...
...BUT I'M WITH YOU, KUROHA.
I WANT TO BE BY YOUR SIDE.
...
BUT DO YOU KNOW WHAT IT MEANS...
...TO COME WITH ME?
GRIP
NO, NOT REALLY.
AFTER HEARING WHAT THREAD-EYES SAID, I THOUGHT ABOUT WHY KILLING PEOPLE ISN'T RIGHT...
...AND I DON'T THINK HE'S WRONG. BUT LISTENING TO YOU, I CAN'T SAY YOU'RE WRONG EITHER.
SO I DON'T KNOW WHICH WAY TO GO.

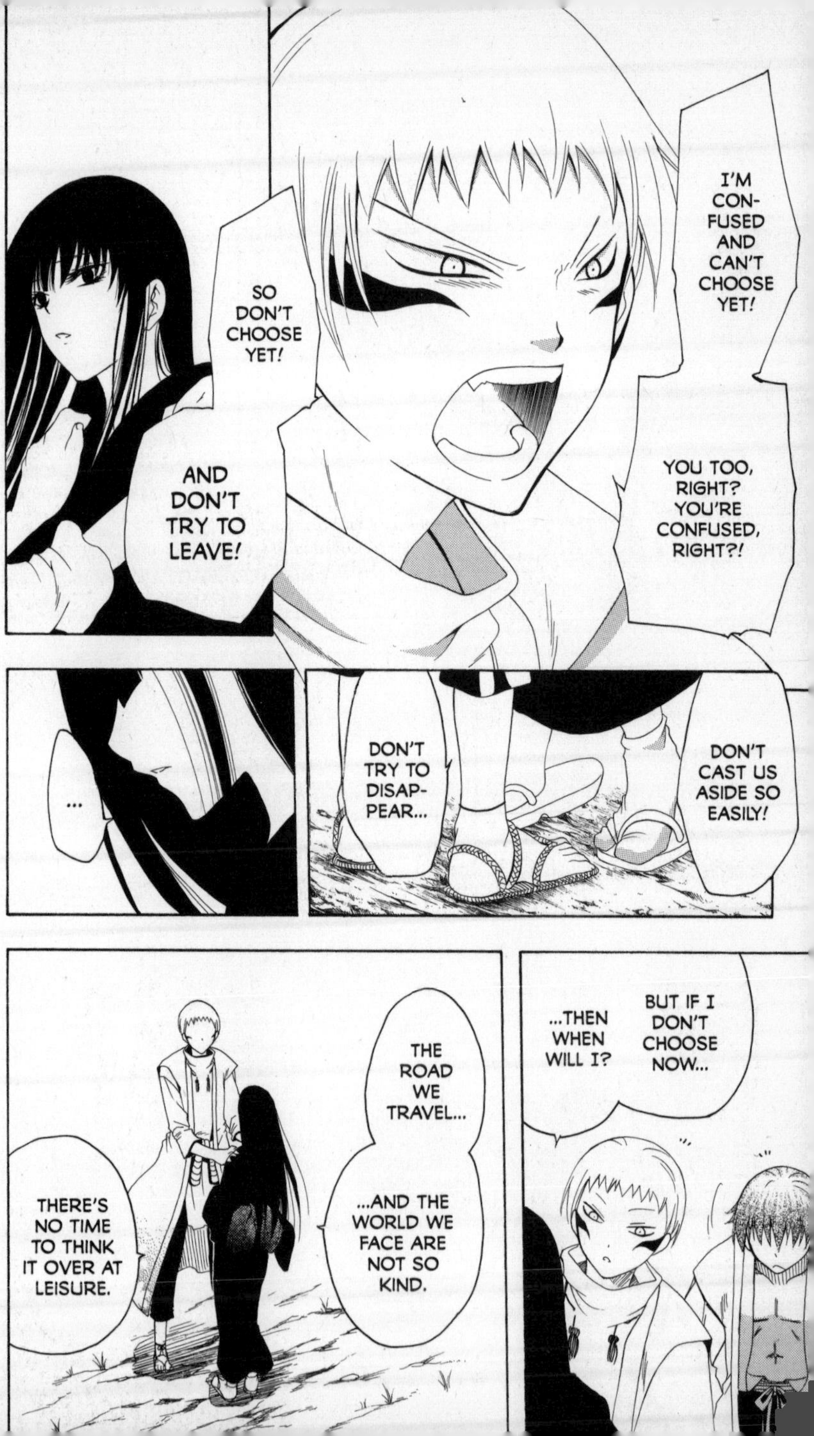
I'M CON-FUSED AND CAN'T CHOOSE YET!
YOU TOO, RIGHT? YOU'RE CONFUSED, RIGHT?!
SO DON'T CHOOSE YET!
AND DON'T TRY TO LEAVE!
DON'T CAST US ASIDE SO EASILY!
DON'T TRY TO DISAP-PEAR...
...
BUT IF I DON'T CHOOSE NOW...
...THEN WHEN WILL I?
THE ROAD WE TRAVEL...
...AND THE WORLD WE FACE ARE NOT SO KIND.
THERE'S NO TIME TO THINK IT OVER AT LEISURE.

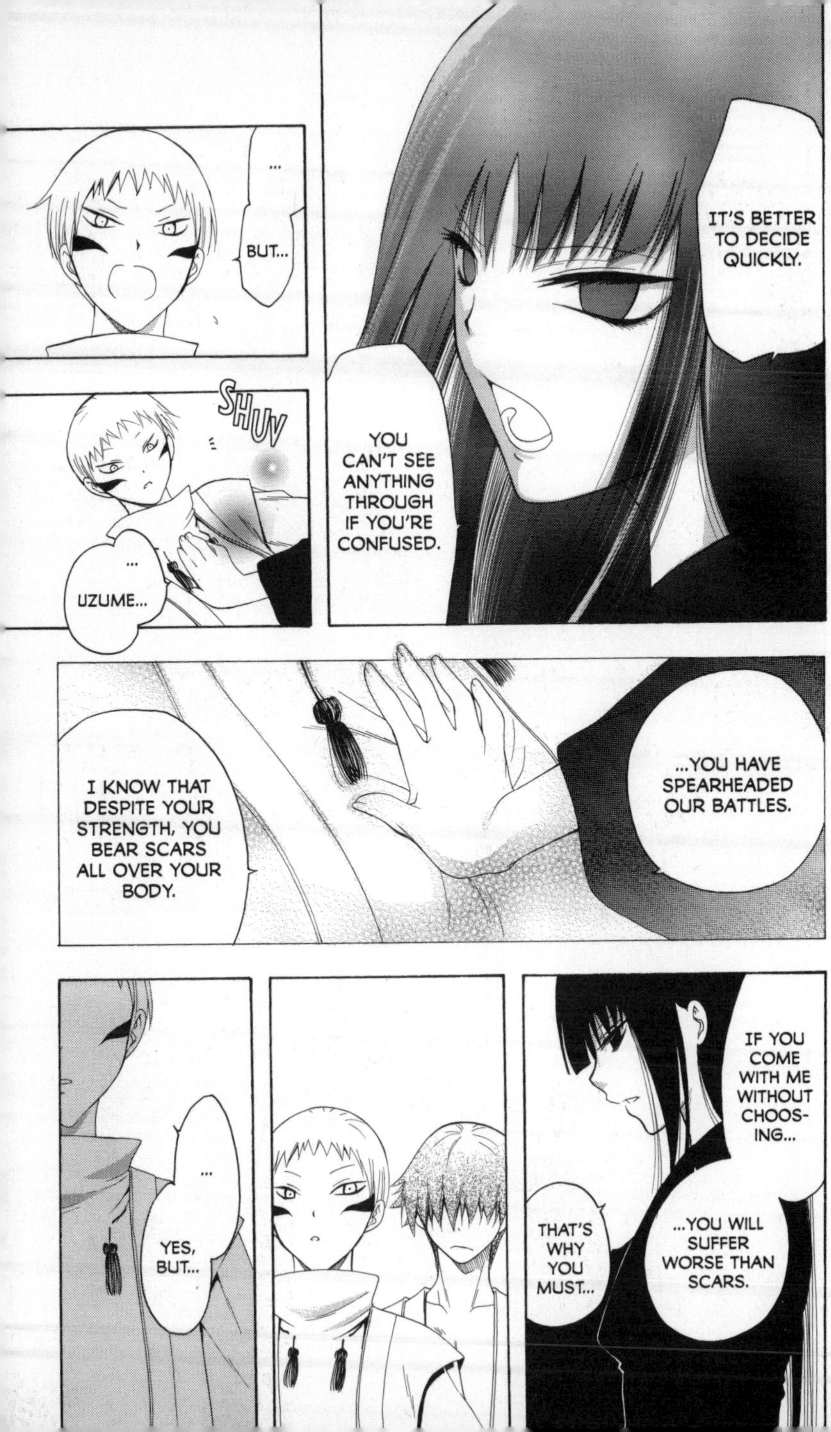
IT'S BETTER TO DECIDE QUICKLY.
YOU CAN'T SEE ANYTHING THROUGH IF YOU'RE CONFUSED.
...
BUT...
SHUV
...
UZUME...
...YOU HAVE SPEARHEADED OUR BATTLES.
I KNOW THAT DESPITE YOUR STRENGTH, YOU BEAR SCARS ALL OVER YOUR BODY.
IF YOU COME WITH ME WITHOUT CHOOSING...
...YOU WILL SUFFER WORSE THAN SCARS.
THAT'S WHY YOU MUST...
...
YES, BUT...

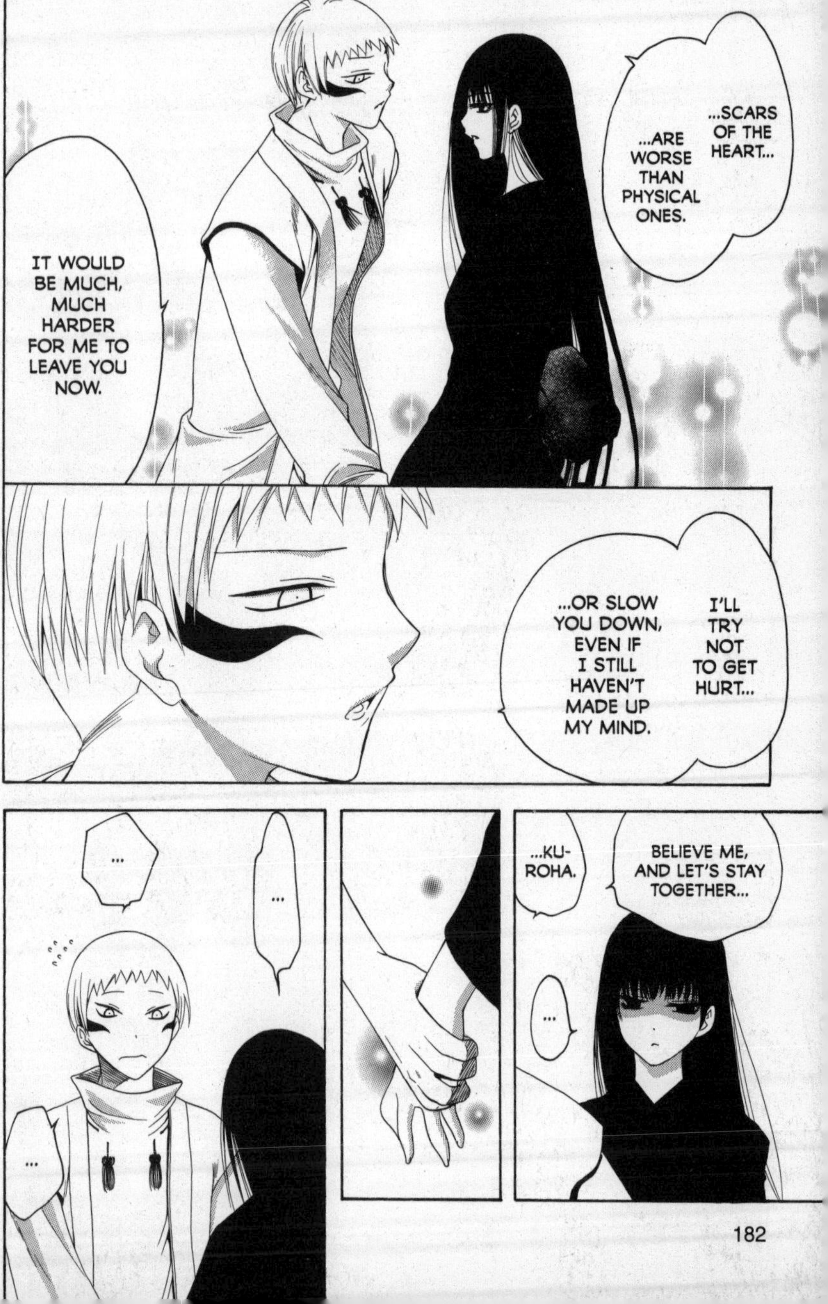
...SCARS OF THE HEART...
...ARE WORSE THAN PHYSICAL ONES.
IT WOULD BE MUCH, MUCH HARDER FOR ME TO LEAVE YOU NOW.
I'LL TRY NOT TO GET HURT...
...OR SLOW YOU DOWN, EVEN IF I STILL HAVEN'T MADE UP MY MIND.
BELIEVE ME, AND LET'S STAY TOGETHER...
...KU-ROHA.
...
...
...
...

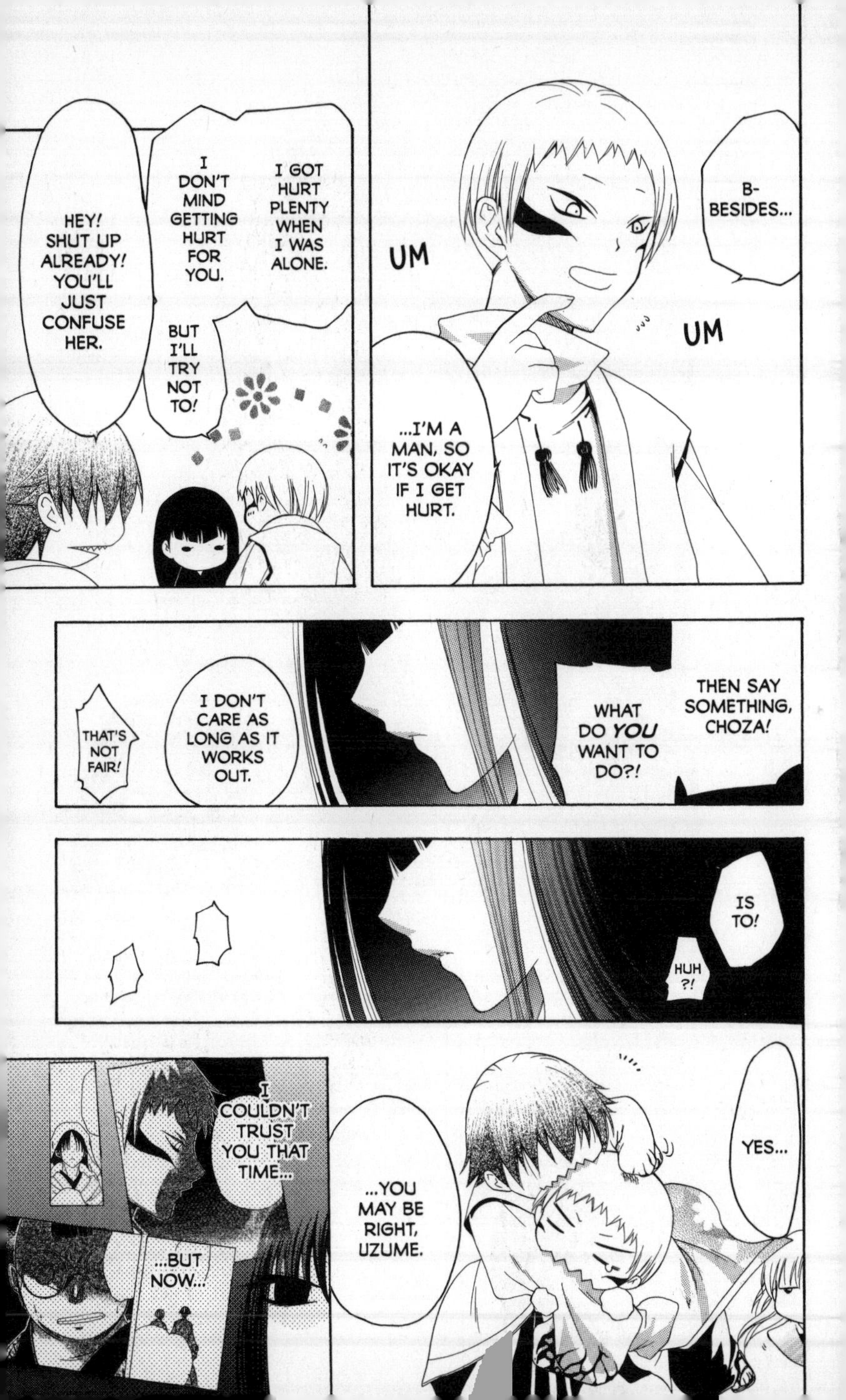
B- BESIDES...
UM
UM
...I'M A MAN, SO IT'S OKAY IF I GET HURT.
I GOT HURT PLENTY WHEN I WAS ALONE.
I DON'T MIND GETTING HURT FOR YOU.
BUT I'LL TRY NOT TO!
HEY! SHUT UP ALREADY! YOU'LL JUST CONFUSE HER.
THEN SAY SOMETHING, CHOZA!
WHAT DO *YOU* WANT TO DO?!
I DON'T CARE AS LONG AS IT WORKS OUT.
THAT'S NOT FAIR!
IS TO!
HUH?!
YES...
...YOU MAY BE RIGHT, UZUME.
I COULDN'T TRUST YOU THAT TIME...
...BUT NOW...

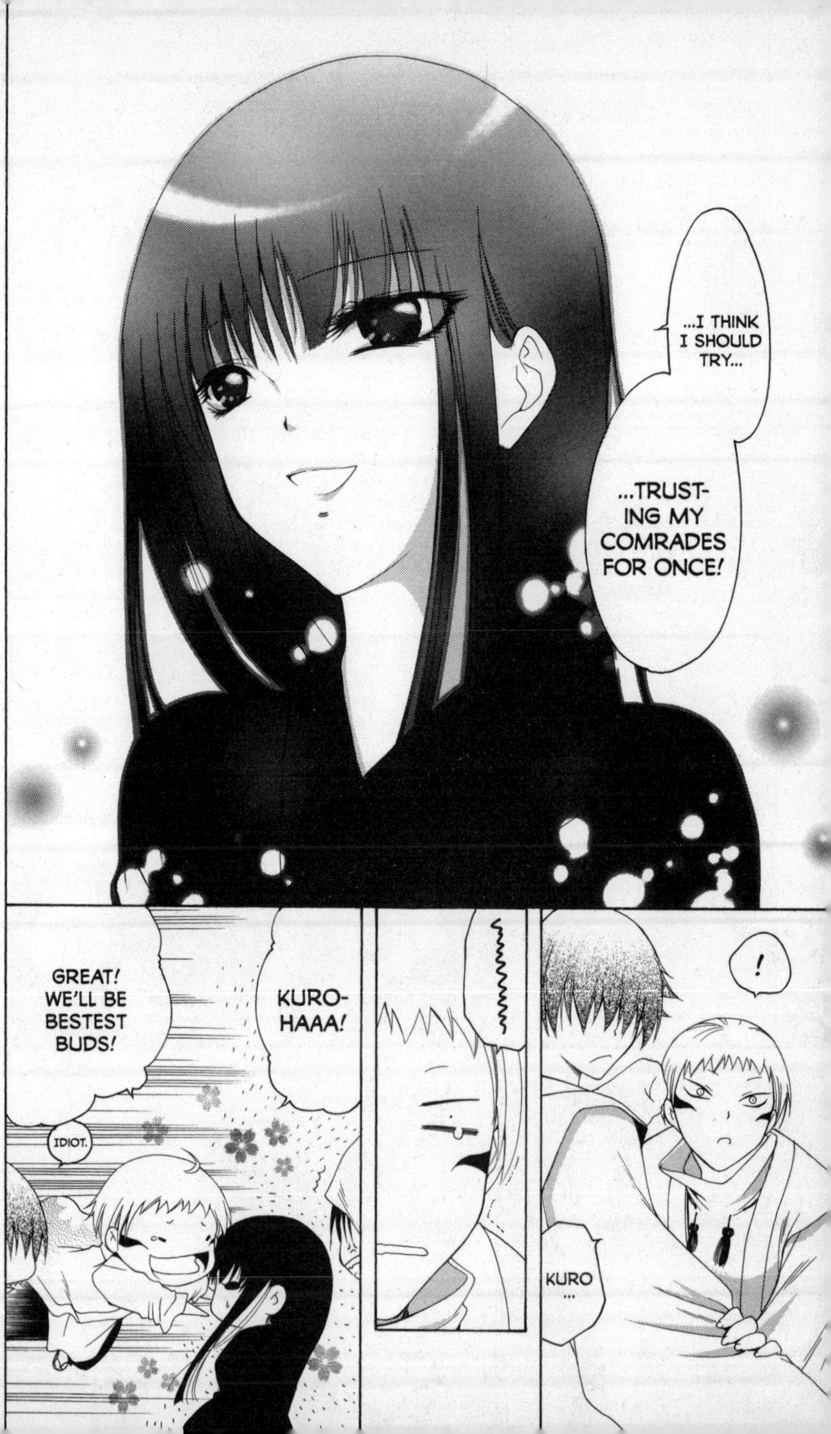
...I THINK I SHOULD TRY...
...TRUST-ING MY COMRADES FOR ONCE!
!
KURO ...
KURO-HAAA!
GREAT! WE'LL BE BESTEST BUDS!
IDIOT.

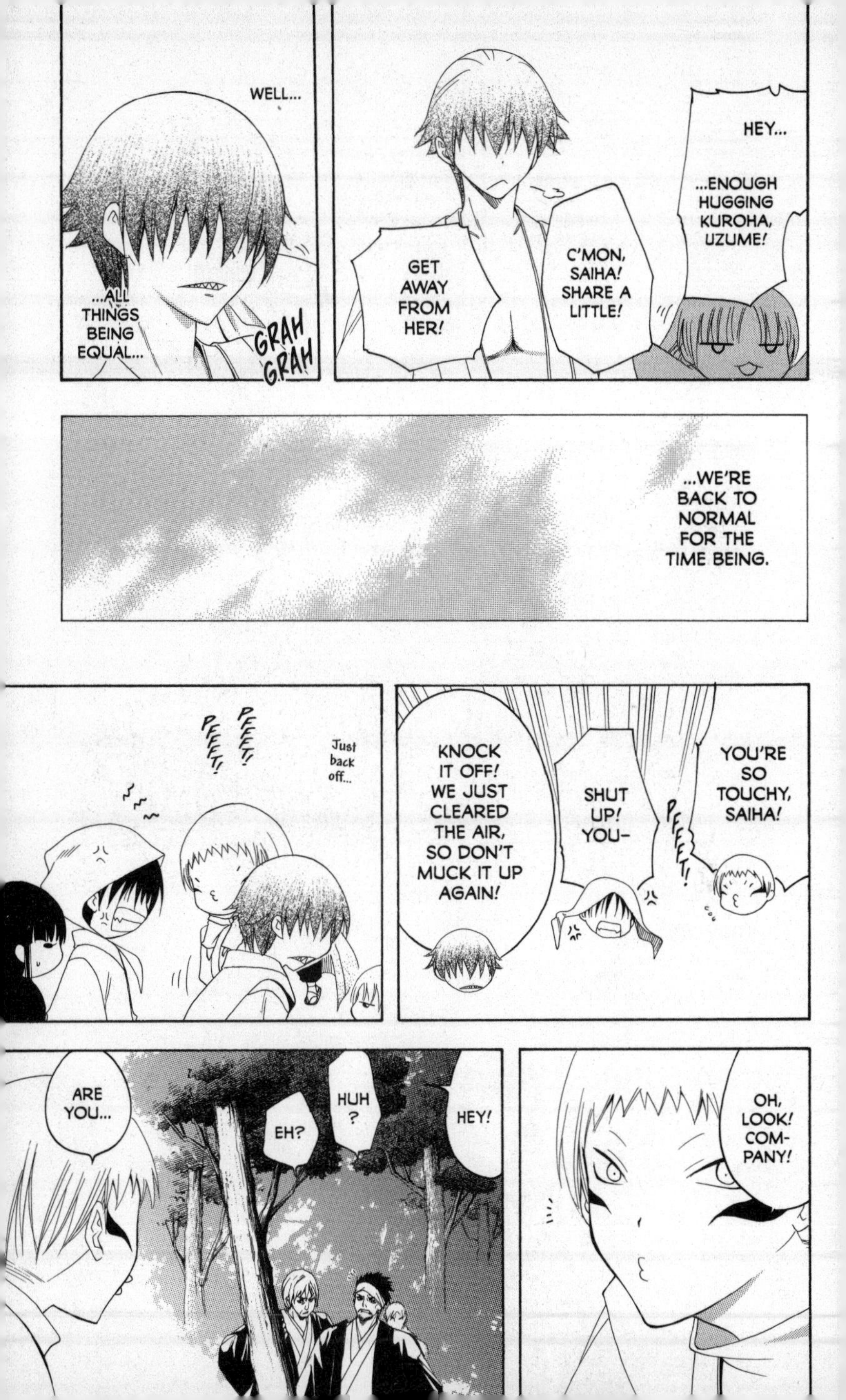
HEY...
...ENOUGH HUGGING KUROHA, UZUME!
C'MON, SAIHA! SHARE A LITTLE!
GET AWAY FROM HER!
WELL...
...ALL THINGS BEING EQUAL...
GRAH GRAH
...WE'RE BACK TO NORMAL FOR THE TIME BEING.
YOU'RE SO TOUCHY, SAIHA!
PFEFT!
SHUT UP! YOU–
KNOCK IT OFF! WE JUST CLEARED THE AIR, SO DON'T MUCK IT UP AGAIN!
Just back off...
PFEFT! PFEFT!
OH, LOOK! COMPANY!
HEY!
HUH?
EH?
ARE YOU...

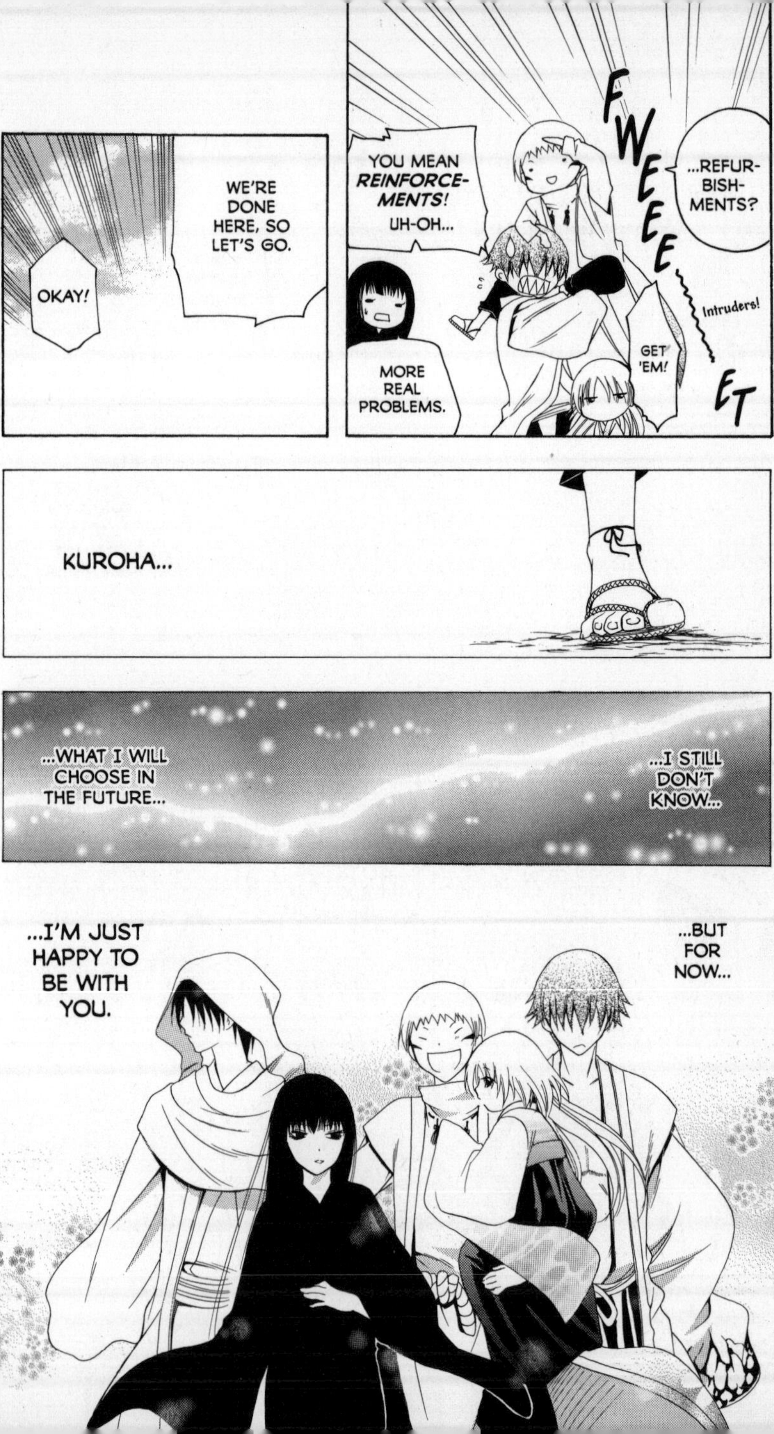
...REFUR-BISHMENTS?
FWEEEEEET
Intruders!
YOU MEAN *REINFORCE-MENTS!* UH-OH...
GET 'EM!
MORE REAL PROBLEMS.
WE'RE DONE HERE, SO LET'S GO.
OKAY!
KUROHA...
...I STILL DON'T KNOW...
...WHAT I WILL CHOOSE IN THE FUTURE...
...BUT FOR NOW...
...I'M JUST HAPPY TO BE WITH YOU.

Bonus Manga

Address:
http://ameblo.jp/iinumayuuki/
Yuuki Iinuma's Blog

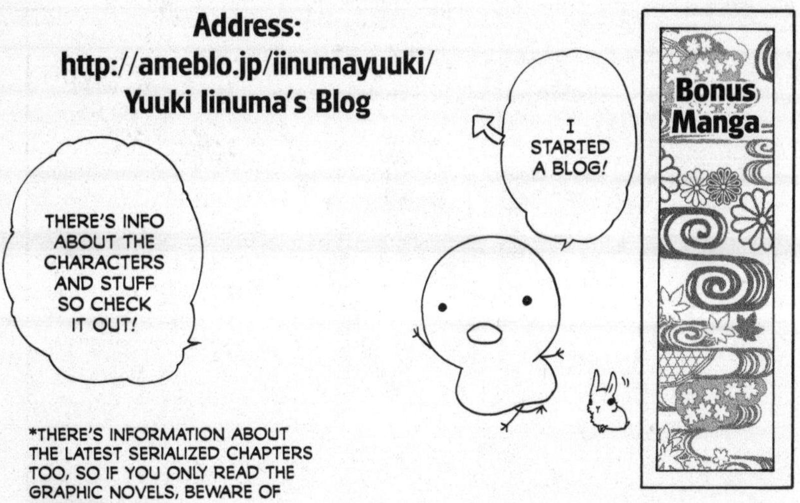
I STARTED A BLOG!
THERE'S INFO ABOUT THE CHARACTERS AND STUFF SO CHECK IT OUT!

*THERE'S INFORMATION ABOUT THE LATEST SERIALIZED CHAPTERS TOO, SO IF YOU ONLY READ THE GRAPHIC NOVELS, BEWARE OF SPOILERS!

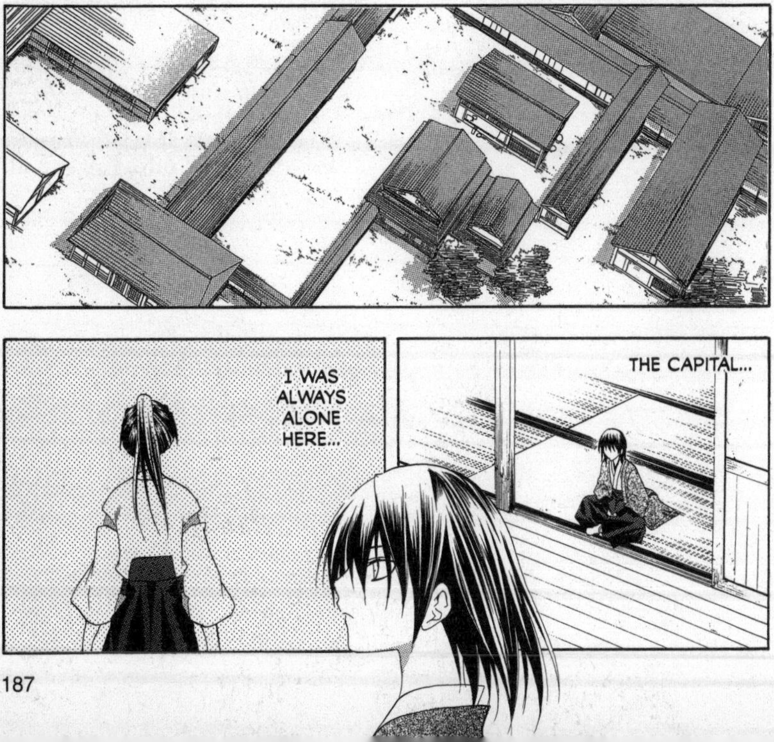
THE CAPITAL...
I WAS ALWAYS ALONE HERE...

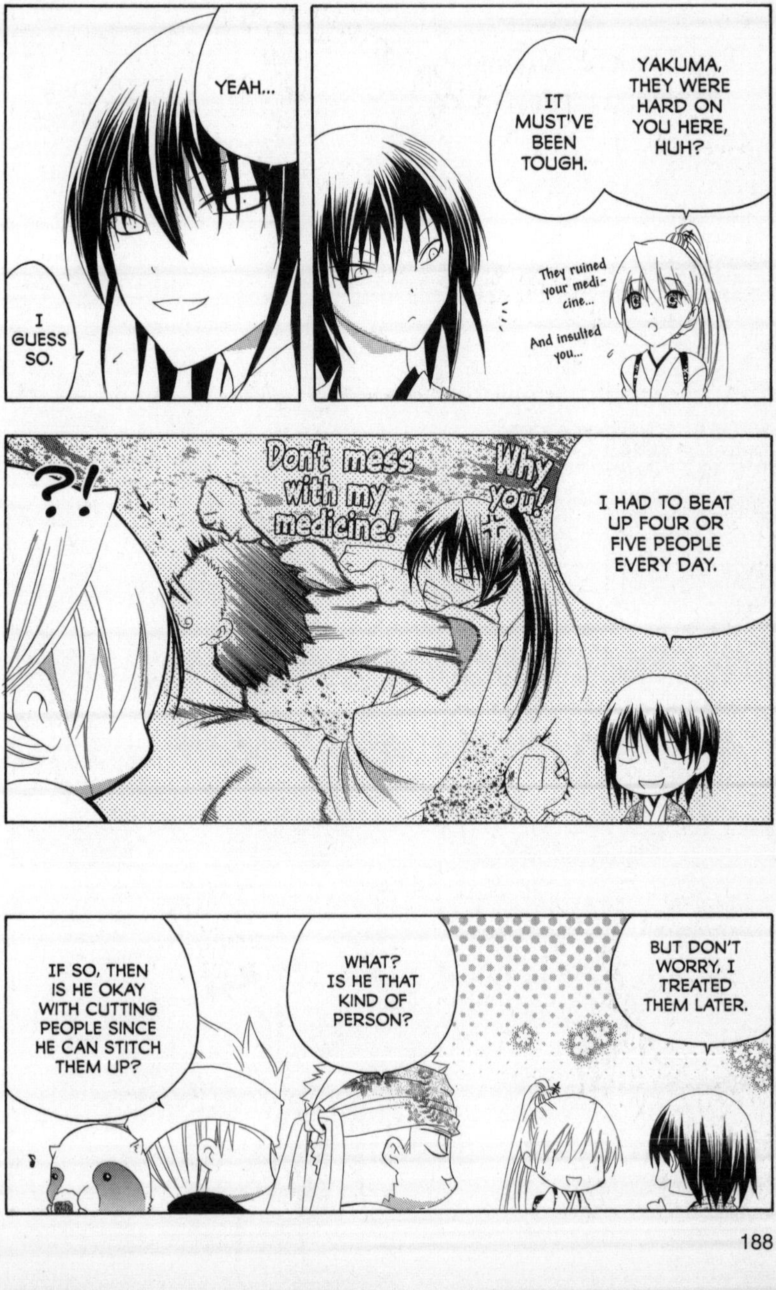
YAKUMA, THEY WERE HARD ON YOU HERE, HUH?
IT MUST'VE BEEN TOUGH.
They ruined your medi-cine...
And insulted you...
YEAH...
I GUESS SO.
I HAD TO BEAT UP FOUR OR FIVE PEOPLE EVERY DAY.
Why you!
Don't mess with my medicine!
?!
BUT DON'T WORRY, I TREATED THEM LATER.
WHAT? IS HE THAT KIND OF PERSON?
IF SO, THEN IS HE OKAY WITH CUTTING PEOPLE SINCE HE CAN STITCH THEM UP?

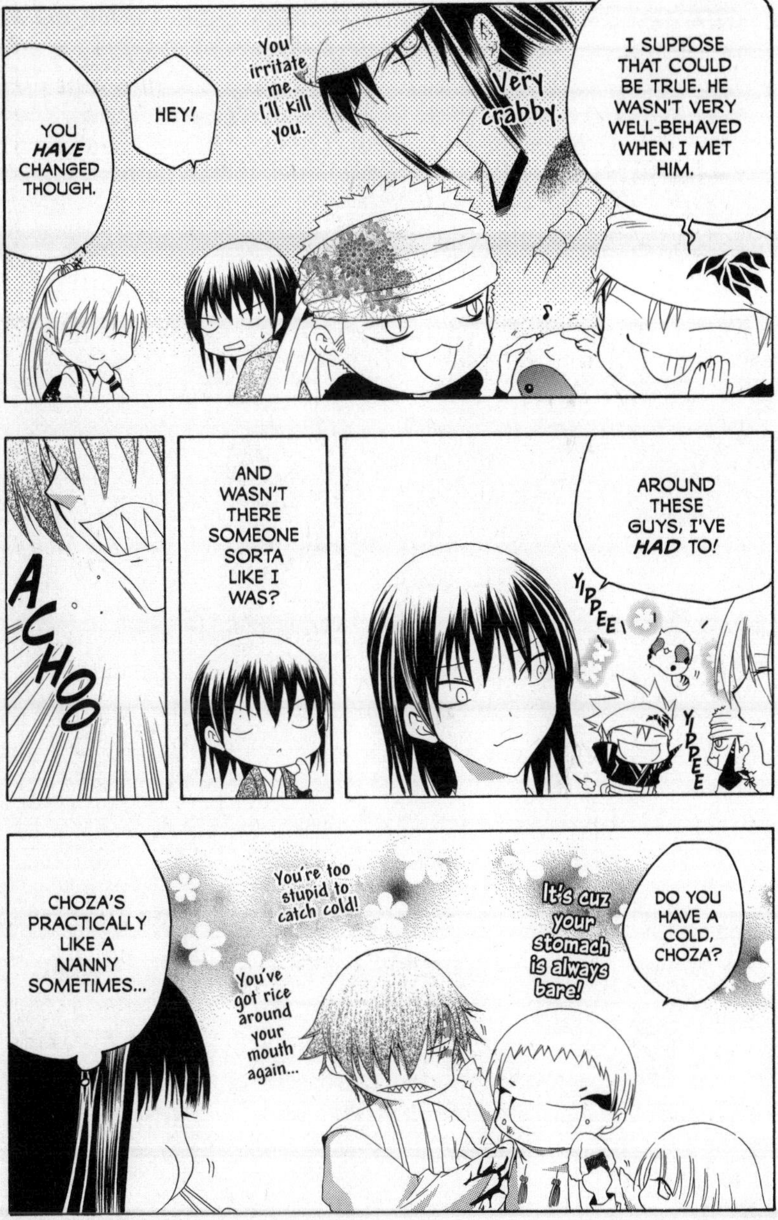
I SUPPOSE THAT COULD BE TRUE. HE WASN'T VERY WELL-BEHAVED WHEN I MET HIM.
Very crabby.
You irritate me. I'll kill you.
HEY!
YOU *HAVE* CHANGED THOUGH.
AROUND THESE GUYS, I'VE *HAD* TO!
YIPPEE!
YIPPEE
AND WASN'T THERE SOMEONE SORTA LIKE I WAS?
ACHOO
DO YOU HAVE A COLD, CHOZA?
It's cuz your stomach is always bare!
You're too stupid to catch cold!
You've got rice around your mouth again...
CHOZA'S PRACTICALLY LIKE A NANNY SOMETIMES...

ITSUWARIBITO
Volume 10
Shonen Sunday Edition

Story and Art by
YUUKI IINUMA

ITSUWARIBITO ◆ UTSUHO ◆ Vol. 10
by Yuuki IINUMA
© 2009 Yuuki IINUMA
All rights reserved.
Original Japanese edition published by SHOGAKUKAN.
English translation rights in the United States of America and Canada
arranged with SHOGAKUKAN.

Translation/John Werry
Touch-up Art & Lettering/Susan Daigle-Leach
Design/Matt Hinrichs
Editor/Gary Leach

Printed in Canada

Published by VIZ Media, LLC
P.O. Box 77010
San Francisco, CA 94107

10 9 8 7 6 5 4 3 2 1
First printing, December 2013

www.viz.com

WWW.SHONENSUNDAY.COM

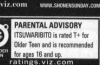

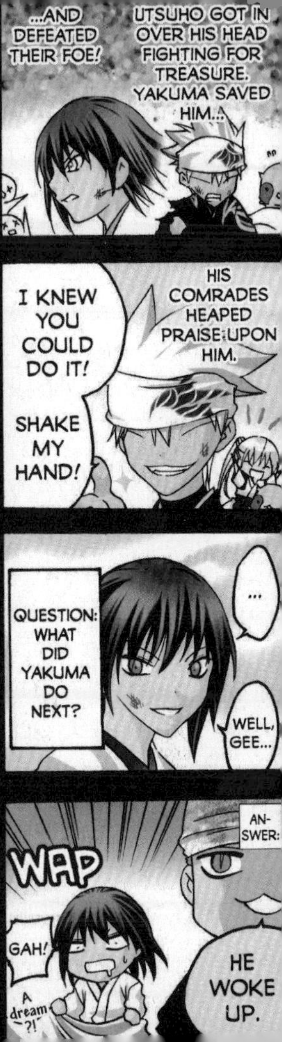
UTSUHO GOT IN OVER HIS HEAD FIGHTING FOR TREASURE. YAKUMA SAVED HIM...
...AND DEFEATED THEIR FOE!
HIS COMRADES HEAPED PRAISE UPON HIM.
I KNEW YOU COULD DO IT!
SHAKE MY HAND!
...
WELL, GEE...
QUESTION: WHAT DID YAKUMA DO NEXT?
AN-SWER:
HE WOKE UP.
WAP
GAH!
A dream~?!

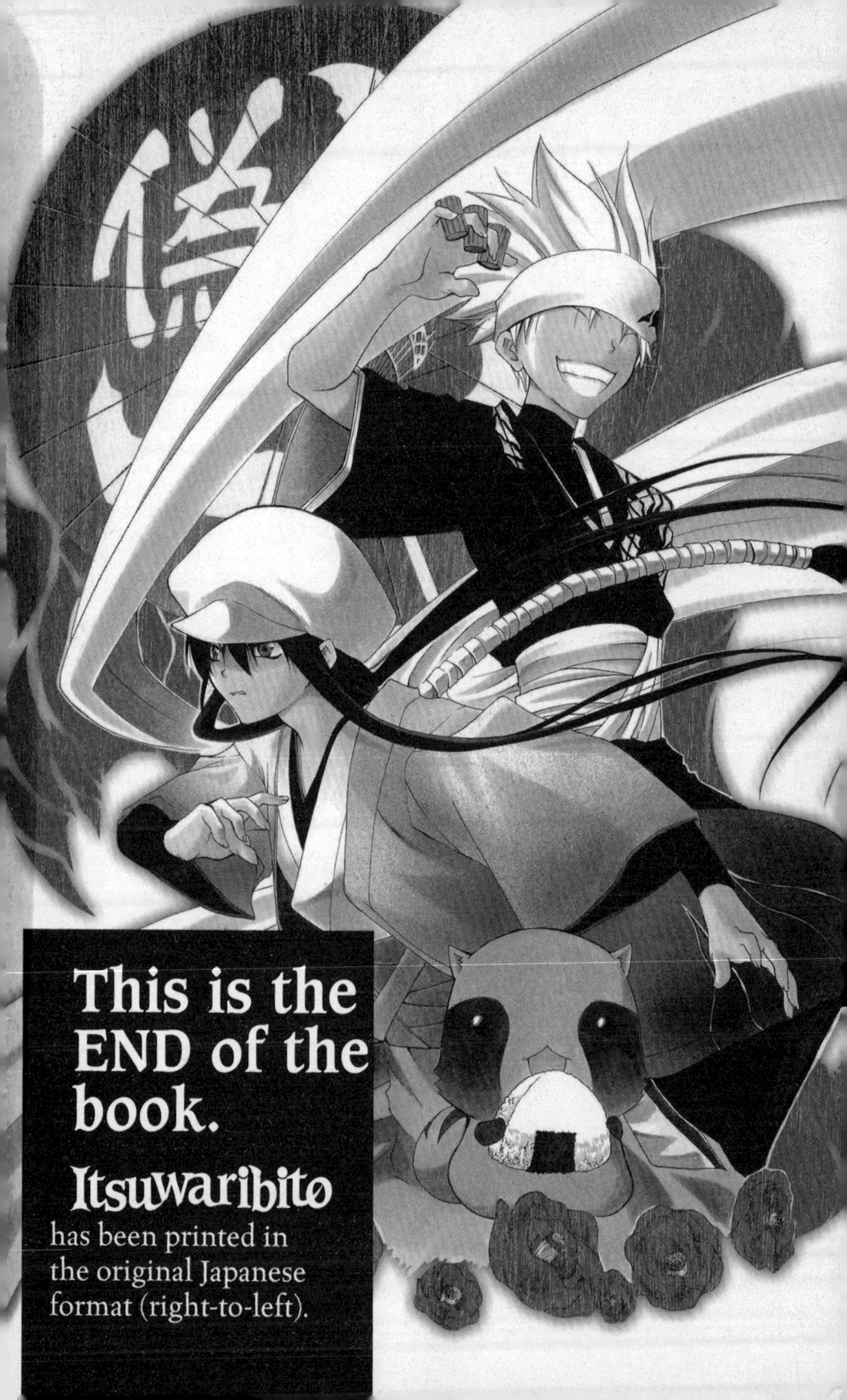

This is the END of the book.

Itsuwaribito has been printed in the original Japanese format (right-to-left).